A GENERAL HISTORY OF EUROPE

GENERAL EDITOR: DENYS HAY

A GENERAL HISTORY OF EUROPE

General Editor: Denys Hay

For many years the volumes of Denys Hay's distinguished General History of Europe have been standard recommendations for university students, sixth formers and general readers. They offer broad surveys of European history, in which the detailed discussion (on a regional or continent-wide basis) of social, economic, administrative and intellectual themes is woven into a clear framework of political events. They set out to combine scholarship with accessibility in texts which are both attractively written and intellectually vigorous. Now the entire sequence is under revision by its original authors – most of the volumes for the first time since they were published – and the books are being redesigned and reset. The revised General History of Europe, when complete, will contain twelve volumes, three of them wholly new.

* *Available in the original edition*
✦ New edition published in the revised format
❑ New title in preparation

EUROPE IN THE HIGH MIDDLE AGES

1150–1309

SECOND EDITION

JOHN H. MUNDY

LONGMAN
LONDON AND NEW YORK

Longman Group UK Limited
Longman House, Burnt Mill, Harlow,
Essex CM20 2JE, England
and Associated Companies throughout the world.

*Published in the United States of America
by Longman Inc., New York*

First published 1973
Second edition 1991
Second impression 1993

British Library Cataloguing in Publication Data
Mundy, John H. (John Hine) *1917–*
  Europe in the high Middle Ages, 1150–1309.–2nd. ed.–(A
  General history of Europe).
  1. Europe, 1100–1453
  I. Title II. Series
  940.17

ISBN 0–582–49395–1 PPR
      0–582–08016–9 CSD

Library of Congress Cataloging in Publication Data
Mundy, John Hine, 1917–
  Europe in the High Middle Ages, 1150–1309 / John Hine Mundy.--
2nd ed.
      p.   cm. -- (A General history of Europe)
    Includes bibliographical references and index.
      ISBN 0–582–08016–9. -- ISBN 0–582–49395–1 pbk.)
    1. Europe--History--476–1492.   2. Middle Ages--History.
I. Title.   II. Series.
D200.M86   1991
940.1'7--dc20   90–42973
                                                              CIP

Set in Postcript Bembo

Produced by Longman Singapore Publishers (Pte) Ltd
Printed in Singapore

CONTENTS

LIST OF MAPS

ABBREVIATIONS

AA.SS.	*Acta sanctorum*
BIMA	*Bibliotheca iuridica medii aevi*, ed. Augusto Gaudenzi *et al.*, 3 vols. (Bologna, 1888–1901)
BGPM	*Beiträge zur Geschichte der Philosophie des Mittelalters*
BuF	*Briefsteller und Formelbücher des eilten bis vierzehnten Jahrhunderts*, ed. Ludwig Rockinger, 2 vols. (Munich, 1863–4)
CICan	*Corpus iuris cananici*, ed. Emil Friedberg, 2 vols. (Leipzig, 1879–81)
CICiv	*Corpus iuris civilis*, ed. Mommsen, Krüger *et al.*, 3 vols. (Berlin, 1912–20)
MGH	*Monumenta Germaniae Historica*
Const.	*Constitutiones et acta publica*
Epp. sel.	*Epistolae selectae*
LL	*Leges*
Ldl	*Libelli de lite*
SS	*Scriptores*
FIG in usum scholarum	*Fontes iuris germanica antiqui in usum scholarum*
SS in usum scholarum	*Scriptores rerum Germanicarum in usum scholarum*
Staatschriften	*Staatschriften des späteren Mittelalters*
PL	*Patrologia latina*, ed. J. P. Migne (Paris, 1844–64)

RIS	*Rerum italicarum scriptores*, new edition 1900 onward
Rolls Series	*Rerum britannicarum medii aevi scriptores*
TUJ	*Tractatus universi juris*

PREFACE

This history is written for college and university students: those who hope to acquire rather more learning than most of their peers. Such young people can understand everything their elders can. The young, however, also differ from the old. Because of innocence or ignorance, they have an advantage: they often comprehend more rapidly. Burdened by experience and learning, older persons often seem to peer in order to judge instead of merely looking in order to understand. 'The old,' said Giles of Rome, 'are naturally sceptical and ungenerous; the young generous and credulous.'[1] But aside from this, all adults, young and old, share a certain intellectual equality. A history addressed to the young is therefore one addressed to a wider audience – the students then, and also their parents and teachers.

The exposition of this book has been interlarded with quotations from primary sources. Occasional Latin technical terms, furthermore, have been retained. This reminds readers of something easily overlooked in today's age of national languages. The Europe treated here was a region divided mainly between the Latin-speaking peoples and the German-speaking ones. Although the latter had once invaded and subjected the Latins, the attraction of the latter's Mediterranean culture had conquered the invaders. Western Europe's universal language had become Latin, and French, a language of Latin stock, was the most widespread literary and legal vernacular. In spite of the importance of the Germanic and Nordic peoples (and, for the time being, the lesser weight of the Slavs and Celts), Latin and its derivatives so dominated the cultural life of Europe that the single adjective best qualifying the word 'Europe' for this period is 'Latin'. This term cleanly distinguishes 'the West' from Greek, Slavic and Arabic Europe, the Near East and Africa.

Many primary sources cited here derive from printed editions of the originals, but this rule is sometimes waived because lack of time obliges me to have recourse to documents and tracts cited in other writers' books. Notably useful here are authors such as Decima Douie, E.H. Kantorowicz and Georges de Lagarde. No matter what the source, however, the translations of Latin and medieval vernacular texts (but not Greek and Hebrew) are my own.

The method of citing primary texts is simplified. Literary texts are usually divided into Books and Books into Chapters, so that the first number is the Book and the second the Chapter, in addition to which is also included the page of the modern edition. Technical citations of law are eschewed because non-specialists generally do not know them. Justinian's *Codex*, for example, is cited as *Code*, not as *C.*, and canon law citations are also simplified. Occasional exceptions to these rules will be noted at the time.

Footnotes are abbreviated. The most succinct references are those to texts taken from books listed in the general bibliography, which is itself divided into groups, one for each Part of this history. They may be searched for there. Other texts or editions are given full references the first time they appear, but are thereafter abbreviated. The book in which they are to be found may be searched for in the general index under an appropriate heading, location, person's name or title of a work.

To make the names cited in this book as familiar as possible, Christian names have been Anglicized, if at all possible. Family names, however, pose greater difficulties. A person often cited below is 'Petrus Johannis Olivi', that is, 'Peter son of John Olivi'. Following the tradition of normal scholarship, Olivi will be referred to as 'Peter John Olivi'. Another example is Remigo, son of Girolamo. The Italian style of 'Remigo de Girolami' will be used.

Special thanks for providing useful references to primary sources used in the second edition are owed to books and articles written by Joan Ferrante, Leah L. Otis and Zephira E. Rokeah, the latter two of whom were my doctoral students, and the first a close colleague at Columbia University. Various scholars in different institutions were instrumental in pointing to other rich primary sources. For the first edition of this book, the most significant of these were Jocelyn N. Hillgarth of the Pontifical Institute of Mediaeval Studies in Toronto, Domenico Maffei of the University of Rome, Kenneth

M. Setton of the Institute for Advanced Studies in Princeton, Sir Richard W. Southern of Oxford University, and Kennerly M. Woody. To both the first and second editions, Julius Kirshner of the University of Chicago and Ronald G. Musto contributed key references from Florentine manuscripts. Thanks are still owed to Peter N. Riesenberg of Washington University in Saint Louis, and Beatrice Gottlieb who read the manuscript of the first edition of this book.

John Mundy
10 February 1990

NOTES AND REFERENCES

1   *De regimine principum* 1, 1, 2 (Rome, 1607), 7.

To Charlotte Williams Mundy

1

INTRODUCTION

THE SUBJECT MATTER

History is often beclouded, and each period has clouds specific to it. Medieval history's cloud is because Europe's culture was then ecclesiastical whereas today's is secular. Secular historians seek to find the origins of the institutions and thought they favour: when looking for today's spiritual ancestors, they vault back over the Middle Ages to Greek and Roman antiquity.

Prisoners of laicism, moderns who favour going to church, mosque or synagogue, experience there only a subculture, one threatened by secularism's greater culture. As a result, the friends of the Middle Ages are as bothersome as its enemies. They are those who, reacting against secular dominance, look back to earlier times in order to criticize the present. After recent European history, one understands their doubts about secularism, but their Middle Ages is often only partially similar to reality. Their idealized community of the medieval town, for example, is clearly partly fictional.

Modern research has defined the differences between classical, medieval and modern times, and contrasted the other-worldly emphasis of late antique and medieval thought with the this-worldly emphasis of moderns and of their predecessors in antiquity. This truthful distinction has, however, encouraged some to inscribe it in stone. To them, the latter promotes rational propositions, those within reach of natural demonstration, whereas the former's are religious, beyond, that is, the reach of the same. This causes some to make institutions coterminous with ideas: the Church *is* religion, so to speak, and the State and other secular institutions *are* reason. This

overlooks the fact that, although there are many differences between the two ways of thinking, they have something in common,
namely their love of indemonstrable propositions. Many present-day
convictions about human free will, moral potential, the necessity of
personal freedom for social and economic advancement, for
example, and mankind's central role in the cosmos are as indemonstrable as any mystery found in Christianity, Judaism or Islam.

Using the ideas expressed in the words 'religious' or 'rational' to
describe motives for human action is both traditional and valid. To
reject either one of them in favour of the other, however, is to
misuse them. Some say, for example, that a person or group acted
only for religious motives; others counter that they were animated
by only rational, economic or material motives. One wonders if
either one standing alone suffices to describe human actions.

These actions vary. Men and women play games. They turn
prayer wheels, recite gods' names, make music, do puzzles or calcu-
lations. When done by one alone, these have little to do with the
society in which a person lives, and seem instead to be means of
testing one's harmony with the nature of things. When one plays
with others or before an audience, however, play becomes a way of
competing or joining with other men and women.

People hope that there is a natural order to which they can fit
themselves, or of which they can make use. This desire is tied to
society, but, rather like play, transcends the particular social world
in which they live because the problems it tries to handle are uniform throughout history. These problems are those caused by birth,
exuberant growth, sickness and death as well as hopes for freedom
and love, and are expressed by a mixture of rational and religious
passions and ideas. The desire to avoid death, for example, causes
humanity both to people the other world with possibly imaginary
souls and to work rationally to prolong life in this one.

The particularities of periods in which individuals live attract historians especially because they distinguish one age from another.
They also bulk large in the sources for historical study probably
because humans spend little time being born, loving or dying and
much in life's routines. Only sleep takes more time than these. Experience nevertheless teaches that the primal activities are more
consequential because humans are mostly moved by the need and
desire to attain love and retain life by finding and using the right
order of things.

Historians should therefore try to recognize the similarities of human desire and need in the many languages, secular or ecclesiastical, technical or commonsensical, scientific or mystic, lent them by transient institutions, philosophies and religions. One recalls, for example, debates among even 'materialist' thinkers as to whether the ideas of their favourite intellectual forebears were mainly drawn from the thought of their time, or instead arose within themselves, having few or no outside sources. Such debaters, one guesses, rehearse arguments as indemonstrable as the old scholastic ones favouring natural or innate capacity versus the need for divine grace, arguments essentially about free will and determination. Once, moreover, the similarities of some modern and medieval propositions about mankind's role in natural history or under the deity are perceived, one can comprehend why humanity is addicted to the indemonstrable.

This addiction presumably derives from need: nobody can be sure that his or her cancer will not kill, and nobody that he or she is loved. All one can do is hope and play games. Although recourse to indemonstrable propositions often inhibits human freedom, history also shows that it sometimes helps it. Most institutions have been built on humanity's natural, reasonable and demonstrable needs for health, material welfare and a measure of freedom in the disposition of talents and goods. In late Rome, however, these normally healthy drives and their concomitant institutions were so overwhelmed by internal disruption and external attack that they became oppressive. Then, the need for relief or freedom forced the people to turn to the other world, the world of the indemonstrable. Although Christianity's obscurantism partly reflected a failure of nerve, it was also a liberating secession from service to state and society and from the often self-defeating race for wealth, learning and well-being. Rome's peoples rejected Greco-Roman earth-centred reason, religion and society.

The institutional precipitate of this once revolutionary attitude was the medieval Church. Empowered by the people, ecclesiastical authority was a counterbalance to lay power, thus making liberty a matter of alternating choice between secular and ecclesiastical authorities, institutions and patterns of thought. If one seemed unduly inhibiting, men and women could and did turn and choose the other. Great though it was, this balance between the two powers was only temporary, its forthcoming disruption announced when the clergy itself, called on to direct the world in practical life during its period of leadership, began to turn from theology to philosophy, from mystery to reason, from the other world to this one.

These being the author's opinions, it is assumed in this book that few or no human activities lack a religious dimension, an appeal to, or a use of, indemonstrable propositions or ideas, and few or none lack an appeal to what can be known or projected to be reasonably likely on the basis of human experience in nature. The study of heresy (beliefs differing from those of the majority) has been confused, for example, by conflicts between those who claim that its genesis was religious and those asserting it was social or economic. The medieval believer, doubter and heretic are described in this book as both religious and rational persons.

There are also divergent ways of viewing the relationship of nations, classes, groups and sexes. Many feel that the powerful always exploit the weak, the warlike the pacific, the rich the poor, and men women. Conjecturing that societies based on violence are bound to lack sufficient solidarity to combat their enemies, others favour an opposing viewpoint, arguing that, instead of abuse, the use of one by the other to their mutual profit is society's cement. Because both of these views are rational and yet wholly indemonstrable, this book avoids choosing sides.

Violence and civilization coexisted in the Middle Ages. Although lamenting servitude, for example, some modern writers, even radical ones, have asserted that without it, there would have been no culture. It can surely be shown that labour is necessary for civilization, and that coerced labour often has advantages over free. Greco-Roman civilization was spread around the Mediterranean and towards the Rhine and Danube valleys in large part by a temporary increase of servitude. But that does not mean that coerced work is always beneficial. History seems to say only that oppression at times helps humankind; at others it harms it.

Many have been so sickened by past savagery that they see no profit in history, which, to them, merely provides models for bad behaviour. This position is weak: to deny hideousness suppresses much of living and all of dying. Others, too numerous to cite, love selectively, explaining away evil and emphasizing the good. Their past is read in terms of their present: good institutions and good people have led to today's fulfilment. In the view of such thinkers, the medieval attempt to extirpate heresy and attack Islam and Judaism was unhappily necessary because the Church created and defended European culture. The subordinate place of women and the exploitation of peasants by townsmen and lords were functional because without their labour there would have been no monuments of art or letters. Partly true, perhaps, these views would have surprised medieval men and women who knew and worried about what they were doing. Jews and Muslims were detested but sometimes admired, serfs scorned but also emancipated, and women brutalized but also loved as equals.

Some also assert that exploitation of others always destroys the unjust. Like the mad, individuals and societies undoubtedly often repeat actions to excess, persisting in behaviour that causes defeat. But is there a necessary link between self-destruction and lack of justice? One can surely exist without the other, as the long duration of awful empires attests, not to speak of some appalling persons. Still, up to today, someone might say, all empires have fallen; but then, up to today, all individuals have died, and surely not because of self-destruction.

Up to today, death has been largely independent of humanity and its institutions, and, because of the fear it inspires, has caused both human invention and destruction. Having given life, nature launches all into a race from oncoming death. Children, men and women are the runners, who combat their neighbours, young against old, men against women, debtors against creditors, families, provinces, nations and races one against the other. But it is also true that, from the brief commerce of these racers, new life derives to run yet further distances, as do exchanges of information, momentary but fond solidarities and relatively long-lived institutions and cultures. Fear also makes one worry about what one does to others, but, given the tempo of death's approach, only hasty and partial restitution can be made.

The history of individuals and societies shows that excess is wrong or self-defeating. Overbourne by death's rush and the hordes driven before it, however, who can know when he or she has passed the limit? An historian of such vertiginous scenes had best avoid moralizing, and instead imitate Benedict Spinoza, who wrote:

> When I apply my mind to history, I intend . . . to deduce from human nature nothing outrageous or unheard of but instead those things that best fit experience. I will inquire into the things pertaining to this science with the same freedom of spirit one is accustomed to use in mathematics, and will sedulously take care not to laugh at, lament, or execrate, but rather understand human actions.[1]

A tendency to read back modern experience into history must also be resisted. An example is the nineteenth-century view that economic expansion is necessarily accompanied by growing human freedom. The opinion is mistaken: Europe's early modern expansion was accompanied by a great increase in slavery. Again, reflecting the imaginary triumph of the bourgeoisie in the French Revolution, not a few historians have believed that merchants were progressive, but churchmen, nobles and peasants backward. Not only simplistic, this overlooks the prohibition of usury, which, along with technological change, made all the difference between medieval and modern economic individualism or capitalism. Lastly, many of the same students, however much they otherwise disagreed, claimed to have found an essential and original difference between northern urbanism and that of the Mediterranean. Serving as capital of a province and housing rural landowners, the ancient city was said to have lived again in medieval Italy whereas the northern city created a new urbanism led by a bourgeoisie free from the trammels of rural society. To some, the medieval bourgeois city was the cornerstone of the progressive modern and capitalist mercantile and manufacturing city; to others it was also an original creation of northern, even German culture. This book argues instead that, in their origins, northern and southern medieval towns were fundamentally similar.

Again, the Church's needs of today have inspired not a few to maintain that apparent assertions of political power by the popes really dealt with moral or ecclesiastical questions. This position disregards the fact that, to many churchmen and popes, the world was to be made into a fit school for teaching humanity how to attain heaven. The Protestant and even Catholic view that, by failing to reform in the period treated in this volume, the papal Church invited its overthrow during the Reformation is surely too narrow. All the people and not just a few clergy planted the seeds of that great transformation, and no amount of the kind of reform envisaged by modern Christians would have prevented it.

Lastly, one regrets that Scandinavia, the Iberian peninsula, southern Italy and Sicily do not bulk large in this book. A still greater lack is that Slavonic Europe and the Greek and Muslim areas of the Mediterranean are hardly touched on at all. The excuse is that a book on western Europe cannot treat everything. A partial compensation is that, with the exception of southern Italy, institutions in Scandinavia, Hungary and nearby Slavonic states were not dissimilar to those seen earlier in the Carolingian period.

SOURCES

Many readers and historians want to see what individual actors did on history's stage. They wish to evaluate the contributions of famous leaders, to see how successful they were or were not, whether or not they foresaw the future before their time or were reactionaries incapable of understanding their present. This is a reasonable desire because life requires models. At the same time, this kind of history can easily become a cult of human fame, a partial equivalent of medieval canonization. Even in modern times, when (until the introduction of the telephone) sources were abundant, this produced dubious history. It overlooks the fact that, quite apart from the natural reluctance to disclose interests or devious motives even to oneself, it is hard for an individual to know what prompted his or her actions. For obvious reasons, it is harder in regard to others.

The student of medieval history also faces a paucity of sources stating the intentions (whether false or true) of actors or describing their intimate feelings and conduct. A few texts, however, do so. The so-called autobiography of Peter the Hermit of Monte Morrone who became Pope Celestine V (pope 1294, d. 1296) is a work astonishingly rich in details about its hero and his milieu. Similarly, the life of the canonized king of France, Louis IX, finished by John, lord of Joinville, in 1309, sketches aspects of the king's behaviour, qualities, dress and speech, not to speak of those of his crusading notables and clergy, with immense realism and candour.

On the whole, however, this kind of material is far rarer in medieval than in modern or contemporary history. This is not so grave a weakness as it might at first seem. Although the texts cited below do not relate what specific individuals said about their actions, they often clearly show their institutional and psychological context. If, then, one does not learn about specific persons, one knows rather clearly what people generally thought about, their ways of acting and their plans for living. Apart from specialized treatises on theology, philosophy, law and government, the two most instructive types were the many histories and the great pieces of literature composed during this period.

HISTORY

Although the elegance of an Otto of Freising (d. 1158) was not surpassed in the period with which this volume deals, universal history was well represented. Other than the English historians mentioned below, good examples are the *Pantheon* of Godfrey of Viterbo (d. 1191) and the *Historical Mirror* of the Dominican encyclopaedist Vincent of Beauvais (d. *circa* 1259). Similar in tradition was William of Nangis (d. 1300), a historian of the royal monastery of St Denis that, from about 1274, began to produce the official vernacular annals of the French monarchy, the *Great Chronicles*. There were also specialized histories with a large chronological range like Martin of Troppau's (d. 1278) papal and imperial history, a version of which was finished by 1258.

Partly because their treatment of antiquity and the earlier Middle Ages was usually distilled from earlier sources, historians were more original though no more truthful when dealing with their own times. Among the best were England's prolific chroniclers William of Newburgh (d. 1198), Roger of Hoveden (d. 1201) and the monk of St Albans, Matthew Paris (d. 1259) whose excellence illustrates how information could be transmitted with accuracy and detail from one part of Europe to another. Each important event evoked its historians. An example is the German monk Helmhold's (d. 1177) history of the conquest of the Baltic Slavs. Among the best historians of the Crusades in the Near East was William, archbishop of Tyre (d. *circa* 1186), gifted in Arabic and Greek, who also wrote a lost, although much cited, account of the oriental states.

'History' did not quite mean what it means today. A famed preacher, James of Vitry's (d. 1240) *Oriental History* is a historical guidebook of the Holy Land and adjacent regions, and his *Occidental History* treated the orders, structure and sacraments of the Latin Church. His works were manuals for parish priests, preachers and clergy on pilgrimage or missions. Again, history was a moral discipline. Moralizers all, historians favoured parties or interests, Matthew Paris, for example, being hostile to both Rome and the monarchy of Henry III. Although informative and often very perceptive, history was primarily partisan, even polemical, and therefore even more openly biased in favour of contemporary causes, if such can be imagined, than professional academic history today.

Some events were covered thoroughly. The Albigensian Crusade of 1209 and the introduction of the Inquisitors into Languedoc in the 1230s, for example, were recorded in the general French and English chronicles. Local and specific histories express almost every possible point of view, save that of the Cathar church. Peter of Vaux de Cernay, a Cistercian who accompanied the crusaders (1212–18), wrote a detailed polemical history, full of colourful propaganda and miracles. A rhymed vernacular history composed by two authors, now called the *Song of the Crusade*, expressed the attitudes of the southerners, especially the second half. Although intolerant, a cool account of the spread and repression of Catharism was given by a chaplain of the counts of Toulouse, William of Puylaurens, in the 1270s. He enlivened his record with natural wonders, but miracles were left to propagandists like Vaux de Cernay. A brief but remarkably accurate history of the early repression of Catharism was given by the Dominican William Pelisson, himself an enthusiastic Inquisitor (d. 1268). Lastly, there is the history of the Dominican order written by the noted Inquisitor and historian Bernard Gui (d. 1331) in which attention was paid to Languedoc and Toulouse, where the order's mother house was located.

Gui was one of several authors from the new mendicant orders who recorded the glories of their founders, the lives of their saints and their learned men, the latter replete with the titles of their works. A mixture of this genre with the chronicle was that by Salimbene of Parma (d. *circa* 1290), one of the most astonishing documents of all. Salimbene's book outlines the history of the Franciscan order from the death of its founder, its internecine struggles and battles with other orders and the papacy. Interested in reforming Church government, he also interpolated a tract *On Prelates*. This was interwoven with a colourful account of the wars between the Italian republics and the Hohenstaufen Empire from 1167 to 1287, and with an intensely personal history of his own entry into the order and life there, spiced with perceptive, if intolerant, details on every divergent religious and political sect.

Town and provincial history was an early speciality of laymen. A notable example was the history of the March of Treviso written by the son of a notary, the grammarian Rolandino of Padua (d. 1276). To this may be added a literature in praise of individual cities. The one cited in these pages is the curiously statistical praise of Milan by Bonvesino of Riva in about 1282. Since lay literacy in Latin was widespread in Italy, these were in that language. As seen above anent the Albigensian Crusade, vernacular history had also begun to make its appearance. An outstanding work was the history of the Fourth Crusade and of the Latin Empire of Constantinople by Geoffrey of Villehardouin, marshal of the Champagne and of Romania (d. *circa* 1213).

BIOGRAPHY AND POETRY

As in Otto of Freising's and his continuator's *Deeds* of Frederick I Barbarossa, biography was close to history. Capetian ideology inspired a life of Philip II Augustus of France by William the Breton (d. *circa* 1224–26). Princely lines were also interested in recording the histories of their families and the deeds of famous ancestors. The canon Breton of Amboise's (*fl.* 1155–73) history of the counts of Anjou and lords of Amboise and that of the lords of Ardres and counts of Guines by the clerk Lambert of Ardres (*fl.* 1194–1203) exemplify this genre. A chaplain composed a vernacular verse biography of William, marshal of England and earl of Pembroke (d. 1219), a work which, if not always truthful in detail, is veracity itself about the milieu of his hero. By the thirteenth century, laymen were in this business themselves, writing both biographies and autobiographies in the vernacular. Among the most celebrated of these were the memoirs of Philip of Novara (d. 1261–64), seignior, jurist and historian of Cyprus and of what was called 'Overseas France'. Joinville's biography of Louis IX, mentioned above, is another.

Career and advancement attracted the élite that set the tone for medieval society. What they wanted were heroes who taught lessons. Some of these, like the twelfth-century *Ralph of Cambrai*, preached the virtue of moderation and the unhappy fate of those ruled by excess. Others, like the earlier and ever popular *Song of Roland*, provided heroes whose suicidal and Christ-like sacrifice was the model of how to win fame by arms. There were also humorous caricatures of martial values, complete with anti-heroes who behaved without a shred of virtue. The religious counterpart of the acquisition of fame by soldiers was the attainment of sanctity by the saints, the Church's heroes. Saints' lives were becoming increasingly historical in this period and large collections of use to preachers were appearing. A celebrated example was James of Voragine's (Varazze, d. 1298) collection of semi-biographies and tales called the

Golden Legend. Related to this literature were such exemplarist semi-historical books as the *Dialogue of Miracles* by the Cistercian Caesarius of Heisterbach (d. 1240), designed to explore for the benefit of novices the hazards, joys, history and heroes of the life religious.

A spate of increasingly specialized tracts on the 'ages of man', manners, chivalry and social and political theory was written by laymen such as Novara mentioned above, Brunetto Latini (d. 1294–5) and the polymath Raymond Llull (d. *circa* 1315). These authors wrote in the vernacular, and this reminds the reader that, in lay letters, vernacular verse initially predominated. In poetry, the individual was the central subject. Influenced by religious thought, themes of spiritual ascent or progress were outlined in poems such as *Perceval*. The subject was easily joined to that of love. In his *Erec and Enide* Christian of Troyes (*fl.* 1150–80) – a poet admired by Dante – taught that true love flourishes only among those who strive to advance in the world. The tests to be overcome by lovers were investigated in Arthurian literature by means of figures like Lancelot and Queen Genevieve. Troubadour verse especially explored the passion and unresolvable longing of being in love. There was, indeed, an enormous literature on the subject, some of it playful and earthy. In 1184–6 Andrew the Chaplain wrote his *On Love*, a witty socio-philosophical encyclopaedia of this topic.

Vernacular writing, moreover, had begun to transcend history, war's heroics and love. Mentioned above, Raymond Llull joined love to theology. Yet another writer in the vernacular was the great poet Dante Alighieri (d. 1321) who began work on his *Divine Comedy* about 1307. During the ten or more years he spent on this vernacular verse encyclopaedia, he took time off to compose in Latin a political and ecclesiological tract *On Monarchy* (around 1313). Widely circulated, the larger part of the *Romance of the Rose* was written in French somewhere between 1270 and 1285 by John Clopinel of Meung on the Loire, presumably a clerk. Not only a lively description of love, of the war between woman and man, of manners and behaviour, John's poem was also a vernacular encyclopaedia of philosophy and theology. A translator of Latin texts, John also provided the lay élite with elegant vulgarizations of clerical thought, such as that of the Cistercian Alan of Lille (d. 1202).

These remarks touch on the relationship of the clergy and laity, a topic outlined in the next chapter.

NOTES AND REFERENCES

1   *Tractatus politicus* 1, 4 in *Opera* (ed. Carl Gebhardt, Heidelberg 1925), 274.

PART ONE
Europe

2

SOCIAL FRONTIERS: CLERKS AND LAYMEN

THE TWO PEOPLES

Impelled by motives described in Mr Brooke's earlier volume in this series and occasionally reviewed here, western Europeans elevated the Church to lead Latin society during the Gregorian age, a period of social and internal warfare extending from about 1050 until 1130. During this slow revolution, a new structure of social and governmental power came into being, and remained to characterize western Europe's apogee in the twelfth and thirteenth centuries. This structure differed from that obtaining in the earlier Middle Ages and from the one that appeared in early modern times. Before the revolution, Europeans had been governed – except on local and familial levels best investigated by historical anthropologists – by empires and quasi-national states, aided by often rebellious but always subordinate churches. After 1300, larger units of political and social power were growing into nation states or other substantial units of government, such as the Italian principates and large German principalities. Here also secular power was coming to rule a subordinate clergy, and eventually, indeed, to replace them partially by lay Levites, the philosophers of modern times.

Although large monarchies lingered into the twelfth and thirteenth centuries, and although, as shall be seen, some states that were to become modern nations were already evolving, most power was entrusted to the ecumenical government of the Roman Church and the local governments of town and countryside. The latter, whether urban or rural, seigniorial or republican, achieved a degree of freedom from central governments they were never again

15

to enjoy. From the days of the Gregorians until the turmoil of the fourteenth and fifteenth centuries, Europe was led by an inadvertent but real alliance between her aristocracies and her churchmen under the See of Peter.

The Church embodied the cultural identity of the 'Christian republic'. Although war persisted, Christendom's true wars were the Crusades, repeated waves of expansion at the expense of neighbouring cultures and religions. The needs of this imperialism encouraged plans designed to realize at home the ideal of a peaceful Christian brotherhood, and the military élite was restrained at home by the idea and law of just war and the peace or truce of God. Just price and the condemnation of usury were employed to protect crusaders and police the marketplace. A propaganda for economic brotherhood helped to build a social corporatism with which to tie the grasping hands of the rich and mighty. In every activity, the expansion of the penitential system and of the courts of canon law testified to the willingness of the people to allow the clergy to regulate and harmonize life on earth.

Not always happily, the clergy were aided by the monastic orders. Indeed, around 1100, the monks were often ahead of the rest. Cistercians were famed for clearing forests and marshes, Europe's best soldiers served in the ranks of the military orders, and new foundations appeared everywhere to house the aged, the sick, the destitute and the fallen. The thirteenth century saw the fulfilment of earlier efforts in education: the building of the university system and parish schools. Friars, monks and parish clergy combined to enhance the role of sacerdotal authority by proclaiming the miracle of the mass and expanding penitential police. In regard to the mass, the cup having been withdrawn from the laity during the Gregorian age, the priestly miracle of transubstantiation was finally codified at the fourth Lateran Council in 1215 and the feast of the Body of Christ spread by papal edict in 1264. The role of the priest in the miracle of the mass and as judge in the court of conscience fortified a confident sense that there existed a direct link between God's eternal ordinance and human institutions, between heaven and earth.

Circumstances seemed to justify this sanguine attitude. Growing population, newly cleared fields, new towns, expanding personal freedom and the conquest of foreign lands made nature herself seem beneficent and earthly institutions fit to help achieve a happy end. Still, this required difficult adjustments on the part of Christians, ones that caused basic changes in the ethos of the Church. Many were still attracted by what had once given freedom in the days of Rome and the State-dominated churches of the earlier Middle Ages: the accent on the other world – the world of heaven against earth, of spiritual against material values, of things felt but indemonstrable against things demonstrable. Moved by success, however, both clergy and laity turned to examine and manipulate the world in which they lived. The receptiveness to Aristotelian and Arabic natural philosophy was an expression of this. Another was a heightened interest in both the ideal and practical forms of ecclesiastical and secular government. Clerical and lay utopians tried to remake the world on the model of the supernal Jerusalem, to make a heaven on earth. Around 1200, this movement attracted such varied groups as the teachers at Paris headed by Peter Cantor (precentor of Nôtre Dame, d. 1197) and the humble craftsfolk brigaded in the mass movement of the Italian Humiliati.

The Austin Friar Giles of Rome (d. 1316) said that government's main objective was to educate men and women to attain heaven. For this, the people must be at peace, possess the material means of living well, and have suitable education.

> A king ought therefore see that the study of letters flourishes in his kingdom, and that many learned men and scholars are there. Where wisdom and letters flourish, surely the whole will thence draw a measure of learning . . . . Indeed, if a ruler does not promote education and does not wish his subjects to be learned, he is not a king but instead a tyrant.[1]

Working in the world led to a gradual shift not only of values but also of clerical institutions. When the State dominated the Church, the monk's contemplative and cloistered life seemed more consequential than the active life. This conviction never wholly died. The abbot Rupert of Deutz (d. 1135) claimed that the apostles had been monks, and that the Saviour did not have them preach, baptize or perform miracles but instead exalt themselves by exemplifying virtue and humbling themselves before others. This is what the later Francis of Assisi (d. 1226) also taught. On the other hand, the Assisan's Franciscans went to work to animate the Church's mission by preaching and stimulating penance at the world's crossroads. This programme was earlier previsioned by Peter Cantor, who likened teaching and preaching to a house. Its foundation is study and reading; disputation and discussion compose its walls; 'preaching . . . is the roof protecting the faithful from the heat and tempests of the vices'.[2]

Preaching was necessary to make the world into a Christian society. Bernard of Clairvaux's (d. 1153) tours to southern France, the Rhineland and elsewhere illustrate how famous preachers were sought after by the local clergy. In the thirteenth century the university replaced the cloister as the training ground for the pulpit, and Paris produced many successful preachers whose sermons were collected for the use of others. Among these were the revivalist Fulk (d. 1202), a parish priest of Neuilly and student of Peter Cantor; Robert of Curzon (d. 1218), professor at Paris and cardinal; Stephen Langton (d. 1228), professor there and later archbishop of Canterbury; and James of Vitry, who died in 1240 as archbishop of Acre and cardinal. The mendicants picked up this torch. Local chroniclers exaggeratedly claimed that a Franciscan spellbinder, Berthold of Regensburg (d. 1272), attracted crowds of a hundred thousand or more.

Scripture and bible history were basic sources for preachers. An example of the latter is the *Scholastic History* of a one-time chancellor of Paris, Peter Comestor (d. *circa* 1179), recounting the bible story with legendary accretions. Scripture was given its great or ordinary gloss by commentators starting with Anselm of Laon (d. 1117) and ending with Gilbert the Universal, a canon of Auxerre and later bishop of London (d. 1134). Thereafter followed commentaries or postils on specific parts of the Bible. Much was done in Paris, where the work of two canons regular of St Victor, Hugh (d. 1141) and Andrew (d. 1175), was later advanced by the circle of Peter Cantor mentioned above. In the thirteenth century, leadership passed to the mendicants, who added much traditional Jewish commentary, especially that of Rashi of Troyes (Solomon son of Isaac, d. 1105). Including postillators as radical as Peter John Olivi (d. 1298), the Franciscans produced the greatest commentator of all, Nicholas of Lyra (d. 1340). These studies prompted dissatisfaction with the sacred text itself. Forever swinging wide, another Franciscan, Roger Bacon (d. 1292), attributed the imperfections of the contemporary Bible to the fact that the Paris bookmakers were laymen, and married ones at that!

The pulpit led to penitence and the court of conscience. The Franciscan Alexander of Hales (d. 1245) and the Dominican Thomas Aquinas (of Aquino, d. 1274) together expounded the doctrine of the treasury of the saints, a reservoir of superabundant grace on which to draw for forgiveness to be granted the fallible. Developing the idea of purgatory, churchmen were confident that the punishments and pardons they assigned penetrated beyond life into the beyond. This system was reinforced by the insistence of the Lateran Council of 1215 on at least one annual confession. Manuals of casuistry appeared, one of the earlier by the Cistercian Alan of Lille in the later twelfth century. About the same time, Peter Cantor issued his *On Sacraments and Advice to the Soul*, whose third book was devoted to cases of conscience. Like a collection of legal opinions was the standard *Summa of Penitential Cases* written between 1220 and 1234 by Raymond of Peñafort (d. 1275). This literature branched out to produce epitomes and specialized tracts. A compilation called *Rules for the Merchants of Toulouse* concerning usury and related topics was culled by a Dominican named Guy from the much larger *Summa of Confessors* of John of Freiburg (d. 1314) written in the 1290s.

The clergy needed manuals to understand the world and their place in it. John of Salisbury's (d. 1189) *Policraticus* touched on all subjects regarding the relation of the faith to secular life and government, but in too elegant and specialized a way to appeal to a textbook audience. More successful were the *Sentences* by Peter Lombard (d. as bishop of Paris in 1160), a manual treating basic questions of theology and Church organization, a work 'canonized' at the Lateran Council in 1215. During the thirteenth century, the encyclopaedic tradition reached its apogee in the Dominican Vincent of Beauvais's *Great Mirror*, a work subdivided into three parts: nature, doctrine and history.

Clergy working in the world soon began to absorb the intense sense of vocation that had marked the withdrawn religious. This inner asceticism and progress in self-discipline was explored by the Franciscan Bonaventure (John of Fidanza, d. 1274) in his *Itinerary of the Mind*. Although spiritual withdrawal still attracted, physical retirement into the cloister lacked the appeal of an active engagement in the world's life. Those fighting the world's evils were soon called superior to the monks confined in their cloisters, and Robert of Curzon claimed that a teacher explaining scripture in the schools deserved a reward higher than that of any Cistercian. The canonist Hostiensis (Henry of Susa, cardinal of Ostia, d. 1271) referred to 'just judges leading the active life without duplicity, a life which, if well conducted, is more fruitful than the contemplative'.[3]

These attitudes exemplify the paradox of Church leadership: the more the clergy led, the more they came to respect the world's professions. Some even admitted that soldiers were more needed than monks. Gregory VII had complained in 1079 to Abbot Hugh of Cluny, who had received a Burgundian duke into the cloister when the papacy needed allies against the Empire, 'you have . . . received the duke into Cluny's quiet and thereby caused a hundred thousand Christians to lack a protector'.[4] Canon lawyers were flattered to hear Boncompagno of Signa (d. before 1250) borrow from Roman law to liken them to soldiers in arms.

Perhaps the clergy could have provided that function themselves, and, to some extent, did, as in the military orders. Directing the life of the world, however, was only part of their ambition. Another was the desire to protect ecclesiastical liberty by gaining freedom from secular authority. Dominant though churchmen seemed after the Gregorian age, they remembered earlier subjection, and, to avoid lay oppression, wished to be their own judges. Since princes and magistrates wanted officers accountable in secular courts, freedom required clerks to withdraw from secular office and the exercise of professions involving them in the lay world. Yet someone had to fill such positions. Paradoxically, then, the Gregorian desire for freedom from lay power not only resulted in Rome leading Europe for a time, but also encouraged a reforming laity and clergy to purge the old clerical cadres holding secular office. This helped create the beginnings of the secular literate or clerical professions during the Gregorian troubles. Not a few early jurists and scribes were one-time clerks who had been married or charged with simony and fled, so to speak, into lay professionalism.

The change should not be overstated, because this was no overnight transformation. Lay literacy in Latin had never entirely vanished. That princes should be literate had always been urged, and there were lay notaries and lawyers in parts of Italy before the Gregorian age. These exceptions, however, merely prove the rule. As the Premonstratensian Philip of Harvengt (d. 1182) said, the word 'clerk' meant 'churchman', and charters, even those written by secular notaries, often referred to the clergy simply as 'literate persons' in this period. As shall be later seen, the separation of the spheres of lay and clerk was long obscured by the lack of trained laymen and by the persistence of the old State-dominated churches of earlier times.

A start had been made, however, and ecclesiastical legislation pointed in two directions. Starting early in the twelfth century and

continuing to the fourth Lateran Council of 1215, churchmen were
forbidden to serve as officers, lawyers and notaries for lay governments and persons. Surgery was altogether closed to them. Church
law also sought to limit clerical education for secular pursuits. By
1163 monks were prohibited from studying civil law and medicine,
and in 1219 this prohibition was extended to parish rectors and
other full-time officers. Lower clerical grades were left free to learn
secular professions except surgery, but clerks were not usually permitted to exercise them except in the military orders, within the
Church itself or, if need be, to help the poor.

LETTERS, PROFESSIONS AND LAICISM

Although often harmonious, the relationship between the clergy
and laity was never easy. Writing around 1300, Alberic of Rosate
(d. 1354) summed up juristic doctrine:

> There are two peoples, one of the clerks and the other of laymen . . . and they
> are two types of diverse nature, one superior and the other inferior . . . . There
> are therefore two governors in Milan, the archbishop who rules the clerks and
> the temporal lord who rules the laity.[5]

The literate professions were on the disputed frontier between the
ecclesiastical and lay nations.

The first secular professions were medicine, law and scribal services. To these were soon added the teachers of the liberal arts,
such as grammarians, and of the sciences like mathematics. Related
to these was a wide range of artisanries such as druggists, surgeons
or barbers and the stationers and book-copiers who sprang up
around the universities. Because many persons were in lower clerical orders and because middle-aged people frequently moved into
clericature, frontiers were never clear. The history of the master
mason Gerhard of Rile, 'master of the fabric' of the cathedral at
Cologne begun in 1248, is a case in point. In 1257 Gerhard became a canon and his wife entered a Cistercian house. By 1268 this
mason had attained the priesthood and four adult children had followed him into the Church.

Lawyers soon expressed lay professional self-consciousness.
Roman law maintained that the Empire and its law were sacred,
postulating that judges who repressed crime shared this quality. Text

appended to the twelfth-century code called *Peter's Excerpts* expressed this idea: 'What is sacred is partly human, like the laws, and partly divine, like the Church. Some priests are therefore divine . . . and others human, like magistrates, who are nevertheless called priests because they administer something sacred, that is, the laws.'[6] A later jurist attributed to Alberic of Rosate the self-congratulatory fancy 'that judges who judge justly are not only to be called priests, but even angels of God, and deserve more than monks'.[7] Circumstances also obliged the Church to admit the equality of lay jurists. As early as 1252, the layman Giles Fuscararius (d. 1289) taught canon law at Bologna, and not a few judges sitting in the papal court and episcopal ones were laymen. Everybody got into this act. If lawyers could be called priests, so also could soldiers, a notion found in Raymond Llull's *Order of Chivalry*, the most popular manual of knighthood and nobility of the age.

The lay spirit went beyond professionalism and added a sense of vocation taken from the cloistered religious. The spread of the monastic ethos to the lay world, at first in the Gregorian age and then again during the mendicant movements of the thirteenth century, will be treated in later chapters. Here it may be noted that this combination of the priesthood of the active life with the monastic contemplative life had begun to give laymen a growing sense of equality with the clergy. Besides, however much they led, clerks often confessed that, in God's eyes, all men and women were equal. Gerhoh of Reichersberg (d. 1169) opined that, rich or poor, noble or servile, merchant or farmer, everyone who has renounced the devil,

> even if he never becomes a clerk or a monk, can be shown to have renounced the world . . . . Every man has his place and every profession without exception has a rule in the Catholic faith and apostolic doctrine suitable to its quality, under which, by fighting well, a man can attain the crown.[8]

Laymen belong to orders, just as do monks, said James of Vitry:

> We do not judge only those who renounce the world and enter an order to be monks, but instead . . . all faithful Christians who serve the Lord under evangelical rules and live ordained under the one highest abbot [Jesus] . . . . There is an order of the married, of the widowed and of virgins. Soldiers, merchants, farmers, artisans and all the other multiform types of men have rules peculiar to each.[9]

Spiritual equality would have meant nothing without some literacy in either Latin or the vernacular. The principal conduits of lay Latin literacy were the professions of medicine, law and the public scribes. Just as the academics stole their black robes from the clergy, so had they taken their language for learning and law. As taught by jurists, notaries and grammarians, a simplified Latin emerged as a juristic and literary vehicle, finding a place between high Latinity and the rising vernaculars beneath. What this meant is easily seen. Around Toulouse in Languedoc, for example, scribal Latin improved, driving the vernacular out of the documents as the professional notariate penetrated villages and small towns in the decades after 1200. In the same region, furthermore, ordinary businessmen habitually collected their own files of Latin documents and could surely read them. In Italy Boncompagno remarked that 'merchants do not need an elegant choice of words because almost all correspond with each other either in their vulgar tongues or corrupt Latin'.[10]

The proponents of this Latin were aware of its character. Introducing his history of the March of Treviso, the grammarian Rolandino of Padua explained why he chose Latin instead of the vernacular: 'I write prose because I can say what I want more clearly in it than in verse . . . [and many] prefer to discover in Latin the sufferings and labours of modern men than to hear of the deeds of the noble ancients in the vulgar.'[11] The relationship of this Latin to the classical language may be seen in Boncompagno of Signa. This notary felt that his Latin was new and improved, and detested the authority of the ancients, especially what he thought was Cicero's needlessly obscure style. 'In [Tully's] rhetorical works, the construction is inept and the position of words intricate, whereby he most clearly contradicted his own instructions, because he there stated that the narrative should be brief and lucid.'[12] Wildly off base, Boncompagno opined that Ciceronian Latin would never regain its place because students no longer studied it. Who, he asked, obeys the professors of rhetoric with their artificial Latin composition? Only an idiot would address a fellow named Pope as 'Mr Servant of God's Servants'.

Although statistics are lacking, the currency of this vulgar Latin can be estimated. Most literature between 1200 and 1300 was written in it. Not only was it used by jurists and notaries but it was also the language of the clergy and their schools. As the examinations recorded in Odo Rigaud's register of visitations in his archdiocese of Rouen from 1248 to 1269 show, rural clerks were not always very literate, and vulgar Latin was easier to learn than classical discourse. Partly because of its flexibility, vulgar Latin was also eminently suitable for technical discourse in philosophy and theology, and it therefore caught on in the schools in spite of John of Salisbury's lamentations.

An assessment of taxes in the upper and lower towns of Carcassonne for the Flemish war in 1304 affords a glimpse of a small city's professional services. Estimated on the basis of four persons per taxable hearth, the population of this modest city was around 9,500 souls. Including nine parish rectors, some 260 clerks lived there. This figure includes monks, friars, the canons and priests of the cathedral chapter, and those in lesser grades, such as hospital workers and inmates, schoolteachers and domestics. The legal professions were represented by forty-three public notaries (solicitors) and fifteen advocates (barristers). Twelve Lombards and thirty Jews offered economic services. Lastly, forty-three nobles and forty military persons inhabited or were stationed in this administrative capital.

Because business required correspondence with home and other Lombards, Lombard males were probably literate in the Latin in which their contracts were written. Most Jews were literate in the vernacular and Hebrew, but few in Latin. That notaries and advocates were literate in Latin goes without saying, but there were differing degrees of competence. Representing clients before the bar, lawyers in the Midi were all university-trained; notaries, on the other hand, had probably been apprenticed to others in the profession. In a university town like Bologna, notaries usually also went through the faculty of arts.

Nine medical doctors were also counted in Carcassonne. There, because of the town's proximity to the medical faculty at Montpellier, most medical doctors were 'physicians' (*physici*), those who had studied Aristotle's physics at a university. These undoubtedly had Latin. Farther north, it is likely that most doctors were medicos (*medici*), men trained by practitioners, just about the same as surgeons who had little or no Latin. The matter was almost one of geographical distribution. Although, as Bonvesino of Riva tells us for Milan, physicians were common enough in Italy's urbanized areas, there were few in the north, even in the Low Countries, where they were largely to be found among the clergy who did not practise for laymen. Along with the legal and medical élites at Carcassonne went the clergy, especially those who had taken higher orders, many of whom had seen the inside of a university and were titled 'master'. Lastly, urban patricians often had some competence in Latin letters.

Most gentlemen were literate only in the vernacular. This also goes for certain groups in the Church, such as the female religious and even secular canons, those whose birth was so elevated that they, like the canons of St Mark's of Venice, were damned if they would learn Latin. This does not mean they were uncultivated. The poetry of the age – vernacular literature was at first primarily poetic – treated almost every theme of interest to an alert mind. Gentlemen of means usually had clergy and scribes in their households to whom they dictated their letters and who read aloud at dinner or other times. A rather exaggerated example is Baldwin, in 1169 count of Guines and lord of Ardres, towns near Boulogne in northern France. The count's secretary was a layman who collected romances and heroic songs. He also translated parts of scripture, sermons, a commentary on the mystical sense of the Song of Songs, Alfred's life of St Anthony, 'a great part of the physical art', Solinus's *On the Nature of Things*, and selections from Augustine, Denis the Areopagite and Thales of Miletus (!) for his patron's edification. Dinner, when reading often took place, must have been a pretty heavy affair up there in Guines.

Vernacular letters grew during the 1200s. A basic text for soldiers, Vegetius's late Roman *On War*, was widely circulated in the original Latin, but parts were paraphrased and incorporated in Spain's vernacular 'mirror' of government called the *Book of the Laws (Siete Partidas)* of 1260. The whole was finally translated into French by John of Meung, whose other translations also testify to the audience for vernacular works: Boethius's Consolation of Philosophy, the Calamities and letters of Abelard and Héloise, Ailred of Rievaulx's Spiritual Friendship, written about 1160, and Gerald of Wales's Topography of Ireland of about 1188.

'An illiterate king is a crowned ass' went the tag. This doctrine spread to nobles and patricians during the time studied in this volume. There was schoolteacher's special pleading here: could one be a soldier and also an amateur of letters? Writing the history of the counts of Anjou, the canon Breton of Amboise defended Fulk the Good, who had celebrated mass in clerical garb on the feast of St Martin of Tours, by saying that, 'although expertly instructed in letters and the grammatical art as well as in Aristotelian and Ciceronian reasoning, this intelligent man was considered the best among the more vigorous knights'.[13] Gerald of Wales (d. 1220) later claimed that the more a man knew of the liberal arts the better was he as a soldier, a point proved by adducing Greece under the Macedonians, Rome under the Caesars and Frankland under the Carolingians! By the time John of Meung wrote his *Rose*, the idea that a gentleman was to be as lettered as he was expert in arms was a commonplace. The wide circulation of Dante's poetic and vernacular works reminds one of Italy's many literate patricians and gentlemen. As significant was the penetration of the vernacular into legal documentation. Generalized everywhere by about 1300, vernacular documents testify to the literacy of the business classes and even of some artisans. In Tuscany, Brunetto Latini wrote a vernacular rhetoric in Ciceronian style for the use of town notaries and chancellors.

Most layfolk, however, were illiterate. Dated no later than 1324, a manual for parish priests makes distinctions: 'literate people can have knowledge of God from Scripture, but ignorant ones must be instructed by books designed for laymen, that is, by pictures'.[14] Besides, many of those who wrote for laymen were clergy. A number of troubadours, for example, were clerical or ended their lives in clerical garb. Noted before, John of Meung may have been a clerk.

The audience of lay letters was grander than the number of literates, and hence literature penetrated below aristocrats and patricians. Modern imagination does a disservice to medieval popular culture by using terms such as 'courtly love'. True, the stories are usually aristocratic in tone, but who would think of public notaries as ideal lovers? Soldiers were the ideal: by risking their lives in war, they showed ability to risk love with all its loyalty and difficult tests. The beloved was also a lady. Never mentioned in the literature, her risk was childbirth, but neither she nor her lover is ever seen changing nappies.

Although lovers in poetry (save a few) were both handsome and rich, there was no necessary class affiliation among those who loved them. Nor can one assign to different classes the genres of love literature, from the courtly fancies of Arthurian romance to the earthiness of the *fabliaux*. The lives of the troubadours compiled in the fourteenth century show that not a few of the most spiritual and courtly poets were burghers, merchants and even artisans. At Toulouse, the two greatest poets were Peter Vidal (*fl.* 1180–1206), the son of a furrier, and William Figueras (*fl.* 1215–45), barfly and son of a tailor. Nobles, moreover, both enjoyed and wrote earthy verse.

The early troubadour William IX, duke of Aquitaine (d. 1127), composed some of the raunchiest stuff on record. The chronicler William of Malmesbury (d. *circa* 1143) reported with mock horror that the duke had a mistress 'whom he so loved that he had the girl's picture painted on his shield, often saying that he wished to bear her in battle as she bore him in bed'.[15] Evidence of the popularity of this literature and its themes is seen everywhere. A Bolognese statute of 1288 ordered singers of French songs not to perform in public places when preaching was under way. Writing on business morality, a Dominican named Guy wagged his finger: 'I advise each of you to read or at least to listen to the [*Rule for Merchants*] in place of the useless fables and romances customarily read in workshops and stores'.[16]

The effects of the invasion of what had once been their near monopoly sometimes prompted the clergy to react. Their doubts about the competence of laymen in philosophy and theology were partly justified because the best of the clergy were better at these subjects than layfolk. The reaction was nevertheless greater than the cause justified, and showed that the clerks wished they could put the genie back in the bottle. Besides, specialists often dislike those in other fields. Churchmen, for example, shared the intellectuals' prejudice against lawyers. Giles of Rome observed that

> all jurists are political idiots. For, just as laymen and plebeians are called dialectical ignoramuses by the Philosopher . . . because they do not argue with artifice and dialectical skill, so lawyers, because they speak of politics narratively and without reason, may be called political ignoramuses. It is obvious how much more highly those who know the political and moral sciences are to be regarded than those who know law.[17]

In almost the same words, this opinion is repeated by the Franciscan zealot Roger Bacon. Although inviting wonder about how people often make their own knowledge the universe's only yardstick, these conflicts between lay and clerical intellectuals are good evidence of the power of secular intellectualism at this time.

In fine, before and during the period with which this volume deals, churchmen led western Europe. Turning towards the world they believed they ruled, they tried to discover what composed it and to create agencies to make it better. In so doing they helped build lay literacy and the lay spirit, both of which were to reduce clerical power and authority later on. In the meantime, however, the two peoples, clerical and lay, were relatively harmoniously balanced. The scales were to tip decisively to secular authority only later during the Reformation and the rise of the national State.

NOTES AND REFERENCES

1   *De regimine principum* 3, 2, 8 (Rome, 1607), 417. The Latin *industres* is translated *sages hommes* in the French (*Li livres du gouvernement des rois* (ed. S.P. Molenaer, New York, 1899), 314.

2   *Verbum abbreviatum* 1 in *PL* CCV 25.

3   His *Summa Aurea*, cited in Kantorowicz, *The King's Two Bodies*, 122n.

4   *Registrum* 6, 17 in *MGH Epp. sel.* II, 351.

5   *De statutis* 2, 2, 17 in *TUJ* II, 29a.

6   *Petri Exceptionum appendices* 1, 95 in Herman Fitting, *Juristische Schriften des früheren Mittelalters* (Halle, 1876) 164.

7   Kantorowicz *The King's Two Bodies*, 122n.

8   *Liber de aedificio dei* 43 in *PL* CXCIV,, 1302d.

9   *Historia occidentalis* 34 (ed. J. F. Hinnebusch, Fribourg 1972) 165–66.

10   *Boncompagni Boncompagnus* in *BuF* I, 173.

11   *Cronica in factis et circa facta marchie Trivixiane (AA 1200–62)* in *RIS* (ed. 1905), VIII, i, 7–8.

12   *Rhetorica novissima*, Prologue in *BIMA,* II, 252.

13   *Chroniques des comtes d'Anjou et des seigneurs d'Amboise* (ed. Louis Halphen and René Poupardin, Paris, 1913), 40.

14   *Speculum humanae salvationis*, Prologue (ed. J. Lutz and P. Perdrizet, Leipzig, 1907), 2.

15   Bezzola, *Les origines et la formation de la litérature courtoise en occident* II, ii 272.

16   Oxford ms Lincoln Coll. Lat. 81, f. 34, and Cambridge ms Add. B. 65, f. 1.

17   *De regimine principum* 2, 2, 8 (Rome, 1607), 309.

3

CULTURAL FRONTIERS: FRANCE, ITALY AND EUROPE

FRANCE

What first strikes one about Latin Europe around 1200 is the apparent leadership of France and Italy. Until the late eleventh century, the Germans and their Empire had been preponderant, and the memory of this circumstance still influenced the perceptions of those living later. Frederick I Barbarossa, the Hohenstaufen emperor (d. 1190), asserted that Europe's other kings were kinglets in comparison with him. Only in 1268, with the extinction of the Hohenstaufen imperial line, would such observations have seemed absurd. By that time, indeed, contemporaries were finally aware of the power of France and Italy: the astonishingly rapid expansion of the Capetian monarchy, the invasion of much of Europe by papal power and its affiliated Lombard merchant bankers and, of course, the defeat of the Hohenstaufen. Still, the foundations of French and Italian success had been laid much earlier with the basic victory of Rome over the Empire, the rise of Italian commercial and industrial power and the emigration of Frenchmen and French culture in the latter half of the eleventh century and the first half of the twelfth century, in short, during the Gregorian age. Curiously, the grandeur of the French and Italians had no sooner been realized than it began to fade. Preaching and writing in Florence around 1300, the Dominican Remigio de'Girolami could say that all Europe's other monarchs were mere kinglets when compared with France's king, whose prince was paradigmatically *The* King, just as Aristotle was *The* Philosopher and Mary *The* Virgin. Barely half a century after he died in 1319, even a loyal Frenchman would have smiled sadly on hearing such a remark.

For the time being, French greatness was assured. Along the northern frontier with the Empire, French speech was penetrating maritime Flanders at the expense of Flemish. French culture penetrated into a Germanic region like Luxembourg, and Capetian political influence was dominant from the royal province of Flanders to the Lorraines by 1300. To the east Capetian success was more marked. The definitive absorption of the county of Champagne into the royal domain in 1284 reminds one that a province whose princes had sometimes looked towards the Empire had become irrevocably French. By 1245 the old imperial territory of Provence had fallen to the house of Anjou, a Capetian cadet line. The occupation of Lyons by France in 1312 completed the occupation of the Saône valley, and French influence penetrated the Burgundies and Lorraines and, beyond them, into the Rhineland and Swabia. One understands why Pope John XXII (d. 1334) believed that King Philip IV the Fair (d. 1314) of France had a good chance of becoming emperor. One may nevertheless not forget that the loyalty of Flanders was doubtful, that Walloon regions like Brabant and the Liégeois were not part of the kingdom, and that other French-speaking areas such as Savoy and parts of the Lorraines and Burgundies lay beyond Capetian control.

The history of the Iberian frontier is not dissimilar. From Carolingian times Catalonia was part of France, and until the 1220s, public scribes there occasionally dated their documents by French regnal years. In the decentralized Midi, a loose confederation under the house of St Gilles-Toulouse had reached from western Provence on the Rhone river to the Agennais on the Garonne, and began to break up in the late twelfth century. It looked as if the Catalans and Aragonese (who joined in 1162) would take over the area from Provence through maritime Languedoc to the Pyrenean counties, and that the rest would fall to the Poitevin Aquitanians, a group joined to the Plantagenet (or Angevin) Atlantic French and English monarchy in the reign of Henry II (d. 1189).[1] As shall be seen, the Plantagenets lost most of their French domains, including Poitou, during the reign of Philip II Augustus (d. 1223), and had no further ambitions to the south. Beginning with the Albigensian Crusade launched in 1209, northern French crusaders and eventually the Capetians themselves intervened in the south. Already failing in Provence, the Catalan–Aragonese hold in Languedoc was erased by the crusader Simon of Montfort (d. 1218) and the death of Peter II of Aragon on the battlefield of Muret in 1213. By 1300, although Languedoc and the mountain counties were restive throughout the century and Montpellier was not lost to Catalonia–Aragon until 1349, most of the Midi had been absorbed by the Capetians. In the meantime, however, a treaty signed at Corbeil in 1258 had split this once unified linguistic and cultural area. There the Catalans renounced all claims to Provence, Languedoc and the mountain counties, while France surrendered its ancient claim to Catalonia. The only breach of the Pyrenean frontier in favour of France came about as a result of the union of Navarre with Champagne in 1235 because, in 1284, the Capetians collected this kingdom along with the northern inheritance of the counts of Champagne.

Rivalled only by Italians, the French were Europe's greatest crusaders, leadership in the Crusades implying excellence in warfare. Certainly, others also exemplified martial vigour. Although the imperialist Alexander of Roes granted the French pre-eminence in learning, he reserved for the Germans the capacity to conquer and govern others. Famed for naval warfare, the Italians were also not bad on land, and during the late twelfth century, popularized the crossbow, whose bolts prompted the introduction of horse and plate armour at this time. By about 1300, indeed, warfare's future course could be dimly discerned in the successful combination of bowmen and men-at-arms by the English in their Scottish wars and in a seemingly fortuitous defeat of Habsburg chivalry by Swiss hillfolk in 1295.

For the time being, however, chivalry ruled the battlefield, and French chivalry, especially that of northern France, was Europe's best. William of Newburgh reports that Richard Coeur de Lion believed French knights were 'sharper' than English because of exercise in frequent tournaments. 'English knights,' the king said, 'should learn the art and use of war [in tournaments] so that the Gauls should not insult them, as being rude and less expert.'[2] The most expert soldiers of the age, the Templars and Hospitallers, were recruited largely in France, and northern France produced the two most brilliant commanders of the age, Richard Coeur de Lion (d. 1199) and Simon of Montfort (d. 1218). Exceptions apart, the military orders in Spain and Germany followed the rule of the Temple, itself inspired by the Cistercians; and the Teutonic order (founded 1190; military in 1198) derived its military rule from the Temple and that for its hospitals from the Hospitallers.

Along with soldiers went emigrants. The great age of French emigration precedes the time treated in this book and lies between 1050 and 1150. Soldiers and settlers flooded from Poitou, Aquitaine, Languedoc and the Burgundies into Spain. Many Spanish towns had French quarters in the twelfth century. In 1118 the king granted Toledo's citizens their customs, describing them as Castilians, Mozarabs and Frenchmen. In successive waves, also, Cluniac monks and then Cistercians penetrated everywhere so that, for a time, many southern French monasteries had affiliates south of the Pyrenees. The first major victory over Islam won by Spanish arms alone was Las Navas de Tolosa in 1212.

Much the same was true on the German frontier: the earlier age witnessed the deeper penetration, although settlement naturally continued. In 1253-5, for example, at the Mongol capital at Quaraqorum in central Asia, the Franciscan missionary William of Ruysbroek met three French-speaking persons swept up in the Mongol raid on Hungary of 1242, a Lorrainer, a Parisian and a Londoner. French settlement in Hungary's nascent towns, however, had reached its peak around 1100. German towns had also admitted these immigrants, especially French Jews. The school of Rashi of Troyes, the celebrated Talmudist and biblical commentator, influenced the rabbis of Mainz, Worms and Speier, and French Jews settled in the Rhineland, the upper Danube valley and also eastern Saxony. Even in the thirteenth century, French was still occasionally spoken by German Jews, leaving traces in Jewish speech from Cologne to Regensburg.

England was another German frontier, and the conquest of 1066 made it a province of French culture. Led by Normans who clung to a Nordic identity setting them apart from the other French, the invasion drew volunteers from all north-eastern provinces from Brittany to the Liégeois. After the conquest, the Anglo-French indifferently referred to themselves as Normans or Frenchmen. Nor did French pressure cease at that date or even at the accession in 1154 of the Plantagenets from Anjou. Although declining, settlement continued into the thirteenth century. The last and unsuccessful French invasion was that of Philip Augustus's son in 1215 at the end of John's turbulent reign, but a lighter French penetration continued, as shown by the importation of officers from as far away as Provence and Savoy into royal service. The French of France believed that they had conquered the English. Abbot Suger of St Denis (d. 1151) reasoned in his life of Louis the Fat that William Rufus of England failed in his attempt to invade France because 'it is not right or natural for Frenchmen to be subject to Englishmen, but only for Englishmen to be subject to Frenchmen'.[3] Not long after 1274 when this sentiment was incorporated into the vernacular *Great Chronicles* of France, it was to appear anomalous.

Populous Italy received fewer French. The earlier movements of the Burgundians and Savoyards were followed by that of a modest number of Normans and other French who helped build the Norman kingdom of Sicily and the mainland principalities around Naples in southern Italy from about 1060 to 1091. The only other penetration of importance was that of the Angevins in the thirteenth century, a subject treated later. Although their language, manners and literature were eagerly adopted in Italy, the French never did there what they had in England, Spain and, to a lesser extent, in Germany, that is, implant city life. In the Mediterranean, French success was greatest in the Near East where they almost monopolized the seigniorial ranks and rivalled the Italians in urban settlement, especially in the Holy Land, Cyprus and parts of mainland Greece. When the Latins were threatened by a Greek and Bulgar attack in 1224, Pope Honorius III (d. 1227) addressed the French to ask aid for Robert of Courtenay, emperor of Constantinople. God, he said, 'has given into the hands of the Gauls the empire of Romania . . . and there a New France, as it were, has recently been created'.[4]

This astonishing explosion spread the French language. French was the tongue of the crusaders and, with its long domestication in the Near East, soon became the *lingua franca* for many who lived in a wide arc from Greece to the frontiers of Egypt. Much later on, a Cypriote told the truth when he wrote that 'after the Lusignans conquered the island, we began to speak French and Greek became barbaric'.[5] The best example of the advance of French at the expense of a Germanic tongue is to be seen in England. There French (though Latin also played a role) suppressed a lively Germanic administrative and literary dialect until well into the thirteenth century. Once it had gained full recognition beside Latin in the ever-conservative language of law, French held its place for ages. Praised by Fortescue in the fifteenth century, by Coke in the seventeenth, its recent demise was still mourned by Blackstone in 1758.

Latin apart, French was also Europe's premier literary language. Although in debt to earlier literature, Arabic, both Muslim and Jewish, early German and Celtic, as in the Matter of Brittany, and to classical letters, the French undoubtedly led the world in this period. Few poets equalled Christian of Troyes, Bertrand of Born (d. 1208–10), Bernard of Ventadour (*fl.* 1180s), William of Lorris (d. *circa* 1240) and John of Meung. The Burgundian Humbert of Romans (d. 1277) remarked that Dominicans given to 'celestial' speech had trouble speaking about mundane things, 'just as Frenchmen . . . cannot easily replace their speech with another because of the nobility of both their language and fatherland.'[6] Better testimony than self-congratulation, however, is that, no matter what their origins, authors who sought wide audiences wrote in French. In his *Treasure* of 1260–6, Brunetto Latini remarks that 'were anyone to ask, since I am an Italian, why this book is written in Romance, in the French tongue, I reply that it is for two reasons, one, that I am in France, and the other, that this language is the most delectable and widespread of all tongues'.[7]

Not that vernacular literature other than French did not exist. Both Spain and Germany boasted native tongues which, indeed, were widely used by rural and urban scribes rather earlier than Italian or French. In both regions also, although about fifty years behind France, poets such as Wolfram of Eschenbach (d. *circa* 1225), Walter von der Vogelweide (d. 1240) and Alfonso the Wise of Castile (d. 1284) wrote in their vernaculars and, however much they owed to French authors, were assuredly their equals. In Italy, easy Latin helped retard the development of Italian, and French, both Provençal and northern, quickly became the language of courts and urban aristocracies. Still, a popular vernacular poetry persisted to burst out in famed verse with the Tuscans Guido Cavalcanti (d. 1300–1), Cino of Pistoia (d. 1336) and Dante. England's literature was still partly in French in the period treated here, but there were limits to English Gallicism. Later a royal governor, Philip of Rémi, lord of Beaumanoir (d. 1296), poked fun at the insular speech of his Anglo-French employers in his youth. As early as the 1260s, middle-English romances appeared, and the author of *Of Arthour and Merlin* remarked that he knew not a few nobles who could speak no French.

Music was closely related to poetry, much of which was sung. Although, except for a few tunes, little secular music can be found, ecclesiastical music is better known. There, the French led in introducing polyphony into plainsong. Leadership in this quasi-secularizing of church music was seen at St Martial in Limoges until about 1150 and thereafter at Nôtre Dame of Paris in the late twelfth century, with Leoninus (*fl.* 1160–70) and Perotinus (*fl.* 1190–1200). By the mid thirteenth century the Rhineland and France's eastern counties were forging ahead and English polyphony was seen *circa* 1275.

The attractiveness of French culture was based on more than power and language. France was the home of the arts of sensibility: manners, style and elegance of dress. Frenchmen lived well in the relatively peaceful thirteenth century. Latini complained that Italians, warring among themselves, build crabbed country houses enclosed by walls and towers, but the French 'build grand and ample houses with large decorated rooms to have joy and delight without war and disturbance', homes surrounded by lawns and fruit trees.[8] No wonder that John of Salisbury called France 'the most gentle and civil of all nations.'[9]

Envy combined with anger to caricature French arrogance and sexual licence. At the time of the conflict over Maimonidean ideas, a correspondent warned against the conservative French rabbis: 'Watch out for the French because they think their best chance of knowing God is when they eat beef marinated in a vinegar [wine?] sauce and garlic . . . . Most of them anyway have two women and their thoughts are incessantly on intercourse.'[10]

There was more to it than comfort and chic. French styles and engineering dominated architecture, both military and civil. Among the most inventive monuments of castramentation were the Hospitallers' Krak des Chevaliers in Syria, completed around 1205, and Richard Coeur de Lion's castle, Gaillard des Andeleys in Normandy. Better known is the invention of Gothic, probably in the Ile de France, a style and engineering technique that spread throughout northern France and the Plantagenet domains on either side of the Channel during the late twelfth century. Replacing or refurbishing older monuments, Gothic began to penetrate Languedoc and Italy around 1220 and Germany by 1263. If Peter of Montreuil, the probable designer of the Ste Chapelle, busied himself largely around Paris, his relative Eudes accompanied his patron Louis IX to Cyprus and there designed several churches. Author of an architectural sketchbook, Villard of Honnecourt was employed from Hainault to Hungary. In 1287 Stephen of Bonneuil left Paris with a team of builders for Sweden. John des Champs brought

Gothic to Toulouse and Narbonne, and in 1266 Peter of Agincourt accompanied Charles of Anjou to southern Italy where, after introducing the French style, he was rewarded by being knighted.

Love of learning was often described as a French characteristic. Assigning the Empire to themselves and the Church to the Italians, a German commonplace gave the university to the French, by which was meant Paris. French law influenced England and penetrated west Germany, and was also imported into southern Italy under its twelfth-century Norman kings and became predominant in the Latin colonies along the coasts of the eastern Mediterranean and Aegean Seas. There a notable monument was the *Assizes of Jerusalem and Cyprus*, a collection of laws and tracts on government, one of whose authors was Philip of Novara, an active memoirist, soldier and statesman of 'Overseas France'.

ITALY

Italy did not lag behind France. Her fleets swept the Mediterranean and her sons and daughters joined the French settling along that sea's eastern shores. When Constantinople fell in the Fourth Crusade of 1204 and the Latin Empire was established in Greece and the Aegean, a quarter of the territory was given to the French emperor and the rest was divided equally between the principal crusaders and the Venetians who had provided the fleet. This effectively gave the latter the upper hand in Bosporan and Greek commerce. The Piedmontese house of Monferrato, moreover, was granted the major fief of the new Latin emperor, the kingdom of Thessalonica. More lasting was the settlement of Italians along the coasts of the Mediterranean and Black Seas where they enjoyed the privilege of extra-territoriality and self-government.

Italian arms never gained overseas victories comparable to those of the French, however, largely because they were employed at home to weaken the traditional power of the Empire in the peninsula. Although imperial suzerainty never wholly disappeared, it gradually became an idea significant in political theory, as in Dante's *On Monarchy*, but relatively unimportant in the practical politics of Italy's principalities and republics. As the jurists, even French ones like Peter Dubois (d. 1312), recognized, these little states admitted 'no superiors in the world'. Their victory over transalpine power was won with the defeat of Frederick I Barbarossa at Legnano and the subsequent Peace of Constance in 1183. The northern Italian maritime cities profited from the struggle over the succession between the Guelfs and the Hohenstaufen after the death of Henry VI in 1197 to weaken southern Italy, the new and powerful imperial ally. Although German intervention continued, the great wars of the age of Frederick II were mainly those of southern Italy against the Guelf townsmen of northern and central Italy who, with French aid, won a crushing victory.

Although Italy might have done better unified under the Apulian or Sicilian Hohenstaufen, contemporary Italians felt no sense of failure. Proud of their newly won liberty, their freedom was what impressed foreigners. James of Vitry described Italians as

> circumspect in council, diligent and zealous in managing their governments, prescient and tenacious in regard to future affairs, refusing to be subject to others, defending before all else their liberty, issuing their own laws and customs under one common captain whom they elect and observing them faithfully.[11]

Besides, if Italy's maritime enterprise ruled the eastern Mediterranean by the end of the twelfth century, the next century saw it rise in the western part of that sea and penetrate into the Atlantic as far north as Bruges in the period between 1271 and 1317. As will be shown in later chapters, also, the spread of Italian merchant-bankers and moneylenders beyond the Alps marked the economy of the thirteenth century.

Italian republics stood together with the papacy against the emperors, and both liberty and profit were won by this alliance. By 1200, during the pontificate of Innocent III, Rome was the diplomatic capital of the Latin west, and by 1300 western princes were well advised to retain ambassadors at the papal court. Many of these representatives were also officers of the Italian merchant-banking houses, especially Florentines. Playing on the classical division of Europe into four great nations – the French, Germans, Italians and Spaniards – Boniface VIII once looked around his court and observed that the Florentines constituted a fifth nation. Besides, the papacy was itself Italian. From the death of the Englishman Adrian IV in 1159 until the accession of Urban IV in 1261, the popes were all Italians and so were most of the curial personnel. Two of the four larger mendicant orders of the thirteenth century were Italian in origin, including the Franciscan, the largest of all. Again, if the

French seemed to contemporaries to exemplify intellectual life with their university of Paris, Italian mendicants invaded that institution's faculty of theology. The first Dominican to teach there was Roland of Cremona (d. 1250), and the names of John of Fidanza (Bonaventure) and Thomas of Aquino speak for themselves.

Although rivalled by the graduates of Montpellier and, in Mediterranean regions, by the Jews, Italians were also pre-eminent in medicine. If France had philosophy, Italy had law: Italians revived Roman law in Bologna and other centres. But there was more to it than that. 'Modernizing' Roman law, the professors created the most influential common law of the medieval period. Although the Gallic spirit, moreover, informed feudal law, Lombard law as systematized by the professors became a normative feudal code for much of western Europe by 1300, being accepted directly within the Empire and indirectly elsewhere. As indicative of Italian leadership were those who taught canon law, the other great common law. Mediterranean in origin, this law was most studied in northern Europe before 1100, but by 1150 this had changed: the great canonists now learned their business in Italy. Lastly, all of these learned studies were based on practical legislative and judicial experience. The statutes and codes of Italy's urban republics constitute the largest body of constitutional materials to be found anywhere in western Europe at this time. Although moderns have lamented Italy's much-divided state, her small republics and monarchies were already models for Europe's later states. William of Auvergne (d. 1249) noted with some astonishment that her republics' heralds were divided into grades for diplomatic purposes, *nuncii* for small matters, *ambassadores* in livery for more significant ones and *ad hoc* representatives or *legati*.

Italy's arts, although still under transalpine and French influence, were beginning to evolve independently. What fired her artists were, first, their hostility to the Germans who had ruled them for so long, and then, after the honeymoon of the mid thirteenth century, their reaction against the French. Italians therefore sought inspiration that did not come from beyond the Alps. For a time, Byzantine art sufficed, but in the long run the most fruitful source was classical antiquity. The turn towards a renewed classicism may be already discerned in the twelfth century, and its effects are to be seen in the spacious independence of the buildings placed in the cathedral complex of Pisa, for example, as well as in specific works, such as the reliefs in the cathedral and baptistry of Parma executed by Benedict Antelami in 1198. Ancient models reappeared: the equestrian relief of Oldrado of Tresseno, *podestà* in 1233, that graced the Palazzo delle Ragione in Milan. In the baptistry pulpit of Pisa, completed in 1260, the Apulian architect and sculptor Nicolas Pisano employed classical models for the figures decorating a Gothic monument. What this means for the emergence of Renaissance art cannot be overestimated. Giotto of Bondone, later city architect for the republic of Florence, was a well-known painter and sculptor by 1300.

Italians did not come by their classicism without borrowing from their neighbours. An example is the history of Latin style. In the twelfth century, the best Latin was usually written north of the Alps, as John of Salisbury attests. Shown by the *dictatores* of Orléans, an elegant if sometimes affected Latinity marked composition there until well into the thirteenth century. Influenced by the practical needs of the legal profession and the notariate, Italians generally favoured simpler styles and found their counterparts north of the Alps only among the academic theologians and scholastics whose lack of style had so offended John of Salisbury. An illustration of this practical or vulgar spirit is Boncompagno of Signa.

In the long run, Boncompagno's suit against classicism was lost. The growing use of the vernacular for legal documents irreparably weakened the base of popular Latin culture. Almost as damaging was the influence of transalpine Latinity, so useful for the pomp of princes. Lawyers did not appreciate this new development, and never quite gave in to it. The Bolognese professor Odofredo (d. 1265) referred scathingly to those who wish to 'speak obscurely and in a pompous style as do the most exalted doctors and also Peter of Vinea'.[12] Still, the self-conscious style of many of Italy's rhetoricians and intellectuals in the late thirteenth century shows that they were about to make classicism their own. The elegance of Petrarch and Boccaccio in their Latin works, it seems, had a long period of gestation, and one of its parents was not Italian.

EUROPE

To sum up, France and Italy led Europe during the twelfth and thirteenth centuries. Their pre-eminence and capacity to influence other parts of western Europe seems odd, however, when their internal constitutions are examined. During a time when French law spread far beyond her frontiers, France herself boasted no monarchy or state comparable to that of England, Norman southern Italy or even the declining Empire. To illustrate the machinery of French government, or lack of it, a few wagons containing all the archives and treasury of the Capetian monarch were captured on the battle-field of Frétéval by Richard Coeur de Lion in 1194. The typical Italian state that produced Europe's common (Roman) law and published its most elaborate statutes was an urban republic, tiny when compared with the states of Spain and England and with Germany's provinces, not to speak of the Empire.

Size was not, however, the principal criterion. Having im-planted Latin civilization in northern and eastern Europe, the great states and quasi-national kingdoms that ruled Europe from the days of the Carolingians weakened in the eleventh and twelfth centuries. The age of empires was over. In spite of the Hohenstaufen revival, the Empire was irreparably weakened by the alliance of the Roman Church with German local princes and Italian towns in the time of Gregorian enthusiasm. Conquering the Moors with French aid, but wishing to be free of their allies, Iberian princes tried to advance a Spanish idea of empire. In 1139 Alfonso VII of Castile was styled emperor, ruling in New Castile, Leon, Aragon, Navarre, Castile, Galicia (Portugal), Catalonia and Provence, and, in 1159, the northern annals of Cambrai spoke of three empires: the Byzantine, the German and that of Galicia (St James of Compostella). Defeated by geography and by papal and French encouragement of separatism in Portugal, Catalonia–Aragon and elsewhere, however, this reminiscence of Spanish unity soon faded. What remained was Spain's insistence on its independence and equality with France and the Empire. Writing in 1210–12, Vincent Hispanus, chancellor of Portugal, reversed Charlemagne's victory sung of in France's *Song of Roland*, by averring that when 'Charles with the French wished to enter Spain, the Spaniards met them at Spain's gates, conquered them in battle and killed the twelve peers . . . . [Whence] Spanish prowess alone obtained the empire.'[13]

In regard to the nations, the princes of Europe's peripheral powers, from the Kiraly or king, like Kaiser, (from the name Charlemagne) of Hungary to the kings of Norway, governed quasi-national states that still resembled Carolingian Frankland in governmental and social institutions. Although their churches were invaded by Rome and their civil institutions transmuted by French feudalism and immigration, England, the states of inland and western Iberia and northern and eastern Germany had, and partly retained, an identity and unity that marked them off from France and Italy. Although conquered by the French, England never disappeared as a nation.

Significant though these retentions were, it was in France and Italy and the parts of Europe hard against their frontiers that the institutions most characteristic of the medieval epoch reached their apogee in this time. On the local level, these were the seigniories of the countryside and the 'collective seigniories' of the towns, both jealously seeking a measure of independence from regional princes or kings. Both types of community were generally governed by aristocracies of wealth, both new and old, of lineage, both newly ascending and traditional, and of experience in government. To simplify complex social structures, local aristocracies had combined with ecumenical popes to weaken Europe's emperors, kings and regional princes.

The harmony of northern and Mediterranean power typical of this period was instanced by the largely amicable relationship of France and Italy. These nations combined during the Crusades to penetrate the Near East at the expense of Greek and Muslim. Although torn by conflicting parties and although her kings were not always the allies of the popes, France – the 'refuge of the popes' was the commonplace – usually buttressed Roman policies, and Rome in turn represented the interests of the Italians, save those of the south. After 1250 this once loose alignment gradually became more rigid as the Capetian house rose to rule the larger part of France and its cadet line of Anjou entered Italy to help the popes destroy the Hohenstaufen. After this, France's kings and Rome's popes were often considered to be Europe's greatest princes, a fact lamented by a German like Alexander of Roes. When Rabban bar Sauma, a Nestorian Christian from Peking, was sent by Persia's Mongol khan to bring the Latins into alliance against Islam, he first visited the Roman pontiff. He then went to Paris to see the king, and, on his way back to Rome in 1288 stopped off briefly at Bordeaux, a town he thought to be England's capital. Of the two princes, also, few doubted the pope was the greater. To Rabban he was Europe's king of kings, a notion common among Europe's Jews. In 1321 Todros son of Isaac remarked that the year of the rising of the Pastoureaux was 'when the lepers were suppressed and evil men appeared before the pope, the king of nations, demanding he destroy the true law'.[14]

Frenchmen and Italians did not advance because of their power and wealth alone; they were also blessed by circumstances. A reason their neighbours accepted leadership so easily was that they were busy expanding Europe's frontiers. The Spaniards fought Islam to the south, their crusaders and military orders remaining in the peninsula. The English were busy along the Celtic fringe, their gallicized nobility being far less enthusiastic about the Crusades than their brothers across the Channel. England's greatest crusader, Richard Coeur de Lion, was the most French of all her kings. Although Swabians and Alpine Germans looked to the south, Germany's northern and eastern inhabitants fought their wars on their own frontiers. If the Teutonic Knights began in the Holy Land, they won their fame on the Vistula and beyond. Europe's centre therefore profited because, in this expansionist age, her peoples looked outside Latin culture for advancement, not within. It was there, on their frontiers, that English, Germans and Spaniards confessed they emulated the French. Around 1108 Magdeburg summoned troops against the Slavs:

> Wherefore, O most famous Saxons, Franks, Lorrainers and Flemish, conquerors of the world, here you can both save your souls and . . . acquire and settle a beautiful land. [God], who has summoned the French to set out from the furthest reaches of the west to triumph by the virtue of their arms against his enemies in the furthest east, will give you the will and power to subjugate these nearby inhuman gentiles.[15]

NOTES AND REFERENCES

1   'Plantagenet' is used for the English Angevines in order to avoid confusion with the cadet line of the Capetians in Anjou active from Provence to Italy and Hungary.

2   Gauthier, *La chevalerie*, 675.

3   *Vita Ludovici grossi regis* Prologue (ed. Henri Waquet, Paris 1864) 10–12.

4   Odorico Rinaldi, *Annales ecclesiastici ab anno MCXCVIII ubi desinit Cardinalis Baronius auctore Odorico Raynaldo* (ed. J.D. Mansi, Lucca, 1747) I, 536a–b.

5   The fifteenth-century Leontios Makhairas cited in Grousset, *L'empire du Levant*, 379.

6   *De eruditione praedicatorum* 7, 39 in J.J. Berthier   (ed.), *Opera de vita regulari* (Rome, 1888), II, 465.

7   *Li livres dou tresor* I, 1 (ed. F.J. Carmody, Berkeley, 1948), 18.

8   *Ibid.*, I 129 (ed. Carmody) 126.

9   Letter 225 in *PL* CXCIX 253.

10 Güdemann, *Geschichte des Erziehungswesens . . . der Juden* I, 73. The letter was attributed to Maimonides!

11 *Historia orientalis* 67 (Douai, 1596), 124.

12 Wieruszowski, *Vom Imperium zum nationalen Königtum*, 67n.

13 Post, *Studies in Medieval Legal Thought*, 486 and 490.

14 His commentary on the tractate *Nazir* is cited in Baron, *A Social and Religious History of the Jews* XI 251.

15 Rudolph Kötzschke, *Quellen zur Geschichte der ostdeutschen Kolonisation* (Leipzig and Berlin, 1912) 10, No. 3.

4

CRUSADES AND MISSIONS

CRUSADES

Holy wars against non-Christians and especially Muslims in Spain and the Mediterranean had begun in the eleventh century, and the so-called First Crusade was launched against the Near East in 1092. Themes justifying these grand aggressions were the superiority of the Catholic faith and the recuperation of lands 'wrongly' taken by Muslims from the Christian Roman Empire in earlier times. For this reason the continuous Iberian Christian war against Islam was called a 'reconquest', and a French lawyer, Peter Dubois, called a tract the *Recovery of the Holy Land*.

Canon lawyers justified the Crusade. Innocent IV (d. 1254) shared the views of Hostiensis, who wrote:

> It appears to me that on Christ's coming all honour, principate, dominion and jurisdiction. . . was removed from infidels and given to Christians . . . whence we firmly state that infidels should legally be subject to Christians and not vice-versa . . . We nevertheless concede that infidels who recognize the dominion of the Church are to be tolerated . . . and [that] such men can have possessions, Christian dependent farmers and even jurisdictions . . . . Other infidels who do not recognize the power of the Roman Church . . . we judge unworthy of kingdom, principate, jurisdiction and all dominion, and those who occupy the Holy Land or other [once-Christian] regions ought to be attacked by authority of the Church.[1]

Earlier times had seen great military success. The first European overseas empire had been built by the conquest and partial European settlement of Palestine and parts of Syria. Fate intervened, however, and the late twelfth century witnessed the first of many Islamic resurgences. Byzantine attempts to recover central Anatolia from the Seljuk Turks failed when Emperor Manuel was defeated at

Myriokephalon in 1176. Further south, the unification of Syria and Egypt under Nureddin and Saladin caused the loss of Jerusalem in 1187 and threatened the rest of the Holy Land. In the western and central Mediterranean, the rigorist sect of the Almohades rallied Muslims. Moving east from Morocco, these Berbers regained by 1160 the coast from Bone to Tripoli, once dominated by the Norman kings of Sicily. Profiting from Christian divisions, the Almohades momentarily unified Iberian Islam and administered a severe defeat to the Castilians as late as 1196.

Thereafter the Muslim counter-attack halted and the Christians resumed their advance. In Spain Almohade progress was already slowed by five recently created Christian military orders and frequent French Crusades, and a grand alliance finally crushed their host at Las Navas de Tolosa in 1212. Thereafter the Spaniards advanced rapidly. By 1238 the loss of the Balearic Islands and Valencia to Aragon cost Islam the central reaches of the west Mediterranean. By mid-century Portugal had taken the Algarve, and Islam had lost half-empty Cordova and populous Seville to Castile. Cadiz fell in 1265, and Italians began to penetrate north Africa economically. Missionaries and merchants from France and Italy were active from Senegal on the Atlantic to Tunis near Sicily. Europe's geographical knowledge grew apace. Spaniards settled the Canary Islands in 1270. In 1291 the Genoese merchant corsair Benedict Zaccaria (d. 1307) joined with others to equip two ill-fated galleys that set out past Gibraltar to circumnavigate Africa. The Azores were marked on a portolan map of 1350.

In the east the Latins turned aside from Islam to shatter the Greeks. Beginning with Cyprus's loss to Richard Coeur de Lion in 1191, Latin arms moved to the Bosporus. A Franco-Venetian Crusade captured Constantinople in 1204, creating a Latin Empire that, although it lasted on the Bosporus only until 1261, left French and Venetian possessions in mainland Greece from Thessaly and Attica to the tip of the Peloponnesus. Some of the Aegean islands and Rhodes, Crete and Cyprus remained Latin dominions into modern times. Westerners had not gained so much Near Eastern territory since the days of the First Crusade. In Syria and the Holy Land the deterioration of the Latin position was arrested, partly by the efforts of Coeur de Lion. Thereafter, in spite of defeats like the Egyptian campaign of Louis IX in 1249, Christian expeditions and the civil wars between the Ayyubid dynasts of Saladin's Kurdish line kept the frontier more or less stable. Threatening war, Frederick II

Hohenstaufen recovered the administration of Jerusalem in 1229 and held it until 1244, six years before he died.

Christian frontiers were also stabilized by the Mongol irruption into the Near East. Although the two worked together only in Armenia, the Mongols conquered Iran, took Baghdad in 1258, ruined Iraq and raided Syria and the Seljuk principalities of Anatolia. The unification of central Asia and China under the Mongol aegis offered opportunities for trade. The khans also ruled their heterogeneous domains with foreigners, and hence when Marco Polo retraced his father's steps and arrived at the Mongol court in 1275, he immediately entered their service, serving as a provincial governor and ambassador until returning home nearly twenty years later. The khans also favoured religious heterogeneity and encouraged Latin missions. From 1245 until 1340 missionaries were despatched eastward. An example is the mission of the Apulian Franciscan John of Monte Corvino in 1294. John translated the New Testament into the Mongol tongue, erected a monastery and two churches in Peking and delighted the khan by buying 150 boys to chant the Latin mass. In 1307 Clement V named him archbishop of Peking.

Fifty years after the Polos, the Franciscan Odoric of Pordenone reported that the Chinese port of Amoy contained a *fondaco* for Christian merchants, a place equipped with a public bath-house and church. The fastest route to China ran from the Genoese towns in the Crimea–Azov region of the Black Sea across the Caspian Sea and thence through Tatary. Writing early in the fourteenth century, Francis di Balducci Pegolotti, a director of the Bardi firm of Florence, reported that the route to Peking was safely open. Italians were also busy in Iran, then controlled by a friendly Mongol khanate. In about 1321 a Dominican observed that Genoese merchants sailed vessels from the Persian Gulf to India and Ceylon, recruiting local sailors and Abyssinian marines. Noting that Egypt was the Christians' main enemy, the friar William Adam from Languedoc suggested around 1313 stationing a squadron off Aden to intercept Red Sea traffic.

After 1300, however, these alluring prospects vanished. Mongol power faded rapidly: Persia returned to Islam and China to a native dynasty. The Muslim people destined to play a major role during modern times already showed its muscle, an Ottoman Turkish force having crossed the Dardanelles to Europe in 1300. To the south the Mamluks, erecting a government built around an élite of slave soldiers, replaced the Ayyubids in Egypt and Syria. Their commander Baybars repulsed the Mongols in the 1260s and re-established the Abbasid caliphate in Cairo. His successors went on to expel the Latins from their coastal holdings in Cilicia, Syria and the Holy Land, where Acre was the last town to fall in 1291. Islam also advanced in the western Mediterranean where a new Moroccan dynasty, that of the Berber Merinids, unified the north African coast, repulsed the Franco-Italian attack of Louis IX on Tunis in 1270, and reinforced the Muslim frontier kingdom of Granada in Spain by raids from 1261 to 1285.

Turning to Europe's north and east, there too, momentary retreat had marked the late twelfth century. In Hungary, for example, the Byzantines made and unmade kings at the height of the Comnenian dynasty and even briefly weakened the hold of the Latin Church. After the death of Emperor Manuel in 1180 and the subsequent collapse of the Greek Balkan Empire, Greek and Slavic Christianity retreated everywhere. In Russia the Mongol assaults of the 1230s and 1240s all but obliterated the southern principalities from Kiev to the Carpathians, and subjugated all Russia save northern Novgorod. Nor did these eastern Christians win much sympathy from the Latins: Roger Bacon coolly said the Ruthenians were 'schismatics' who practised the Greek rite.

The Germans profited, partly because there was no strong state to resist them. Once-powerful Hungary weakened throughout the thirteenth century and was not pulled together again until the accession of a Neapolitan–Angevin dynasty in 1308. Poland was divided and did not unify until well into the fourteenth century, and of the pagan peoples near the Baltic, only the Lithuanians showed signs of creating a state. Even the disasters afflicting these regions helped the Germans. Mongol raids on Poland and Hungary from 1241 onwards increased their princes' need to import Germans to build cities and modernize courts and armies on the model of western chivalry.

German penetration of eastern Europe was often peaceable, but where the populations remained staunchly pagan, it was different. Wars against the Wends came early when the Germans resumed the push over the Elbe. By the thirteenth century they were settling the Vistula valley and had thrown outposts along the Baltic shore as far north as Riga, founded in 1198. From 1208 on, the Teutonic knights took leadership, absorbing two military orders already active in Livonia and Prussia. Around the Baltic and North Seas, and in the northern Mediterranean, the forerunners of the Hanseatic merchants were appearing. From towns as far apart as Cologne or Utrecht in the west and Reval in the east, the merchants of the Gothland Society dominated the once Scandinavian port of Wisby, and by 1229 had settled in Russian Novgorod with rights similar to those of a Mediterranean *fondaco*. Led by Lübeck's merchants, Germans established other *kontore* in Bruges, Bristol, London and England's east-coast ports by the 1260s. By 1293 Lübeck's leadership in northern Germany was recognized, and the Hanseatic League just around the corner. After a victory by German cavalry in Scania in 1134, Scandinavian princes hastened to modernize, importing knights and modelling local institutions on German ones. The last Danish maritime Empire succumbed to German attack in 1227, and Scandinavia was thereafter partly opened to German exploitation.

With the exception, then, of what may be called German Europe where expansion continued, Latin Europe halted before or around 1300 and began to retreat thereafter. This inspired redeployment. The Grand Master of the Teutonic Order, for example, remained at Acre to 1291 and then retired through Venice to Prussian Marienburg in 1308. Chivalry partly followed this movement, and Prussia became the magnet for crusaders. On the whole, however, the failure of the Latin effort against Islam disturbed Europe deeply.

Renascent Muslim power profited from changes within Latin Europe. In the past, war had moved toward the frontiers. French culture and arms, for example, invaded England until the early thirteenth century, and the Anglo-French expanded at the expense of Britain's Celtic fringe. From 1152 onwards the English penetrated Ireland, conquering Leinster and the Pale and raiding throughout the island, and by 1284 the remnant principality of north Wales was irrevocably crushed. By 1307 England's attack on the curious Anglo-Celtic and even quasi-French power called Scotland seemed about to result in the annexation of that kingdom.

A shift ensued, however. If Henry III's campaigns in France were flops, they nevertheless secured Capetian recognition by 1258 that Guienne and adjacent areas were fiefs legitimately held by the English king, thus halting the Capetian conquest of the Plantagenet continental domain. From the 1290s the English again began to intervene in Flanders. Steps towards the Hundred Years' War, the intermittent combats from 1292 through to the 1330s were hardly English victories because the county of Flanders remained French long after these skirmishes. By the Peace of Athis in 1305, in fact, the French acquired Douai, Béthune, Lille and St Omer, and avenged their earlier defeat at Courtrai in 1302 by crushing the Flemish townsmen at Cassel in 1328. But France's hope of incorporating the rest of Flanders into the royal domain was forever finished. In sum, although the English had yet to invade the Continent and lay claim to the French crown, Capetian France had ceased expanding.

In the British Isles the English had themselves been set back. If Wales was too far gone to raise its head, Ireland was not, and in spite of several major efforts, English holdings gradually shrank in the later thirteenth century. The rising under Robert Bruce from 1307 to the victory of Bannockburn in 1314 revivified Scottish independence.

In spite of conflicts at home such as those between the German emperors and the Italian towns, or the Plantagenets and Capetians over France's Atlantic provinces, furthermore, Europe's great war before 1200 had been the Crusade. This may be seen in the numbers of effectives in the field. Richard Coeur de Lion won his spurs in France and lost his life there, but won his laurels as a captain in the eastern Mediterranean, where he commanded armies two or three times the size of those he led at home. By 1200, however, the largest armies were to be found at home, especially Italy, during the Hohenstaufen wars. War had come home to roost.

In 1150 Italian navies had swept the waters of the eastern Mediterranean, and largely French crusaders occupied its easternmost shores. Between Italy's maritime cities and the Holy Land had lain two powers, the Greeks at the height of the Comnenian revival and the Norman state of southern Italy and Sicily, whose mutually destructive battles over Epirus, Macedonia and Antioch were unremitting. The first of the two powers to fall was Byzantium, beset not only by the Seljuks in Anatolia but also, from 1186, by the Balkan revolts of the Bulgars. At about the same time the Latins began to attack the Greeks, an attack culminating in the catastrophe of the Fourth Crusade in 1203–4, from which the Greeks never recovered. About the same time, Italian maritime republics aided a Hohenstaufen invasion of southern Italy and Sicily, profiting from the ensuing wars from 1190 to 1215 to win substantial trade concessions and rights of extra-territoriality. During the thirteenth century, the struggle between the more urbanized north and centre of Italy against southern Italy – a Latin state with Greek and Muslim components – intensified. The victory went to the north, resulting not only in the defeat of the Hohenstaufen in 1268, but also in Sicily's secession from the mainland part of the south Italian state in wars from 1282 to 1302.

The victory of the popes and their Lombard allies was won at the cost of increased foreign intervention in Italy. Beset at Rome, Innocent IV fled to Lyons on the Rhone. Although he later returned and his successors usually resided in Italy from 1245 to 1312, the general councils that had formerly been summoned to the Lateran were held in the Rhone valley. Northern Italian strength having proved insufficient to defeat the Apulians, Sicilians and German imperialists, Innocent invited the French to settle the question. From 1261 – the year in which a French pope, Urban IV, was elected – to 1268 the Angevins spearheaded the final assault on Hohenstaufen Italy.

Nor were the French Italy's only invaders. As the Germans failed, others filled Ghibelline ranks. A weak Castilian intervention preceded the entry of the Catalans and Aragonese at the time of the Sicilian revolt against the Angevin French in 1282, known as the Vespers. These interlopers did not stop in Sicily but pushed on into the Aegean, establishing a duchy in Thebes and Athens in 1311. The struggles between Italy's maritime powers intensified, further weakening Latin power in the Near East. The Greeks retook Constantinople in 1261 partly because of Genoese hostility to Venice's monopoly of Bosporan commerce, and the combat between these two republics helped cause the loss of the Syrian and Palestinian coasts to Islam. Only the largest naval powers could hope to compete any longer. Genoa crushed Pisa's fleet at Meloria in 1284 and devoured her commercial empire thereafter. Marseilles' flourishing trade suffered the same fate during the Angevin and Catalan struggles over Sicily.

In brief, by fighting among themselves the Latins helped Islam halt western expansion by the end of the thirteenth century. This was accompanied by a change in the ideas of Christendom and the Crusade formulated during the Gregorian age. On the defeat of the Empire, the conception of a Christian republic rose above that of membership in a secular state. When Urban II launched the war to 'recover' Jerusalem from infidel hands in 1092, he also weakened the justification for wars within Europe, even surrendering or relaxing the sanctions against 'heretics' and 'schismatics' that had marked the Gregorian wars in the Empire and against lay domination of the

Church. To win that war, Urban's step was a compromise, even a retreat, but it enabled the papacy to assume the leadership of Europe's expansion after the Gregorian civil war. Not that the holy war did not continue to find application within Europe itself. Abbot of Cluny, Peter the Venerable (d. 1156), wrote to Pope Eugenius III that his local enemies were 'false Christians, worse than Saracens', to be fought with Christian arms.[2] The popes used the Crusade indulgence against Roger II of Apulia–Sicily in 1135, Ireland in 1152 and the king of Leon in 1197. The war launched against the Markward of Anweiler, Hohenstaufen regent in Sicily, in 1199 was institutionally a Crusade. The historian Matthew Paris even assumed that the campaign of the French prince Louis against John of England in 1213 was a papal holy war. But all this was secondary: the true holy war was the Crusade against Islam and other non-Christian peoples.

Around 1200 holy war began to turn back in earnest into Europe. The Fourth Crusade of 1204 against the 'schismatic' Greeks was first deplored by the pope but soon applauded because of hope for the union of the churches. Closer to home was the Crusade launched in 1209 against the Albigensians which soon became a war of the northern French against Languedoc. The return to the Gregorian pattern of religious wars at home awaited the final struggle between the popes and the Hohenstaufen from 1240 on. Innocent IV prohibited preaching the Crusade for Jersualem in Germany in order to draw troops to the Italian front. The Angevin attack on the Hohenstaufen was declared a Crusade, as were the successive Capetian and Angevin wars against the Catalans and Sicilians from 1282 on. The popes had become so used to calling their wars Crusades that Boniface VIII launched one in 1297 against his enemies in the college of cardinals and the papal states, including the Colonna family. Dante derided him as 'the prince of the new Pharisees, whose every enemy was Christian, waging war near the Lateran, not with Saracens or Jews, only with Christians'.[3]

Dante's complaints were not unique. Many were disturbed by this seeming perversion of the Crusade. Matthew Paris accused Innocent IV of sabotaging Louis IX of France's wars to advance his Italian policy. In 1265, when in France, an archbishop of Tyre observed that it was bad when the pope redirected to Sicily those pledged to the Holy Land, but worse when money raised for Jerusalem went to support Angevin wars in Italy without the consent of the donors. The popes wanted to resume the Crusade, but believed they first had to defeat the Hohenstaufens and stop – by winning! – Europe's internecine wars.

The failure to defeat Islam encouraged an oft-expressed belief that corruption and sin impeded the Christians. Peter Cantor argued that sin could not be eradicated by conquering others, only by purifying one's own soul and society. Doubts about their leadership made some believe that, to succeed, the cause must be entrusted to the 'just' or the poor in spirit. Already evident in the First Crusade, this idea eventually took on all sorts of forms, of which the most egregious was the 'Children's Crusade' of 1212. Initially designed to stir faith, popular preaching from the Loire valley to that of the Rhine evoked a curious youth march towards Jerusalem. Greeted by Innocent III (d. 1216) and others as praiseworthy, because fervid youth shamed the indifference of age, the movement petered out with several thousand displaced persons, and charges that merchants or Jews had sold them into Muslim slavery.

Not dissimilar ideas about the force of innocence were expressed by the Pastoureaux, who rose to crusade for Louis IX during his captivity in Egypt in 1251. Initially encouraged by authorities like the queen mother, these Holy Innocents were not children but rather 'the poor'. They also remained at home, roughing up townsmen, the well-to-do and Jews. Movements of this type had been known in the west before, an example being the Capuciati of Puy in 1182. Also initially encouraged by the pope, this group was organized to defend the peace threatened by unemployed soldiers when fighting ended between the Capetians and Plantagenets. Like the Pastoureaux, the Capuciati became violent and were suppressed. A difference between the two movements, however, is worth underlining. The Capuciati tried to restore peace, the necessary counterpart of the Crusade: God's peace at home, God's war abroad. The Pastoureaux and those who merged into the peasant and artisan revolutionaries of the fourteenth century differed: theirs was God's war at home.

Finding scapegoats was no monopoly of the poor; all society played that game. Blaming the fall of Acre on the misbehaviour of its defenders was a case in point. The Templars were especially chosen for obloquy, an order suffering popular dislike for many reasons. Its houses served as treasuries for kings, for example, whereas the rival Hospitallers ran hospitals. The real reason the Templars were singled out, however, was that, as the earliest and greatest military order, they symbolized Christendom's defeat.

People said that most of their members were to be found at home, not at the front, something they had in common with all armies. The prestige of the order had been falling consistently, and the French crown had begun to attack it in 1287. Serious persecution started in 1306, the order was abolished in 1312 and the grand master and his staff were executed in 1314. Like other victims of escapism, the knights were charged with everything: heresy, materialism, sorcery and sodomy with man and beast. The abolition of the Templars was the first successful attack by lay power on an order of the regular clergy.

Secular princes had found popular support for taking command of the Crusades away from the popes. As the head of what seemed Europe's greatest power and heir of Louis IX, canonized in 1297, the Fren h king thought himself the natural leader of the west. Philip IV's councillors wished to unify the military orders, make their prince grand master, assume the crown of Jerusalem and lead a united Europe in a great Crusade. France's leaders had come to believe that their interests were identical with those of the Holy Land and the faith. The secular notion that the nation is the Holy Land was being born.

MISSIONS AND TOLERATION

Opposition to Crusades always existed, because religion was held to be voluntary, not to be imposed by force. Some even thought that religion and secular government were so far apart that infidels not only enjoyed natural rights but also that pagan dominion over Christians was justifiable. As the Crusades failed, these themes were reinvigorated during the thirteenth century. Franciscan radicals, Salimbene said, were happy when their prophecy of Louis IX's failure was fulfilled in the disaster of Damietta in 1249. Roger Bacon argued that Crusades involved the Church in secular wars, proving his point by the French Crusade against Catalonia–Aragon. Besides, they do not work. Even when unbelievers are beaten, Christians lack troops to hold the conquest. Infidels and pagans

> are not converted by war, but instead slain and sent to hell. . . . [Those] who labour for their conversion, especially the Teutonic Knights, really wish to reduce them to slavery, as Dominicans, Franciscans and other reliable men

throughout Germany and Poland have clearly ascertained. The pagans therefore defend themselves, not because they have a better religion, but because they resist violence.[4]

Missions seemed the better way. Francis of Assisi preached to the Egyptians in 1219. After his conversion in 1265 the Majorcan Raymond Llull lectured everywhere to encourage missions and language studies to make them possible. He was at Vienne in 1311 when the council recommended (in vain!) that Oxford, Paris, Bologna and Salamanca teach Arabic, Greek, Hebrew and Syrian. He visited Armenia, Cyprus and north Africa, and was believed to have been martyred in Algeria in 1315. Raymond of Peñafort, general of the Dominicans, urged Thomas Aquinas to write his *Against the Gentiles* in 1261–4 for use in missions, asked Spanish kings to finance language schools and echoed a decision of the order's general chapter of 1250 that they should teach Arabic, Greek and Hebrew. Careers were built around these techniques. The Dominican Raymond Martin was employed in Aragon investigating Jewish texts in 1264. In that year and again in 1269 he preached against Islam in Murcia and Tunis, and retired as lector in Hebrew at his order's school in Barcelona in 1281. The Preachers created a Society of Missions in 1312 which, together with the United Brethren, a group of sympathetic Greek Basilians, ran missions in Persia and Armenia in the early fourteenth century.

Hopes for voluntary conversion were vibrant. The reunification of Christendom, also, seemed about to be attained. Part of the Armenian Church joined Rome in 1198, and Latin influence in the Balkans rose to culminate in a momentary unification of the Bulgar Church with the Roman in 1204. Greatest achievement of all, Constantinople united with Rome at the second Council of Lyons in 1274.

The movement failed, and a reason was that the Latins twisted the arms of those they wished to bring to the 'Way of Truth'. They were sometimes open about it. A pagan fort on Germany's eastern frontier was summoned in 1227, for example, in this way: 'If you want peace, renounce idolatry and receive the true peace, which is Christ,' and the defenders of another replied: 'We know your God is greater than ours because he has forced us to worship him by conquering us. Whence we beg that, sparing us, you mercifully impose on us . . . Christ's yoke.'[5]

They were sometimes covert. When Constantinople fell in 1204,

Thomas Morosini replaced the Greek patriarch of that city and, importing Venetian canons, planned to replace all Greek prelates with them. Although initially appalled, Innocent III himself forced the Greeks to subscribe to Latin beliefs – so vigorously that soon only one bishop remained in his see – and fostered the entry of Latin missionaries, at first Cistercian, then mendicant. What could happen to Greek churches, moreover, is seen in Cyprus after the Lusignan dynasty was established in 1192. By 1220 Greek clerks were obliged to swear oaths of obedience to Rome, and two years later the island's four Greek prelates were ordered out of town and settled in the countryside. A Latin attack led to papal 'arbitration' in 1260 in which the pope abolished the Greek metropolitan, entrusting his functions to the Latin archbishop of Nicosia, and assigned the clerical tithe to the Latins. No wonder the union with Rome lasted only eight years!

Nor could relations have been different: religions were contemporaries, definition of citizenship both in Europe and elsewhere. Rooted in unbelief or indifference towards religion, however, tolerance nevertheless existed. The Holy Land's French aristocracy was more tolerant than newly arrived crusaders. Saladin was something of a hero to western gentlefolk, and Dante reserved for him a pleasant place in hell. In Wolfram of Eschenbach's romance *Parzifal*, the heathen Feirefiz fully equals the hero in chivalry, and besides, they are close blood relatives. Moved by a desire to purify the Latins, Peter Cantor praised Muslim absorption in prayer, monotheism, detestation of idolatry, lack of 'images' and 'sacrifices' in its 'temples'. He also praised their sobriety, noting that Saladin scorned the drunken Christians. He also encouraged giving alms to an indigent pagan or Jew rather than a Christian who could get by.

Tolerance was not widespread, however. Responding to Muslim allegations that the Trinity showed Christians to be polytheist, lawyers like Innocent IV and Hostiensis asserted that Islam itself was idolatry and polytheism. Dante repeated an old story that Islam derived from Judaism and Christianity, but this made it worse, as being a heresy. James of Voragine, archbishop of Genoa, states that a Jacobite archdeacon or Nestorian monk converted Mohammed from idolatry into Christian heresy. Gerald of Wales explained why Muslims eschewed pork: they were judaizing. Wine was also prohibited because Mohammed, when 'drunk, since he had preached filth . . . fell . . . in the street and was bitten by pigs'.[6] Both Jews and Muslims thought clerical celibacy exposed young boys and girls to risk, which, in turn, made William of Auvergne, the bishop of Paris, claim that Muslims thought themselves free 'to use or abuse all possessions, abuse male slaves and even many animals'.[7]

Christians and Muslims often enslaved prisoners of war. James of Vitry described what happened when Damietta fell in 1220. Four hundred rich captives were exchanged for Christians; the rest were sold as slaves, the children being bought by James himself for conversion to Christ. The chancery of Eugene III (1145–53) drafted a letter to a Muslim prince, thought so elegant that it found a place in a German formulary book:

> Eugene bishop etc. to a king or sultan of the Saracens. We do not greet you, not because we do not wish your health, but because you do not believe in the true health, that of Christ Jesus crucified for the salvation of humankind, and because you do not cease injuring those who profess Christ.[8]

As if diplomacy were not difficult enough!

Facing religion's pressures the natural religious tolerance or indifference of secular monarchy was weakened. Conqueror of Toledo in 1085, Alfonso VI of Castile described himself as emperor of the 'two religions' when addressing Muslims, and a successor, Ferdinand III (1217–52), had Arabic, Castilian, Hebrew and Latin inscribed on his tomb. In the code called the *Usages of Barcelona* the prince promised to defend the rights of all citizens, Christian, Saracen, Jew and 'heretic' (those, perhaps, adhering to the Mozarabic rite). Such attitudes were seen when Christians invaded Spain's Islamic areas and were aided by rebellious Muslim and Jewish populations. 'Divide and rule' is good counsel for a monarch, and minorities, moreover, often provide useful officers and troops. Alfonso VIII of Castile (d. 1214) was criticized by Innocent III for paying Muslim officers with church tithes. Similar censure fell on Andrew II of Hungary (d. 1235) for employing Ismaelites (Asiatic Muslims) to suppress magnate opposition, and was repeated against his successors of the Arpad dynasty. Frederick II Hohenstaufen's Muslim military colony at Lucera in the Capitanata infuriated Rome.

Overcoming princely resistance, laws barring Muslims from public office, from owning Christian slaves or domestics, against publicity for their cult and social intercourse with Christians spread from the late twelfth century, inspired by the Roman pontiffs. By the early fourteenth century similar legal impediments were imposed on Greek 'schismatics' in Sicily by the Catalan Frederick III

(d. 1337). This law or what was behind it affected everything. Alfonso X of Castile's poetry and even his *Book of the Laws* were remarkably intolerant compared with earlier Spanish letters.

In fine, like Greeks, Muslims living under Latin rule rightly viewed missionaries as agents of a persecution to which they were, or were about to be, subject. In the past, Muslims had often summoned Latins to help solve internecine squabbles; by 1300, however, they had learned better – for a time. They had been alerted to what their fate would be

WAR AND MISSIONS

During the thirteenth century, missions failed just as the Crusades had. Enthusiasts, however, did not readily surrender hopes that there would no longer be 'gentile or Jew, circumcised or uncircumcised, barbarian or Scythian, slave or free', only Christians.[9] Roger Bacon proposed recasting education and society so that 'all the nations of the unbelieving predestined to the life eternal will be converted to the efficacy and glory of the Christian faith'.[10] Like Llull's, his universal science would help missionaries explain the truth to deaf ears. Aquinas had shown the language to use: when you argue with Jews, centre on the Old Testament, with Manichaeans on the New, but with the others who use neither, natural reason will work. Bacon agreed that philosophy was common to all, and since he believed it in accord with religion, it would bring humanity to Christ. Language instruction, however, was needed.

Llull had once shared this view, learning Arabic to serve as a missionary. By 1295, however, he knew it was insufficient. So recalcitrant were Muslims that missions had to be assured a fair hearing, and he therefore recommended a Crusade for free speech in his plan of 1308, one owing much to a book of about 1291 by Fidenzio of Padua, a Franciscan in the Holy Land. The canonists Hostiensis and Innocent IV had in fact opined that Muslims contravened natural law by refusing free entry to Christ's 'good news'. Some therefore favoured outright conquest. In his *Recovery of the Holy Land* of 1306, Peter Dubois urged this course because it would be vastly profitable. He packaged religion in materialism. Spices etc. would be cheaper after the conquest. Educated young westerners would intermarry with Muslims, showing them how good it could be. The Mamluks' Egyptian subjects, especially women, were enslaved and would revolt when freedom's banner was waved. A reformed Church was to educate young women and men for eastern settlement. Political unity under the king of France, a European congress and permanent international arbitration, with the Roman pontiff as final arbiter, would still war in Europe. Others played war games. In 1321 the Venetian senator Marino Sanuto proposed unifying Europe under both pope and French king. He also hoped for an alliance between the Tatars and Latins to attack the strategic base of Islamic power in Egypt, and looked forward to the conquest of the Indian Ocean.

These schemes all shared the notion that the faith needed coercion. History, indeed, had shown that, apart from Mongol Asia, missions succeeded only where Latin power dominated. Even the momentary union of Constantinople and Rome in 1274 was motivated by Emperor Michael VIII Paleologus's fear of Charles I of Naples's (d. 1285) plan to restore the Latin Empire on the Bosporus. The Sicilian Vespers of 1282 and resultant loss of Sicily to the Catalans enabled or obliged Emperor Andronicus II to drive out the unionists and withdraw obedience from Rome. Marsiglio of Padua (d. 1342) summed up this failure:

> It cannot be shown from sacred Scripture that an infidel can be forced to confess the Christian faith . . . and it follows that, if an overseas expedition is made to force infidels to do so, such an expedition should never be considered meritorious. If the expedition, however, is made to force infidels to obey civil commands of the Roman prince and people and pay their taxes as they are supposed to by law, such an expedition, I think, should be thought meritorious because its objective is the peace and tranquillity of all citizens.[11]

Marsiglio had not only junked holy war, he had inadvertently justified the secular ones of Europe's modern colonial empires.

That hostility to one's enemy stimulates is shown by the great fruit borne by the knowledge Christians obtained of Muslim writings. Llull modelled his hero Blanquerna on Muslim mystic hermits (or *sufis*). The *Mir'ag* or *Ladder*, a mystic voyage by Mohammed into heaven and hell, was translated into Castilian by a Jewish doctor at the court of Alphonso X, and into Latin and French in 1264 by Bonaventure of Siena. Bonaventure did so that Christians might 'know that rash assaults against Christ by Mohammed were as wrong-headed as they were ridiculous, and that, when compared with such lies, the truth of the Christian faith will seem all the more appealing'.[12] Without this and other pieces of Muslim popular piety, however, Dante's *Divine Comedy* would not have had its distinctive architecture. Even in retreat, then, Latin Europe still hungrily devoured the wisdom of other cultures, thus accumulating technical competence that would astonish the world in early modern times.

At this time, however, the Latin retreat was real; indeed, it was sometimes a rout. There was more to the failure of Christian missions than is stated above. In 1332–33 those – largely Italian – attending a service in the Franciscan church of Tabriz in Persia heard a radical friar, George of Adria, describe Pope John XXII as the Antichrist. The Latins were exporting not only their faith but also their civil wars, and these show that, at home as abroad, the Church's mission was faltering. Aspects of this are examined in the last three chapters of this volume.

NOTES AND REFERENCES

1   *Commentaria in quinque libros decretalium* (2 vols, Venice, 1581, rprt) II, 128ra–9vb, cited in Robert Benson, 'Medieval Canonistic Origins of the Debate on the Lawfulness of the Spanish Conquest' in *First Images of America* (ed. Fredi Chiappelli with M.J.B. Allen and R.L. Benson, Berkeley 1975) 333.

2   Norman Housley, 'Crusades against Christians: their Origins and Early Development, *c.* 1000–1216' in *Crusade and Settlement* (ed. Peter W. Edbury, Cardiff, 1985), 24.

3   *Inferno* 27, 85.

4   *Opus maius* 3, 3, 13 and 4, 2, 1 (ed. J.H. Bridges, Oxford and London 1897–1900), II, 121 and 200.

5   The chronicle of Livonia in *MGH SS in usum scholarum*, 48 and 80.

6   *De principis instructione* 1 17 in *Roll Series* LXXXI, viii, 68.

7   *De universo* in Paris National Library ms lat. 15756, 84r a–b.

8   *Baumgartenberger Formularius* in *BuF* II, 731, dated about 1302.

9   *Colossians* 3:11.

10   *Compendium studii philosophiae* I in *Rolls Series* XV, 395.

11   *Defensor minor* 7, 3 (ed. C.K. Brampton, Birmingham, 1922), 18–19. This work of 1342 summarized the *Defensor pacis* of 1324.

12   Francesco Gabrieli, 'New Light on Dante and Islam' in *East and West* IV (1953), 175a.

5

THE JEWS

DIVISIONS AND EDUCATION

The law dealing with Muslims was an adaptation of late Roman and Visigothic legislation on Jews. This people was the only group in the Latin west, except in a few peripheral and recently acquired regions, permitted to hold a faith other than Christian. More numerous under Islam, Jews were also not so unique in the multinational and multireligious area of Arabic culture.

Although massacres of Jews in the Rhineland had marked the early Crusades and Muslim Spain in the first half of the twelfth century, these had ceased. Around 1200, both in the north and in the Mediterranean, Europe's Jews flourished as never before. The greatest centres of Jewish life were found outside of the Latin west in Byzantine and Arabic areas, but this was changing, partly because Sicily and most of Spain had been conquered, and partly because Islam was fading. Europe's Jews were few in number, the heaviest populations being along the Mediterranean frontier. In 1343 the Jews in Palma (about ninety per cent of their co-religionists in Majorca) were a trifle over eight per cent of town population. Up north, hardly more than three thousand lived in England in the late thirteenth century, a well-to-do group drowned in a population of five or so million.

Jews had long been richer than the peoples among whom they lived. As intermediaries between Islam and Christendom they helped transmit the teachings of Mediterranean culture. Although this function was fading and Jewry was itself becoming parochial, Jews were more literate than most of their Christian neighbours, thus reinforcing a sense of cultural superiority. They had also found a way of living with the Latins. An example was the abrogation of polygyny by the ruling of Gershom of Mainz (d. 1028), one echoing the ban on polygyny for Roman citizens. Surrendering social practices, however, they held all the more firmly to religion.

Mediterranean Jews probably enjoyed an ampler culture than northern ones. From the south – one thinks of Maimonides (d. 1204), an Andalusian who lived mostly in Cairo in Egypt – came an influential Aristotelian natural philosophy. Typically, French and German rabbis condemned this thought. In Italy, Languedoc and Spain things were different, although intellectual battles took place there, too. The history of philosophy was paralleled by the practical art of medicine. Whereas Jewish doctors were rare in the north, the reverse was true in the south. Busy in Spain and Languedoc, Italy's popes and southern princes employed them.

Mediterranean Jews were also more given to messianism and mystical thought. Although Eleazar Rokeah (son of Jehudah, d. 1223–32) of Worms produced an encyclopaedia of quietist ethics, messianic numerology, folklore and superstition called the *Book of the Devout*, he was from the Italian family of the Kalonymides active in Speyer, Mainz and Worms. Besides, if German or Ashkenazic Jewry vaunted its Hasidic mysteries, Spanish or Sephardic rabbis, along with those of Languedoc, led in the similar tradition of the Kabbalah. The author of the *Zohar*, Moses son of Shemtob (d. 1305) of Leon, lived in Guadalajara, and although he voyaged all over the Mediterranean from Syria to Italy, the prophetical messianist Abulafia (Abraham son of Samuel, d. after 1291) was raised in Saragossa and Tudela. Abulafia also represents a special messianic and prophetical tradition. Although northerners speculated about the date of the Messiah's coming, they usually put it off; in the south, they brought it nearer. In 1263 the Kabbalist Nahmanides (Moses son of Nahman or Rambam) of Barcelona and Gerona stated in a debate with Paul Christiani, a Dominican apostate from Judaism: 'When the end of time comes, the Messiah will go to the pope at God's command and ask him to liberate his people.' Perhaps this caused Abulafia to go to the pope in 1280 and plead Jewry's case.[1]

Jews were not intellectually sealed off from the world. There was a Jewish minnesinger, Süsskind of Trimberg. As soon as Walter of Metz had finished his verse encyclopaedia *Image of the World* in 1245, the Londoner Deulecresse (Chaim son of Deulecret) translated it into Hebrew. Mediterranean Jews were especially open-minded. They created a secular love poetry which, just as did Muslim, influenced Christian verse. Writing on ethics in 1278 the Roman Jehiel son of Jekutiel cited not only Scripture and the *Talmud*, but also the philosophers Aristotle and Porphyry and a saying of Frederick II Hohenstaufen. In the early fourteenth century, Leo Romano (Judah son of Moses, b. 1292), a courtier of the Angevin Robert I (d. 1343), translated not only Arabic texts but also a Hebrew version of selections from Augustine, Albert the Great and Aquinas. Intelligent Jews, he said, 'believe that true knowledge is going to other peoples, especially Christians'.[2] Leo's older cousin Immanuel son of Solomon (grandson of Jekutiel of the Roman Zifroni family, d. 1330) was a poet in Hebrew and Italian, a friend of men in the circle of Dante and Cino of Pistoia. He also wrote a mystical commentary on the *Song of Songs* and a collection of satirical verses on religion, love and Jewish life called the *Mehabberoth*. He is a bad Jew, he says, but not thereby a Saracen or Christian. Take the best from each faith: Christian eating and drinking is good, Moses required few fasts, and one can debauch with Mohammed. Love is the only complete lordship, knowing no law, no mass, no prophet.

Jewish communities had synagogue schools. Most youths left school either at the age of thirteen, the age of religious majority, or at sixteen. Not a few dropped out before that, as is seen in the *Hukke ha-Torah* of Languedoc, where, if a pupil is weak, the teacher is to take him to his father and say: 'God may enable your son to do noble things, but, for learning, he's too stupid.'[3] No provision was made for females, although a few girls were trained by rabbinical fathers. From the age of five, students began with languages (the local vernacular, Hebrew and Aramaic), examples being drawn from the Bible, itself studied in subsequent years. From ten to sixteen, parts of the *Mishnah* were read. After that during seven years in which the pupils lived with their teacher, material from the whole *Talmud*, that is, both the *Mishnah* and the *Gemara*, and rabbinical commentaries were studied.

The *Hukke ha-Torah* has led some to think of Jewish universities. That most rabbis came from rabbinical families or married into them, however, shows that Jews were educated in the homes of learned men. Standard in Arabic culture, this educational method was also normal in Christendom where apprentices (*discipuli*) were sent to live with master artisans, and young gentlemen learned manners, arms and sometimes letters in the courts of local magnates. What made the university different from Islamic, Jewish and Latin lay education was celibacy. This partly freed the life intellectual from bondage to family, and so strong was it that it marked even secular law and medicine in which most professionals were married.

Formal education was limited to scripture and the *Talmud*, but philosophy and natural science flourished, especially among Jews in Islam. As in Muhammedanism, however, Maimonides's attempt to graft philosophy on to the law, as in the *Mishneh Torah* of 1180, was not well received. Things were different among the Latins where, by 1300, university students had formal instruction in Aristotelian thought. In Jewish education, then, everything centred on the law, and hence the tone of rabbinical literature was analogous to that of Latin legal writing. Abraham of Posquières (son of David or Rabad, *fl.* 1150–70) from Montpellier glossed five of the *Mishnah* tractates, twenty-four of the *Talmud* and pioneered in commenting on the *Midrashim*. He also published *Responses* on particular questions, and, of course, criticized Maimonides's *Mishneh Torah*.

Abraham seems narrow until one remembers that an encyclopaedia like the *Talmud* contained not only law and observances, but also examples of ethics, magic, prophecy, indeed all sorts of subjects. The unification of such heterogeneous material into texts like the *Talmud* suited an Arabic Mediterranean society divided into national–religious 'castes', and was also of use to Jews as a European minority. The urge towards unity contrasted sharply with the Latin bent in the opposite direction. Although Raymond Llull attempted to join all knowledge into one grand scheme, a united body of learning, tradition and law never emerged, probably because religion did not sufficiently define a nation or a people in Latin Christianity. There were many nations under its aegis, and within these, the separation, even mutual hostility of Church and State encouraged institutional autonomy. Hence, when growing wealth made it possible, the different disciplines – theology, law and grammar – became specialities, creating special faculties.

GOVERNMENT AND ECONOMY

Jewish communities had a limited right of autonomy or self-government. Their civil litigation was usually settled by Jewish judges, the *dayanim*. Civil cases between Jews and Christians usually went to the defendant's court, although in England and northern France these were often arbitrative panels, half Jewish, half Christian. In some Italian statutes and John of England's legislation of 1201, criminal cases – those involving the shedding of blood – came before Christian courts. This meant intrusion into the Jewish community even in a case such as adultery between Jews, a case specified in a law of Cologne in 1252.

The institutions of Jewish self-government were similar to those of Latin guilds and small communities. Government by elders was the rule, and judges and councillors frequently chose their own successors. In theory, however, the adult male members of the synagogue chose the rulers. Writing to the Jews in Saragossa in 1264, Rashba (Solomon son of Adret) of Barcelona remarked that a community is not legally bound to choose either the wise or the rich for its canonical seven councillors. Constitutions varied, he said, and there are 'places where business is run by the elders . . . . Others where . . . [they] can do nothing without consulting the people and obtaining their consent, and still others where individual leaders can do as they see fit'.[4] Such councillors were to raise the taxes required by government, and here too practices differed. Answering a query from Montpellier, Rashba remarked that the senior community sometimes dominated but that elsewhere, as at Tarragona, Villafranca and Montblanch, the larger centre was obliged to consult the lesser ones when assigning taxes.

According to medieval Roman lawyers, Jews were citizens, but from the days of Christian Rome and Visigothic Spain, they were prohibited from holding public office and land. Encouraged to lend money, however, they were granted the right to use or rent land pledged to them for debt. There were exceptions. In 1239 Frederick II Hohenstaufen granted the Jews from the island of Gerbi, settling in Palermo to introduce indigo and henna, a portion of the royal date groves – few Arabic-speaking town-dwellers lacked a date-palm – and the right to rent lots for houses with leases of from five to ten years. Save in Spain or Italy, however, Jews never became farmers or landlords, but leased vineyards, dairies and other facilities for domestic consumption and ritual needs.

Jews usually served Christian princes. In England, Sicily and Spain they were the possessions – called 'special serfs of our treasury' in Sicily, 'chattels' in England – of the kings, who jealously guarded their monopoly. In the mid twelfth century, the *Laws of*

Edward the Confessor reported that 'all Jews . . . must be under the guardianship and protection of the king; nor may any of them be subject to a richman [baron] without the licence of the king, because Jews and all their property are the king's'.[5] In centralized monarchies, princes appointed leaders for the Jews – as Frederick II acceded to the request of the Palermitan Jews and ordered his governor to appoint an elder from among them – or even appointed a head of the nation's Jews like the 'Jews' bishop' in England, an officer sometimes replaced by a synod. England's community was ordered in 1241 to choose delegates to meet at the Worcester parliament to negotiate a subsidy to the king.

Where political power was decentralized, as in France, Jews fell under local lords. In 1235 a count of Boulogne blandly willed to 'his' people the property of 'his' Jews in reparation for 'his' sins. A Capetian effort to claim them all met great resistance, and the crown settled for treaties from 1198 to 1210 with the counts of Champagne and those of Saint-Pol and Nevers and again in 1230. The participants prohibited luring Jews from another's Jewry, stipulating that those who moved should be returned. Small wonder that, writing in the late twelfth century, Isaac son of Samuel of Dampierre referred enviously to the fact that elsewhere than in France 'Jews have the right to reside wherever they wish, like nobles.'[6] The Empire was not yet so decentralized. Although Frederick II gave rights over Jews to the princes, he none the less issued a general privilege for them in 1236, and until late in the century Germany's Jews insisted that they were not citizens of local communities, but instead of the Empire or at least of a substantial principality. A rabbi who had served all over Germany, Meier son of Baruch (d. 1293), claimed that the Jews 'are not dependants obliged to pay taxes wherever they happen to be, as gentiles are, but are like nobles'.[7]

Princes profited from 'their' Jews by forced loans, ransoms to avoid confiscation and taxes. Hard pressed by war with the Plantagenets, Philip II Augustus first ransomed them and then drove them out in 1182. This expedient failed because they migrated to France's greater feudatories and enhanced the revenues of the Capetians' rivals. They were therefore readmitted sixteen years later. Jews were used or abused, in short, according to need. Matthew Paris's wisecrack about the pledging of the Jews by Henry III of England to his brother Richard of Cornwall in 1255 illustrates the attitude: those whom the king had skinned the count would eviscerate.

In spite of this, princes had no desire to kill geese laying golden eggs and rarely initiated attacks on the Jews. Normally, Jews were useful officers, especially tax collectors, and their permitted usury had many functions. Since Jewish loans were publicly registered, a government, although often both defrauded and defrauding, roughly knew what the wealth of a Jewish community was. In return for enforcing their contracts, it siphoned much of the lucre into the treasury. Besides, princes could buy recalcitrant magnates by cancelling debts, or force obedience by insisting on payment. Facing a hostile Christian population, Jews were dependent on their princely masters. If popular hatred exploded, however, princes tried to reap the profits from persecution and confiscation.

The opponents of princes hated Jews. England's baronial opposition attacked them from the Great Charter of 1215 until the expulsion of 1290. The expulsion from France in 1315 coincided with the nobles' league of France and the Champagne against arbitrary royal government. Towns also attacked their Jews when rising against their lords. Otto of Freising tells us that in 1146 Bernard of Clairvaux silenced a wandering monk at Mainz who stirred up revolts of the people on the pretext of attacking Jews. Once princely or seigniorial power was reduced and urban aristocracies built oligarchies, however, they made peace with the Jews. It was then the people's turn, and, as the plebs gained a measure of political power around 1300, Jewry's great trials began.

Even in the expanding economy of the twelfth century, Christian merchants drove Jews out of commerce except in the Mediterranean and along Europe's eastern frontiers. Paced by maritime Venice, northern Italy's towns led the world in exclusionary legislation. At Perugia in 1279, a newly elected *podestà* took oath to refuse entry to Jews. This, combined with the prohibition of the ownership of land, obliged Jews to specialize in lending money. Ecclesiastical attack on Christian usury may have had something to do with this increase. The fourth Lateran Council of 1215 required Jews to restore 'grave and immoderate usuries', because 'the more the Christian religion curbs the taking of usury, the more does Jewish perfidy become used to this practice, so much so that, in a short time, Christian wealth will be exhausted'.[8] Tax collectors and moneylenders could not escape popular hatred. Abelard (d. 1142) had his fictional Jew say that, not being permitted to own land, 'what remains to us is usury, that we sustain our miserable lives by taking interest from the others, which makes us hateful to them'.[9]

Moneylending or usury was not enthusiastically engaged in by all Jews. It was forbidden among Jews, and the right to collect usury from Christians was also actively debated. Although usually permitted by Christian authority, many, including Thomas Aquinas, claimed it was immoral. When asked why Jews, since they had no other way of making a living, should be punished for it, Aquinas coolly replied they ought not be allowed to profit from crime. Some Jews justified taking usury from Christians: around 1204 Moses of Paris (son of Jehiel, grandson of Mattathiah) permitted it because the brotherhood of Jew and Christian had been sundered, an opinion dismissed by Joseph the Zealot (son of Nathan Official) of Sens. Still, just as some Christians allowed usury taken from Muslims, Maimonides permitted usury to defeat the enemies of the faith. In 1246 Meier son of Simon of Narbonne adopted a familiar Christian expedient of trying to pass usury off as interest.

And Jews were moneylenders. Notarial registers from Perpignan in Roussillon in the late thirteenth century contain a total of fourteen acts showing Jews active in commerce and local trade as against 1,643 lending money to Christians. Of the 220 Jewish adults mentioned in these acts, at least eighty per cent were moneylenders, and of those mentioned twice, ninety-three per cent were in the business. Perpignan, however, corrects a misapprehension about usury, namely that these loans were only to the poor or improvident. Perpignan was a new town at that time, and most Jewish loans there were to successful businessmen. One concludes that Jews were wanted in growing but underdeveloped areas. They accompanied the Germans in their drive to the east and were welcome there. Once a region was built up, however, Christians, such as the Lombards in France and England, replaced Jews in the 'big money'. At that time Jews were forced into humble trades and petty usury or pawnbroking which, although profitable and necessary, evoked popular hostility. Roussillon is an example. Although suits against Jewish usurers were brought into ecclesiastical courts from about 1261, Catalonia's princes stoutly protected the Jews' right to lend at interest. In the early fourteenth century, however, popular and judicial actions began a systematic attack on the Jewish community, leaving it impoverished by the next century.

The Jews' most active enemies were the people and churchmen. This was because churchmen were the ideologues of the age, who voiced its passions, and because the people, the humble many, suffered poverty more than others and hence their anti-Judaism was more virulent. Rescinding the expulsion of 1306, the French crown readmitted the Jews in 1315 and tried to protect them. This policy failed because of the popular movement of the Pastoureaux from 1319 through the early 1320s that, beginning in Languedoc, swept all France. Shouting utopian slogans, mobs of deracinated workers, farmers and others massacred Jews and lepers in the hospitals before turning against the rich and towards inevitable repression. Such was the backdrop for the royal expulsion of the Jews in 1322. To judge from their early expulsion from England and northern France, in short, the Jews' torment also had to do with the growth of centralized states. Princes lacked resources partly because their aristocracies refused the subsidies they needed. Even had he no wish to harm Jews or Muslims, a prince would necessarily profit from their expulsion or impoverishment, and people often take pleasure in doing what they cannot help but do.

The attitude of Latin princes towards Jews is therefore worth examining, as are the pressures they underwent. Exponents of Christian brotherhood and utopia had harsh words for them because they tolerated and profited from Jews. By allowing them to take usury from Christians, the prince was the real usurer. Aquinas opined that Jews must restore usuries and that, if princes lost because of this, they had only themselves to blame. 'It would be better for princes to make Jews earn their livings by working, as in Italy, rather than allow them to live idly enriched by usury.'[10] The Dominican was exaggerating: in southern Italy, especially Sicily, Jews were often artisans, even farmers, but that was rarely true in the north, and then only in the least-favoured occupations. James of Vitry urged Latins to emulate the Muslims:

> Saracens . . . hold [Jews] in greater hatred and contempt than do Christians. For while the detestable avarice of Christian princes supports them for material profit, permits them to have Christian servants and allows them to despoil their Christian subjects by immoderate usuries, they are allowed to live among the Saracens only when they work with their hands at the most abject and vile professions, are servants and slaves of the pagans and live in the lowest possible condition.[11]

Few princes publicly defended their relationship with the Jews. They either argued that things are necessarily imperfect in this world or asserted, as did Otto III, duke of Burgundy, in 1205, that papal law against employing them in public office was an invasion of the secular sphere. When, as they sometimes did, they went over to the popular ideal, it was a bad day for Jews. Forwarding the canonization of Louis IX of France, the dead king's chaplain, William of Chartres (d. *circa* 1280), praised his king:

> As hateful to God and man, Jews he so detested that he could not even see them, nor did he want to turn their property to his own use, saying that he did not want their poison, and that he did not want them to exercise usury, but instead gain their livelihood in licit professions or commerce . . . . When many of his councillors tried to persuade him to the contrary, asserting that the people could not live without loans, cultivate land or exercise professions or commerce, and that it was better that the Jews, who were already damned, should perform this damnable function than Christians who would, for this very reason, oppress the people with even heavier usuries, he answered as a Catholic, saying: 'Concerning the Christians and their usuries, that pertains to the prelates of the Church. To me pertain those of the Jews, because they are under the yoke of my servitude . . . . Let the Jews give up usury or leave my land.'[12]

Although Christian and Jew often lived at peace, Abelard knew how Jews felt. His Jewish spokesman said 'we are thought worthy of such contempt and hate by all that whoever injures us believes that action to be the highest justice and the greatest sacrifice to his God'. After sleepless nights, Jews arise and go fearfully among enemies, and even the princes 'who rule us and from whom we buy protection at such cost desire our deaths because it is then more permissible to seize our possessions'.[13] Social relations were well-nigh impossible. Jocelin of Brakelonde's history of Abbot Samson of St Edmunds recorded that, in the late twelfth century, a sacristain of Bury St Edmunds

> was called father and patron [by the Jews], who delighted in his guardianship, having free entry and egress, often going about the monastery by the altar and reliquary while solemn masses were being celebrated. They put their money in our treasury under the protection of the sacristan, and, even more absurd, their wives and children were received in our almshouse during wartime.[14]

And at times, things were far worse than that. The fiscal and constitutional crisis shaking England's monarchy in the late thirteenth century prompted a round-up by the beleaguered monarch of Jews and others for economic 'crimes' such as coin-clipping. In the period 1278–9, about 600 Jews were brought for trial to the Tower of London. Anywhere from 280 to 293 of them, just under ten per cent of all England's Jews, may have been executed!

CONVERSION AND PERSECUTION

To judge from Abelard and Raymond Llull, even sympathetic Christians believed the Jews were punished for the Saviour's fate. Asking whether a people must defend a person unjustly condemned, Peter Cantor answered that it was not that they had killed Christ, but rather that, as Augustine of Hippo said, they had not tried to save him. Augustine wrote:

> 'The Jews sinned mortally in allowing Christ to be crucified because they blanched . . . when their numbers protected them. They could have rescued him'. . . . [Peter concluded] Christ would not have been crucified if that people had united to oppose it.[15]

As punishment, God made them a people without a prince, everywhere humiliated and oppressed. Having refused the Lord's 'my yoke is easy, and burden is light' (Matthew 11:30), they were left bearing the heavy burden of an old law, one both superstitious (taboos on food, menstrual blood, etc.) and materialist (circumcision versus baptism). Abelard's Jew says: 'the precepts of [our] law are so tangled with difficulties that we are crushed as intolerably by its yoke as by the oppression of other men. Who, for shame and pain, does not abhor or fear to receive this sacrament of our circumcision?'[16]

Although secondary to the religious and social themes, racism reinforced hostility. As in Islam, racist concepts abounded, and colour and appearance were much commented on. Blond, white and blue-eyed are the usual heroes and heroines of medieval literature. What appear like black Carthaginians made the final attack on the martyr Roland, and even so open a man as Marco Polo, who was entranced by Chinese women, described black Africans as demonic looking. Caesarius of Heisterbach's book for novices in the Cistercian order several times refers to the Jewish 'stench', which, however, can be washed away by baptism.

That Jews hated them was a common Christian suspicion, as was the notion that malevolent envy was a Jewish characteristic. New expressions of these ideas appeared during the Gregorian and crusading periods when Europe's sense of Christian citizenship was strengthened. Around 1141 the story of the Christian boy, a Holy Innocent, murdered by the Jews makes its appearance. So popular was this fiction that, in 1181, Abbot Samson of St Edmunds managed to conjure up his own boy martyr. In 1255 England's justiciars said that the murder of Hugh of Lincoln – a fabrication – implicated all Jewry. Written for a king of a partially Jewish society whose forebears had been notably tolerant, the *Book of the Laws* of Alphonso X of Castile blandly noted that it was said that Jews crucified Christian boys on Good Friday.

Paralleling a desire for a more exact definition of civil and social status among Christians themselves, legislators and jurists separated Jews and Christians ever more sharply. Borrowing from Late Roman and Visigothic legislation, the Church led in formulating this new law during the pontificates of Alexander III (d. 1181) and Innocent III, especially the Lateran Council of 1215. The intention was partly protective: the Jews' right to keep faith and property was asserted by Calixtus II (d. 1124) and repeated by pope after pope. The anti-Jewish tale of the ritual murder of Christian boys was repeatedly attacked, especially by Innocent IV in 1247 and 1253. In Rome, where the pope was prince, each pontiff issued a constitution enshrining Jewish liberty on accession.

The other objective was to keep Jews in 'their place'. It was customary at Rome for them to exhibit their scrolls of the law during the pope's solemn parades, a practice soon adopted by Europe's secular princes. Saluting the law, the pope observed aloud that the Jews, by not cleaving to Christ, had failed to obey it. The theme of Jewish servitude surfaced in a papal letter of 1205 reminding Alfonso VIII of Castile that, by appointing Jewish officers, he was putting the handmaid before the mistress. In the same year, Innocent III requested France's princes to repress the 'excesses' of the Jews 'lest they presume to lift up their necks, submitted to the yoke of perpetual servitude, against the reverence due the Christian faith'.[17] By 1215 a battery of laws prohibited relations between Jews and Christians, employment of Christian servants, building of new synagogues and holding public office. Imitating Islam on this point, they were also to be visible: 'Jews and Saracens of either sex . . . should wear clothing to distinguish them from Christians, and not go out in public on Easter.'[18] In 1215, also, as has been seen, Jewish moneylenders were required to restore usuries under pain of 'indirect excommunication', a way of stopping commerce between Jews and Christians first mentioned in a papal letter of 1198.[19]

As missions rose in importance, Judaic texts were studied with greater care. This led to an attack by Gregory IX two years before his death in 1239 because the *Talmud* and rabbinical commentaries had passages hostile to Christianity. In 1240 a 'debate' between Nicholas Donin, a convert to Christianity, and some rabbis took place at Paris before the queen mother. The rabbis were permitted only to answer charges against their faith, and two years later, several wagons full of their books were burned. Although, as his biographer Joinville tells us, Louis IX would have preferred to run the Jew through, he ordained in 1254 that they should cease from usury, blasphemy and sorcery and that their books should be burned. Even silence was held against them. Robert of Criklade (d. *circa* 1161), a Benedictine at Oxford, said that the ancient Josephus's silence about Christ was a Jewish plot to hide the evidence that condemned them.

In Catalonia–Aragon, Paul Christiani of Burgos, a converted Jew who became a Dominican, petitioned Clement IV against the *Talmud*, and in 1267 the pope requested that the king establish a commission. The commission 'corrected' but did not burn this and other Jewish texts because the missionary friar Raymond Martin said they were useful for Christ's cause. A 'debate' took place in Gerona in 1263, one similar to that in Paris mentioned above. The intellectual quality of such 'debates' is shown by the fact that the Jewish leader at Paris, Rabbi Jehiel, and his peer at Gerona, Nahmanides, fled to Palestine shortly after the exchanges. In 1242, furthermore, the crown of Aragon obliged its Jews and Muslims to hear Christian missions and, in 1263, give preachers access to mosque and synagogue. In 1278 the popes granted the Lombard Dominicans the same right. Knowledge of each other's beliefs had served to increase the hostility of the different religions.

These anti-Jewish ideas influenced areas such as Germany, where they had not been known before. The ritual murder accusation was first heard of there in 1235. Written some time between 1215 and 1235, Eike of Repkow's law code, the *Saxon Mirror*, does not mention the conception of Jewish servitude but the *Swabian Mirror* of 1274–5 speaks of it at length. Jews had usually been treated like Christian merchants in older law, but now things changed. Promulgated in 1265 by the archbishop of Mainz, the statutes of a group of rural lords and towns on the Rhine, Main and Lahn rivers stated that the peace must be upheld for all inhabitants, adding 'even for Jews'.[20] Although protecting Jews against townsmen, Frederick II, outdoing the pope because at war with Rome, may have been the first to introduce the notion of Jewish perpetual servitude into imperial law. Confirming Vienna's liberties in 1237, he excluded Jews from holding public office, 'since, from earliest times, imperial authority has proclaimed perpetual servitude to be the punishment of the Jewish crime'.[21] In Germany as elsewhere, however, secular law only reluctantly followed ecclesiastical. If churchmen derived Jewish servitude from Christ's death, secular law often preferred another traditional explanation for slavery's origin: war. Titus defeated and captured the Jews, hence the emperor's right to their service.

That Jewry law became ever more hostile is exemplified by the statutes of Avignon in the early fourteenth century. Jews were locked in the *Juzataria* on Christian holy days and not allowed outside when Christ's body was being paraded. No 'Jews or whores should dare touch fruit or bread exposed for sale; if they do, they must buy what they have touched'.[22] Race crime was revived. A passage on treason, adultery and arson in the English lawbook called *Fleta* included the following: 'Apostate Christians, witches and others of that kind are to be drawn and burned. Those cohabiting with Jews and Jewesses, those engaged in bestiality and sodomites are to be buried alive.'[23] A provincial council at Avignon in 1337 listed cohabitation with Jews, Muslims or beasts among crimes confessors could not absolve without episcopal consent.

Not surprisingly, living on the same street or in the same quarter of a town became more advisable, indeed obligatory, for Jews. This was no radical change because, except for the wealthy who liked more spacious places, ordinary folk often lived near work and synagogue. Besides, Islamic society provided models for separate town and village quarters, which were, if not common, known in the west. Northern Spanish towns had French quarters with their own law, and Slavs and Germans did not initially live together. The French Jews invited to settle in Speyer by the prince archbishop in 1084 were delighted by his provision of a walled area. German Jews settling the valleys of the Oder and Warta rivers were not offended by the insistence of a provincial council of Gniezno held in Breslau in 1267 that they live apart. Relations had nevertheless worsened. The fathers at Breslau kept the Jews apart to preserve Christians from 'corruption'. Earlier, the bishop of Speyer had wanted them protected from the 'animal herd' of their Christian neighbours. What made a quarter into a ghetto was not enclosure so much as coerced enclosure.

In the late thirteenth century, Jewish conditions varied widely. In Spain and other Mediterranean regions, notably the islands, they were protected by numbers and by the fact that they were only one of several religious minorities, Muslim and sometimes Greek. In eastern Europe, where their economic services were much in demand, they were not only protected but privileged. There, serfs were subject to particular lords but Jews, like nobles, held of the prince alone. Eastern town law was still sometimes beneficent. In 1297 the Brandenburger lord of the town of Stendal ordered that 'Jews shall enjoy the common law of the city and are to be treated by the [town councillors] as are their own burghers.'[24] In England, France and northern and central Italy, however, they were impoverished, as in Italy, or expelled, as from England in 1290 or royal France in 1306 and again in 1322. As Jews were pushed toward Europe's frontiers by expropriation and expulsion, the distinction between northern Jewry and that of the Mediterranean was further reinforced.

The slow deterioration of their position evoked varied reactions among Jews. One was rage, and hence, although the polemic of the two faiths was always crude, it plumbed new depths at this time. Compiled from earlier French sources, especially the work of Joseph the Zealot in the 1260s, the anonymous German *Nizzahon vetus* of around 1300 exemplifies this. The apostle Peter is there called Peter the Ass, a teaching not unknown among Christians, where Peter, who represented the active life and the Roman hierarchy, was sometimes portrayed as a bumbler in contrast to John, the apostle of contemplation, apocalyptic understanding and intellectualism. Few Christians, however, enjoyed the notion that Christ was a common criminal, the Hanged One, or the story of his bastardy from the whore Mary, referred to throughout as *Haria*, from the Aramaic 'ordure'. Not, again, that such was unheard of among Christians. According to the French jurist and publicist Peter Dubois, Boniface VIII, when dying, was urged to give his soul to the Virgin. He replied: 'Silence fool, I don't believe in that she-ass or her foal.'[25]

Bad in a Christian, it was unforgivable in a Jew. As they learned how Jews doubted the Saviour, mocked the Virgin, the Trinity, etc., inquisitors went after not only the *Talmud*, but all sorts of books. In his manual of 1323–4, Bernard Gui recommended destroying works by Rashi of Troyes, Maimonides and the rationalist polemist David Kimhi son of Joseph (*fl.* 1160–1235) of Narbonne. A result was that Islam's Jews in Spain, reversing their stand of the early twelfth century, praised Saladin for liberating Jerusalem in

1187, and Europe's community generally favoured Islam thereafter. They also wanted to go 'home' to Palestine, the land from which they thought Rome had expelled them. Fleeing persecution, Nahmanides went to Jerusalem, finally settling in Acre where he died in 1267. He believed that the Messiah would come on the return of the Jews, and curiously, that the land would then itself bloom: 'nowhere in the world is there a land once as good and prosperous which is now as desolate. Ever since we were exiled from it, it has accepted no nation or tongue, and, though all try to dwell in it, none succeed.'[26]

Defencelessness also inspired self-hatred. By failing to teach the law, by irreverent noise in synagogues, etc., said Isaac of Corbeil in 1277, the Jews had brought it on themselves.

> We must learn from the Christians who, although they have the wrong faith, stand silent in their houses of prayer . . . . Our fathers have told us and we have seen it with our own eyes that many synagogues have been destroyed or changed into churches because they have not been treated with due respect.[27]

A parish priest would have been struck dumb by this observation. According to Berthold of Regensburg's Lenten sermons, Christians really made noise, upsetting the elevation of the Host with flirting and gaming.

Some Jews converted voluntarily, but their erstwhile community reacted strongly against them, and helped those converted by force to escape. Because converted Jews relapsed not infrequently, laws applying to heretics were soon applied to them; by 1271, inquisitors were charged with hunting them down. Although opposed to forced conversion, Nicholas III stated in 1278 that converted Jews must remain Christian, having come, however unhappily and unlawfully, to the better faith. About 1280 the law doctors of Pavia, Bologna and Ferrara recommended that those who aided or promoted an escape were liable to the death penalty. Those providing food or shelter were to be fined, exiled or excommunicated.

As the treatment accorded the numerous New Christians in the kingdom of Naples shows, conversion was no easy answer. A royal decree of 1311 required them to leave their quarters and integrate with Christians. Later legislation reversed this, ordering them to live apart because they might judaize Christians. One suspects that, although names change easily, habits and economic functions do not, especially in an ever more competitive economy.

Given this history, it seems strange that persons otherwise astute like Roger Bacon were convinced that it would not be difficult to convert the Jews. He opined that 'an infinite number of Jews among us have perished because no one knew how to preach to them or to interpret the Scriptures in their tongue, or to dispute with them . . . . O! ineffable loss of souls, when it would be so easy to convert innumerable Jews.'[28] This Franciscan was surely moved by utopian fancies, ones he shared not only with intellectuals but also with the people. But the people in movements such as the Pastoureaux were impatient. Urged by material poverty and oncoming death, these humble eschatologists looked for signs of coming bliss, and if the Jews had to be converted to provide them, they would see to it that they were.

Members of a tiny minority domiciled among a hostile majority, however, Jews were unwilling converts. Individuals aside, the social role and history of the Jewish people made its inner harmony dependent on being apart. When threatened, Jews rarely converted, and the consequent persecutions thus increased the rhythmic cycle of pogroms, expulsions and impoverishment that marked later medieval Jewry. On a time, Latin crusaders had gone to fight unbelievers abroad; they now chased Jews around at home.

As with Muslims, toleration of Jews was rare, and the level of discourse between the faiths was rarely high. Reflecting the events described earlier in this chapter, Thomas of Cantimpré claims that, in the 1250s, a nameless prelate and royal councillor persuaded the king of France not to burn Jewish books. For this God killed him with a sudden (typically medieval) stomach 'flux'. The Dominican went on: 'Note, dear reader, that all oriental Jews think that Jews who, against Moses' law and the prophets, receive and copy the book called the *Talmud* are heretics and excommunicates. And nevertheless this archbishop of Christ's law had defended such books!'[29] The knowledge Christians obtained of Jewish writings nevertheless bore great fruit. Although, as noted above, north European rabbis did not much read Maimonides's *Guide for the Perplexed* of 1190, Thomas Aquinas wrestled with it and the Dominican Neoplatonist Master Eckhart (d. before 1329) swore by it, and Rashi of Troyes influenced biblical studies through the work of Nicholas of Lyra. Curiously but typically, the work of both authors had been condemned by the inquisitor Bernard Gui.

NOTES AND REFERENCES

1 Scholem, *Jewish Mysticism* 128.
2 Güdemann, *Geschichte des Erziehungswesens . . . der Juden* II, 157.
3 *Ibid.* I 96: 'schwer von Begriff.'
4 Haim Beinart, 'Hispano-Jewish Society' in *Cahiers d'histoire mondiale* XI (1968), 227.
5 *Gesetze der Angelsachsen* (ed. Felix Liebermann, Halle, 1901) I, 650.
6 Baron, *A Social and Religious History* XI, 18–19.
7 *Ibid.*
8 *Liber extra* 5, 19, 18 in *CICan*. II, 816.
9 *Dialogus inter philosophum, Judaeum et Christianum* in *PL* CLXXVIII, 1618.
10 *De regimine iudaeorum ad ducissam Brabantiae* 2 in *Opuscula philosophica divi Thomae Aquinatis* (ed. R.M. Spiazzi, Turin, 1954), 250a.
11 *Historia orientalis* 82 (Douai, 1596), 160.
12 *De vita et actibus . . . Ludovici noni* in *Historiae Francorum scriptores* (ed. François Duchesne, Paris, 1636) V, 471.
13 *Dialogus inter philosophum, Judaeum et Christianum* in *PL* CLXXVIII, 1617.
14 *Cronica Jocelini de Brakelonda de rebus gestis Samsonis, abbatis monasterii Sancti Edmundi* (London, 1951), 10.
15 *Liber casuum conscientiae* No. 340 in *Summa de sacramentis et animae consiliis* III 2a (ed. J.-A. Dugauquier, Louvain and Lille, 1963), 417–18, and Augustine's *Enarratio in Psalmos* 81, 4 carried in the *Glossa Ordinaria*.
16 *Dialogus inter philosophum, Judaeum et Christianum* in *PL* CLXXVIII, 1618.
17 *Liber extra* 5, 6, 13 in *CICan* II, 776.
18 *Ibid.* 5, 6, 14 in *ibid.*
19 *Ibid.* 5, 9, 12 and 18 in *CICan* II, 814–16.
20 *MGH Constit.* II, 612, No. 444.
21 *Historia diplomatica Friderici secundi* (ed. J.L.A. Huillard-Bréholles, Paris 1852–61) V, pt I, 57.
22 *Coutumes et règlements de la république d'Avignon* (ed. M.A.R. de Maulde, Paris, 1879), 200, tit. 137.
23 *Fleta* 1, 35 in *Selden Society* LXXII (London, 1955), 90.
24 Otto Gierke, *Das deutsche Genossenschaftsrecht* I (Berlin, 1861), 261.
25 Text No. 34 in Etienne Baluze, *Vitae paparum Avenionensium* (ed. Mollat, Paris, 1917) III, 162.
26 Arye Grabois, 'The Idea of Political Zionism in the 13th and early 14th Centuries' in *Festschrift Rëuben R. Hecht* (Jerusalem, 1959), 68.]
27 Güdemann, *Geschichte des Erziehungswesens . . . der Juden* I, 84–5.
28 *Opus maius* 3, 13 (ed. Bridges), III, 120.
29 *Bonum universale de apibus* 1 36 in Paris National Library ms lat. 3585, 5v.

PART TWO
Economy

6

FOUNDATION AND GROWTH

THE LAND

Agricultural expansion moved into high gear in the early twelfth century and continued through the thirteenth, accompanied by technological improvement: horses for traction, improved harnesses, the introduction of water– and windmills and the spread of the three-field system. The people of this age perfected and spread a technology bequeathed them by their fathers; only the use of horses for ploughing and the spread of windmills may be assigned to the twelfth century.

Growth was especially marked on the frontiers from Spain to Slavdom. Partly settled earlier, central Spain's high plateaux were still filling up. The eastward push in Germany was resumed after the wars of the Gregorian age. Aided by Dutch and Flemings, farmers crossed the Saale and Elbe, going toward Transylvania and the Tatra range. Settlement stood still in the Lusatias, central Brandenburg and Mecklenburg up to about 1200; then, bypassing the plains of Bohemia and Moravia, it moved forward through Pomerania, into Silesia and into the north Vistula valley. Tidal marshes were drained along the North Sea and Baltic coasts. Although Holland and the Zuyder Zee were untouched by 1300, cultivation at the mouths of the Rhine, Meuse and Scheldt Rivers had advanced at the expense of the sea almost as far as today. Monasteries pioneered: over two-thirds of the Abbey of the Dunes' land at Hulst in the Scheldt estuary consisted of land reclaimed from the sea. River valleys were opened: the Milanese dyked and cleared the central Po valley by about 1300. Clearing valleys both increased the cultivated area and converted swampy streams into navigable rivers.

Although the Alps, Pyrenees and other mountains bordering the Mediterranean basin had important stands of timber, Europe's great forest lay to the north. There, bounded by Arctic seas and tundras and southern mountains and steppes, a vast wood extended from England into Russia. By 1300 the western reaches of this belt had been split into large segments. Although the royal forest was not all wooded, England's king claimed that the whole county of Essex lay within his forest. Partly won from the forest, the region between the Rhine and Loire rivers, especially Flanders and Brabant, had become north Europe's most urbanized part, the world's first example of inland urbanism not located on irrigated river valleys. This region was also the centre of the most widely spread national culture of this age, the French.

So well had nature endowed the northern plain that one wonders how the Mediterranean basin could equal it. The south's dry climate and light soils supported less cereal production, and land could not be used as intensively as up north, where a system of using two-thirds of the arable annually was commonly adopted. Northerners were also beginning to use horses for ploughing because, although they cost more than oxen, they were faster. Morocco, Lombardy and the Castilian plateaux were famous for horses, but only the damper northern soils could feed enough of them for agricultural use. Horses were not even much employed for transportation in the south, asses, supplemented by mules, being the usual beast of burden. Besides, except in favoured areas like Lombardy and alluvial valleys in southern France, central Italy and Catalonia, nature's wealth enabled northern farmers to live in larger villages than those of the south.

Northern advantages were not fully realized, however, until modern times. Too many forests remained to be thinned, too many swamps to be drained. Intensive agriculture had penetrated only the alluvial soils of northern France and parts of western Germany. In England, the three-field system had spread only to heavy soils of the south and east and plough horses were not used everywhere. Moreover, the Mediterranean held its own against the still underdeveloped north, partly because of geography. Northern transport was chiefly overland, whereas the indented coasts of the Mediterranean's many peninsulas and islands offered cheap sea transport. Inadequacy of food storage and the need for dietary variety also aided Mediterranean agriculture. The north depended on southern dried fruits, rice and sugar, and preservative spices came across the inland sea.

Mediterranean techniques were also highly developed. Dry-soil irrigation was common in the Near East, Africa and Spain, where Valencia's canals were famous. Lacking summer moisture, Milan's upland plain was irrigated by the waters of the Ticino, brought about forty miles in the canal called the Muzza built between 1179 and 1257. Ranching in the Mediterranean's dry savannahs produced horses, beef and wool. In Castile from the 1260s, the *Mesta*, an organization of landlords, shepherds and merchants, functioned under royal sponsorship. Forty years later its wool competed with England's and Burgundy's in both Tuscany and Flanders. Because of the small urban population, the Mediterranean still supplied its needs for agricultural products, with the exception of timber. Sicily and Apulia produced enough cereal to help feed northern Italy's mercantile and industrial towns, Apulia exporting nearly 690,000 bushels in good years during the early fourteenth century.

As markets grew, so did specialization. The Italian Salimbene was astonished to see that farmers around Auxerre in 1245 raised nothing but wine, selling it to buy food. By 1300 wine production was concentrated in the Bordelais, Poitou, Burgundy and the valleys of the Moselle and Rhine. Regional specialities involved international relationships. Wool for cloth manufactured in Flemish shops came largely from England, though Brabant, Burgundy and Spain also contributed. Woad, the dyestuff used there, came from the Rhineland and Picardy and also, by 1300, from the Garonne valley from Agen to Toulouse. Wine sold in Flanders came from the Rhineland, the Bordelais and Poitou. In short, England, Flanders and the Rhine and Garonne valleys had strong economic links, a reason for the struggle over Flanders between England and France.

Regions and towns favoured mixed production. Townsfolk often cultivated a field or two for vegetables or wine for the household, and the rich had substantial farms providing produce, storage facilities, summer recreation and counting-houses for rural usury. Agriculture was regulated. Around 1300, Mantua's magistrates tried to stabilize their county's 9,000 acres: sixty per cent in arable and pasture, thirty in vineyard and other crops and six in timber. Because the town could make do with its own, Messina's magistrates prohibited wine importation in 1272 and 1294.

Walter of Henley in the early thirteenth century, Robert Grosseteste (d. 1253), bishop of Lincoln, and the Bolognese lawyer Peter

Crescenzi early in the fourteenth century wrote tracts on farming. Agronomy was still in its infancy: Crescenzi was interested mainly in law, his agronomy a bare epitome of Columella, and Grosseteste really wrote about household management. Most practical of all, Walter of Henley was interested mainly in estate management; ploughhorses he thought impractical 'because the malice of plough-men will never allow a team of horses to go faster than oxen'.[1]

This agriculture supported a substantial population. Figures for the decades around 1300 indicate densities not materially surpassed until the agricultural and industrial revolutions of modern times. The area within modern France's frontiers may have contained around twenty million souls. Agriculturally rich, England supported around five million in 1300. Italy boasted about eight million of which about two and a half were in the south and Sicily. Some heavy populations are seen. In 1281 the town and county of Padua contained about 90,000 souls, with about a third in the town. Town and country had about 100 per square mile, that of the latter alone about 65. In 1255 the region of Pistoia supported about 114 per square mile. Parts of Flanders surely surpassed these figures.

This population rested on a fragile base. Fertilization was primitive, crop alternation rare, metal tools in short supply and so was animal traction. Even in crowded Italy, a team of oxen equalled the value of a peasant's farm. A result was that yield per acre was often low. Cereal production on the lands of the bishop and chapter of Winchester, for example, was about five times higher around 1914 than in the thirteenth century. Still, modernity itself admitted wide variations, an acre in the Po valley producing about twenty-six bushels of grain around 1900, a sharp contrast with Sicily's twelve. In 1879 the yield of grain per acre in the region around Mantua had only doubled since the thirteenth century. Around Marseilles in 1812 the return on seed grain planted over a ten-year period was about four and a half to five, only a trifle higher than that expected by the Hospitallers there five hundred years earlier. Yield per acre, moreover, was not so important then because farmyard fowl, small beasts and garden crops weighed more in the balance than today. Nor was the need for exports as great, because town population was relatively small. Unlike today, also, the hunt was a source of food.

A study of famines in western Germany and the Low Countries shows that, while the twelfth century suffered about five general crises, only local difficulties were experienced for a century after the hardships of 1215–16, themselves alleviated by importing eastern German grain. Not that shortages did not strike. England underwent six years of them in this period, three of them falling together from 1257 to 1259 to make a famine. Difficulties aside, west Europe's climate was markedly benign through the thirteenth century, and the food stocks increased until around 1300. French hospital regulations provided for meat thrice a week and eggs or fish on other days. Workers building a bell tower at Bonlieu in Forez in 1300 were provided liberally with bread, beans for soup, eggs, cheese, meat and wine. Well-to-do, the canons at Maroeuil in Artois in 1244 received bread, three eggs and three herrings or a portion of salt meat daily.

Eating well, however, is not enough. In spite of spicing, salting and smoking, food storage was in its infancy. The cold wave of the early fourteenth century showed how much humanity could suffer from a reduction of food production for more than a year. Besides, full bellies do not alone determine health; medical care is also needed. Excepting minor cures, good diet and some surgery, medicine helped little until modern times. The death rate was high, especially among the lower classes. Statistics from Winchester indicate that in 1245 the life expectancy of a twenty-year-old rural worker who had escaped the high mortality of childhood was twenty-four years. The age distribution was also quite unlike today's. Although longevity was not rare, infants and children died like flies.

Population pressure became acute before 1300 and untilled land of good quality became rare. This threatened forests. In heavily settled northern France during the thirteenth century, landlords protected their woods from overcutting and abrogated villagers' rights to pasture their beasts there. By 1300 the mountains around the Mediterranean were losing their forests. From England to Italy grain had been planted in marginal, easily exhausted soils. Villages were bursting at the seams. In 1241 the inhabitants of Origgio near Milan cultivated fifty-five per cent of their land; by 1320 only sixteen per cent was left untilled. The population of nine villages near Nice rose from 414 households in 1263 to 722 in 1315. Subdivision of farmland is seen at Weedon Beck (Northants) where the number of tenants rose from 81 to 110 between 1248 and 1300. Larger holdings also suffered, an inheritance of about 240 acres at Rozoy in the Isle de France being subdivided into seventy-eight parcels. Excessive subdivision blocked rational use of the land and prevented implanting new technology. Government regulation grew apace in urbanized Italy, whose republics regulated labour, crops, contracts and marketing. Population pressure paralleled by increasing litigiousness within communities led to social troubles like the Pastoureaux of France and the risings of the 1280s in the Low Countries that foreshadowed the social wars of the fourteenth century.

Although agrarian growth was slowing, population increase until shortly before the disasters of the 1340s makes it probable that contemporaries were unaware of it. Their expectations were those of earlier ages. Besides, the turn of the century showed signs of continued progress. Germany continued to expand. Pomerania was settled in the thirteenth century, and heavy settlement in East Prussia and adjacent regions did not begin till after 1280. Opened to colonization in the late thirteenth century, Silesia by 1350 boasted around 1,500 new settlements. Rounding out also kept alive a feeling of growth even in areas of older settlement. In northern France the twelfth century witnessed an enormous implantation of new villages. In the south, as emigration to Spain from the valleys of the Garonne and its confluents ceased, a new village movement got under way. From around 1230 until 1350, over 400 planned towns and villages were founded, though some failed to grow.

THE TOWNS

The medieval town reached its apogee in the 1320s. It was not large, a population of 5,000 being substantial in this period. Bigger towns existed, however, and one region where they were typical was centred in and around the county of Flanders. Flanders had many towns with from 10,000 or more souls in a rather small area. The population of Ghent may have reached 60,000, Bruges was possibly 35,000 and Ypres 15,000 to 20,000. Between the Rhine and Loire valleys and extending over the Channel to southern England there were other important towns. Cologne had perhaps 30,000 inhabitants. Set among modest towns and surrounded by rich plains, Paris rose to about 80,000 in 1328. Although England was a region of small urbanization, it, as in early modern times, had a huge metropolis: London, with perhaps as many as 90,000.

Lombardy, Liguria, Venetia, the Romagna and Tuscany were probably Latin Europe's most urbanized regions. Venice's population reached about 90,000 in 1338 and Milan was of almost the same magnitude, Genoa being somewhat smaller. The patriotic chronicler John Villani estimated Florence's population at 90,000 before the plague. Pisa had 50,000 in 1315. Like Flanders, what made Italy impressive were the many substantial towns in small areas. Other than Florence and Pisa, for example, Tuscany boasted four solid towns: Siena, Lucca, Pistoia and Arezzo. This contrasts with other Mediterranean regions where occasional large cities like Naples and Palermo (50,000 inhabitants) and the metropolises of Alexandria and Constantinople focused economic life in spaces without other important towns.

A hub of communications and a manufacturing centre, a town's relations to the countryside were many faceted and included government, defence, education and transport. Princes planted towns to develop their territories, to 'build the region', as the founding charter of Jüterbog in Brandenburg said in 1174. At Leipzig in 1160, burghers immigrating to Posen were urged to acquire and exploit rural properties. Poland's grand duke valued towns so highly that in 1253 he gave Posen jurisdiction over seventeen nearby villages. When Aquila was founded in the Abruzzi around 1254, its episcopal prince provided 'that a city of one body be constructed from outlying villages and lands, which, as dispersed members . . . were unable to resist the attacks of our enemies and unable to afford each other mutual aid'.[2]

Town and countryside were not rigorously separated in this period. Many town dwellers either worked the land or invested in it. After 1250 almost two-thirds of the new loans by Jews to Christians in Perpignan were made to countryfolk, and in the late thirteenth century, Lombards lent money in rural France from Normandy to the Lorraines and Hainault to Dauphiny. At his death in 1229 the self-made Pons of Capdenier, patron of the Dominican order in Toulouse, left over 300 documents devoted to his interests in lumber, animal husbandry and agriculture. Even large cities were somewhat rural. Florence's industrial proletariat worked seasonally in the fields and nearly a third of the debts occasioned by the crash of the Peruzzi merchant bankers in Florence in 1347 were paid by selling landed property. Typical was the Champagne town of Provins, which in the early fourteenth century had a population of eight to ten thousand in town and eight villages outside. In a plebiscite sixty-four per cent of the votes were cast by townsmen and thirty-six by villagers; about a third were in textile industries and nearly a fifth in agriculture.

If towns were somewhat rural, villages were somewhat urban. Mining was a village industry, as was woodwork for export. Besides, restrictions imposed by artisan guilds could impede urban industry, driving new processes into the less organized countryside. In the thirteenth century Flanders' export woollens were manufactured not only in cities but also in small towns or villages like Dixmuiden and Poperinghe. Combined with geography, technology sometimes even benefited villages more than towns. In the late twelfth century the introduction of watermills into England weakened urban fulling, moving it to the countryside with ample water-power in Yorkshire and Wales. Castelfigline near Florence boasted a guild of tailors, and in 1350 Fabriano in the March of Ancona was famed for quality paper. Villagers sometimes made fortunes acting as part-time moneylenders and merchants. Around 1180 the lord obliged the tavern keepers of Ferrières in the Gâtinais to shut their shops during his 'banal' wine sale because they were brokers for foreign buyers.

Still, innovation was more frequent in town. Living at a hub of communications, townsfolk were in closer contact with invention elsewhere. As long as the economy grew, also, city industry was strengthened by other urban functions. Villages were invaded by town moneylenders, lawyers and notaries. In spite of rural monasteries, the clergy were concentrated more heavily in town than the balance of urban and rural population warranted. Secular government also had its seat in towns.

Townsfolk were more informed than rustics, more talkative, more ambitious and, on the whole, lived more interesting lives. Some in the countryside, however, were not simple villagers, notably the clergy and the well-to-do. When nobles inhabited villages – and they often moved to town in winter-time – their horizons were broader because they travelled. Most tournaments, litigation, festivals, clerical synods, etc. were held in or near towns. Chivalry's poet, Christian of Troyes, introduced Erec and Enide at a duel in a bourg, and had them complete their ascension to royal crowns in a city. A wider contact with the world was possessed by town citizens than by villagers. In 1202, when the burghers of Tournus in Burgundy asked for abolition of a tax on marriage, they did so 'because it appeared infamous and strange to foreigners'.[3]

Each seeking maximum gain, townsfolk battled countryfolk. In urbanized Italy and Flanders, towns victoriously reduced the countryside to subservience, but elsewhere they did not. A vexing question was that of tolls on bridges, rivers and overland routes. Often originated to fund transport facilities, tolls were rarely voluntarily abolished and easily multiplied. Those along the Rhine increased from about nineteen in 1200 to about fifty-four in 1300.

The urban desire for untrammelled trade is only one side of the picture, because, just as did rural lords, towns imposed tolls. Besides, tolls siphoned off profits from interregional commerce to advance local interests and also, inadvertently, protected local industries and even independence. The consuls of Toulouse waged war against twenty-three seigniories and local communities from 1202 to 1204. They fought not only to abolish tolls, but also to subject the villages, opening them to exploitation. Italy's urban republics did the same, and also sought to make sure that the 'county' provisioned the town cheaply.

Such conflicts should not be overstressed because economic growth cushioned rivalries, expanding areas of mutual interest. If town moneylenders hurt villagers, they also aided their search for freedom from their lords. Besides, this was no simple struggle between town and countryside because great cities, modest towns, villages and hamlets had differing interests. By 1300 commercial growth and the revival of the centralized state had created a pattern of growing large cities while middling towns stabilized or shrank, villages amalgamated and small hamlets withered.

Friction existed also between areas of heavy urban development and those of light. Some time after 1200 most north Italian towns were faced by a need to regulate grain supply, and by 1300 most of them had permanent bureaux fixing prices and distributing grain. Siena's grain bureau dates from the early thirteenth century and precedes by about fifty years the first such agency in Flanders' Ghent. In 1261 2,200 tons of Sicilian grain entered the port of Genoa alone. By the early fourteenth century, a grain merchant opined that her 'county' could feed Florence for only five months of the year, and in 1320 the republic owed the Acciajuoli firm 40,000 gold florins for Sicilian grain. The Hohenstaufen and Angevin wars saw a radical change in the relationship of southern to northern Italy. In the late twelfth century Apulia–Sicily was an active maritime power; some of her industries, such as silk, were widely reputed; and her state was the grandest in Italy. By 1300 all had changed. Sicily and Naples had been divided between the

Catalans and the French, and the sea had been wholly lost to the northerners. Luccan and Florentine silk was better known than that of Palermo, and northern townsfolk ate Sicilian and Apulian grain.

It comes as a shock to realize just how small the largest towns were. No western city in 1300 came near the size of ancient Rome (300,000 to a million). In ancient and medieval times, furthermore, both the Near East and China boasted centres with perhaps as many as a million inhabitants. Technology's relationship to geography plays a role here. Ancient and medieval alike, great cities were either seaports or located in irrigated valleys like the Nile, and the inadequacy of overland transport prevented their rise in inland areas until the age of the railways. Still, neither geography nor technology explains the smallness of the medieval town. In 1300 Venice and Bruges were great ports but neither equalled ancient Rome.

Another comparison is useful here. In 1500 Paris was over three times as large as it had been in 1300, yet France's overall population was probably smaller. This ability to support larger urbanism was not primarily caused by technological advance. Although Atlantic traffic had increased, carting was more common and canals had just begun to supplement medieval river routes, basic techniques were not much advanced. The late-medieval innovations, – gunpowder, printing, new types of sailing vessels, etc. – had only a gradual influence on living standards. It is likely, in fact, that the Frenchman of 1500 lived scarcely any better than his forefather of 1300.

There was a change, however, to which the inventions mentioned above give a clue. They were all connected with warfare and the growth of government. It may therefore be that the growth of larger states and the concomitant concentration and mobilization of resources and manpower were the reasons that made the great city possible. The existence of unitary states also explains why Romans had been able to maintain great cities in spite of backward technology. The small size of the medieval town may therefore be explained by the absence of centralized states.

INDUSTRY AND COMMERCE

At its peak around 1300, European manufacturing, as was true until late in modern times, was especially devoted to textiles. Although linen came second, wool cloth was Europe's biggest export. In

1313, 92,500 seals were stamped in the town of Ypres to be affixed to bolts of woollen cloth. Initially importing cotton from Syria, a cotton industry began in central Italy in the early fourteenth century. To these export industries may be added leather and furs.

Something like heavy industry also existed. With around 30,000 inhabitants, Toulouse produced 1,000 mail coats, 3,000 gorgets, 3,000 helmets and 600 crossbows for the king in 1295. In the mid-fourteenth century Ghent boasted about 5,200 weavers and fullers out of a population of around 60,000. In 1292 Paris, a capital and consumer-centred city, had about 130 professions:

> twenty-seven per cent in clothing and personal furnishings
> seventeen per cent in metallurgy
> seventeen per cent in textiles and leather goods
> fourteen per cent in food and consumables such as firewood
> eight per cent in furniture
> four per cent in building and related arts
> two per cent in medicine and sanitation
> ten per cent in banking, brokerage, bookmaking and the public baths.

The smaller town of Poitiers registered only nineteen guilds in the early fourteenth century. Represented by three organizations, riding equipment and harnesses was the most developed industry. There were also ropemakers, locksmiths and tinsmiths. Four guilds prepared leather goods and textiles. No less than six sold foodstuffs and fuel, to which may be added two guilds of publicans and inn-keepers. Doubling as bankers or moneylenders, goldsmiths led the financial life of the town.

Substantial industry required a lively commerce in basic commodities. In some years around 1300, England exported up to fifteen million pounds of raw wool, and a year's export of about twenty-five million gallons of wine from the Garonne valley was recorded. French wine went everywhere. In 1229 it found a market in Muslim Tunis (!), and in 1291 quantities were shipped to the Genoese towns on the Black Sea. Exotic commodities were moved in bulk, as is illustrated by the accounts of a Hanseatic merchant at Stockholm in 1328. Preparing for a wake, a princely family bought one and a half pounds of saffron, twelve pounds of caraway, ninety pounds of almonds, one hundred and five pounds of rice and four of sugar, all from the Mediterranean, especially Spain and Italy. Asia contributed four and three-quarter pounds of ginger, a pound of cinnamon and three pounds of galingale, while Africa provided half a pound of grains of paradise, good for hot toddies. The shopping list included three large barrels of wine, one from the Rhine and two from Bordeaux. Having sourly described the mock grief of his compatriots at funerals, Boncompagno of Signa remarked that Englishmen and other northerners 'mix drink with their tears until they're drunk, and thus are consoled by being happier than usual'.[4]

Growing commerce sparked improvements in transport. Mediterranean sailors adopted northern Europe's rudder and square sail in the late twelfth century, and Alexander Neckham mentioned the navigational use of the compass by 1187. *Portolani* sea guides accurately 'mapped' the Mediterranean coast. Point-to-point sailing was frequent in that sea, but, as was true until yesterday, most shipping hugged the coast. Until the great galleys of the fourteenth century, ships were small, although the Italian marine boasted a ship (*nave*) 110 feet long with a cargo capacity of 630 tons. Contact by sea between the Baltic and North Sea area and the Mediterranean was sporadic in the twelfth century. Exemplifying Italy's rise, her mariners first voyaged to northern waters in 1277, and by about 1314 regular sailings to Flanders and England from Genoa and Venice were scheduled. Along with this, Italians began to take service in Spain and France and hence diffused Mediterranean maritime law and lore.

Inland transport was based partly on rivers, especially downstream, and, with exceptions such as Milan and Florence, no inland cities not on navigable rivers grew large. France's major inland towns were all situated on navigable rivers – Paris, Rouen, Orléans, Lyons and Toulouse. Farmers around Auxerre shipped wine to Paris via the Seine, and those around Toulouse used the Garonne to get their wine, wool and woad into the Atlantic market. German rivers flow from south to north and, when combined with the Baltic sea, drew eastward-moving immigrants north towards the sea. The indifference of northern and eastern Germans to the affairs of the Empire on the Rhine and in Italy was caused by this geography.

Medieval roads were rarely paved, save in town where there was heavy pedestrian traffic. This remained true of Europe until yesterday, and a primary reason was the use of horses and asses, whose hooves were harmed by paving. The thirteenth century witnessed a growing use of cartage, the four-wheeled wagon with pivoted front axle supplementing the two-wheeled cart from about 1250. Cartage, however, had a long way to go. Even the famous Septimer pass in the Alps was unsuitable for carts until after the mid-fourteenth century. Year-round cartage in some areas, however, had already resulted in planking and paving muddy stretches. The highway between Florence and Pisa was paved in 1286, and embanked to avoid spring floods. An engineering feat was the opening of the St Gotthard pass in the Alps in 1237, a route soon eased by a stone bridge. Villages, towns and princes legislated about roads, even providing for shade trees. Bridges were often financed by ecclesiastical institutions and builders sometimes formed temporary fraternities, and, as 'pious places' in canon law, bridges received small donations in private testaments. Used for maintenance, bridge tolls also often supported hospitals associated with and sometimes built on them.

Overland transport had improved enough since antiquity to make the urbanization of west Europe's inland reaches possible. In Roman times overland bulk haulage doubled the price every hundred miles; in the thirteenth century, the increase was about a third. Shipping remained cheaper. In 1283, for example, the *San Niccolo* carried grain from Sicily to Pisa, increasing the original price at only about eight per cent per hundred miles. Transport and travel were nevertheless relatively slow. Five to ten miles a day was common for pack trains. Mounted parties made eighteen to twenty miles a day. Less sure, sea transport was faster. In season the length of the Mediterranean could be traversed in one to two months. These estimates do not illustrate maximum speed. A galley is said to have gone from Pisa to Sardinia at an average of a hundred miles per day in 1313. Around 1300 couriers of Tuscan merchant-banking firms counted five days from Avignon to Paris, eight to Bruges, thirteen to Venice and ten to Valencia. In short, all Europe could be informed of an event in about a month.

Transport and travel were seasonal. On unpaved roads, what could be carted in summer had to be sledged in winter. Storms all but shut the North and Baltic Seas for three months yearly. The Mediterranean was better off: Marino Sanuto, a Venetian senator, thought of stationing a squadron off Alexandria to intercept that port's year-round commerce. Venetian statutes in 1284 nevertheless forbade the state convoys to sail from 1 December to 1 March. Commerce generally slowed during the winter, and this rhythm was also reflected in fairs. Although local markets continued uninterrupted, Toulouse's fairs ran from mid-Lent to early December. Even the fairs of Champagne and Brie, where the Lombards met the rest of Europe's merchants to exchange commodities and thrash out a primitive balance of payments, submitted to the same rule. The six fairs successively held in Troyes, Provins, Bar on the Aube and Lagny on the Marne petered out from November to January. Only commercial centres like Genoa and Venice were active year round, though even there the tempo slowed.

PLANNING, BUILDING AND LIVING STANDARDS

Most homes and workshops were humble and small, rarely over two storeys, and usually not made of stone. In timber-rich regions they were built of wood or wood and stucco, often being roofed with straw. Brick and adobe were common in the Mediterranean. What first struck the eye, however, were a town's towers and spires. Monuments of jealously guarded independence, town and village walls cost heavily. Monumental stone or brick architecture was another huge investment, most of the major western churches having been built by the early fourteenth century. By then Toulouse, a town of around 30,000, boasted five great churches, one the size of Chartres, not to speak of many less significant monuments. So decorated were these communities that Henry II (d. 1189), witnessing the burning of his natal city of LeMans, cried out that, since God had stolen from him the place he loved most in the world, 'I'll pay you back as much as I can by taking from you what you most love in me!' – namely, his soul.[5]

Building exalted the arts. John Pisano and Giotto were architects and also painters and sculptors. Virtuosity was rewarded, a master mason of Bologna, being acclaimed a 'noble and famous architect' in 1234, and a Florentine who undermined the walls of Poggibonsi in 1220, were exempted from taxes. When Orvieto employed Lawrence Maitanis in 1310, it gave him twelve gold florins annually, the right to have apprentices, citizenship for self and family, fifteen years' exemption from military service and taxes, and a noble's right to bear arms. Art had been assimilated to letters in Italian towns, because Maitanis' privileges were those granted professors of the liberal arts. A contract in 1294 provided that the apprentice residing with a Florentine master painter would 'zealously perform whatever the said master ordered him to do in the theory or practice of the said art'.[6]

Specialization did not prevent disaster. The choir of Beauvais cathedral collapsed in 1284. It rose to a height of 150 feet, the world's highest hall until steel construction, and took nearly forty years to rebuild. Building was often slow, but rapid work was not unheard of. Richard Coeur de Lion constructed Gaillard des Andeleys in just over a year in 1197–8. Even though the castle fell in 1204, it justified his boast: 'By God's throat, if that castle were built of butter and not of iron and stone, it would defend me against [the king of France] and all his power.'[7] In 1159 the Genoese built a wall of 5,520 feet including four towers in fifty-three days.

Village and town statutes accented cleanliness and orderliness in the disposition of rainwater, garbage and ordure. Slaughterhouses and some industries were placed either outside town or downstream. San Gimignano had two street sweepers for each quarter. Public service was owed by property holders, and duties in town and country differed. The custom of Milan in 1216 obliged rustics to maintain public roads, irrigation canals and the like; townsfolk were to busy themselves paving, illuminating streets and digging cesspools. Impure air, it was thought, induced illness: in 1237 the *podestà* ordered all Florence's streets paved to be 'cleaner, more beautiful and healthier'. Similar motives inspired Philip Augustus for Paris in 1198, though with less immediate results. In Siena the first street map for planning purposes is heard of in 1218, and the first building code was dated 1262. Like the law on highroads, this legislation was modelled on Roman law but grew to surpass its model, determining the width of streets, uniformity of facades, etc. Old laws destroying buildings as punishment for crime were questioned. Urging that 'so noble a city should not be deformed by ruins, especially since men and not property have sinned', the count of Toulouse petitioned Pope Gregory IX to have the law rescinded anent condemned heretics, but was refused in 1236.[8] A Luccan statute of 1309 was more enlightened: 'Lucca's appearance should not be deformed by the destruction of houses and towers.'[9]

Social class affected town planning. In Tuscany, for example, Ghibellines were lukewarm about it, being satisfied with their own commodious town houses, of which the towers of San Gimignano are reminders. Because humbler folk lived more in the streets, the popular, or Guelph, party busied itself enlarging public squares and ecclesiastical and public buildings. Men of this political complexion also wrote books praising their cities, an example being Bonvesino of Riva about Milan in 1288.

In old centres planning was limited to ameliorating existing centres, but new ones and enlargements were formally laid out. In the New City added to Hildesheim in 1216–20, the rectangular street grid contrasts sharply with the often unplanned older town. The most popular plan was the simple rectangular or square grid, often adapted to an irregular exterior wall for reasons of defence, as in Neubrandenburg in 1248. Roman planning favoured hexagonal or octagonal circumferences for defence, and this is seen in not a few gridded centres, as, for example, the lower town added to Carcassonne in 1247. Planned cities took time: Aigues Mortes was begun in 1244 but its walls were still being built in the 1270s. In 1290, when the king and the Cistercians planned Grenade on the Garonne (named after Spain's Grenada), the fortifications were laid out and places set aside for a central market, church and public hospital.

Town planning was not specialized. The sculptor John Pisano served as town planner in Siena and Pisa. The clergy, knights, notaries and simple burghers directing settlement in eastern Germany planned towns and villages and published customary laws. In planning, there was no distinction between village and town. Although jurists distinguished between cities housing episcopal sees (*civitates*) and towns or villages (*ville*) or fortified villages (*castella*), *villa* was also a generic term describing any community big or small. Furthermore, since settlers wanted urban amenities, founders were not likely to advertise villages, and hence mere villages were often called towns (*ville* and *burgi*) and were granted urban privileges. In eastern Germany and Poland, some were even grandly called *civitates*. Many a new town in hilly Cornwall was smaller and had fewer conveniences than old villages in the rich plains of East Anglia. An example of this planning is Revel near Carcassonne. Founded in 1342, this gridded and hexagonal little town was to have public mills, a prison and a square, arched and colonnaded, on which the town hall was to be located.

Planning gave attention to public health. Lucca in the early fourteenth century published a statute book of sanitary regulations, and village custumals often included similar provisions. Public bathing was part of this: twenty-six public bath-houses were listed in the tallage of Paris in 1292. As important was the attack on sickness, old age and burial costs. Revel's planners did not neglect charity: 'The consuls and university of the said town may construct . . . two houses of piety [hospitals] in suitable places wheresoever they see fit, each containing a half arpent of land in which the poor of

Christ shall be received.'[10] Protected by canon law, hospitals were diverse in organization, some being attached to monasteries or cathedral chapters and others private or municipal. Leper houses and private old folk's homes were often self-governing. Although military, the Hospitallers and Teutonic knights were famed for hospitals. Founded in 1198 the Trinitarians devoted a third of their budget to repurchasing captives from Islam and the rest to hospitals.

Save for leproseries, hospitals did not usually specialize. Some did, such as Metz's maternity hospital of the early fourteenth century. Characteristic of many, however, is St Catherine's in Esslingen in 1232, where the poor, passing strangers, needy women in labour, orphans and sick were received. Many hospitals for the aged were small, housing the apostolic number of thirteen inmates. Some were larger: Strasbourg's St Leonhard's had fifty prebends for the aged, besides offering other services. Nürnberg's Holy Ghost housed about 250 patients in 1341. Towns sometimes had considerable facilities. With a population of under 30,000 in 1262, Toulouse had seven leper houses and fifteen hospitals. One hospital contained fifty-six beds, another was surely larger; most housed a dozen or so aged folk. Villages were not far behind. In 1210 Isle Jourdain near Toulouse possessed two small hospitals and one leper house. Larger Jewish communities also had hospitals, one in Regensburg in 1210 and another in Cologne.

Given the prevailing medical knowledge – in 1308, suddenly taken ill, Albert I of Habsburg was hung up by his feet! – hospital care consisted of rest, bathing and wholesome diet. Diagnosis was provided by lay doctors: Roger of Molins' Hospitaller statutes in 1181 stated that a doctor 'who knows the quality of excrements, the diversity of the sick and can administer the remedy of medicines should be hired in each hospital'.[11] Private help was supplemented by the state: in Milan around 1300 town doctors were paid to give care to the poor. Hospital staffs of clerical and nursing personnel often formed chapters with voting rights. In 1220 the Hôtel Dieu of Paris was staffed by four priests, four other clerks, twenty-five sisters and thirty lay brothers. Ideally, hospital staffs treated the sick and poor as Christ. The Hospitallers called their patients 'sick lords' and the statutes of the hospital of Aubrac in 1162 told its staff to 'take care that . . . the poor always precede as lords, while you follow as serfs'.[12]

Hospitals and religious houses also provided services to young and old oblates. At Toulouse those wanting care and residence when sick or old acquired retirement plans. In 1233 a man entered the Hospital as a permanent resident, receiving bread and water as a brother. He was to be kept 'well dressed and shod, including Stamford cloth, and equipped with breeches and shirts in summer and winter' for life.[13] Presumably sick, a cutler retired into the Hospital in 1242, leaving two houses and other property to his heir, a minor son. Under the guardianship of fellow craft members, the boy was to reside at the Hospital for ten years to be educated in letters. The estate was to pay for teachers, books and clothing, and a hundred shillings if the young heir ceased study or left the order at the term's expiration. So extensive a system explains why Raymond Llull mistakenly crowed in 1308 that 'Christians build hospitals to receive the poor, the sick and travellers, and have one, two or even three in each city, but I never heard that Saracens have more than two hospitals, one at Tunis and the other at Alexandria.'[14]

Expanding economy brought a better standard of living. Economic growth, however, is rarely uniform among social classes, and rage against economic individualism marked 1200. Criticism of new wealth abounded, the commonplace being that gold dictates everything. Writing in the 1220s, the biographer of William the Marshal of England contrasted the spartan beginnings of his champion – he travelled with two servants! – with the luxury of the lowest squire of his own times, voyaging with a pack animal laden with clothing and creature comforts. The rich castigated the humble, the prior Geoffrey of Vigeois in the Limousin lamenting around 1184 that

> our barons used to wear common cloth, so that Bishop Eustorge and the viscount of Limoges and Comborn when travelling wore lamb skins and fox furs that an artisan would be ashamed to wear today. Since then, rich vestments of divers colours have been invented, strangely cut in spheric figures with little pendant tails and tassels . . . . Now boots, once rare and reserved for gentlefolk, are worn by anybody. Once, men shaved their heads and grew beards; now peasants and workers grow long hair and shave their beards. As Merlin remarked, the walk of women has come to resemble a serpent's undulations because of the mad length of their trains . . . . Cloth and furs cost twice what they used because nowadays humble folk wear clothing suited to the greatest lords of past times. [In contrast] the old-timers daily found something left on their tables with which to nourish the numerous poor . . . . Today, these onetime hosts of the castles are often obliged to go about begging themselves.[15]

The prior's complaint is characteristic. Both the poor and old rich found a common enemy in the new rich, and the *nouveaux* were often townsmen. Around 1200 John of Flagy's romance *Hervi* records the marriage of the daughter of a duke of Lorraine – the father had silenced her plaints lest he lose his debt-ridden lands – to a rich bourgeois of Metz. John saw to it that the issue of this union had nothing to do with trade but preferred hunting, fighting and love, as became a gentleman.

The people of the recent past had experienced periods of economic crisis. From the 1170s to the mid 1220s the economy faltered with the usual accompaniment of wars and shortages. After 1250 a series of difficulties culminated in a downturn from 1278 to 1285. Surely related to change in climate, renewed troubles appeared just before 1300 and were not exorcized until 1319. These troubles, however, were soon repaired and nobody could have dreamed what the disasters of the 1340s would bring. All over Europe new village emplacements and town walls were planned to absorb the projected population increase. Experience had misled the planners, however: those walls were not filled until the eighteenth century.

It was also hard to judge: what seemed decline was sometimes growth. An instance is the rapid withering of the fairs of Champagne and Brie during the early fourteenth century. Although hurt by the French wars in Flanders, these fairs failed mainly because of economic growth. A meeting place for Europe's two main urban areas – that centred in Flanders and that in northern Italy – Champagne was admirably located as long as the main commercial route was the Rhone valley. As seen above, however, the sea route between Italy and Flanders came into use in the late thirteenth century and new Alpine passes also multiplied routes from Germany to Italy. Once, Italian merchants visited the Champagne, but by 1300 they resided permanently in all important northern cities, including Paris, a town that had absorbed much Champagne business. In fine, the decline of the fairs of Champagne and Brie was really a sign of economic maturity.

NOTES AND REFERENCES

1   *Le dite de Hosebonderie* (ed. Elizabeth Lamond, London, 1890), 10.
2   Lousse, *Société d'ancien régime,*208–9.
3   Duby, *La socitété aux XIe et XIIe siècles dans la région Mâconnais* 400.
4   *Boncompagnus Boncampagni* in *BuF* I, 141–2.

5   Gerald of Wales, *De principis instructione* 3, 24 in *Rolls Series,* XXI , iii 283.

6   Published in Braunfels, *Die Staatsbaukunst in der Toskana*, 225.

7   Gerald of Wales, *De principis instructione* in *Rolls Series* XXI, viii, 290.

8   *Register* II, 1245, No. 4758.

9   Braunfels, *Staatsbaukunst in der Toskana*, 45.

10   J. Ramière de Fortanier, *Chartes des franchises de Lauragais*, (Paris, 1939), 576.

11   Léon Le Grand, *Statuts d'hôtels-Dieu et de léproséries* (Paris, 1901), 12.

12   *Ibid.*, 17.

13   My 'Charity and Social Work in Toulouse', *Traditio* XXII (1966), 263–4n.

14   *Disputatio Raymundi christiani et Hamar saraceni* 2, 25 in *Beati Raymundi Lulli opera* IV ((Mainz, 1729, rprt) 474b–5a.

15   *Chronique* I, 73 in *Recueil des historiens des Gaules et de la France* XII, 450.

7

ORGANIZATION

RURAL ENTERPRISE

The manor, or great farm, required a balance of labour and land. Excluding forests, pastures and commons, a manor's territory was divided into strips or fields assigned the demesne, and those held by tenants. The demesne was the main farm, and those who worked it were the landlord's 'family', a household ranging from gentlemen agents to servile domestics, and the tenantry, free or servile, paid by land allotted them by the lord in return for labour on the demesne. In Bavaria a typical lord assigned tenants three or four times more land than he retained in demesne.

Even great manors were rarely self-sufficient. Many essential commodities, – salt, metalware, millstones, stock animals, etc., – were imported. While landlords favoured autarky and disliked buying commodities from outside, they enjoyed selling. In the thirteenth century, Glastonbury, Peterborough, Ramsey and other large English monasteries pushed the export of wool and grains. The peasants of Ramsey Abbey near Ely performed carting services as far south as London and Canterbury.

The great farm was not universal in Europe, partly because manors always varied widely in size. Those englobing whole villages were few, even in the parts of Germany or England famed for manorial exploitation. Over half the villages of Leicestershire contained more than one manor, and one had as many as five. Besides, small farms always existed, and much of Europe's geography was inimical to the community farming of the manorial system. Mediterranean dry soils did not require the heavy ploughs and community traction needed on the rich but heavy northern soils. Although large estates with dependent peasantries existed in the south, open fields were rarer than in the north and demesne less important for landlords. Mountainous and hilly areas, broken terrain and recently drained areas favoured independent more than community farming. Certain types of crops – dyestuffs, wine and olives – did not lend themselves to manorial farming.

For whatever reasons, and they shall be discussed below, the great farm was undoubtedly declining. In Bavaria monastic and seigniorial demesnes were breaking up into a number of smaller units rented to lesser knights or estate bailiffs, some of whose farms were substantial. A second stage occurred during the later thirteenth century, when a wealthy yeomanry exploited farms averaging about fifty acres. A similar process had taken place in France, where modest knights, substantial bailiffs, burghers and well-to-do farmers built semi-independent farms. Change was gradual. On eight manors of the bishop of Winchester, thirty-seven per cent of the land was in demesne in the second half of the thirteenth century; the figure was about twenty-four per cent in the early fourteenth century.

Although many farms were composed of strips and parcels of land mixed among the allotments of the villagers in large open fields, others were concentrated, especially in cleared land. Parts of the north European plain began to look quite modern. During the thirteenth century in Burgundy, gentlefolk left the villages inhabited by their parents, building modest manor houses in the midst of their own farms or 'domains'. These small farms were less self-sufficient than large manors. Handicrafts played a smaller part, and to pay for industrial goods from nearby towns, crops were tailored to fit market needs.

Landlords increasingly relied on salaried labour, and, being less necessary, tenants' work was either commuted into rents or sold. At Pasignano near Florence, for example, the monastery housed fourteen monks and the demesne was farmed by nearly forty lay brethren, the equivalent of a lay landlord's 'family'. The rest of the cloister's land was rented to sixty-nine tenants, whose labour services were of so little value that the abbot alienated them in 1242. Elsewhere such services were long retained. Although the Alsatian monastery of Marmoutier had replaced fieldwork by rents early in the twelfth century, transport services and help at harvest and haymaking were required until well into the thirteenth century.

This change transformed the relationship of tenant and landlord.

Save for jurisdictional rights and commutation charges for old services, a landlord's right was best expressed in terms of land rent. Documentation changed: registers balancing allotments given to tenants against service were replaced by current leases, to be discarded when new ones were issued. As long as rent was not lost, it mattered little who used the land, the replacement of tenants even being welcome because mutations were taxed. Instead of being community planners, landlords were becoming rentiers.

Old manors often briefly regained ground. In the thirteenth century England's larger monasteries, assured of grain and wool markets, resumed the direct management of their lands, expanded demesnes and even increased the labour owed by their peasants. The late thirteenth century, however, witnessed a renewed decline. Although sales and other contracts relaxing tenurial restrictions were widespread in England, they were more common in recently settled areas and around towns than in the manorial regions of the Midlands. *Meierrecht* and types of tenure evidencing the disintegration of old manors were common along the Rhine, but began to penetrate north-west Germany only during the late thirteenth century. The difference between the later and earlier ages was one of degree, not of kind. The great manor had never entirely dominated rural life, and the smaller units still relied partly on manorial service owed by tenants.

Like semi-independent farms, flexible land tenures gradually spread, ranging from England's burgage tenure to Languedoc's commoner's fief. The same was also seen east of the Elbe river, where field labour was not required of settlers from the mid-twelfth century on. Because town and village were not far apart, many of England's boroughs were mere villages just like 'new towns' across the Channel. An example in the Low Countries was Herenthals, founded by the duke of Brabant in 1209, settled by farmers called 'burghers' owing hereditary rents and minimal services.

Frontier settlement together with urbanization have been held to explain the appearance of semi-independent farms and the weakening of the manor's community enterprise. The argument is partly correct. Trans-Elbian Germany was free of manorial services until the late thirteenth century, and urbanization encouraged a division of labour between town and countryside. Village workshops slowly surrendered industrial production to towns, and farmers raised commodities designed for the markets of a somewhat urbanized world. An aspect was the use of money (gained in exchange for export crops) by countryfolk. In 1245 ordinary cultivators on farms of the Bavarian monastery of Baumberg paid fifty-eight per cent of their charges in money, while those with vineyards paid ninety-eight.

Urbanization and the frontier, however, effected change only in favourable circumstances. Eastern German settlement was channelled through newly founded towns, and manorial services and tenures did not penetrate there at first. Things changed later as economic growth halted and then retreated. Like those of early modern Spanish America, eastern Europe's cities of around 1300 served a pre-manorial function, that of encouraging settlement. Too precocious to last, the towns, save for some ports, were then reduced in early modern times by the rise of the rural great manor with its semi-industrial workshops. In times of economic growth, however, things evolved differently. In early medieval western Europe, the spread of the manor, heir to Rome's fading urbanism, constituted a pre-urban stage. In the later stage, whose high point is being treated in this book, towns moved to the fore, and both manor and village industry declined.

Nor did economic growth, the settlement of new lands and urbanization always lessen coercion, as was evidenced when the manorial system spread into north-west Europe, a great economic advance for regions beyond Rome's frontiers. This had also been the case in antiquity (the post-Punic Roman republic) and in more modern times (Europe's colonial expansion), when slavery accompanied the settlement of new lands, economic growth and urbanization. The question is therefore why coerced labour did not grow in this age of rapid economic growth and urbanization.

A reason was that circumstances and institutions opposed a rational use of humans as machines: oppression existed, but slavery was not practicable at this time. Churchmen insisted on individual responsibility; hence, slave or free, all women and men owed charity to Church and society and had the right to marry and have issue. Although this did not prevent servitude, it impeded the efficient use of human labour. Similarly, political particularism drew seigniors towards martial and governmental functions and away from a purely economic use of their farms and dependants. England's renewal of manorialism in the thirteenth century, for example, was partly because the king's near-monopoly of government encouraged lords to exploit the economy more vigorously. In that circumstance, seigniorial decentralization meant a measure of freedom for serfs.

Slavery also requires plentiful recruits. Unlike conquering Rome and early modern Europe, entrepreneurs at this time had no easy way to replace superannuated humans. The Church forbade enslaving Christians, and except for some Baltic peoples who were anyway being rapidly converted, Europe had no large reservoirs of non-Christians. Such were found around the Mediterranean, but were protected and used by an Islam still holding its own against the Latins. Apart from a few bonanzas like the fall of Damietta in 1219 and the conquest of Majorca in 1232, a thin trickle of largely female slaves from Africa and the Black Sea was all Europeans got their hands on. Slaving was profitable, however, the Genoese having entered the Black Sea trade to Islam from Kaffa in the Crimea in the late 1260s.

If servitude was relatively unprofitable, selling freedom was not. In an expanding economy, farmers were willing to pay for liberty. Commutation of services into money spelled freedom because the real value of money shrank in the price rise of a growing economy. The change was gradual: in 1181, of the twenty patrimonial manors of St Paul's of London, six offered dues in kind, eight in kind and money and six wholly in money. Slowly, a landlord's own farm began to outweigh the dues and rents collected from dependants. In 1267 a lord's demesne near Mâcon in Burgundy provided an annual income of about a hundred pounds; villagers holding tenures contributed only five.

Peasants wanted hereditary land. In 1233 at Pasignano in Tuscany, of the families holding of the monastery, those of eight knights and town patricians may be excluded. Of the remaining tenants, six were non-hereditary while fifty-five were perpetual tenants paying fixed quit-rents for farms both hereditary and alienable at will. Ideally, farmers wanted freehold land. Although known in Frisia and Scandinavia where manors were still uncommon, this ambition was rarely fully realized. Around towns, especially Italy's urban republics, the abolition of seigniorial rights and depreciation of rents enabled farmers to free their farms.

Even if commutation of services into money meant eventual loss for landlords, it was profitable. In a growing economy where land remained to be cleared, alert lords wanted capital, and money rent received from old parcels could help develop new lands from which little had come in the past. Landlords, in fact, often insisted on money payments, and farmers, short of cash, were not always happy. New exploitations had many advantages besides rent. During the late thirteenth century, farmers settling in eastern Germany usually paid an entry fee. Fees collected for the use of mills, wine presses and other common facilities built by seigniors were profitable. In brief, as long as land remained for settlement or more intense exploitation, rent fixing and the commuting of rents and services into money was a means of selling old investments in order to buy new. It is worth noting, however, that while many landlords profited, some lost out. In the mid twelfth century Cluny's houses, committed to old contracts, suffered crisis, while new Cistercian ones flourished.

As rents were increasingly fixed, rent value sank in comparison to the real value of land. Long-term rent contracts were described as sales, and possession or use-right came to be nine-tenths of the law. Not that rents were meaningless, because, although slowly declining, they were steady investments for rentiers. Active entrepreneurs and landlords, however, often acquired use-right to lease it again for a sum representing a true return. In 1281 only fourteen per cent of the revenues of St Peter's monastery in Ghent came from hereditary leases, eighty-six from short-term ones. Land was also leased to be improved, to have tenants plant new crops, and, if labour was plentiful, landlords favoured short-term sharecropping leases. Rural and urban investors also provided herdsmen with animals or ploughmen with oxen or horses and shared the profits.

At Pasignano in Tuscany in the early thirteenth century, most villagers held of the monastery, paying hereditary quit-rents and some services. By 1300 the situation had altered radically. Already weakened in 1242, services disappeared altogether when Florence abolished them in 1289. Meanwhile, the monks tried to acquire the use-right to their lands. Of about fifty farms, half had been largely lost to them, being leased perpetually at fixed rent. The other half, however, was held by farmers on short-term leases who paid as much as half their grain crop. In this and other regions agriculture had moved far from the manors of the past. The relationship of lord to dependant had turned into one of investor to worker. Far more free than before, farmers got seed, animals and capital but were more exposed to the ups and downs of the market. When economic growth slowed around 1300, the deleterious side of the farm worker's relationship to the capitalizer became apparent. No longer inhibited by manorial laws, also, division among heirs split the peasant's farm, making it less viable in an increasingly competitive economy.

As new land ran out and few new technologies improved productivity, crisis became inevitable. In parts of France and south-west Germany, obligations reminiscent of manorial servitude were reimposed. Generally, however, entrepreneurs in areas of dense settlement expanded production by pushing farmers off the land. In this circumstance, serfs with quasi-hereditary land were disinclined to buy liberty. Up to about 1300, France's kings were slow to free their serfs. Enfranchisement was expensive: the serfs of Pierrefonds paid Louis IX (d. 1270) five per cent of the value of their real property, those of Paray ten per cent of the value of their movables. During the Aragonese and Flemish wars from the 1290s on, the crown stepped up its efforts to sell liberty. Under Louis X (d. 1316) it even tried to force peasants to buy it. Serfs in the Toulousain, from whom the treasury hoped to get a third of the value of their goods, held back. The best it got was six to thirteen per cent, and even then many refused to buy freedom. Liberty had become too costly.

As the thirteenth century aged, landlord and tenant relations were less and less happy. Competitiveness, however, still stimulated invention more than social war. Rural credit mechanisms, for example, changed radically. In the past, a form of mortgage was common: those wanting capital pledged property for loans, surrendering the income of the pledge as interest on the loan. Since real property was thereby risked, this contract was practical only when land was cheap. As land became dear, circumstance joined with ecclesiastical censure of this frankly usurious contract to push out the mortgage. Capital, one soon discovered, could be obtained without usury: rents on land or means of production could be sold, giving creditors anywhere from five to fifteen per cent annually. First seen in the twelfth century, this flexible contract gradually spread. What could not be foreseen was that, in the later difficult economic circumstances, rents became perpetual and crushing burdens.

COMMERCE

Commerce was at once universalist and particularist. Merchants were inhabitants of particular communities, not Italians so much as Luccans or Pisans. When harmed by foreigners and refused redress, their fellow citizens granted them the right to exact reparation from any denizen of the other town or region. Although rare in quasi-national England or the royal lands of France, marque and reprisal was known in Italy's independent cities. The jurist Alberic of Rosate remarked that, although opposed to natural law, it had a place where there was no superior government. It was also used in towns like Toulouse in Languedoc, Arles in Provence and Cologne in the Rhineland where political decentralization gave communities freedom to protect their own interests. Overlapping authority sometimes made trade a chancy affair. In 1303 a Milanese merchant on his way to Flanders was seized by a Rhenish lord because the emperor, sovereign of both, owed him money!

Communications being what they were, few merchants were sedentary. Lombards travelled to Flanders and Germans to Barcelona in the course of a season. Once out of their home regions, merchants were among foreigners. Around 1300, a rich noble like Benedict Zaccaria of Genoa owned industrial shops in Genoa and Florence, raised mastic on Chios, mined alum in Phocaea and, as merchant and corsair, ranged from England to the Holy Land. He could look after himself, but ordinary merchants needed protection against rampant localism.

Protective institutions had therefore appeared. Foremost were fairs, times and places under special law designed to protect merchants. Merchants from warring communities abode together under the fair's peace, marque and reprisal being in abeyance. Bartholomew of Exeter's (d. 1184) penitential records papal legislation censuring those who harassed pilgrims and merchants, even those molesting the latter with unwarranted tolls. By threatening exclusion from the all-important fairs of Champagne and Brie, the counts of that region and their successors, France's kings, issued efficacious safe-conducts to Lombards coming to the fairs.

Lombards visiting the Champagne usually voyaged in caravans. Well-travelled routes spawned special associations. In the early fourteenth century, the hanse of the Loire river consisted of twenty-two guilds, towns and seigniors interested in this artery. Others were designed to control particular trades. By the early thirteenth century the London hanse included fifteen Flemish towns whose merchants imported English wool. Another hanse united those of seventeen cities handling the sale of manufactured cloth at the Champagne fairs. Italians at those fairs created a society to prohibit members from suing each other in foreign courts. The Pisans captured by the

Genoese in the naval battle off Meloria in 1284 formed a 'university' with its own seal. When domiciled in Islam, Latins lived in jurisdictional enclosures analogous to ghettos. The two large Venetian settlements in Mamluk Alexandria enjoyed self-government but were locked at night from the outside. Established in 1261, the Genoese community of Pera across the Golden Horn from Constantinople soon outstripped the capital itself. Self-governing, it offered citizenship in Genoa's overseas Empire to Greek, Near Eastern and Latin applicants. Similar but smaller institutions were seen in the west. Around 1300 Lucca had consulates (merchant hotels, really) in London, Bruges, Paris, Montpellier, Avignon, Genoa, Venice, Rome and Naples. Similar were those of the Germans in London and Bruges, where they won extra-territorial rights in 1250 and 1252.

Common economic interests bred leagues of cities. Such were the Cinque Ports in England, with their commonly elected mayor and councillors, whose authority was confirmed by the crown in 1278. Leagues were more free-wheeling where central power was weak, the most famous being the Teutonic Hanse. It began around 1230 with an agreement between merchants from Hamburg and Lübeck. By 1265 other towns agreed to adopt the latter's maritime code, and in 1293 twenty-six communities met at Rostock to expand this agreement. By 1300, the Hanse dominated commerce in the North and Baltic Seas.

In the thirteenth century commerce weakened the contrast between universalist and particularist elements. Prizing the profits to be made from foreigners, townsfolk protected them. Inns were regulated to assure pilgrims and merchants of honest treatment. Innkeepers mediated between foreign and native businessmen, and soon brokers emerged, appearing in southern Germany, the Rhineland and Flanders during the first four decades of the thirteenth century. Italy was more advanced: a schedule of brokers' fees was published in Genoa in 1204, and in 1233 Pisa counted over 165 such specialists. It also became possible to run a business from a distance – to be, in effect, sedentary. A courier service created by Lombards at the Champagne fairs helped. Italian merchant-banker firms established networks. The Florentine Acciajuoli had forty-one factors abroad in 1341, mostly in Italy but others were stationed from London to Nicosia and Tunis. The great Peruzzi boasted 150 factors spread even more widely through Europe, north Africa and the Near East.

Growing trade led to uniform commercial law. By the late twelfth century Italian codes had so influenced each other that one may speak of a common Mediterranean maritime law. Derived from Byzantine and Italian models, Barcelona's code influenced law in much of Europe. The Plantagenets spread the *Rolls of Oleron* from the Bay of Biscay to the narrow seas, a source for later Flemish sea law. Lübeck's code ruled the North and Baltic Seas, a version with 250 articles being sent to the Teutonic Order in 1254. These codes fought particularism. The ancient law of salvage gave finders the profits of storm or navigational error, sometimes even allowing shipwrecked foreigners to be ransomed, an affront to Christian brotherhood militated against by papal conciliar decrees from Gregory VII to the third Lateran Council of 1179. By 1200 the law of wreck and wrack had been mitigated in the Mediterranean, save on the frontier between Islam and Christendom. In the north progress was slower, and Gerald of Wales contrasted English barbarity with Roman civility. The Hanseatic towns were granted exemptions from wreck and wrack by treaties with England in 1228 and Flanders in 1253.

Although marque and reprisal continued, it had lost its sting in Italy, the individual's right having become so hedged about by treaties between the republics that it had become like modern international reprisal. A similar change took place north of the Alps. In 1271 Deventer asked Cologne to abrogate personal marque and reprisal lest an individual's malice upset trade. Magdeburg's twelfth-century code legislated against the practice, and its law was adopted in Brandenburg, the March of Lausitz, Silesia and Pomerania.

Reinforcing this were dual citizenship and domiciliary rights, both reflecting frequency of contact. In 1249 Cologne and Trier agreed to be 'one people' to promote wine sales. Dual citizenship, usually non-political, was common in Italy and elsewhere. Similar was the right to reside and trade, an example being the Lombard privilege. Although Italians, or Lombards as others usually called them, had begun settling in France early in the thirteenth century, the privilege was not seen until the latter half of the century. In Germany the oldest was that of Trier in 1262, and, reflecting the fading of the Champagne fairs, the first Flemish one dates from 1281. By about 1325 most Rhenish, Swiss and south German towns accorded Italians residence rights. In the tallage roll of 1292 Lombards were the wealthiest Parisians: two had taxable incomes nearly twice that of the richest local patrician clan. The French crown still claimed foreigners' inheritances so that, when Gondolfo, Paris's greatest Lombard, died in 1300, it took four years before his heirs freed what remained of the fortune from royal custody.

The Lombards invaded Europe's economy in the thirteenth century. This was due partly to Italy's location in the centre of the Mediterranean basin, midway on the axis of trade running from Flanders to the Middle East. Italian industry, moreover, equalled that of the north. A further stimulus was the link of Italian, especially Tuscan, merchant bankers to the papacy, serving as its main collectors and creditors. A partial schedule published by Martin IV (d. 1285) assigned Tuscany and Liguria to the Buonsignori of Siena. England, Scotland and most of Germany and Slavonia went to eight Florentine houses; Portugal and parts of Spain to three firms from Pistoia and Lucca; and the Squarcialupi of Lucca drew the consolation prize – the northern islands, including Greenland, where hides and whalebone served in lieu of money.

The Italians replaced the Jews in providing credit, making their expulsion from England and France possible. In the visitations of Odo Rigaud, archbishop of Rouen, from 1248 to 1269, most monasteries' creditors were still Jews. Rigaud himself borrowed from Lombards, however, and by 1300 most French monasteries were in debt either to local moneylenders or to Lombards. By 1291 resident Lombards paid the French crown twice the revenue it got from Jews. Even on the lower levels of moneylending, Lombard usurers were busy in France. In 1260 three Luccan merchants, capitalized by three sleeping partners, opened a pawnshop in Poigny near Troyes. These usurers were careful about the natives, ordering their factors living 'in the said store not to sleep with the servant who lives with them'.[1] The distinction between petty usury and big business was recognized in Italy's mature economy. Pistoia and Florence taxed petty moneylenders but never touched their great merchant bankers, who were, as John Villani (d. 1348) called them, 'the columns of Christianity'.[2]

The Italians did not win everywhere. Jews remained economically powerful in the Iberian peninsula and in eastern Europe. Active in England and Flanders, Italians never penetrated the Germans' northern seas. By 1300 the frontier between German and Italian mercantile enterprise had been fixed in Flanders, where it remained for centuries. Elsewhere the emergence of local businessmen hurt the Lombards. By 1300 local moneylenders aided by the Lombards' debtors in France enabled, or possibly compelled, the crown to expropriate and expel them. Such actions were sporadic – 1268–9, 1274, 1277, 1291 – and soon rescinded, but show the beginning of a desire to do without foreigners: the Pastoureaux hated Lombards almost as much as they did Jews. Local society had begun to arm itself against medieval universalism, paralleling the beginning of the national State and the decline of papal authority in Latin Europe.

In the meantime and for long, Lombards were useful. An example is to be seen in the Florentines Albizo and Musciatto Guidi who, together with their brother Niccolo, entered French royal service in 1289, where they helped modernize the fiscal administration. It was 'Biche et Mouche', as the French called them, who raised the florins from the Peruzzi firm with which were hired Raynald of Supino's soldiers who attacked Boniface VIII at Anagni in 1303.

BUSINESS, CREDIT AND INDUSTRIAL STRUCTURES

A marriage of labour and capital, business created many types of contracts. Modernized by Italy's jurists, Roman law was a source for these, and also provided a 'common law' normative everywhere in a divided world. Another source, evidenced by terms like 'risk', was Mediterranean Islamic and Jewish practice. Lastly, basic contracts derived from early agrarian practice.

Many have argued that land is retrograde, inhibiting economic individualism and imposing hereditary right as a norm. Not all landed contracts were hereditary, however, and benefices or fiefs were only salaries, not necessarily directly based on land. When money was available, fiefs were paid in cash. Writing on Italian government in the 1240s, John of Viterbo called the pay given public officers a 'salary or fief'.[3] This use of 'fief' was rare in northern Europe, being associated by this time with hereditary landed remuneration. Even there, however, England's king bought allies in the thirteenth century with cash pensions known as 'money fiefs'.

In rural contracts, the party providing land and equipment was termed the 'lord', and the tenant was to deliver a share of the crop to the lord's home or shed, there to be weighed on the scales. An industrial parallel is seen in clothmaking statutes from Toulouse in 1227. The raw wool supplier was described as 'lord or lady'. Finished goods were to be delivered to the lord or lady's house, there to be weighed. Issued before the building of textile guilds, these statutes favoured entrepreneurs by regulating in their favour the putting-out or domestic system.

The partnership or 'society' joined capital to labour, the partners sharing profits and risk. Sharecropping was described by Italian jurists as a 'quasi-society', risks being shared because a tenant was insured against loss caused by weather and warfare. Other contracts were similar, an example being a contract whereby investors put money or animals with a farmer or shepherd to share the profit. Seigniorial rights could also be shared. Most new towns and villages founded by Alphonse of Poitiers in Languedoc after 1250 were partnerships with local lords. In 1198 conflict between the bishop of Viviers and the count of Toulouse over the silver mines of Largentière ended in a partnership. Family communities wherein relatives shared the profits and duties of a common inheritance were frequent.

How close these forms were to each other is seen in Beaumanoir's customs of the Beauvaisis where commercial and political partnerships, family societies and even the community of man and wife are all lumped together in a chapter on 'companies'. If Italian jurists were beyond that stage, they still discussed the Lombard communitarian family and always insisted that a commercial 'society' was a brotherhood. Great jurists like Azzo (d. *circa* 1230) and Accursius (d. 1260) also found in Roman law a 'law of brotherhood' making all partners brothers, equally responsible and exposed to risk. Lacking this quality, societies or contracts were termed 'leonine', reflecting the tale of the lion who ate the shares of the beasts with whom he had agreed to hunt.

In Toulouse the cathedral canons sued the armed guards of a farm in 1191 for breach of 'society' because they fled when an enemy appeared. In 1218 a dying father put capital bequeathed to a minor son in a company for a term of seven years, ordering his executors to receive yearly accounts from the active partners. Most partnerships were small, but some large. Among the latter were maritime societies whose expensive ships and cargoes were financed by being divided into a number of shares. As early as 1197, a Venetian vessel was capitalized by a hundred shares. Mines were financed by shares, those of the Swedish copper mine of Stora Kopparberg being first mentioned in 1288. Large-scale business enterprise used the same methods. Although the average number of partners in a

Tuscan merchant-banking firm was around five, some had five times as many. External capitalizers were also employed here. In 1331 the capital of the Florentine Bardi consisted of fifty-eight shares, of which about thirty-six per cent was held by six family members and the rest by five outsiders.

Most partnerships were short-lived. Maritime ventures were often for one voyage, and even great merchant-banking societies were constellations of transitory partnerships. Large-scale milling or mining, however, required companies of longer duration. The Bazacle watermills in Toulouse were operated separately, each being owned by a group of partners, some millers and some simple investors, clerical or lay. The operators gradually joined to face lawsuits and carry out common designs, in 1177 combining to build a barrage across the Garonne river to increase the flow. In 1193 a spokesman acted for all Bazacle partners in a lawsuit, thus beginning a company that lasted until 1925. Continuity was also lent by family tradition, as in merchant-banking firms. When the Florentine Scali crashed in 1326, they had been in business for over a century.

Functional specialities appeared everywhere. In 1307 the Florentine Alberti merchant bankers gave branch partners maintenance, a share of profit and a salary. Practical business required a combination of partnerships, contractual relationships and hired labour. Florence's Peruzzi both employed managers all over Europe and invested in sixteen industrial and commercial companies. John Boine Broke (d. 1286 or 1287) of Douai joined partnerships for merchant ventures, put out his wool for manufacture and ran his own dye works and drying house with hired labour. Salaried workers are heard of at the Bazacle mills in 1291. In 1388 – a time when business was not as good as half a century earlier – the Strozzi-Credi wool workshop in Florence employed about fifty persons, of whom a quarter were permanent staff, fifteen per cent apprentices and the rest dayworkers. Brotherhood sometime resisted specialization. The shareholding miners of the Tuscan silver mine at Massa Marittima together elected masters to direct the pits, and a partner who neither worked nor sent a replacement was to surrender his share in the company. Similar restrictions were imposed on investors by millers at Douai and elsewhere. It was, however, already normal in mines and mills for one partner to provide capital and another labour. When, in 1294, the abbot of Admont held shares in Steiermark iron, he was obviously not a miner or smelter.

The distinction between active and inactive partners was early adopted in maritime companies because the capital needed exceeded that possessed by the merchants or seamen aboard the vessel. Shares were sold to sleeping partners, investments that could be sold, pledged, willed and divided like other property. In large family merchant-banking firms, investors were often partners for profit, having nothing to do with management. This stretched the fabric of the 'society' because partners were responsible for the actions of their associates. In small companies, partners were protected from loss because they knew its members well. In 1256 Rolandino Passaggeri's notary's manual tells that a partner must agree 'not to contract debts or give credit without the consent of the other partners, and to show, see and give accounting of the partnership whenever the other partners require it'.[4] In large companies, lesser partners needed and demanded a voice. When, after a period of difficulty, the Buonsignori rebuilt the Great Table of Siena in 1289, the seniors pledged to conduct the business in line with the decisions 'of the majority of [the family] and of the other partners of the said firm'.[5]

As firms became larger and directors separated from the investing partners, stronger controls evolved. Jurists came to describe them as fictive persons, and hence distinguished between the capital of a company and the private fortunes of its partners. In 1301 the Florentine wool guild or *Calimala* provided that a creditor of an insolvent partner could not attack the firm itself, merely take the debtor's shares. In 1298 the Buonsignori junior partners petitioned the republic to intercede at the papal court, to grant a moratorium on payments and asked that 'no partner . . . be obliged to pay the debts of the said company above or beyond his share of the capitalization'.[6] Initially rejected, the principle was accepted by 1310.

After 1250 government regulation grew rapidly in Italy. Founded in 1234 or 1235, the *Maona* of Ceuta, a Genoese chartered company, assembled investors to arm a fleet in return for sharing booty. By 1346 the *Maona* of Chios–Phocea – a huge 'society' divided into 2,013 shares valued at a hundred pounds each – gave the government of the conquered islands to the shareholders. The Venetians preferred government management. The senate ordered its merchants in Alexandria in 1283 to combine to corner the cotton and pepper trade and, before 1300, sponsored the building of great galleys and instituted a convoy system for them. Given a monopoly of carrying spices, silk and other light and valuable goods, these vessels were increasingly owned and operated by the government.

Chartered companies were near relatives of the *montes* created by governments to raise money. Heard of from the 1160s, *montes* derived partly from the assignment of public revenue to pay debts owed creditors and partly from the forced loans characteristic of urban and seigniorial public finance. In Genoa in 1164, a *mons* of seven shares was created by assigning revenues for eleven years, the shares being divided among six creditors, who purchased anywhere from two full shares to a quarter of a share, each being alienable and negotiable. The system underwent huge expansion. Shares in harbour duties, the state salt monopoly – indeed, all revenues – were assigned to raise money. By about 1180 they were assigned in perpetuity and became heritable, though government retained the right to repurchase and regulate the rate of return. Although formally forced loans, governments advertised the annual return, and investors began to clamour for them. In short, a system analogous to a funded debt had been created. Government-regulated or managed companies and funds also reinforced the idea of limited liability because investors in government debts or companies risked no more than they had invested.

Love of free enterprise led Genoa to differ from other towns. By 1323 her companies had become autonomous with directors elected by the shareholders. This freedom was not to be won in Venice, where the old *montes* were consolidated into a state-managed fund as early as 1262. The State's emergence as a major economic operator shows the superiority of Italian fiscal techniques. No northern ruler was able to establish a *mons* in the thirteenth century or even fourteenth century, and even the largest northern towns had only begun to sell shares of municipal income.

Another way to capitalize was an outgrowth of placing money or valuables in safekeeping. Churches and monasteries, especially Templars and Hospitallers, were traditionally used for this purpose. Worried about secular lawsuits, in 1198 the pope's rule for the Trinitarians prohibited this order from receiving specie in deposit. Templars and Hospitallers were allowed to, but could not pay interest. The lay banker's great advantage was that he enticed clients by offering not only protection but also profit on deposits. In 1215 Boncompagno of Signa listed the kinds of deposits:

> Some deposit property with the religious, others with laymen who are believed good, others with innkeepers of whom they have heard report or with whom

they are staying, and still others with merchants or moneychangers. Some then deposit only for safekeeping and others for both safekeeping and profit . . . .[7]

Deposit contracts soon became ordinary investments for widows, gentlefolk and ecclesiastical institutions. In Perpignan in 1286 a businessman was given money by a noblewoman

> in deposit . . . in order to do business with the said money together with my own, either personally or by agents in France, Flanders or elsewhere, from this date for a year or more as it pleases both of us, and I will faithfully give you three parts of the profit . . . retaining the fourth . . . for my labour.[8]

Depositors also entrusted their means to the Italian merchant-banking firms at rates which were known in the market.

Deposits had many advantages. Although not free of ecclesiastical censure, they were not looked on with the disfavour of outright usury. In civil courts investors did not share responsibility for the actions or debts of those with whom they deposited: if depositees failed, depositors became their creditors. Deposit for gain was so flexible that during the thirteenth century it replaced loans and various kinds of partnerships. The meaning of this for capitalization is illustrated by the larger Tuscan companies. From 1300 to 1303 over a million gold marks were deposited with the Spini firm by the papacy. In 1318 the assets of the Florentine Bardi were over ten million gold marks, a sum eight times larger than the firm's original capital. A Genoese lawsuit of 1200 shows that businessmen had 'call' deposits, ones where depositors received no interest but could withdraw at will, the banker meanwhile investing the capital. Bankers soon encouraged reputable depositors to overdraw, hence investing in loans, short and long term. Lacking figures, the quantity of credit created cannot be estimated, but it must have been huge.

Even though guilds and governments combined to produce banks, they were not yet highly specialized. Tuscan firms were only partly banks, being principally mercantile houses investing in commerce, industry and land. Smaller operators on the local level were what the Tuscan merchant bankers were on the universal. Possibly once a serf, Arnold of Codalet became one of Perpignan's richest men in the period from 1276 to 1287. He invested in trading ventures from Seville to Flanders, and speculated in local seigniorial and ecclesiastical revenues. He received both call deposits and investment deposits from local businessmen and rentiers, thus serving as a one-man banking and investment house.

Interest rates were high around 1300. In Catalonia the legal maximum was twelve and a half per cent for Christians and twenty for Jews. On commercial credit, Genoa permitted twenty-five per cent and Venice set the maximum at twenty, as did the Champagne fairs in 1311. For what moderns would describe as consumer credit, higher rates were allowed. Under the Flemish Lombard Privilege of 1281, Italians were permitted forty-three per cent, and moneylenders exacted appalling rates from the poor. A Lombard at Nîmes was charged in 1289 with having extorted 202 per cent. State finance also sometimes involved staggering rates. Losing the war, Frederick II promised to pay his Roman bankers anywhere from thirty-six to forty-eight per cent.

Moderate returns on investments were common, however, and overall rates of profit were not great, perhaps because the high cost of capital was partly compensated for by the high rate of gain. Around 1300 land rents brought annual returns of anywhere from five to ten per cent. Those who deposited for gain with businessmen in Perpignan expected about ten per cent. The government debt of Genoa offered subscribers from seven to ten per cent while Florence's gave anywhere from five to fifteen. After paying off the seven or eight per cent owed on depositors' investments, the Peruzzi partners averaged a profit of just under sixteen per cent in the period from 1308 to 1324, a time of prosperity. The usual percentage on deposits with mercantile firms in Florence ranged from six to ten per cent yearly, and, to judge from the books of the Del Bene firm, the return of partners in the wool industry oscillated between seven and fifteen.

Business required ancillary agencies of which some were ecclesiastical, although, as seen above, the direct participation of the Church was fading. The Languedoc hearth tax raised by the pope in the Albigensian Crusade in 1212 had been deposited with the Templars. The French crown used the Paris Temple as a treasury until 1295, but the Tuscans had taken this business by mid-century. Although the decline of the Temple was related to the failure of the Crusade, Tuscan merchant bankers also won out because they offered better service. They served as revenue collectors, employed bills of exchange, essential instruments in a decentralized economy, and deposits placed with them yielded a return. They also operated on as grand a scale as did the Temple. Whereas the Scoti of Genoa had aided Simon of Montfort modestly during the Albigensian Crusade, by 1266 a combine headed by the Buonsignori of Siena advanced Charles of Anjou 160,000 pounds of Paris, a sum considerably larger than the total debt of the French crown to the Temple in 1286.

Specie, moreover, no longer had to be transported. Improving on the methods of the Templars, merchant bankers devised paper transfers. A primitive bill moved credit from Genoa to Alexandria in 1155. Papal collectors in London used bills of exchange issued by the Bardi to carry credits to Rome. Non-negotiable promissory notes were generalized, a collection of 7,000 such for the period from 1249 to 1291 being discovered in the archives of Ypres alone. As early as 1200 interbank transfers were common in Italy, and by mid-century Italian merchants at the Champagne fairs normally used them. When embargoing the export of goods and money to Italy during the conflict with Boniface VIII in 1301, Philip the Fair took care to prohibit credit transfers by merchants' letters and deposits.

Coinage became more uniform and stable as commerce grew and the State developed economic power. By 1300 England had reduced the number of mints from over forty to twelve, and even France, initially burdened by almost three hundred, cut this to thirty by 1315. Coin values increased and various types corresponded to Europe's principal economic areas. Before 1200 the English minted the great silver penny (Sterling) which became a standard in the Hanseatic North and Baltic Seas. In 1192 the Venetians issued the great penny, whose weight and style, only slowly received in Venice itself, was adopted by many towns in the peninsula and also replaced Norman south Italian coinage. Italian-style coinages spread everywhere. The great penny of Tours imitated an Italian model in 1266, and was itself copied by many coinages in the Rhineland by 1300. At about that time the king of Bohemia invited Florentine mintmasters to introduce their models in his realm.

Gold coins, the first since Carolingian times, made their appearance. In 1149 the Genoese stamped a few gold coins that never caught on, and even the Emperor Frederick II's *augustales* had little economic significance. The Florentine florin of 1252 and the Venetian ducat of 1284 really established gold coinage. Writing in the late thirteenth century, the Dominican preacher Remigio de 'Girolami praised his city's coin:

The [florin's] nobility is shown in three ways: first, by its metal, because the gold in Sicily's *tarena* is good, that in the *augustalis* better, but that in the florin best; second by its engraving, because on one side it has the lily, a thing of great excellence . . . and third, by its currency, because it circulates throughout the world, even among Saracens.[9]

All was not bliss, however. Although the economy continued to flourish, public finance was shaky around 1300. Trying to extend their authority without adequate support from a still decentralized society, princes ran into debt, sometimes ruinously. By 1290 Guy of Dampierre, count of Flanders, owed the Lombards a sum equalling nearly a quarter of the annual take of the French royal treasury, and his resulting powerlessness invited France and England to intervene in industrial Flanders. Weak public finance gradually affected all the economy. Undertaken for profit, the mutation of 1295 was the first significant breach of the stability of France's royal coinage since the beginning of the century. In spite of howls of rage by those whose savings had been wiped out, and protestations by the clergy in 1303–4 and nobility in 1314 and 1316, devaluation of coinage soon became normal government policy in France and in much of Europe. In short, a crisis reflecting undeveloped national public finance preceded the general economic difficulties of the fourteenth century.

NOTES AND REFERENCES

1   Thomas W. Blomquist, 'Luccan Bankers in the Champagne' in *Journal of European Economic History* 14 (1985), 531.
2   Armando Sapori, '*Compagni mercantili toscane*' in *Studi in onore di Enrico Besta* (Milan, 1937) II, 136.
3   *Liber de regimine civitatum* 21 in *BIMA* III (Bologna, 1901), 225.
4   *Summa artis notarie* 1, 6 (Venice, 1583) I, 141v.
5   Sapori, '*Compagni mercantili toscane*' in *Studi . . . Enrico Besta* II, 126.
6   *Ibid.* II, 127.
7   *Boncampagnus Boncompagni* in *BuF* I, 173.
8   Emery,*The Jews of Perpignan*,194–5, No. 147.
9   C.T. Davis 'An Early Florentine Political Theorist: Fra Remigio de'Girolami' in *Proceedings of the American Philosophical Society* CIV (1960), 688.

8

USURY AND CORPORATISM

ECONOMIC BROTHERHOOD

Churchmen were of two minds about the marketplace because scripture enjoined: from each according to his means; to each according to his needs.[1] In the aftermath of the Gregorian age, utopians tried to make the world into a Christian society where men, like monks of old, lived in brotherhood without private property. This teaching paralleled the rise of nascent guild hostility to economic individualism around 1200 and the gradual secularization of the monastic idea. A student of Peter Cantor, Cardinal Robert of Curzon, professor at Paris and papal legate in 1213, wrote:

> So many evils cannot be purged unless a general council of all bishops and princes is convoked under the lord pope, where the Church and princes together will instruct all, under penalty of excommunication . . . to work either mentally or physically, and to eat only their own bread, that is, the bread won by their own labour, as the apostle commanded, and that there be no idle or pushing fellows among us. Thus would all usurers, factious men and robbers be removed; thus would charity flourish and the fabric of the churches be restored; and thus would all be brought back again to its pristine state.[2]

Some doubted that the ideal could be realized. Robert of Curzon's legatine mission to France was ended abruptly by Innocent III in 1216 because the king opposed his attack on usury, the clergy disliked the utopian rhetoric of his councils and the well-to-do detested his crusade preaching to the poor, children and even the sick. If common possession was sanctified in divine and natural law, Gratian's *Decretum* admitted that society is forced to choose between two evils, that of private property or the greater evil of violence or anarchy. Caesarius of Heisterbach knew how to trim it. He praised Ensfrid, dean of St Andrew's in Cologne, because he took from the rich to feed the poor. Others, however, could not do so because 'the saints are allowed many things not permitted to those not holy. Where God's spirit is, there is liberty!'[3] If the poor were aided, private property was permitted, and, indeed, some justified it more than others. It was only postlapsarian to Duns Scotus, but Aquinas found it even in the state of innocence. Giles of Rome rehearsed Aristotle's arguments against Plato's communism: we have more incentive to do well with what we ourselves own, and brothers often fight over common inheritances. Still, it is a pity because

> had men not corrupt appetites . . . and were they not prone to evil, it would be good . . . to have property in common, because the more in common it is, the more divine it is . . . . As things are now, however, it is useful for a community's citizens to have private property, because . . . men are not normally perfect.[4]

Some also confessed that merchants performed necessary social functions. A passage by Honorius (*fl.* early 1100) defines their honour: 'You minister to all nations because you bring what they need through the perils of roads, rivers, thieves and the dangers of solitude. All men are your debtors to render prayers for your labour.'[5] Giles of Rome's schedule of salaries 'for labour' includes gains from special knowledge. He even lauded the morally dubious case of the philosopher who cornered olive presses in the off season to rent them at high rates when needed.

Compromise aside, the clergy viewed those in other social orders sourly, probably because moral censoriousness is the usury the religious mind exacts from others of the world's inhabitants. Carried in Peter Lombard's *Sentences*, a passage from a council at Rome of 1078 conveys this severity:

> If a soldier or trader or one devoted to any profession that cannot be exercised without sin should come to penitence when snared in serious sin . . . he should know that he cannot perform true penitence by which to obtain eternal life unless he leaves business or gives up his profession . . . . That he should nevertheless not despair, we urge him to do whatever good he can in the meantime that omnipotent God may light his soul to penitence.[6]

The final sentence shows how the clergy policed the marketplace by means of the court of conscience.

CHURCH AND USURY

Ecclesiastical legislation expressed the churchman's hope for economic brotherhood and willingness to press hard on laymen. Following the law of brotherhood, Christians were not to lend at usury to other Christians. As Gratian put it around 1140: 'Usury exists when more is asked than is given; for example, were you to give ten shillings and seek more, or one measure of grain and require something more.'[7] *La Somme le Roi*, a vernacular tract of 1279, lists moneylenders, mortgagers, heirs who refuse restitution of usury by penitents, helpers of Jews or other usurers, businessmen taking advantage of buyers and those exploiting debtors.

Exceptions were made for the poor and for minors, that is, wives and widows. The consuls of Genoa's chamber of commerce were not too bold when they promised to uphold all sentences rendered by the archiepiscopal court except those 'concerning usury given to minors from money . . . that guardians have placed to advantage'.[8] In a decretal often cited to justify the deposit contract Innocent III instructed the archbishop of the same town to permit a poor citizen to invest his wife's dowry with a merchant to sustain matrimony's burdens. The Church itself was also the pauper. When, as will be seen, mortgages were forbidden, churchmen were expressly allowed to use them to redeem church property from lay hands. This exception was soon extended to include the recuperation of patrimonies wrongly lost to lay families.

The law on usury did not spring up overnight. The principle was known in antiquity, but did not seriously invade the lay world until the Crusades. The need to protect crusaders from creditors then elicited papal and conciliar legislation. Following the introversion of the Crusade itself, the accent began to shift. Churchmen, exemplified by Robert of Curzon at the Council of Paris in 1212–13, moved from protecting crusaders to converting the whole world into a truly Christian society. This affected both secular business and clerical practice. Although mortgages were long suspect because creditors collected as usury the fruits of pledged property, monasteries, military orders and chapters had regularly invested in these contracts. After their condemnation by the pope in 1180, they did so only in exceptional cases. In 1163 when Alexander III wrote to an archbishop of Rheims asking him to protect a debtor against usury, it seemed that, as in Roman law, moderate usury was tolerated. After the Lateran Council of 1215, however, that excuse could be pleaded only by Jews.

The Church developed new enforcement agencies. Episcopal tribunals changed in the late twelfth century from synodal bodies of laymen and clergy to courts under a professional judge called the Official, and the new court actively prosecuted usurers. At the Council of Toulouse in 1229, testaments not witnessed by churchmen were declared suspect, thus indirectly insisting upon deathbed restitution of usury. At the Council of Lyons in 1274 notorious usurers were denied Christian burial until restitution was made. At that of Vienne in 1311–12, the famous canon *Ex gravi* crowned the edifice by condemning princes or magistrates who protected or permitted usury, declaring heretical those pertinaciously defending this sin.

This law changed business practice. In the twelfth century jurists frankly mentioned usury. Widely used in southern France and Italy, the code called *Peter's Excerpts* regulated the relationships of creditor and debtor in a chapter called 'If anyone owes a sum to his creditor, that is, capital and usuries, and pays any part of the debt, he may choose at the time of payment whether he wishes it to count for the usuries or for the principal.'[9] Writing in 1215, Boncompagno of Signa casually recorded a letter form requesting intercession to obtain a loan at usury, which included the following promise: '[the debtor] will give satisfactory security to the creditor . . . for both capital and usury.'[10] Furthermore, a lax interpretation of the law of brotherhood of the business partnership was current. The glossator Alberic of Porta Ravennate (d. early 1190s) proposed that partnerships where one partner bore the risk and the other shared the profits were licit. If the great canonist Hostiensis echoed Alberic's argument later on, his was a minority voice. Contemporary practice is shown in Rolandino Passaggeri's treatise for notaries, where he warns them not to condone usury by writing partnership documents 'in which only gain and not both the gain and loss are mentioned'.[11]

Jurists rarely mentioned usury save to condemn it, and town statutes, like those of St Gilles in 1233, warned notaries to avoid it. Sometimes, as at Toulouse, the change occurred with dramatic rapidity. A common contract, the usurious mortgage vanished in the 1190s. The loan with usury was more durable, disappearing only during a period of intense factional strife within the town. From 1206 to 1215, Bishop Fulk, once a merchant and troubadour in Marseilles, created a White Confraternity to evoke popular support for the Crusade and against heretics and usurers. Although the heretics were scarcely touched and the Whites were speedily countered by a Black Confraternity, Fulk was successful against usury. During this time testamentary restitutions became normal and loans vanished from documents.

As the prohibition of usury became prominent, so also did penitential restitution. The practice was old and tied to the Church's view of the rich, whom, Honorius warned,

> God wanted you to be the fathers of the poor. Remember, you came naked into the world, and naked you will leave it. Because you must leave your riches to others, hasten now to build up heavenly treasures by the hands of the poor . . . . Decorate churches with books, robes and other ornaments, restore those destroyed or deserted, enlarge the prebends of God's servants . . . . Build bridges and roads thus preparing your way to heaven, and provide lodging, food and clothing for the poor, sick and wandering, thus buying eternal riches for yourselves.[12]

Systematic testamentary restitution, however, did not begin much before the 1180s, but thereafter spread rapidly. Rolandino listed the various types under the following rubrics, of which the first three are *certa* and the fourth *incerta*:

1. Open or public restitution to known persons.
2. 'In fear of infamy', covert restitution by the penitent's confessor to known victims whose names are listed in a closed codicil externally authenticated by two witnesses.
3. General restitution by the penitent's executors to those who can prove usury against him.
4. Distribution of a sum of money by the executors to pious causes for the souls of those whom the usurer has harmed.

Obviously open to abuse, such distributions 'are to be made only with the consent of high authority, such as pope or bishop'.[13] Everyone knew of the problem. In his biography of Louis IX of France, John of Joinville complained that the devil invented restitution in order to corrupt the clergy.

Restitution was a rendering of accounts by an individual in the sweat of the deathbed; gifts for salvation (*pro anima*) during a life of crime could not replace it, and hence what moderns call philanthropy was condemned as one of the seven deceptive types of restitution by a council at Ravenna in 1317. Such gifts could not be rejected, however, because few confessors could deprive of hope those who expressed an intention, however imperfect, of healing the wounds they had dealt the pauper or Christ. In 1310, when the capital stood at £147,000, the Peruzzi gave £2,500 for pious causes. The partners of this merchant-banking firm were not thereby wholly excused from deathbed restitution – at least, not in theory. In 1254, for example, a pope gratified the Austin Friars of Todi:

> Inclining to your prayers, we permit . . . you to receive for the erection of your church up to £500 . . . from those of . . . Todi who have extorted usuries or acquired other things illicitly and cannot discover to whom restitution should be made. Nor do we wish that those who have given you the said usuries should be held to make other restitution for them.[14]

Writing between 1254 and 1262, the Franciscan Claro of Florence asked whether those who invested in town revenues bought during a war and who profited tenfold in the subsequent peace are obliged to restitution. 'They are to be excused,' he says, 'because of their risk and danger and are not held to make restitution to the town, but none the less ought to give very fat charities from their profits'.[15]

The growth of moral rigorism requires explanation. Although labour was sometimes permitted, ecclesiastics were forbidden economic activity except as rentiers. This was reinforced, if not imposed, by the division between the two peoples, clerical and lay, that compelled ecclesiastics to surrender functions for which they could be held responsible by civil power. Rentiers, however, are disadvantaged in burgeoning economies. Churchmen therefore looked for ways of eliciting lay charity, and moral rigorism combined with social utopianism was a way of sharing in the growth.

Restitutions and pious giving made the medieval town into a jewel by building 'pious places', churches, cloisters and bridges. The expansion of parish education and hospital care for the sick and aged was financed by the same. The attack on usury, moreover, may not have slowed economic growth. Rent sales (*census*) replaced the mortgage and, being simple sales, were not usurious. They also, relative to the ever-mounting value of land, reduced the price of capital. The banning of the loan with usury multiplied the use of business partnerships, and stimulated the evolution of the deposit contract. This suited economic maturity, a time when the price of capital tended to diminish as risk declined.

These benefits, however, were unintended by churchmen, and

rigorists did not want businessmen to escape easily. Henry Goethals of Ghent (d. 1293) declared rent sales usurious, and the deposit contract was even more frequently attacked. The lengths to which rigorists went is shown by the canon *Naviganti* of 1236, wherein Gregory IX refused any profit to those who lent money to merchants even if they shared the risk. Although laxists like Cardinal Geoffrey of Trani in 1245 argued that this referred only to maritime loans, rigorists used it against any and all business. Still, the opinion earlier advanced by Peter Cantor may have been the more probable one: 'Were [one] to invest money and share both the loss and the pain . . . that would not be usury.'[16]

The banishment of usurious contracts from public records did not mean that moneylending ceased. The contracts were converted into loans without usury. Innocent III in 1206 permitted a debtor to gratify a creditor with a gift, as long as there was no intention to cheat. Roman law's distinction between usury (a creditor's profit on a loan) and interest (a loss to the creditor by a debtor's non-fulfilment of contract) was more significant. Even in canon law, a putative penalty could be spelled out in loan contracts. Raymond of Peñafort believed that, 'if the penalty is . . . placed in the contract by the common consent of the parties, to the effect that, through fear of it, the debt will be paid on a certain day, usury is not committed, so long as the intention is good'.[17]

Two interpretations of interest were possible, however, and casuistry about intention could thereby enter the equasion. Typical of twelfth-century civil law, the code called *Peter's Excerpts* allowed a deceived party to 'recuperate the price together with the interest, that is, the loss he has suffered because of the sale, and the gain he could have made with his money'.[18] To some, such as Hostiensis, damaged parties could recuperate only their loss and not the putative gain they might have made. Noting that entrepreneurs lending to towns or persons thereby forewent a probable profit, however, Peter John Olivi suggested compensation. He argued that:

> since money or property . . . is put to work for a certain probable gain, it not only has the simple quality of money or goods, but, beyond that, a certain seminal quality of generating profit, which we commonly call capital, and therefore not only does the simple value of the object itself have to be returned, but also an added value.[19]

Rejecting Aristotle's familiar 'barren money', this radical Franciscan noted that the added value was created 'by the industry of merchants; and so [the value] is not from the money itself but instead from its owners' industry'.[20]

The examination of intention took place in the court of conscience, where the market's hot urges were cooled by the rigour or fanned by the laxity of the confessor. The latter's opinions, however, were informed by the community's consensus, and the size of the penalty or the rate of covert usury was also set by the market. These estimates had nothing to do with the doctrinal prohibition of usury, but were closely related to confessional practice and ecclesiastical courts. Those prosecuted or denied burial were usually described as 'manifest and notorious usurers'. An archbishop of Pisa in 1323 defined such individuals as 'notorious in law because they have confessed or have been condemned for usury, or notorious in fact because they have given evidence of involvement in this business in a way which no subterfuge can hide, as when they have a counter or table ready for this business'.[21]

GOVERNMENT AND USURY

The Church's penetration of the marketplace reflects the weakness of secular government in the post-Gregorian epoch. As the State began to renew its powers, however, conflicts of jurisdiction arose. In 1205, for example, Philip Augustus of France questioned the right of church tribunals to prosecute usurers without royal consent. He was defending a profitable practice: in 1143 Louis VII sold a privilege to the burghers of Tours for 30,000 shillings, which promised not to punish them 'for usury, ill-gotten gain or any other multiplication of money'.[22] This attitude enraged Peter Cantor. Christian usurers licensed by princes are rightly called Jews, he said, 'because princes . . . do not permit them to be charged with any crime, saying, "These are our Jews." But they are worse than Jews because Jews are permitted by scripture to take usury from a foreigner, but not from a brother, which is what Christian usurers do.'[23]

Some princes and lords, however, favoured the Church's stand. With undeveloped tax systems, they were happy to get a share of the take. The *Exchequer Dialogue* and the tract on England's laws attributed to Glanville (d. 1190) show that England's kings quickly received church law, surrendering the prosecution of living usurers to the Church but claiming the inheritances of dead and unrepentant ones for the crown. In France reception was slower but, if the code named after St Louis represents actual practice, the rewards were more widely shared: 'When a usurer is found in the territory of a baron or elsewhere, and it is proven against him, his property goes to the baron. His sin is then punished by Holy Church.'[24]

No more usurious than rural millers, estate bailiffs and rich landlords and seigniors, townsfolk were nevertheless especially disturbed by the law on usury. Many were moved by the utopian hope for economic brotherhood, but others rejected ecclesiastical rigour because investment was their livelihood. The interplay of economics and republican government was curious. A changing group as the newly wealthy moved into authority, the well-to-do generally ran the republic. Although the poor obviously lent both commodities and money, what preserved them for virtue was their incapacity to be vicious on a sufficient scale. Although many with old wealth were also usurers, their interest in public office and hostility to the new rich veiled their economic aggression. Censure was therefore directed largely against the new rich, those demonstrably involved in hard or manifest usury. Usury was therefore political, and its practice and repression led to violence, as in Toulouse during the Albigensian Crusade and frequently in Italian cities. Although nobody could question the canons, governments necessarily applied them reluctantly. If rigorists often berated Italian merchant bankers, their republics protected them; and if moralizers questioned their debt societies (*montes*), they defended subscribers by the fiction of the forced loan.

Because every kind of state and most social elements require investment, the law appeared irrational to some. In his influential *Summa of the Confessors*, the Dominican John of Freiburg followed Hostiensis in saying that, where laws contradict each other, those more humane or rational are to be preferred. God, went the commonplace, demands nothing impossible. Elaborating on arguments earlier expressed by Azzo, Cino of Pistoia commented that

> the emperor who rules the people and the world sees that men are not as charitable as they ought to be, and the poor consequently suffer hunger . . . . Because, as I have said, divine law is to be interpreted by human law which allows an evil in order that worse be avoided, he thought it equitable for usury to be asked.[25]

Moderate theologians joined lawyers in this position. Thomas

Aquinas opined that practical needs (especially of the poor) made concession necessary. The principle was: 'Sometimes practical law permits something unjust lest the community bear greater inconvenience, just as God sometimes permits evil lest the good that He knows will derive from evil be impeded.'[26] Still, usurers, Jewish or Christian, are to restore their usuries if the wronged debtors are known. Most debtors, however, are unknown or, as they said, 'uncertain'. For uncertain debtors, Aquinas went on, a prince may tax the Jews for the common good – in effect, government may license usury and profit from it. The learned professor then added: 'And what has been said of the Jews is to be understood of . . . all others who busy themselves in usurious pravity.'[27] It may be concluded that a secular magistrate or prince who permitted usury was not heretical so long as he did not assert that his action was without sin.

The Church was itself Latin Europe's greatest government, and in consequence, although utopian voices were heard in Rome, finance outshouted them. Examples of what the latter meant in the forum of conscience are easy to find. In 1297 Boniface VIII wrote to the Florentine Franzesi merchant-banking family, noting that

> because . . . much . . . property is known to have come into your hands by means of usury and evil and illicit contracts . . . we, benignly considering that you are uncovering your guilt in this matter by a humble and spontaneous confession for the exoneration of your consciences, and wishing . . . to provide for you of the great clemency of the apostolic see, remit and concede to you that . . . you may licitly and freely have and retain all you have acquired in this way.[28]

Among the Franzesi mentioned were the 'Mouche and Biche' who harmed Boniface so greatly in the conflict with the French king!

In conclusion, a reader may recall that the text the clergy expounded is hard. 'But love you your enemies, and do good, and lend, hoping for nothing therefrom; and your reward shall be great, and you shall be the children of the Highest: for He is kind to the unthankful and the evil.'[29]

ECONOMIC CORPORATISM

That the mortgage and loan with usury were driven out of circulation is puzzling. Some have explained it by saying that these contracts provided capital for consumption: loans being made mainly to the poor, improvident gentlefolk or declining monasteries. This is doubtful. Jewish loans at usury in Perpignan in the 1290s went to members of all classes and successful businessmen were among the borrowers. At Toulouse before the Albigensian Crusade, income from mortgages (*pignora*) constituted a substantial part of a landed family's wealth. Magistrates at Narbonne, Marseilles and Pisa financed government by borrowing at usury until 1200. Such contracts were so necessary that, when banned, substitutes soon replaced them, and, where they could not be replaced, gained a half-life as licensed usury. Would it not have sufficed to police these functional contracts by means of the just price?

Clerical moral rigorism could not alone have imposed this inconvenience on an unwilling society. Lay adherence was linked to the Crusade where debt protection was among a Crusader's privileges, and in 1214 Innocent III told Philip Augustus that Crusades could not be mounted unless usury was suppressed. The clerical programme's propaganda of brotherhood and social utopia also appealed mightily to the rising trade and craft guilds. A result was that the denigration of private property characteristic of the monks momentarily spread to lay society.

Guilds reflected the desire of crafts- and tradesfolk to pool strength to protect and increase labour's rewards. There was little especially medieval about this, nor was it limited to economics. Charity was maximized by organization and crime also: Tours had a beggars' guild in the late twelfth century and youth gangs or clubs were common in Italian towns. It is worth recalling, moreover, that the guild movement was to be long-lived: the associations described below were the forerunners of a corporatism that grew in France through the seventeenth century and dominated German labour as late as the revolution of 1848.

Guilds were usually new in the late twelfth century. In 1200 Paris had a powerful merchant guild and four or more trade and craft organizations. From 1261 to 1270, the *Book of the Professions* of Paris registered the statutes of 101 trades and crafts. In 1292 there were 130, and in 1313 no less than 157. The rapidity of this expansion gave guildsmen a sense of adventure that never again marked Europe's corporate structures.

In northern Europe association was first expressed in brotherhoods providing protection to traders and others whose itinerant occupations placed them outside of ordinary communities. In 1200 the Danish guild of Flensburg was primitive enough to obligate brethren to aid the flight of a member who had slain a stranger. Similar merchant guilds or hanses soon combined economic functions with jurisdictional or governmental ones, and guild membership became citizenship. In the late thirteenth century membership in the merchants' guild of Bedford, near London, was tantamount to community citizenship. Most northern towns, however, had gone beyond this stage. As they appeared, craft and trade guilds took their places beside the merchants, and as a result, political functions were separated from economic, the merchants' association becoming only the 'first among equals'. Not without power, however: Paris came closest to self-government when her merchants' association farmed the royal office of provost in the late twelfth century. In Italy and adjacent regions things were different. There merchant associations had also played a role, but by the early thirteenth century they had become analogous to modern chambers of commerce with economic police powers. In the custom of Milan of 1216 the chamber of commerce had jurisdiction over the town mint and markets, and its statutes and judicial decisions were read annually in the citizens' general assembly.

Guild domination of urban political life sometimes built oligarchy. In 1240 members of the Hanse of London, plutocratic and patrician entrepreneurs in the wool industry, monopolized high public office at Bruges. Much the same may be said about Florence's entrepreneurial associations of the wool and silk guilds and that of the bankers. The difference between these later associations and earlier primitive ones is that, although political office was sometimes limited to their members, town citizenship was not confused with guild membership.

All owed service to prince or community. In 1158 the tanners of Toulouse promised to build siege artillery in wartime, and twenty years later the stonemasons of Nîmes served the artillery, receiving 100 shillings for each wall breached. During the Albigensian war, Toulouse's butchers were to accompany the militia and sell meat at fixed prices on credit. The Garonne boatmen stated in 1231 that they owed the count river transport services. Florentine construction guilds helped the republic draft building codes and inspect buildings, and provided engineers and artillerymen for the army at Montaperto in 1260.

Particular trades or crafts organized, and, as industrial specialization grew, their guilds split apart. In 1227, for example, Toulouse's woollens had one association; shortly before 1300 five guilds shared the industry, each with a different speciality. Scission took place because the small scale machinery available at this time made household workshops compatible with efficient production. These workshops contained, besides sleeping or capitalizing partners, a master or owner, wife and children, several day workers and a few apprentices – seven to a dozen. Mining and watermilling surpassed these limits, and so did textiles, an industry to be explored below.

In brief, the crafts' and trades' vision of economic heaven was an independent shop with a small staff and family participation. Guilds tried to make the mean the norm of the profession and often prohibited members owning more than one or two tables or shops. In England's Beverley around 1200, the weavers excluded members who became rich enough to qualify for the drapers' or merchants' guild. Meticulous regulation of raw-material purchases, production methods and prices shows that mutual suspicion is the price of economic brotherhood. Guilds were monopolistic, excluded foreigners and early exhibited a trend towards hereditary membership. In the late twelfth century Parisian butchers limited ownership of tables to families already in the guild. Similar motives multiplied training stages, accentuating the 'mystery' or 'mastery' of a craft. The crown of that edifice was the obligatory masterpiece, which was not general in Paris until the fourteenth century. Technical conservatism was also normal. In France and England, old handmill guilds waged a futile struggle against water-powered fulling mills. Just before 1300 German cloth guilds fought the introduction of the spinning wheel. When economic growth slowed, also, the relation between master and worker worsened because the latter had no chance to become a master with a shop.

Guild technological conservatism and monopoly excited resistance by consumers and import-export interests. Governments refused to exclude immigrants and fought guild attempts to regulate the sources of raw material and prices of finished goods. By the end of the thirteenth century guilds had won their place in the sun, but were falling under ever more intense scrutiny. At the same time, the appearance of state-chartered companies, the spread of protectionism (Pisa, for example, in 1303 prohibited the import of semifinished woollens to protect local industry) and the delineation of navigation acts, like that of Barcelona in 1286, were compatible with guild corporatism. As long as its cartel impulse was subordi-

133

nated to the common good, the guild was a means by which society mobilized itself for economic battle. Especially around the Mediterranean basin, the economic structure that was being limned around 1300 was that of the mercantilist State.

CORPORATISM AND SOCIETY

Guild scission was not simply a response to technology, it was also caused by the resistance of small owners and craftspeople to exploitation by the wealthy. The issues were many, centring around partnerships and putting-out contracts between entrepreneurs and artisans. Capitalists also supplied equipment and town statutes prohibited artisans from pledging tools to secure loans. Legislation also protected imprisoned debtors: Beaumanoir mitigated it by proposing that, if debtors 'have nothing, he who keeps them in prison must give them bread, wine and soup as much as they can use at least once a day'. His maximum term was forty days, longer ones being 'contrary to humanity'.[30]

Masters and dayworkers often battled. A burgomaster of Provins was slain in 1281 when journeymen clothworkers protested an increase in hours, and twelve years later laws against their associations were again promulgated. Entrepreneurs' associations fought those of artisans. At Leicester weavers and fullers formed guilds in 1264 and 1275 to bargain with the drapers of the guild merchant. London's merchants in the late thirteenth century claimed that the weavers had raised prices without notice, cut the number of looms, engaged in a slowdown and, in effect, struck by extending Christmas holidays into January.

Similar conflicts also afflicted larger industries, those resembling capitalist industrial organization. The Bazacle watermills of Toulouse have already been seen, and by 1291 their personnel were divided into shareholders, a legal and managerial staff and workmen who, in that year, were forbidden to form a guild. In the Florentine wool industry around 1200 one heard only of weavers, dyers and finishers. In those early days, also, even big entrepreneurs rarely thought in terms of factories, but instead capitalized others' shops or manufactured indirectly by putting out. Although no true factory system appeared, it has been seen above that some productive units were quite large. More significant were industry-wide entrepreneurial organizations. By the 1290s two such guilds were in place, the *Arte di Calimala*, specializing in importing unfinished cloth, and the *Arte della Lana*, whose members imported raw wool. Under the *Lana* were no less than fourteen different crafts, some in guilds, like weavers and finishers, and others, dyers and carders, employed by putting out. In regard to the latter, *Lana* entrepreneurs both provided raw material and equipment and had police authority. The workers tried to organize, and struggle was constant. 'Moral' regulator of the marketplace, the Church was involved: bishops generally favoured the *Lana* and Franciscan popular preachers the workers.

The *Lana* also policed entrepreneurs because, by using workers not under its control, members and interlopers could profit from substandard labour. This also touched the countryside because villages provided 'black market' labour. Things became very casuistical indeed. Preaching in 1304, the friar Jordan of Rivalto excoriated the bishop's attack on peasants weaving illegal cloth, because he intended aiding the poor. This Franciscan, however, inadvertently comforted the most voracious entrepreneurs. Since Florence's merchant bankers dealt in both international finance and wool and *Lana* partnerships, this corporation's struggles affected all Europe. Conversely, France's embargo on exporting raw wool and commercial paper to Italy during the battle between Philip the Fair and Boniface VIII affected Florentine political stability.

In the urban north, Flemish patricians had long battled artisans and labourers. Although prohibited, strikes were frequent, and, as early as 1242, patrician-ruled towns combined to prevent the emigration of workers seeking better conditions. From the 1280s into the early fourteenth century social and political troubles, both rural and urban, shook the whole area. The crafts tried to take over town government, thus annoying France, Flanders' overlord. Opposed by his independent town patricians, the count allied with the people and the English. A shortage of English raw wool in 1297 sparked risings in Douai and Bruges that toppled patrician government and led to the victory over the French at Courtrai in 1302. Although French authority was soon re-established, these conflicts began the persistent social combats that marred late medieval Flanders. In 1300 this was not yet perceived because, occasional violence aside, prospects looked good. If government increasingly intervened in the economy, the guilds invaded government, thus giving artisans a larger part in managing their communities.

Guilds even benefited journeymen. According to the Parisian

Book of the Professions, swordmakers were judged by six craft guardians, four masters and two journeymen. Journeymen officers among the bronzeworkers were two out of five. Journeymen fullers were still better off: two of the four guardians were journeymen, and in annual elections journeymen chose the guardian masters and masters the journeymen. At Douai the issues disputed by merchant drapers and the highly trained shearers were settled in 1229. The shearers agreed to forego the strike but kickbacks were prohibited and pay for work done was fitted to prices by a simple device. When prices rose, the shearers were to petition town-appointed inspectors to present their case to the town council; were they to fall, the merchant drapers were to do the same.

Craftsfolk tried to reduce working hours, and their efforts were modestly successful. Paris's *Book of the Professions* forbade night work in all but eighteen of the 101 crafts registered, citing lighting and the need for repose. Holidays multiply in any society, and in Paris by about 1300 obligatory religious holidays had risen to twenty-eight or thirty, giving, when Sundays are counted, about eighty days of rest annually. To this can be added anywhere from twenty to thirty half-holidays for lesser feasts and the Saturday half-holiday, favoured by the clergy as preparation for Sunday's observances. Each craft also had traditional holidays: the shearers at Arras took four days at Christmas, eight at Easter and eight at Pentecost. The average working week in the region from Paris to Artois has been estimated at four to five days. The year 1300, however, was not labour's time of bliss. Work days ran from dawn to dusk, with perhaps an hour off for meals. Hours varied seasonally, from seven or eight in winter to fourteen in summer, salaries being adjusted accordingly: Brussels' wool spinners earned twopence-halfpenny a day in winter, threepence in spring and autumn and fourpence in summer.

Guilds enjoyed ceremonial banquets, parades, inductions of new masters and gifts to charity. Members' funerals were subvented and free training given to sons of impoverished masters. Such services were tailored to particular needs. Some of Modena's smiths were wandering tinkers, and their statutes in 1244 therefore state that 'if anyone of the said association falls sick from the Alps to the Po and from Bologna to Parma, guild officers must bring him home . . . at the expense of the profession'.[31] The ordinances of the Parisian furriers of vair in 1319 required an entry fee of one shilling and sixpence plus dues of a penny per month. For this sick members received three shilllings weekly, three for convalescence and three more on returning to work.

Guild social service was supplemented by burial societies. Linked to the Church, these charities resisted entrepreneurial pressure better than guilds: when, in the late thirteenth century, the Florentine dyers' guild was quashed by the *Lana*, their charitable confraternity still remained. Churchmen's attitude toward these sodalities was mixed: it supported them in the early twelfth century; fifty years later it often questioned them. A council at Rouen in 1189 complained that churches were crowded with their altars. Similarly, those who made apostolic poverty into a labour ideology, like the Humiliati in northern Italy, were sometimes suppressed, as in 1178. By 1201, however, papal policy had changed and invited these and similar groups. Propagating Christian utopianism, the Humiliati were successful for a time, and at Florence in 1239 they had a community of brothers and sisters in the cloth industry. About the same time communities of female Beguines and male Beghards spread like wildfire through Flemish, French and Rhenish towns. In 1250 Cologne boasted about a thousand Beguines.

In time these movements weakened. Lay artisans objected to their competition, and the growth of secular guilds removed part of their reason for being. Although the mendicants favoured economic corporatism and aided charitable agencies helping artisans and labourers, the Church was not wedded to any one social group. Besides, if the humble got the charity, the rich played a role in the confraternities, being there, one suspects, in order to dominate. The utopian labour movement had outlived its usefulness, and was often driven out of business. Lay guilds obliged a synod at Arras in 1275 to prohibit Beguines weaving, dying cloth and cobbling, and two years later the Florentine Humiliati retired from industry. Although Beguinages persisted in the Rhineland and Low Countries well into modern times, they had become economically marginal. A petition of 1295 to the town council by the Brussels *Beguinage* requested the same return for their labour as the members of secular guilds had.

Princes also responded to the rising power of artisans and shopkeepers, and often encouraged guild creation, so much so that some towns in backward regions had more developed corporate structures by the mid thirteenth century than great urban republics. A reason was that princes' officers were often recruited from the nobility, a group suspicious of the new rich. To Joinville, a noble of vast wealth, the oppression of the poor by the rich amply justified Louis

IX's removal of the provostship of Paris from the merchant guild and its assignment to a royal officer, Stephen Boileau. This action was also applauded by crafts and trades who had fought the patricians since 1250, and they were rewarded by Boileau's publication of their guild ordinances in the *Book of the Professions* of 1261. Princes also often espoused the corporate principle, extending it into the political order. In 1257 the king of Aragon gave the crafts and trades the lesser half of Barcelona's great council's two hundred seats, the same percentage as that given the patricians, a lesser but swing vote being entrusted to the merchants. Urban republics were as yet reluctant to grant these elements such extensive representation.

Princes were not actuated by love of the poor because, loving only themselves, they were opportunist. When aristocracies dominated towns, princes supported the people; when the situation was reversed, they favoured the rich. When the commons seemed about to take over Barcelona in 1285, the king of Aragon crushed them brutally. In this time, however, kings usually supported guilds because patricians had led towns seeking independence. The merchant guild's loss of the right to farm the provost's office obliterated what little self-government Paris had had.

In urban republics guilds advanced more slowly but eventually attained the same heights, and in fact their corporatism became the constitutional basis of the State. By 1282 the Florentine government was run by the seven greater guilds: the medical and legal professions, bankers, and entrepreneurs' associations of the silk and woollen industries. By 1292 middling guilds, butchers and masons, and even some lesser ones had entered, only dyers, carders and other proletarian ones being excluded. The time was not propitious for further democratization, however, because, around 1300, the majority of the people had obtained much of what they desired. A significant minority, however, sometimes swollen by immigration from the countryside, remained deprived of economic and political fulfilment. Over a hundred years of intermittent social war passed before these latecomers, inspired by the century-long success of ascending lesser social groups, abandoned hope. Add a tightened economy to this tragedy, and some causes of the turmoil of the unhappy but inventive fourteenth century may be glimpsed.

NOTES AND REFERENCES

1   *Acts of the Apostles* 4:32–5

2   Georges Lefevre, 'Le trait 'De usura' de Robert de Courçon' 33, and 2 Thessalonians 3:10–12.

3   *Caesarii Heisterbacensis monachi ordinis Cisterciensis Dialogus miraculorum* 6, 5 (ed. Joseph Strange, Cologne, 1851), I, 352.

4   *De regimine principum 2, 3, 6 (Rome 1607), 36162.*

5   *Speculum ecclesiae, Sermo generalis ad mercatores* in *PL* CLXXII, 865. Honorius may have been from Autun, Canterbury or Regensburg.

6   *Decretum* 2, 33, 3 *de penitencia* 5, 6 in *CICan* I, 1241.

7   *Ibid.*, 2, 14, 3, 4 in *CICan* I, 735 and Deuteronomy 24: 19–20.

8   B.N. Nelson, 'Blancardo the Jew' in *Studi in onore di Gino Luzzato* (Milan, 1949) I, 115n.

9   *Exceptiones Petri* 2, 29 and 31, and also 1, 5 in C.G. Mor (ed), *Scritti giuridici preireneriani* (Milan, 1938) II, 115 and 54.

10   *Boncompagnus Boncampagni* in *BuF* II 167.

11   *Summa artis notarie* 1, 5 (*de locatio et conductio*) (Venice 1553), I, 123v.

12   *Speculum ecclesiae, Sermo generalis ad divites* in PL CLXXII, 864.

13   His *Flos testamentorum* in *Summa artis notarie* I, 226v–7r.

14   *Bullarium OESA* No. 116 in *Augustiniana* 13 (1963), 499 referring only to *usurae incertae*.

15   *Casus conscientiae Fr. Clari de Florentia* 30 in Bibl. Naz. Flor. ms B. VII, 1166 (Conv. Soppr.), 3Sr.

16   *Liber casuum conscientiae* 3, 3, III, 2a (ed. Dugauquier), 181, paragraph 213.

17   *Summa de poenitentia et matrimonio cum glossis Ioannis de Friburgo* 2, *de usuris* 5 (Rome, 1603, rprt), 231.

18   *Exceptiones Petri* 2, 15 (ed. Mor), II, 108 and *Digest* 7, 47, 1, 2.

19   Julius Kirshner and Kimberly lo Prete, 'Peter John Olivi's Treatises on Contracts of Sale, Usury and Restitution', *Quaderni fiorentini* 13 (1984), 268.

20   *Ibid.*, 269.

21   Emilio Cristiani, 'Note sulla legislazione antiusuraria Pisana (secolo XII–XV)' in *Bollettino storico pisano* XXII (1953), 13.

22   Heinrich Büttner, '*Frühmittelalterliches Städtewesen in Frankreich*' in *Studien zu den Anfängen des europäischen Städtewesens* (Lindau, 1958), 186.

23   *Verbum abbreviatum* 50 in *PL* CCV, 158 and Deuteronomy 23:19.

24   *Etablissements de St Louis* 1, 91 (ed. Paul Viollet, Paris, 1881), II, 148–9.

25   From his *Super codicis* cited in T.P. McLaughlin, 'The Teaching of the Canonists on Usury' in *Mediaeval Studies* 1 (1939), 92–3.

26   *De malo* 13, 4, 6 in *Opera omnia* XXIII (Rome and Paris, 1982), 256b.

27   *De regimine Judaeorum* 3 in *Opuscula philosophica*, 250b.

28   *Registres de Boniface VIII* I, 627, No. 1661.

29 Luke 6:35.
30 *Coutumes de Clermont-en-Beauvaisis* 51, 1539 (ed. Am. Salmon, Paris, 1900), II, 279–80.
31 P.S. Leicht, *Storia del diritto Italiano – Le Fonti* (2nd edn, Milan, 1943), 322.

PART THREE
Society

9

WOMEN AND MEN

MARRIAGE AND LOVE

Married women of all classes were often addressed in documents as 'mistress' (*domina*). Such was not the case with men: few, save notables, were addressed as 'mister' (*dominus*). Women's ability to give life made husband and wife equal, and in theory, like a man, a woman was free to choose her mate. Marriage therefore required no more than the free and voluntary agreement of a woman and a man along with consummation. Nuptials were customarily blessed in church, celebrated by a feast and a priest's blessing of the pair in bed, the place of birthing. The doctors of law at Toulouse around 1300 were asked: was a young woman who played, when bullied and tipsy, the 'game of man and wife', legally married? No, they found, because she had been tricked. In the Pauline texts glossed by churchmen, if a husband owned his woman, a wife owned her man. According to a Franciscan active around Paris, equality was needed in marriage. Gilbert of Tournai (d. 1270) urged couples not to marry for profit, beauty or lust.

> They should live together happily and honestly honouring God and generating children to serve Him . . . . When they are equals, they live in peace, but when they marry for a dowry or property, they always fight. If you wish to marry, marry an equal . . . . This is a social love . . . because the pair are equal partners.[1]

Because wives usually outlived husbands, marriage gave women a time of power: widowhood, when, unless she had grown sons, a woman acceded to authority over family, property and means of production. From noble to serf, however, everything depended on the liberties won from prince or seignior. Limitations aside, powerful middle-aged women appear in every class. A royal example is Blanche of Castile (d. 1252), mother of Louis IX of France, whose long widowhood and regency were a great success. She had, however, a weakness: excess of motherhood. She so dominated her son that he hardly dared lend his body to his wife.

Women also healed or, rather, nursed. A knight's widow from Puylaurens testified about the fall of Montréal near Carcassonne in 1240. When the French assaulted the walls, Ermengarda and 'other noblewomen' were carrying stones for the defenders' artillery. A clamour arose: the French had broken in. The women dashed into a house to take refuge, but, 'just as [Ermengarda] sat down, she heard it cried out in the square that her brother Isarn had been wounded. [She] straightway went out, hunting about until she found him.'[2] Although never university-trained physicians, women were midwives having a near-monopoly of childbirth. In hospitals women were almost as active as men, partly because physicians were not hospital members and also because hospitals were like monasteries, run by administrators, nurses and sometimes even inmates. A marriage contract involved the hospital of St Antoine at Toulouse in 1202:

> I John the hospitaler, marry you Sibil; and I, Sibil, marry you John and give my body to . . . the hospital to serve God and the poor . . . . I Raymond Calvet [master of the hospital] receive the said Sibil as sister and participant in the said hospital . . . [pledging] that I will receive no man or woman in the said hospital without their consent, and that John and . . . Sibil are to be the masters of the said house after my death and that of my wife Ricarda.[3]

Women have always been loved, but much depended on age and class. In the 1180s, Andrew the Chaplain recommended wasting no time on peasant girls; just push them over. Adam de la Halle (d. 1286–88) disagreed: his heroine was Marion, a peasant maid endowed with natural reason, courtesy and taste who rejected a rough knight in favour of her rustic Robin. Because magic, moralizers hastened to channel sex. Philip of Novara tells of a handsome young woman (twenty to forty years old in his scheme) who collected jewelled knives from her successive lovers. In middle age (forty to sixty) she began to buy love by surrendering the knives until none was left. Others were shrewder: sex and love were not enough for a happy marriage. Christian of Troyes' *Erec and Enide* linked sex, love, friendship and career to fulfil a marriage.

Christian's age created a positive cult of love in which lovers were truly equal. In woman's work like healing, Iseult is as competent as is Tristan in hunting and making war. She sacrifices as much and commits as many crimes for love as does he. Aucassin believed a commonplace that men love particular women while women love any useful man, but Nicolete showed him he was wrong: women's fidelity equals men's. Christian of Troyes Erec and Enide are made to rebuild mutual respect and love in their marriage by means of accomplishment. Enide undergoes tests of loyalty, courage and social wisdom, just as does her husband.

Love's cult was so mighty that it almost pushed sex aside. Perhaps echoing clerical ideas, the troubadour's 'love from afar', like humanity's love of God, expressed an overwhelming longing for the unattainable. In *Tristan and Iseult* the lovers have no home on earth, only in heaven. Captured by love's magic, they violate all social canons: marriage, friendship, family and loyalty to Church and king. This argument was refuted in *Aucassin and Nicolete* wherein the lovers triumph over family, religion (Nicolete being Saracen) and society to build anew true love, family and society. In its easy way, the poem echoed mystical teaching wherein the ability to love with the flesh gave evidence of a capacity to love spiritually.

Focused by monks, male ambivalence towards women was experienced as rarely before or after. The charm of a girl's figure and the lilt of her voice tempted both Peter Damian (d. 1072) and Peter, the hermit of Monte Morrone, elected Pope Celestine V in 1294 and canonized in 1313, and both converted their attraction into scatological rage. Philip of Novara was cooler. Carnality led older men, prompted by fear of death, to seek 'all sorts of unnatural perversions. Just as pride is the vice of the poor and covetousness that of the rich, so is lust the vice of the old.'[4]

Male complaints about women were sometimes plaintive. *Mahieu's Lamentations* argued before 1292 that marriage is harder and worthier than celibacy. Women are impossible: they talk too much. Why did the Saviour first show himself to women after resurrection? Because he wanted everyone to know about it fast. Why did Jesus not marry? He knew better. Celibates concocted the prohibition of divorce. Mahieu asked the Lord: your daughter Eve betrayed you; can you imagine what your wife would have done? The law is unfair: the Saviour ordered what He himself did not dare do. Capitulating, the Lord avows that married men will have a higher place in heaven because they have suffered more. He adds that He had sanctified the married state by allowing his mother to marry, 'but I did not tonsure the monks or constitute any monastic order'.[5]

Mixed feelings about the flesh were well-nigh universal, shared by both men and women. They ranged from flagellation to a cult of the body, the laity leaning towards the latter and the religious towards the former. James of Voragine believed it edifying to report that, when asked why he had not healed his daughter Petronilla, the apostle Peter replied that she was too beautiful to live. Still, physical beauty counted, even titillating blasphemously: by lifting her skirts, the virgin Nicolete miraculously made a sick man leap up off his bed. The clergy castigated the banners and shining armour of the knights, but Dante's *Convivio* urged men and women to dress well and cultivate beauty of body as well as of mind. The clergy themselves wrote much of the romantic literature of the time, but were of two minds about it. Surely hopelessly, a penitential of Peter Cantor's school distinguished between two types of public entertainers: 'Those frequenting drinking bouts and lascivious parties singing dirty songs are damnable . . . . Others . . . singing the deeds of princes and lives of saints, and solacing men in sickness and distress . . . can surely be borne, as Pope Alexander says.'[6]

Even clerks were of two minds. Writing for layfolk, the chaplain Andrew's *On Love* and John of Meung's later continuation of the *Romance of the Rose* flatly asserted the natural impossibility of celibacy. The layman Peter Dubois, John's contemporary, opined that celibacy had been instituted by the old and decrepit in antiquity. Besides, clerks were not as white as the driven snow. In Andrew's intentionally humorous dialogue between a lady and a gentleman (who happens to be a clerk), the latter argues that heavy petting is better than copulation because less likely to cause pregnancy. Both are forgivable, however, being 'natural' since love alone inspires virtue. 'I'll prove to you,' he says, 'that a clerk is a better lover than a layman because he is more prudent.' Unbelievable, replies the lady: knights are at least virile and clerks are disfigured by tonsure and 'as though clothed in female dress'. They can't even give lovers' gifts, she adds, because they shouldn't have anything to give. Who wants stolen goods?[7]

Peter Damian charged that heterosexual carnality led to homosexuality. Perhaps so, but a way of avoiding women is to be homosexual, and love among males is ventilated in the sources. Just after 1300, the inquisition of the bishop of Pamiers, who died as Bene-dict XII in 1342, discovered a gay 'defrocked' Franciscan and hanger-on at the newly founded 'university' in the small town of Pamiers and the young scholars with whom he had relations. This 'loser' also pimped for a prior and canon of St Sernin of Toulouse, a dignitary who used his book porters to meet intimate needs from time to time. The same testimony records a cobbler in Pamiers and a squire of the same persuasion in the nearby countryside. Perhaps the adepts of this minority divergence were obliged to congregate, hence come to town, for reasonably frequent contacts.

Judging from this, also, homosexuals gravitated to educational institutions where celibacy obtained, but celibacy did not necessarily inspire homophilia. Some time in the 1260s, testimony about forty-two of the monks in the monastery of Lézat south of Toulouse was recorded. Almost half were said to have been, or to be, sexually active. Three were merely defamed of having had relationships with women, three were said to have favoured female religious from a nearby house, and specific women were named in the cases of no less than fourteen. Eleven were said to have had issue, six being charged with having had specific children from specific women. Only two were described as given over to 'sodomy', a practice clearly considered a 'fault' by the monks. According to one, the charge that a prior named Hugh 'was a sodomite was repeated se-cretly . . . and was said out of envy and a desire to harm him.'[8]

To return to men and women, highly prized though it was, childbearing inhibited women. The exposure of unwanted children was prohibited and voluntary abortion was not only forbidden but risky and largely inefficacious. Birth control was effectively reduced to being a function of the ages at which union took place, modes of sexual intimacy between the sexes and the mistreatment by par-ents and servants of the very young, especially, to judge from later evidence, females. A second hardship for women were accidents in birthing and childbed fever which may have resulted in higher death rates among adult females than among men in spite of war, hunting, heavy labour and riding.

Childbearing also tied women to property and family. In farming populations, the need for labour encouraged trial marriage to see if a pair could have children. Especially among the wealthy, marriages were arranged by parents. Family solidarity and property impeded the freedom of lovers, of men almost as much as women, especially when a family was rich, noble or princely. Although the sources say very little about the private lives of kings and princes until Joinville wrote about Louis IX of France, the will to win drove a prince as mighty as Henry II of England to marry Eleanor of Aquitaine (d. 1204).

Although she bore him eight children, this princess was ten years older than her spouse and they were anything but a happily married couple. Another impediment to attaining the ideal was imposed by servitude and service. Although accenting uterine succession and hence showing the role of women in servile families, dependency impeded freedom because no serf could marry without a lord's permission. Within the aristocracy the same was sometimes true. When, after long service to both Henry II of England and his son Henry, William the Marshal's suit was pleaded before Richard Coeur de Lion on the grounds that his father had given William the heiress to the county of Pembroke, Richard exclaimed: 'By God's legs, he did not give her to him! He only promised to. But I'll give her to him all free, both the machine [the woman] and the land!'[9] Peter Cantor denounced such practices because they contradicted scripture: 'If any woman wishes to marry, let her marry in the Lord' – freely, that is.[10]

A final impediment was that women often married older men. Men of middling means waited until they had acquired or inherited property or businesses before marrying. Established older men, furthermore, were unlikely to marry women their own age, and therefore many women married spouses ten or twenty years their senior in their first marriages. The disparity in age also helps explain why women – teenaged children – were subjected to physical discipline by their husbands, but was not all bad. Unattractive and insecure young women did better in the market of the overaged than in that of the young. The marriage of a young woman to a failing older man at the peak of his wealth could lead to a kind of equality, especially if a propertied widowhood came to pass.

This kind of union did not attract poets or most young women and men. No romance has lovers who are not exquisitely young. There was fear here too: an old man will be cuckolded by a young wife, a theme seen as early as the eleventh-century poem *Ruodlieb* where an old spouse sits in a privy watching his wife and a young man through a knothole. More elegantly, Philip of Novara disliked this kind of marriage because 'for if [the male] has the desire, he certainly does not have the capacity'. Even marriage between old

folk was disgusting: 'Two rotting bodies in one bed are simply un-
bearable.'[11]

Theft compensated for lack of freedom. Joined to the religion of
love described above, adultery became central. To Andrew the
Chaplain true love could not exist in marriage and marriage was no
excuse for not making love. Here, however, all depends on luck
and especially wealth. No poet bothered to count Iseult's children,
and what may be passed off as love among the rich is bare adultery
among the poor. Or was (is) it? In Italian towns, the people often
loved the French, their songs, their manners and loose ways, and so
did young knights and patricians who 'lived nobly'. Those whom
'Gallicism' offended, even though they too had heard the siren
songs, were lesser gentlefolk, burghers and substantial farmers, those
with modest property and social ambitions. These worthies drew up
laws against sumptuous clothing and conspicuous consumption and
especially looked askance at adulterous love.

Being rich, the aristocracy was more broadminded than the
middle classes, but there were limits. Careers were more important
than love. In spite of professional ambition, Abelard (d. 1142) finally bit the bullet and married Héloise (d. 1164), but they could
not live it out. We know little about the child of this famous pair,
but he was raised back home in Brittany by Abelard's sister and
vanished into history saddled with a didactic poem by his father and
the awful name of Astrolabe. Adultery was always punishable in law
and husbands were sometimes allowed to slay lovers caught in the
act. Relationships involving a wife heading a household or court
with juniors disrupted social order and merited exemplary punishment. Not long before 1296 a Toulousan apprentice was conde-
mend to death for this offence, although being a minor below
twenty-five years of age was never executed. In 1314 a scandal
involved two gentlemen and two princesses at the court of Philip
the Fair of France, and resulted in the death of the two men and
the disgrace of the women. In southern France and elsewhere,
adulterers were often forced to 'run the town', nude amid the
howling crowd. It was nevertheless the town fathers who, at Toulouse, hobbled the prince's right to confiscate property by making it
impossible to catch anyone in flagrancy.

Lovers were not what these magistrates loved; property was. But
they also could not but have understood that love was fraught with
ambivalence. Two of chivalry's greatest heroes, Lancelot and Tristan, were the lovers of their king's wives. Translated from the

Arabic, the *Romance of Sidrac* averred that 'the hottest woman in the world is colder than the coldest man', and that wives had been unfaithful before and still brooks bubble and flowers bloom.[12] A southern French vernacular romance exhibits similar 'wisdom'. Because the king paid attention to his wife Flamenca, Archibald fell into a jealous rage. Constantly watched, the young wife was allowed out only to go to church. There she ran into a secular canon, literate, martial in bearing and background, polite and deeply sympathetic. Archibald had so busied himself with the king at the gate that he failed to watch the postern. One day, however, the lover blithely rode off to war, and this study of the inefficacy of rage came to a happy end.

MEANS, LITERACY AND RELIGION

Most brides came with a dowry from their family and received a smaller marriage gift from their bridegroom or his parents. These two parts together made up a marriage portion which, after the death of the husband, provided for the care of the widow. The administration of the portion was entrusted to the husband who, however, could act only with the consent of his spouse and of her friends. After the husband's death, also, a widow was often appointed manager of the estate until the children reached majority. To recuperate her portion, a widow had precedence over all other creditors of an estate.

A family owed a daughter with male siblings no other endowment than her dowry. Real property, means of production and professional preference went to male heirs, and the daughter's portion was often money. The lord of Isle Jourdain in Gascony west of Toulouse inserted a passage in his testament of 1200 designed to limit the number of heirs to his seigniories and properties. With the express consent of his lord, the count of Toulouse, present at the rendering of the will, the baron testated that 'if there is a legitimate male son, no woman or daughter will ever again have any portion of the said heredity, but instead the daughters will be married with money'.[13] This exclusion was made not only by magnates, but by members of every class no matter how high or low. The poet and lawyer Cino of Pistoia put it succinctly: 'In almost all Italy customs and statutes state that sisters with brothers do not succeed. Their fathers or brothers are therefore obliged to dower them according to the family's dignity and wealth.'[14]

Once married, a daughter, like a son, was emancipated, as the custom of Montpellier said in 1204. The system of dowries for brides together with marriage gifts brought by their young spouses had one great advantage: pairs were endowed when young instead of waiting for parents' deaths when both had grey hair. Besides, parental power was limited and burdened with responsibility. The duty of parents to support and educate children was almost sacred. Jurists agreed that magistrates could adjust the details of both divine and natural law, but they could not change essences. A pope, the commonplace went, could never dispense from scripture, nor a legislator from the duty of parents, especially fathers, to raise and educate children. In regard to daughters, parental duty was to see them married or placed, at smaller cost, in a religious order.

However excellent the system was, marriage portions did not suffice. A recent study of matrimony in Toulouse and cost of living in the first half of the thirteenth century lists about 136 wives, ranging from society's top to bottom. A third to a half of the widows there recorded had either to work or to make special arrangements with persons or institutions. Had the poor been fully represented in the sample, the percentage would surely have been far higher.

Although the value of woman declined with age, remarriage was a way of handling lack of means. But work was best. According to the Parisian mid-century *Book of the Professions*, widows of trades- or craftsmen carried on deceased husbands' professions if they did not remarry out of the craft. In marriage contracts, working women arranged to have their share of joint acquisitions returned on their husbands' deaths. Evidence from later times shows that women were a significant part of the labour force. In 1179–82 the 'brothers and sisters' had equal rights in the turners' guild at Cologne. Parisian guild statutes indicate that some crafts were wholly female and that women, especially widows of craftsmen, could be admitted to the mastership in some woollens guilds. Where guilds participated directly in town government, women even played a minor role in political life. In Provins in the mid-fourteenth century, twelve per cent of the voters in a political plebiscite were women.[15]

Although women's work in field, barn and garden is to be added to the above, their labour failed to persuade contemporaries that they were equal to men. Part of this was caused by the different bodily endowment of the sexes. Women did not normally plough, hunt or do heavy metalwork or building, and hence crowded into less profitable labour. They also rarely went to war except to urge men on, help them plan for it and lament or rejoice in their departure. Maiming and killing was what war was about, and size counted. Some women were, however, suited to it. Although guildswomen usually provided substitutes for watch and ward, Wismar on the Baltic in 1292 boasted one *domina* Adelaide, who pledged herself 'to serve watch as long as she lives just like any other citizen'.[16] Soldiering, however, was not women's business: giving life was their role, not giving death.

Male size also explains why husbands beat their wives. Beaumanoir had thrice heard of wives slain by their husbands for adultery, and recommended that, if a woman misbehaved or refused to obey a 'reasonable command . . . a husband may chastise her reasonably'.[17] Giles of Rome took from Aristotle the sentiment that men dominate beasts, males females and adults young. Women were ruled because they 'normally lack men's prudence. There are some who are more intelligent than men, but that is rare . . . and hence women ought naturally be subject to men.'[18] Women were also believed to be more inclined to flinch than men. Writing on criminal law, Albert of Gandino (d. 1310) remarked about judicial torture that, if it is to be applied to a father and child,

> begin with the child in the sight of the father, because the latter will then speak up more quickly . . . . Likewise, first torment women . . . because, being of greater constancy, men will confess more slowly, but women are quicker because their hearts are momentary and unstable.[19]

In banking and moneylending, physical strength mattered little, and women were in business. Once restitution for usury was enforced, women's testaments restoring 'ill-gotten gains' appear. Even in these fields, however, women were disadvantaged. Law discriminated against them, adjudging their testimony inferior to men's, and businesswomen had to pay for legal counsel to speak for them in court. This was partly because women were rarely as literate as men and were therefore treated in law as dependants, almost as children.

Some were literate, however, partly because, although excluded from sacred orders, women were active in both orthodoxy and heterodoxy. Between 1245 and 1251 no less than thirty-two female convents were incorporated into the Dominican order in the German province alone. At Strasbourg in 1257 twelve cloisters housed about three hundred sisters, and many laywomen were associated with the new mendicant orders. Convents, although inspected by male clergy, were self-governing institutions with elected abbesses. Even at peak, however, there were far fewer female religious than male. Unlike monks who usually had Latin, moreover, nuns often had only the vernacular, though some were distinguished in Latin letters. Dying in 1179 as abbess of Rupertsberg, Hildegard of Bingen was not only famed for visions but was also an indefatigable traveller and correspondent with theologians, emperors and popes.

The clergy were of two minds about women's intellect. Giles of Rome remarked that, because of their weak endowment with reason, they surrendered to their passions more easily than men. This Austin friar would surely have enjoyed the opinion of Humbert of Romans. Glossing the apostle Paul, this Dominican put it thus:

> I do not permit women to preach for four reasons. First is their lack of intelligence which they have in smaller quantity than men; second is the subjection imposed on them; third is that, if a woman does preach, her appearance will provoke lust . . . and fourth is the memory of the first woman who . . . taught but once and turned the whole world upside down.[20]

Literate or not, laywomen were to stay out of religious debates. Esclarmunda, sister of a count of Foix, widow of a lord of Isle Jourdain, witnessed a legal document in 1198, something never done by her sex. But even this exceptional princess, when speaking up during a discussion between the orthodox and heterodox at Pamiers in 1207, was abruptly told by a monk to be quiet and look to her spinning.

To others, however, the picture was different. Addressing the nuns of Godstow, Archbishop John Peckham of Canterbury (d. 1292) repeated the worn sentiment that, the more fragile their sex, the more worthy their virginal penitence. Some did not condescend, however, and knew that there was iron in women. Does not scripture report that weeping women adhered to the crucified Christ more firmly than his fleeing disciples? This quality had inspired Robert of Abrissel (d. 1117) to found the order of Fontevrault (rule adopted in 1115), whose abbess supervised two convents of professed religious, one female and the other male, as well as two houses of lay sisters for those sick in body (lepers) and sick in mind (fallen women).

Saints' lives and clerical biographies show that mothers frequently pushed their sons towards the ecclesiastical life. Saying that women

heard sermons more regularly and went to confession more willingly than men, the Franciscan preacher Berthold of Regensburg told
no secret. Everybody knew that women were more devoted to
saints' cults and more credulous in regard to miracles than men.
Humbert of Romans loved the 'flaky' quality of female devotion.
Decrying clerks who refuse to study scripture because they can
make no sense of it, this Dominican urged them to imitate

> matrons and devout women who do not cease from daily reading the psalms
> merely because they do *not* understand them. Indeed . . . sacred scripture, even
> when not understood by readers, has power against spiritual wickedness, just as
> do the words of enchantment against the serpent, even if the enchanter does not
> understand them.[21]

Men led the Church, but the true believers were especially women,
sometimes embarrassingly so as Dominicans in the Rhineland felt
when their female houses and tertiaries multiplied enormously.

Like the clergy, however, women were famed not only for belief
but also for manipulativeness. Belief's function is therefore to be
examined. Perhaps women profited from, and even stimulated, the
hostility of the two worlds of men with which they dealt: the
clergy and the laity. Exercised over women, a layman's power was
immediate, sexual, deployed in greater physical strength, and practical because it involved property and the maintenance or abandon-
ment of children. The clerk's authority was at a remove, rarely
sexual and, in regard to the relationship of women to husbands and
lovers, idealistic, even unreal, as when it insisted on those Pauline
texts that proclaimed the freedom of women to choose their mates,
and, within marriage, asserted their equality with their husbands.
Clerical judgment, in fact, often affronted practical experience. It is
therefore no surprise that women peopled the clerical order with
chosen sons and enthusiastically seconded their erstwhile children's
practice of winning their battles with the laity by means of sen-
timental obfuscations or appeals to the miraculous. To force the
argument a trifle, women were never more practical than when
they were at their most credulous.

The Latins were convinced that their women were better off
than their Islamic and Jewish sisters. A theme well represented in
Caesarius of Heisterbach's often brutal stories was that Jewish girls –
to him, incidentally, they were often exceptionally pretty – wished
to marry Christian boys or have them as lovers. In his scheme for
conquering the Near East, Peter Dubois argued that Muslim men

would be entranced by that superior product, the educated western girl, and claimed that eastern women, held in the bondage of polygyny and purdah, would welcome crusaders. Peter was a warrior in the long battle between Heleno-Roman monogyny and Near Eastern polygyny, an institution that had spread widely in late antiquity and the early Middle Ages, and was only in this period again beginning another decline. The Latins proudly claimed that divorce on a husband's initiative was impossible among Christians, asserting also that women did not attend mosque or synagogue and that no attention was given to their education.

The daughters of gentlefolk and patricians often learned vernacular letters at home or in convents. According to the Dominican Jordan of Saxony (d. 1237), Dominic of Osma founded his first house at Prouille in 1206 partly because the gentry in the Midi could not pay for orthodox convents and sent their daughters to the Cathars for education. In 1320 four of Brussels' ten lower schools were for girls. One is therefore not surprised that Mary of France who wrote her *Lays* at the Plantagenet court from 1165 to 1190 was a major poet, and that biographies of females were among those of the troubadours published in the late thirteenth century.

For layfolk in general, however, learning was a waste of time in view of women's duties around the crib and the hearth (not to speak of the fields and workshops), duties that, except among the rich, were far more onerous than today. Women were also excluded from the literate professions, partly because these had evolved out of the clerical order and long retained clerical qualities. There were exceptions. When sick the canonist John Andreae (d. 1348) is said to have had his daughter Novella lecture his students, although he veiled her from them by a curtain. Female teachers of vernacular letters are heard of in towns and so are scribes, but women did not attend the university and guilds of notaries excluded them.

A sure proof that women were less considered is that they were poorer on average than men. A tax list for Toulouse dated 1335 shows that women were 8.7 per cent of the heads of household but their share of the wealth was only 6.3 per cent of the total. Relatively illiterate and poor, then, women, especially those of the lower classes, made out not only by work but also by using their attractiveness. Concubinage was common in this age. In the countryside south of Toulouse in the 1240s, one even sees an unmarried woman describing her lover as *her* 'male concubine'. Still, it can be shown that most concubines were female and both poorer and younger than their men. Rural gentlemen had mistresses from the families of their farmers and town patricians from among the humble. An example is Berengar Astro of Toulouse who had two legitimate children by his wife and a son from his mistress Saussia, with whom he lived. Late in life, Saussia was married off to a man of her class and had two legitimate daughters by him. Named John, Berengar's natural child used his father's family name, married a wealthy widow and died in or before 1246.

A yardstick of a concubine's position is the treatment of natural children. John Astro came from a clan whose women were do-wered with 1,000 to 1,500 shillings; his father left him only 500, a sum paid by his legitimate half-brother only when dying. True, on the highest level natural children did well, especially female ones, perhaps because they could be dowered without affecting family office and property. Male illegitimates were excluded from inherit-ances, but it was not always easy. In late 1259, litigation erupted between a lord of Isle Jourdain and his cousin-german, the lord asserting that the latter had no right to inherit 'because you are not a legitimate heir of the barony. You are the son of a subdeacon who was prior, canon and archdeacon in the cathedral of Tou-louse.'[22] What is odd about this long drawn-out case is that the mother of the noble lord of Isle was the much-respected India, natural daughter of Count Raymond VI of Toulouse (d. 1222).

Prostitutes were more discriminated against than concubines. Statutes against ostentatious lewdness, prostitution, gambling and other street disorders are seen everywhere. Wishing to 'out-pope' the pope in regard to 'moral' matters, Louis IX and his brother Alphonse of Poitiers (d. 1271) were hard on this profession. The latter even rescinded the traditional right of his provost in Poitiers to protect prostitutes in return for a fee, and when doing so gratui-tously called the women 'stupid'. Social need, however, led princes and magistrates to listen to Augustine's warning: every palace has its cesspool, and whores are necessary lest men fall into even 'worse vices'. A lawsuit at Montpellier of 1285 noted that the town's pros-titutes had often been harassed by their neighbours. Acting on the advice of the town council, the royal governor ordered that

> the said women should reside on the [outlying] street commonly called Hot Street . . . [and promised] to the advocate in the court for Guirauda of Bziers and Elys of Le Puy there present, and to each and every prostitute now living or

wishing to live in this town, that the said women . . . will remain now and always under the protection of the lord king and his court.[23]

Once permitted, prostitution had to be regulated and the retirement of personnel provided for. Innocent III thought it meritorious of laymen to marry one-time prostitutes, and a number of orders specializing in them, like the German sisters of Mary Magdalene (founded 1225), appeared. Usually associated with hospitals where the 'reformed' women worked, these 'repentant sisters' were characteristic of the state-regulated prostitution in the late medieval town.

To conclude, although women were obviously often happy and fulfilled, the judges who wrote the code called by Bracton's name borrowed a truism from the Italian jurisconsult Azzo who flatly said: 'Women differ from men . . . because their condition is worse than theirs.'[24]

NOTES AND REFERENCES

1   D'Avray and Tausche, 'Marriage Sermons' 47 (1980), 114–15.

2   My *Men and Women at Toulouse in the Age of the Cathars*, 120.

3   My 'Charity and Social Work in Toulouse' in *Traditio* XXII (1966), 248n.

4   *Des quatres tenz d'aage d'ome* 4 (ed. Marcel de Fréville, Paris, 1888), 95.

5   Langlois, *La Vie en France au moyen-âge* II, 277– 83.

6   Gauthier, *La chevalerie*, 656.

7   *De amore* 1, 6, G (ed. E. Trojel, Munich, 1964), 189–90.

8   My *Men and Women at Toulouse in the Age of the Cathars*, 51.

9   *Histoire de Guillaume le Maréchal* (ed. Paul Meyer, Paris, 1891–1901), v., 968ff.

10 1 Corinthians 7:39.

11 *Des quatres tenz d'aage d'ome* 4 (ed. Fréville), 95.

12 Langlois, *La Vie en France* III, 250.

13 My *Men and Women at Toulouse in the Age of the Cathars*, 29.

14 His *De nuptiis* in Mayali, *L'exclusion des filles dotées*, 47.

15 Félix Bourquelot, '*Un scrutin du XIVe siècle*' in *Mémoires de la société nationale des antiquaires de France* XXI (1852), 455ff.

16 Wachendorf, *Die wirtschaftliche Stellung der Frau in den deutschen Städten* 32.

17 *Coutumes de Beauvaisis* No. 1631.

18 *De regimine principum* 1, 2, 7 (Rome, 1607), 65.

19   *Tractatus de maleficiis* 12 in Hermann Kantorowicz (ed.), *Albertus Gandinus und das Strafrecht der Scholastik* (Berlin and Leipzig, 1926), 158.
20   *De eruditione praedicatorum* 2, 12 (ed. Berthier), II, 406, and 1 Timothy 3:4.
21   *Expositio regulae Beati Augustini*, Ch. 142 (ed. Berthier), I, 429.
22   My *Men and Women at Toulouse in the Age of the Cathars*, 78.
23   A. Germain, 'Statuts inédits des Repenties du couvent de Saint-Gilles de Montpellier' in *Mémoires de la Société archéologique de Montpellier* 5 (1860–9) 124–6.
24   *De legibus et consuetudinibus Angliae, introductio* (ed. S.E. Thorne, Cambridge, Mass., 1968) II, 32, citing Azzo's *Summa* on the *Institutes*.

10

WORKERS

FARMERS

Latin Europe's social orders were often described simply. There
were three: clergy, warriors and labourers. A Dutch saying sourly
described them, saying:

> I pray for you,
> I fight for you,
> I lay eggs for you.[1]

Poverty and malice, preached the Franciscan Berthold of Regensburg, made peasants into 'naked' fish devouring each other.
Some thought farmers little more than 'stinking serfs', as the poet
and lord Bertrand of Born said. Manualist of chivalry, Raymond
Llull casually stated that nobles protected 'society because, for fear
of being destroyed by knights, the people . . . cultivate the land
and, terrified of soldiers, fear kings and princes'.[2] The Italian prelate
and townsman Giles of Rome likened rustics to 'barbarians, quasi-
forest folk, who do not know how to govern themselves and are
therefore natural slaves'.[3]

Rural folk were not always disparaged. In the early twelfth century, Honorius praised them: 'What about farmers? Most will be
saved because they live simply and their sweat feeds God's people' –
a sentiment later repeated by the Dominican Vincent of Beauvais.[4]
The poet Adam de la Halle's *Robin and Marion* has a knightly bully
defeated in love by a gentle peasant boy. The theologian Peter
Cantor asked who is wise, the rich, lawyers or men of letters?

None of these; the wise man is the farmer. But this wisdom rested on a fragile base.

Farmers ranged from free to slave, and the origins of this inequality interested contemporaries. In his customs of the Beauvaisis, Beaumanoir catalogued the causes of servitude. Poverty or the incapacity to bear arms had caused some persons to be given to saints and the Church, and others to be oppressed by the powerful. Some slavery resulted from capture in war, a belief that rang true in a time when captured Muslims were enslaved. These ideas came from Roman law where people were either slave or free. This dichotomy was not always considered accurate. Although tempted by Roman theory, the English author of *Fleta* admitted that, although true 'in law', it was not so 'in fact'. Less pedantic, Beaumanoir stated that servitude had many conditions – hard, light, sometimes personal and sometimes attached to tenure.

This fuzziness was caused by the social organization of the time. Since late Rome, free and slave had been coming closer. Humans were viewed as parts of a regulated society in which all were bound to service, rich and powerful and poor and humble. Each person had a function or duty and each an appropriate reward. The Church advocated this sociology, its spokesmen paralleling heaven's hierarchies with those of the world, saying that true liberty was service to God, Church, prince and people. In 1103, for example, Cluny's monks called their serfs 'rustics who, liberated from the yoke of servitude, have been bound to the service of the blessed Peter'.[5]

Although already old, the seigniory with its relative independence from kings and great princes was still being implanted in frontier regions. Although usually also a landlord, a seignior was the head of what was, in effect, a small state. This state was one or more villages or a substantial town with dependencies, like Montpellier under its dynasts, all named William. Ideally, a lord's powers included economic rights over forest and uncultivated lands, and common facilities like mills and wine presses. He usually protected a church or churches and nominated their clergy. He commanded and judged the community's inhabitants, and, with understandable exaggeration, Beaumanoir said barons with fiefs in the county of Clermont exercised all justice, civil and criminal.

The seigniory erased the line between slave and free because lords governed all inhabitants. It mattered not from whom they held their land or to whom they were bound. Words like 'rustics' and 'labourers' replaced terms that more exactly delineated a person's particular tenurial or personal situation, and phrases such as Beaumanoir's 'men of the seigniory', embracing both free and servile elements, seemed apposite. An imperial peace ordinance for Bavaria in 1152 stated that rustics were to carry bows not swords or lances, nor, free or servile, were they permitted judicial duels. Clothing was to be grey or black, and none but nobles was to drink wine. Taxes, like the seignior's tallage, and community services or labour were generalized. The free became subject to marriage taxes and were obliged to sue in seigniorial courts, losing the right to appeal to royal or regional courts. In France the term 'villein' soon designated any village inhabitant, free or servile. In England, where the seigniory was not so developed, it referred only to dependent members of manorial households.

Levelling was never complete. Common in parts of France and northern Italy, it was unusual in parts of Germany, England and Spain. The seigniory was there faced by vigorous central governments protecting the free because justice was profitable, but that also had the effect of freezing servile groups into place. A result was that Europe boasted a wide variety of social structures. In Scandinavia and sections of northern Germany, where the seigniorial system was only beginning to penetrate, the free were numerous and independent but slavery was still to be seen. In intermediary zones like England and much of Germany, slaves no longer existed, although deep servility marked peasants in villenage. Parading young villeins for the lord to cull for domestic service was an annual event in English manors. On the other hand, England's monarchy arrested the decline of the free, who customarily attended the hundred court, one at least formally royal. The same obtained in parts of Germany, but the weakening of the Empire led to the growth of the seigniory in the west and south.

Even where seigniorial authority was deeply rooted, however, the community rarely embraced a whole village, and some inhabitants were still designated as servile, excluded from community membership. Villeneuve le Roi had been granted the free custom of Lorris in 1163, but in 1246 Louis IX freed 326 rustics there. Administrative officers, often recruited in the village, formed a group apart and so did clergy and local knights. Craftsmen were deemed so necessary that they were sometimes held in bondage after ordinary farmers were freed. Although rustics performed guard duty and went to war, they were, as the texts had it, an 'unarmed multitude' in comparison with knights. A Bavarian peace ordinance of 1244 allowed them to bear arms only when 'defending the fatherland', pursuing criminals or parading on the village's patron saint's day. The *Exchequer Book* attributed theft, homicide, adultery and other crimes to the innate drunkenness of England's peasants, and Beaumanoir coolly described rustics' rights as 'what they have of freedom'.[6]

When aided by the beneficent economy described earlier, seigniorial uniformity led to an awareness of common interests. Liberty was most advanced in parts of France and Italy where the seigniory won its earliest victories because, although there was solidarity among nobles vis-à-vis superiors, they competed savagely among themselves. Each seigniory was a jealous little state whose ruler tried to multiply the number of his citizens. Older communities were weakened by freedoms offered in new ones, and although the old often wished to recover fugitives, new ones defended them. A Franconian Rhineland peace ordinance of 1179 provided that a lord with 'a man whom he claims as his serf . . . must plead his case before the judge of the village [where the fugitive resides]'.[7] Nor was this easy: in Alsace such a lord was required to bring seven close relatives of the fugitive on his mother's side to prove the case by oath. In short, competition among seigniors made the old saw 'town law makes free' almost as true of village as of town.

Greater lords found profit in granting freedom to those in the bondage of lesser ones, and, outside of the royal domain, France's kings sold liberty. Stirred by franchises won by the town of Laon and five villages in the nearby commune of Bruyères, fourteen villages grouped around Anizy le Château owned by the bishop and chapter took advantage of an episcopal vacancy in 1174 to buy a commune on Laon's model from the king. A newly elected bishop revoked this grant, and a war ensued in which the town of Laon, a royal monastery and the villagers were defeated by the bishop and local barons. The king then sequestered the bishop's temporal. Fearful for the balance of power, England's king and his allies in Hainault hastened to force France to revoke the commune in 1179. Similar events transpired in 1185, when Philip Augustus granted the right to a new commune. After much peasant emigration, Anizy won her liberties in the mid thirteenth century, and several other villages of the group won theirs shortly thereafter.

That the kings of France were not disinterested lovers of liberty is shown by their grudging grants in the royal domain. A lengthy legal battle between Ste Geneviève of Paris and the inhabitants of Rosny sous Bois began in 1178 when the chapter obtained a royal charter asserting the farmers' servile status. Rosny carried its suit to the higher authority of Rome, and over the years no fewer than five popes supported it. Too remote to be efficacious, papal power failed, and the peasants 'voluntarily' disavowed free status in 1226. Such were the times, however, that by 1246 the village was freed in exchange for an annual tallage of sixty pounds.

Although reluctant to free their own serfs, townsmen usually supported peasant liberty for mixed motives. Italy's urban republicans wanted villages to share their system. Rural enfranchisements were rounded out by general ones like those of Vercelli in 1244 and Florence in 1289. Typical of their imagery, when Bologna freed the remaining rustics of her county in 1256–7 six thousand names were inscribed in the citizens' registry called the *Book of Paradise*. There was exploitation here as well. Townsmen also wanted to rupture seigniorial jurisdictions impeding their rule of the countryside, and besides, often wasted little love on farmers. Giles of Rome recalled Aristotle's saying that the wise should govern the stupid: '[Rustics] lack intelligence and hence are to be ruled by others . . . . Following this opinion, [town] citizens, being more prudent and intellectual, have the right to wage just war against rustics if they refuse to be subject.'[8]

Countryfolk wanted to limit what they owed their lords. In 1208 new settlers at Ntre Dame of Paris's village of Braye were, 'like other villagers, to have suitable equipment to go with the lord of Braye or his sergeants on campaign . . . with this proviso, that they return home each night'.[9] They also wanted to fix or abolish fiscal charges. Among these were fines of justice, especially the lord's right to confiscate property for high crime. Taxes or inhibitions on transmitting property were aimed at. Typical was mainmort at Orly near Paris, where it originally meant the ecclesiastical lord's right to dispose of a peasant's property at death. Mainmort had become a tax on inheritance, and by 1252 a witness testified that it meant that 'if anyone were to die without an heir of his body, his property would go to [the lord], otherwise not'.[10] The ultimate liberty was mobility: to marry freely and leave a community. A clause in the liberties of St Bauzeil near Foix in 1281 shows part of this. 'If an inhabitant wishes to leave the said town in order to reside elsewhere, unless he has committed a manifest crime

. . . we give him free power and licence to go wherever he wishes with all his property.'[11]

Lords were reluctant to grant such privileges, however, because they weakened or even destroyed their little states. In 1258 a lord of Montgaillard near St Gaudens provided that 'we enfranchize and manumit all our serfs living in the said village as long as they remain in it. If, however . . . they leave, by that act they revert to their pristine servitude'.[12] In Lorraine, Austria and Bavaria, lords of overcrowded communities encouraged serfs to move to nearby towns or villages in return for annual remitments, but were reluctant to let the free go. When founding new villages, moreover, lords sometimes prohibited the settlement of farmers from their other communities.

Franchises were usually recorded in customals or charters whose publication became common in regions like northern Italy, Provence, parts of France and the Low Countries during the twelfth century. Customals were relatively rare in Germany between the Rhine and the Elbe and in England even in the next century. Each area experienced cycles. In the Seine basin near Paris, new communities gained them during the twelfth century, but older communities benefited only from 1245 to 1275. The movement was strong around towns and in areas of new settlement, such as eastern Germany. In the mountainous and lightly populated county of Comminges sixty villages won charters from 1202 to 1300. Franchises were not homegrown; many, if not most, emulated town constitutions. Between 1160 and 1303 the laws of Louvain were adopted by many villages in south-east Brabant, and, in their respective areas, the laws of Liège, Douai, Namur and St Pol had the same success. Although inspired by urban models, some were products of princely legislation. Such were the liberties of Lorris of 1155, adopted by royal foundations in the Isle de France, and those of Beaumont en Argonne of 1183, issued by the archbishop of Rheims and eventually adopted by about five hundred villages, mostly in the Champagne.

Some inhabitants rose faster than others. In 1233 in the village of Pasignano outside Florence, of the seven gentlemen holding of this monastic seigniory five were knights, and of these the most consequential was the 'noble knight Mister Tolosano'. His family was first seen in 1130, when his grandfather, a smith, acquired property in freehold. By 1156 the cash rent of his holdings had been fixed, and in 1202 the abbot enfranchized Tolosano's father. In 1233 his relatives in Pasignano included a smith and several humble farmers, and at nearby Poggibonsi a lawyer cousin. Nor was this exceptional. Durand Blanot, whose brother was a peasant, was a sergeant serving Cluny's monks at Voranges in the Mâconnais. His first son enfeoffed land to a knight and educated a son at Paris. This boy became a master and canon of Ntre Dame, finishing his career as judge for the archbishop of Lyons from 1274 to 1287. Born about 1220, Durand's second son went to read law at Bologna, returning to enter the duke of Burgundy's service. Knighted by the duke, he acquired the liege fief and seigniory of Uxelles in 1268, thereby replacing a fading baronial family.

Although work and moneylending were the bottom rungs on the ladder of rustic advancement, arms, law and the Church were the next. England's church boasted at least three prelates of peasant origins: Robert Grosseteste, bishop of Lincoln (d. 1253), Robert de l'Isle of Durham (d. 1283) and John Peckham, primate of Canterbury (d. 1292). To Philip of Novara clergy and chivalry were the most worthy and profitable professions. Through arms, one could rise to empire, and

> by the clergy it has often happened . . . that the son of a poor man becomes a great prelate, and is rich and honoured, and becomes the father and lord of him who was lord of him and his; and rules and governs everyone, and can even become pope, and be father and lord of all Christendom.[13]

Some hated this, and one such was Werner der Gaertner, a monk of Ranshofen around 1250, who wrote about a peasant named Meier Helmbrecht who was corrupted by war, grew his hair long like a noble, drank wine and wore a sword. Pride went before Meier's fall. In an age when it was profitable to make free men and women, however, clerks often relegated to second place doctrines of service, hunting instead for texts to prove the usefulness of liberty. Some were found in Roman law, where the basic notion was that, in nature, equality and freedom ruled. Ulpian said: 'In the law of peoples, slaves are considered as nothing, but not so in natural law, because in natural law, all men are equal,' a text echoed by all the lawyers.[14] Some believed that humanity's pristine liberty could be restored. A prologue to an emancipation in Castelsarrasin in 1268 reads: 'In nature all men are free, but the law of peoples made some slaves. Because a thing easily returns to its nature, however, learn that we, moved by piety . . . freely manumit our serf.'[15]

Using Roman law, Rolandino Passaggeri has a master grant his dependants 'all right of patronage, restoring their ancient birthright and freedom in law, calling them Roman citizens and finally returning them to the primeval law in which all men were born free.'[16]

In Bracton and *Fleta*, the law of peoples had not destroyed humanity's natural freedom, only obscured it. Boncompagno of Signa wrote: 'No one is said to confer liberty but rather to strip off a veil of servitude by which freedom is cloaked.'[17] Enfranchizement was more than restoration; it was also innovation. When the Florentines removed the last traces of servitude in their county in 1289, the harangue began:

> Because liberty, in which the desire of each man depends on his own will and not on that of another, and by which cities and peoples are defended from oppression and their laws improved, and because freedom is much honoured by natural law, we, therefore, wishing not only to maintain but also to increase it, declare . . . .[18]

As in the English codes cited above, freedom is the natural faculty of each person to do what he or she wants.[19]

When the priors of Florence spoke of an increase in liberty in 1289 they were referring to the notion of progress, the 'renovation to the better' seen in the mass. In the *Saxon Mirror*, Eike of Repgow dismissed as worthless attempts to find a biblical justification for slavery, concluding 'that man belongs to God and anyone who takes possession of him sins against the power of the Omnipotent'.[20] In 1311 the king of France enfranchized the bondsmen of the Valois, observing that, 'as beings formed in the image of our Lord, men ought generally be free by natural law'.[21] Two years earlier a royal scribe had copied a model manumission from a monastery in Soissons:

> Since our Redeemer . . . wished to assume human flesh so that, by his divine grace . . . he could restore us to our pristine liberty, it is right that those whom nature created free in the beginning and the law of peoples placed under the yoke of servitude should be restored by the benefit of manumission to the liberty in which they were born.[22]

To these ideas may be added pride of nation or race. Many peoples claimed descent from Rome's founders, Aeneas and the Trojans, and both French and Germans asserted they were Franks. Claiming Lyons for France in 1307, the lawyer Peter of Belleperche

(d. 1308) opined that it had been the ancient capital of the Gauls, a people who changed their name to Franks when they threw off the yoke of Roman servitude. A royal ordinance of 1315 began:

> According to natural law all men are born free, but by certain usages and customs long introduced and maintained to the present in our kingdom, and perhaps because of their predecessors' crimes, many of our common folk have fallen into the bondage of servitude . . . which much displeases us, we, considering that our realm is called the kingdom of the French, desiring that the fact truly accord with the name . . . have ordered that. . . .[23]

Emancipation accompanied economic growth and seigniorial competition, and, being paid for the liberty they gave, emancipators profited. A count of Joigny freed a family in 1328, and did so

> in remuneration and pure guerdon of good and agreeable services, gentilities and kindnesses that they have given . . . and still assiduously do daily without ceasing . . . in pure and special grace, by God and in pure charity and piety . . . and for the sum of 200 in cash.[24]

Money was not everything, however: 'Tis heaven to see others happy when one is happy oneself.

Earlier chapters noted that increasing friction marked the relationship of landlord and tenant around 1300. Seigniors grasped their remaining prerogatives more firmly, enlarging them whenever possible. All rural populations were affected, but not all equally. Some villages had been so completely freed that seigniorial authority could not be restored and within others individuals had risen too far to be reduced. Such divisions exacerbated social divisions in areas where the seigniory had once brought about a measure of social fusion.

The new distinctions rigidified partly because those already free wanted to distinguish themselves from their less fortunate brethren. An illustration is the term 'bourgeois'. Often earlier employed to describe settlers in new villages, it was now restricted to village notables, notaries, merchants or well-to-do farmers. Intellectual formalism was also fashionable, and jurists tried to fix each man and woman in the systems they created. They expatiated on Rome's indelible servitude and used Roman phrases like 'men of the body' for those owing service. Even a governor little touched by the schools like Beaumanoir divided the rural population into three groups: gentlemen, the free of the seigniory and serfs.

The schools' influence was not wholly baleful. *Fleta* notes that, according to the law of peoples, masters had the right of life and limb over slaves, but that Roman law had deprived them of this. The custom of Burgundy allowed those in 'servile servitude' to disavow their lords if threatened with death or lack of maintenance. Not that serfs had it easy. A Freising lawbook of 1328 tells us that masters who killed serfs with swords or clubs were to die, but flogging was different. If a man died the same day, the master was liable; thereafter he was not, because people were rarely whipped to death, and besides, terror was needed to get work out of serfs.

A further beneficial result of the study of law was the formulation of distinctions between 'liberate servitude', 'servile servitude' and slavery. Beaumanoir defined the serf's 'estate':

> There are several states of servitude. Some serfs are so subject that lords can take whatever they have . . . and, rightly or wrongly, imprison them as long as they wish, being held to answer only to God. Others are treated more gently because . . . lords can require nothing except the taxes of their servitude unless they misbehave.[25]

The taxes were rent, tallage, inheritance dues and fees for marriage. Beaumanoir then observes that these happy serfs are to be found in France, especially in the Beauvaisis; the others in foreign lands. He was not inventive. Robert of Curzon had earlier contrasted serfs in France with the slaves of Apulia and Sicily who were, he said, bought and sold like cattle. The word 'slave' to define this rare social category was being adopted by Italian and French jurists from the Empire during the thirteenth century.[26]

TOWNSMEN

Townsfolk were not wholly free of servitude. Early in the thirteenth century around Namur they were never called 'freemen', a term there restricted to nobles, and the same was earlier true in much of northern France. A reason was that trading and manual labour were thought inferior to administrative, martial and clerical activities. When England's William the Marshal accosted a runaway monk with a noble damsel, he was not perturbed by their irregular liaison, but confiscated their money on learning that they were going to town to put it out at usury. The *Treasury Dialogue* said that a freeman who wanted to trade or lend money became nothing but a merchant. Such a 'degenerate knight or other freeman should be punished by another than the common law of the free'.[27]

Key words like 'bourgeois' and 'citizen' designated not only town dwellers but villagers as well. Urban battles for liberty were similar to those of the villages, and rivalry between seigniors helped towns advance. In 1152 a monk lamented that the citizens of Vézelay, 'abjuring their legitimate lord [the abbot], allied with a tyrant [the count of Nevers] . . . to create an execrable commune . . . casting the yoke of ecclesiastical liberty from their necks'.[28] Both townsmen and villagers tried to lessen charges, tallage and forced loans, quartering, hospitality rights, inheritance and marriage controls and military service. Like a village's, Lübeck's inhabitants of 1163 were to defend the town but were excused from outside expeditions. In 1223 the countess of Nevers surrendered mainmort to her subjects of Auxerre so that 'their heirs and successors . . . should possess . . . their parents' inheritances without trouble or tax'.[29] If the principle of 'town air makes free' was upheld more vigorously in towns than in villages, it was restricted there also. In 1191 a lord confirmed the liberties of Landrecies, but specified that none of his own serfs should be admitted there.

Town and village also differed, money being more common in towns. The annual tallage paid by each villager at Busigny in 1201 consisted of a measure of oats, a loaf of bread, a hen and sixpence; in 1191 the citizen of Landrecies gave a shilling for his burgher right and fourpence for the lord's tolls. Everything was on a larger scale in town. Fishing villages provided smacks for service; towns offered warships. In 1191 the crown of Sicily allowed Gaeta to cut its military assessment from two galleys to one, save for the general defence of the kingdom. What was social in a village became political in town. In Burgundy a maltreated serf could abjure his lord. In 1282 the federated towns of Stendal, Tangermunde and Osterburg in Saxony gained the right to seek another lord if harmed by theirs. Townsfolk's liberties were won more rapidly and were greater than those of villagers.

Distinctions between town and countryfolk gradually sharpened. By the thirteenth century the word 'labourers' had lost inclusiveness, being now applied only to farmers. The term 'bourgeois' spread widely to describe townsfolk, being restricted in villages to those professional or rich persons who did not live like farmers. When the jurist Alberic of Rosate posed the question 'who are to be called citizens and who rustics?', he answered: 'They are called citizens who were born in a city [or town] . . . they are called rustics who were born in a village, hamlet or castle.'[30]

Most towns initially consisted of several nuclei, a princely, comital or episcopal walled town, for example, a recent merchant settlement and agglomerations near monasteries outside the centre. Sometimes aided by their lords who wished to weaken enclaves of independent seigniorial authority, townsmen gradually integrated these more or less independent segments. Once a unified community sense had emerged, however, princes and lords changed their minds. Fearing Parisian unity under its merchants' guild, France's kings maintained the independence of no less than five jurisdictional areas in town and suburb, including those of the royal monastery of St Germain des Prés and the Temple.

The formation of a social community created a measure of equality and common membership. Citizenship was obtained by birth and retained by sharing tax and defence burdens. It was also extended to newcomers, after a suitable wait, who participated in common duties. Communities also exiled persons for crime or political reasons. Citing the glossator Accursius, Alberic of Rosate defined exile as a 'kind of expulsion from the common good; hence, in a certain sense, a secular excommunication'.[31]

Equality was rarely complete. Leaving aside clergy, most towns began with at least three social elements: an administrative cadre, at once martial and rarely averse to trade; a merchant group, privileged, as were Jews, to travel; and artisans and other workers, even agricultural ones, who were sometimes in manorial servitude. All owed service to prince and community, knights being better remunerated than others, and artisans humbler than merchants. In the early twelfth century, the old relation of artisan to merchant could still be seen in Germany. Merchants there often derived liberties from, and owed service to, higher lords, even the emperor, than did artisans, who depended on a local lord or church. The unification of merchant and artisan was therefore expressed by the latter acquiring the liberties, especially mobility, possessed by the former. In 1120 the founding charter of Freiburg in Breisgau specified that all inhabitants were to be merchants and enjoy the merchant power. Although this use of the term 'merchant' persisted in frontier urbanization, it was usually replaced by either 'citizen' or 'bourgeois', words referring to all members of the community, mercantile or not.

Common citizenship, the condition of being bourgeois, was accepted in regions of rapid urbanization around 1150, but elsewhere the struggle for a unified social community still went on. The lord included in the liberties of Auxerre granted in 1223 a passage reading: 'I manumit altogether and perpetually those other citizens of Auxerre . . . who are not of free condition, so that, the opprobrium of servitude being wholly removed, they may freely leave and return whenever they wish.'[32] Few western towns of any size, however, contained many inhabitants in seigniorial servitude. Some were wealthy, of course, and others poor, but this did not vitiate the principle of equality before the law. A provision in the statutes of Avignon in the 1240s provided that 'the good carpenters are of no worse condition than any others of this city'.[33] The phrase 'good men' used in the early thirteenth century to designate individuals in any social group, elevated or humble, reflected this desire for social equality.

More difficult to assimilate than the humble were the prince's or seignior's officers. Before 1100 such servitors everywhere lived in town and ranged from toll collectors to sergeants, knights and even substantial notables, like viscounts. They also often combined different functions. The 'proud knights' of Puy in central France whose towers were levelled by the bishop and people in 1102 operated the town mint; an élite, in short, both military and monetary. Such service groups gained freedom at different times, and some evolved into nobilities. At Worms in 1190 the town council consisted of twenty-eight bourgeois and twelve ministers. By the thirteenth century, the latter semi-servile officers had become knights or nobles. Some ministerial groups became bourgeois. At Cambrai the ministers claimed their offices and emoluments were hereditary. In 1135 the dispute between them and their episcopal lord was arbitrated. Those who held fiefs were given them hereditarily; those without forthwith became bourgeois. By 1205 even the superior ministerial group had moved toward the bourgeoisie, being termed 'sergeants of the bishop of Cambrai who are merchants'.[34]

As Salimbene of Parma remarked, nobles in northern France lived in the countryside, whereas in Italy they lived in town. He was right, but modern historians have elevated this observation into a difference between northern or Germanic towns and Mediterranean or Italian, the latter supposedly being 'classical'. Even in this Franciscan's time, however, things were more complex. In Italian Savoy and Sicily few towns boasted noble citizens, and such was also rare in Castile and western Iberia. Nor was the northern frontier clear. Many Rhenish and south-west German towns counted knights among their citizens. Zürich's council was composed in 1127 of 'ministers and citizens' and 'knights and citizens' in 1225 and Oppenheim's in 1287 was evenly divided between knights and burghers. Although knightly citizens were rare in Flanders, northern France and the Low Countries, nobles exempted from town jurisdiction often resided in cities. Sometimes, as in St Quentin or Bourges, they lived in the old nuclei thereby showing that they had once been part of the community.

One might think that, when towns were large and powerful, nobles were citizens. Size alone, however, was not enough. In south-west Germany and Languedoc urbanization was relatively light, yet knights were citizens. In Flanders, where great cities lay thick, nobles did not often live in town, and when they did, were rarely citizens. What helps explain such differences is the capacity of princely government in the period up to 1200. Weak little states were found in southern and eastern France and, in the Empire, political control was feeble in a wide belt reaching from northern Italy up the Rhone and the adjacent Alpine areas to the valleys of the Meuse and Rhine. Princely policy was based on the principle 'divide to rule'. When nobles lived in town, princes often bolstered distinctions that separated them from the other denizens. The Emperor Henry VI's privilege to Florence in 1187 surrendered much but insisted on the knights' exemption from communal taxes, and a similar provision was included in the Capetian privilege given Noyon in 1181. Princes tried to prevent knights from living in town or serving as citizens. In the statutes granted Abbeville in 1184 the count of Pontivy stipulated that 'the bourgeois . . . may not receive in their commune any of my vassals or anyone having a free fief in my domain'. Nor were rural seigniors allowed to join communes, as they often wished to. In 1179 the count of Troyes expressly ordered that 'no castellan living near Meaux may join that commune save with my permission'.[35] Frederick Barbarossa's edict for Trent forbade its citizens to force anyone to reside in town or compel 'those who live outside in open or fortified villages to be subject to their power and jurisdiction'.[36]

Where towns grew rapidly and central government deteriorated, these inhibitions failed. The best examples are found in Italy, in Lombardy, Venetia, the Romagna and Tuscany, although other regions boasted some success. Knights there domiciled in town profited from the faltering of the emperor's power to lead their communities to political freedom. Cities also often obliged rural seigniors to join. At Reggio in 1169 a rural magnate and numerous lesser knights confessed themselves citizens, pledging to reside in town for four months each year in wartime and two in peace. A Sienese statute of 1262 listed a hundred county families obliged to maintain domiciles in town. In short, even though knightly aristocracies long retained privileges, they had been integrated into the community. In 1164, when the Lombard League was formed against the emperor, town ambassadors pledged the support of all inhabitants, excepting only clerks, criminals, madmen, the mute and the blind.

Where towns were weaker or local princes retained more authority, townsfolk reacted differently. Unable to assimilate nobles domiciled in town or oblige rural ones to live there, town fathers sought either to exclude them altogether or restrict them to certain parts of the town. All domiciled at Noyon in 1181 save clerks and knights owed taxes and military service, hence knights were too privileged to be citizens. In the midst of his French wars, England's King John (d. 1216) promised Rouen's citizens that knights would not spend more than one night in town except at the king's express command or because of illness. The founding charter of Freiburg in Breisgau of 1120 proposed that 'no ducal minister or knight will live [there], except with the inhabitants' consent'.[37] Cityfolk even made a virtue of necessity by prohibiting intermarriage between themselves and nobles, as in the founding charter of Lbeck in 1163 and the custom of Cologne. Although the exclusion of nobles in parts of northern Europe weakened urban political power, it also created an ethos of bourgeois self-consciousness that was to be of great significance later on.

Once attained, unity began to weaken. A reason was the rise of the 'people' and social corporatism. In the thirteenth century, class, guild and professional affiliation began to replace old individual citizenship. At Toulouse, constitutional documents had usually referred to the citizens simply as the 'good men of the City and Bourg', the two parts of the town. In 1226, however, an edict described the citizenry as knights, burghers 'and other good men', and a contemporary poem as 'the knights, bourgeois and commonalty' or 'the knights, bourgeois and artisans'.[38] These distinctions penetrated private documents around 1250: before that, knights and burghers were not identified as such; after that, notaries were careful to do so.

Demarcating function, style of life and wealth, social position became all-important. Vital of Canyellas, a jurist and bishop of Huesca, defined the word 'bourgeois' just before 1250:

> Citizens are those who live in cities or towns equal to cities; of which group those are called burghers who, although they have masters and workers through whom they exercise professions, do not work with their own hands. There are, however, some who, although they do use their hands, are not excluded from the order of the burgesses, such as cloth merchants and moneychangers, and especially lawyers, medical doctors, or surgeons, and others equal or superior to these.[39]

Well-to-do townsmen believed that trade or work with the hands was demeaning, but these worthies did not have it all their way. When the 'people' rose in Italy and the Low Countries, artisans were proud of their blue nails and rarely lost an opportunity of maligning those they called 'the idle'. Besides, nobles looked down on bourgeois. Raymond Llull said:

> Almost all crafts- and tradesmen want to be bourgeois or want their children to be. But there is no estate so perilous as that of the bourgeois, nor that lasts so short a time . . . . No man lives so short a life as the bourgeois. And do you know why? Because he eats too much and does not exercise enough . . . . No man is so annoying to his friends as a poor bourgeois, and in no man is poverty quite as shameful as in a bourgeois. No man gains so little merit or enjoyment from the charity he gives as does a bourgeois.[40]

Nobles not only scorned them, they feared them. James of Vitry told townsfolk that their

> communities or rather conspiracies . . . oppress their neighbours violently. If thieves and usurers are held to restitution, how much the more should these violent and pestiferous communities be held to it because they . . . weaken neighbouring knights and steal the jurisdiction of their men from them.[41]

As towns grew, a quasi-noble aristocracy emerged from the bourgeois: the patricians. Often busy in business, they acquired rural properties and intermarried with the nobility from whom, indeed, some of their ancestors had sprung. They built lineages contrasting sharply with modest middle-class and artisan families, whose substitute was their guilds. As described in an Avignonese document of 1251, they were 'honourable bourgeois who are accustomed to live as knights' and who went to war armed as such.[42] Such were found not only around the Mediterranean, but also in the Low Countries, northern France and western Germany. In Metz in the late thirteenth century eight dominant lineages were divided into about 220 individual families totalling about a thousand members. Such wealthy clans had poor relations. A cloth finisher was a son-in-law of the distinguished Colon family, and a daughter of the knight Gervase of Lessy had married a baker.

As noted above, the urban rich were not only businessmen but also acquired land, the most secure of all investments. In northern and central Italy the acquisition of farms by bourgeois or town knights served to tie countryside to city. Elsewhere, where towns had extended power only over limited regions, this ambition hurt them. Having rural properties, patricians often withdrew from citizenship and, while continuing business in town, contributed no taxes and service to the community whence their wealth derived. The financial stringency afflicting northern French cities in the late thirteenth century was caused by this, but the problem had existed earlier. In 1197 the crown granted Roye 'that townsmen who . . . acquire fiefs, thereby becoming noble, and are not knights should either become members of the commune or vacate the town'.[43]

Facing marked social differences, a judge's problem was no longer to make the punishment fit the crime but instead to make it fit the status and means of the criminal, a matter to be studied later when examining law. Furthermore, just as growing social complexity had produced a far above the average burgher's standard of living, so it had also created a proletariat. Composed of youths, recent immigrants and other marginal folk, this group was only slowly and never completely absorbed into the inflexible structure of trades, industries and professions. Such persons grew in number during the economic tightening around 1300, posing a threat of delinquency or civil violence. Especially severe corporal punishments were therefore devised for these 'vile' or 'base persons' without regular employment and of bad habits. Paradoxically, urban growth had created such diversification of social status and wealth that the old vocabulary of equal citizenship no longer suited the town. The demise of equality, furthermore, signalled the weakening of the community solidarity that had enabled towns to win so many victories over reluctant princes.

NOTES AND REFERENCES

1   Lousse, *La société d'ancien régime* I, 103.
2   *Livre de l'ordre de chevalerie* (ed. V. Minervini, Bari, 1972), 130.
3   *De regimine principum* 2, 3, 15 (Rome, 1607), 385.
4   *Elucidarium* 2, 18 in *PL* CLXXII, 1148–9.
5   Duby, *La société . . . dans la région mâconnais*, 248.
6   *Coutumes de Beauvaisis* 45, No. 1451 (ed. Salmon), II, 233.
7   Heinrich Mitteis, '*Stadtluft macht frei*' in *Festschrift Stengel* (Münster, 1952), 352.
8   *De regimine principum* 2, 3, 7 and 15 (Rome, 1607), 365 and 385.
9   Verriest, *Institutions médiévales* I, 157.
10   Bloch, *Rois et serfs*, 30.
11   Verriest, *Institutions médiévales* I, 226.
12   *Ibid.*
13   *Des quatres tenz d'aage d'ome* 15 (ed. Fréville), 10.
14   *Digest* 50, 17, 32 and *ibid.* 1, 1, 4 and *Institutes* 1, 2, 2. The phrasé 'law of peoples' translates the Latin *ius gentium*.
15   Bloch, *Rois et serfs*, 150.
16   *Summa artis notarie* 1, 7 (Venice, 1583), I, 157v, a gloss on *Digest* 1, 1, 4.
17   *Boncompagnus Boncompagni* 5, *BuF* II, 155–6.
18   Villari, *I primi due secoli della storia di Firenze*, 190.
19   All used *Digest* 1, 5, 4: *libertas est naturalis facultas eius quod cuique facere libet, nisi si quid vi aut iure prohibetur.*
20   *Sachsenspiegel* 3, 42 (ed. C.W. Gärtnern, Leipzig, 1732), 409.
21   *Ordonnances des Rois de France de la troisième race* XII, 387.
22   Bloch, *Rois et serfs*, 154, itself derived from Pope Gregory I's Letter VI, 12 in *MGH Epp. sel.* I, 390.
23   *Ordonnances des Rois de France* I, 583.
24   Bloch, *Rois et serfs*, 136.
25   *Coutumes de Beauvaisis* 45, Nos. 1451–3 (ed. Salmon), II, 233–6.
26   The term derived from Latin *sclavus* for Slav.
27   *Dialogus de scaccario* 2, 13 (eds. A. Hughes, C.G. Crump and C. Johnson, Oxford, 1902), 146.
28   Guilhermoz, *L'origine de la noblesse* (1902), 385.
29   Verriest, *Institutions médiévales* I, 223.
30   *De statutis* 2, 177, 17 in *TUJ* II, 49ra.
31   *De statutis* 4, 1, 9 in *TUJ* II, 66ra.
32   Verriest, *Institutions médiévales* I, 223.
33   *Coutumes et règlements d'Avignon* 208, No. 158.
34   Ritter, *Ministérialité et chevalerie* 86. The word 'minister' translates the Latin *ministerialis*.
35   Both in Ennen, *Frühgeschichte der europäischen Stadt*, 261.
36   *Ibid.*, 257.

37   Ennen, *Frühgeschichte der europäischen Stadt*, 260.
38   My *Liberty and Political Power in Toulouse* (1954), 378.
39   *Los fueros de Aragón* (ed. Gunnar Tilander, Lund, 1937), 380.
40   *De doctrina puerili* cited in Langlois, *La vie en France au moyen âge* IV, 353.
41   *Sermo II ad burgenses* in A. Giry, *Documents sur les relations de la royauté avec les villes de France* (Paris, 1885), 146.
42   *Coutumes et règlements d'Avignon* 269, No. 16.
43   Ennen, *Frühgeschichte der europäischen Stadt*, 257.

11

NOBLES AND SOLDIERS

SOLDIERS

As in city militias, soldiers were of two kinds – horse and foot. Although not in the vernacular, in Latin the word for 'horseman' had gradually come to mean 'soldier' (*miles*), thus showing that mounted troops had become more valuable than infantry. Because the military also headed secular government, the ample range of the soldiery embraced all of the 'feudal' hierarchy. Beneath titled nobles such as counts and viscounts came Flanders' and England's barons, sometimes called 'rich men', Castile's 'rich men', Limousin's 'princes', Burgundy's 'castellans' and Lombardy's 'captains'. In the *Usages* of Catalonia whose provisions on these matters date from the late eleventh century, viscounts were valued as equal to two *comtores*, four vavassors or sixteen knights. A knight was estimated to be almost 500 times richer than a rustic, and rode and ate white bread. At Toulouse in 1128–35, the value of the war-horses given the Temple by a group of worthies ranged from 1200 shillings to 240, with an average of 528. In brief, cavalry in the early twelfth century ranged from heavy to light in terms of mounts and equipment.

This broad group was also divided by status. To be termed 'noble' initially meant to be 'free', and relatively few members of the martial order were nobles. In the 370-odd villages of the county of Namur in the mid-twelfth century, only about twenty families were noble. Beginning in the eleventh century first in France and Italy, however, magnates and afterwards knights gradually became free. This meant that they held their fiefs or salaries hereditarily and paid no taxes except aid: ransom for their lords, dower for their daughters and for knighting their sons. Judged by peers, they also limited the court or military service they owed, in northern France the usual obligation being forty days of free military service. Well into the twelfth century, however, past memories were alive. When Louis VI freed his sergeants (the word means 'servant') in Laon in 1129, he specified that they were free to become clerks, knights or burghers. In the 1180s the book named after Glanville still claimed that a peasant, when emancipated and knighted, was free only vis-à-vis his master and other peasants but not those of any other social order. The compilation named after Bracton in the next century maintained the contrary.

Past servitude still meant much to knights. They owed an expensive and dangerous service, and, like farmers under manorial law, were not usually allowed to alienate the property held as salary for their labour. Young men of military family, moreover, were attached for training to the courts of princes and barons from about the age of fourteen, becoming members of the household. Great princes had large households. In a tournament at Lagny on the Marne in 1180, young King Henry, son of Henry II of England, fielded twenty-seven Normans, twenty French, twenty Flemings, fourteen English and six Angevins. Baronial households were smaller. In 1166 Walter Waleran of Wiltshire owed the king twenty knights, eight of whom were household. Composed of young men trying to please their masters to get brides and lands, households were the élite of a medieval army. Just as lesser knights relied on them, great nobles still depended on kings for the transmission of their fiefs in spite of hereditary right. The ameliorations they wanted are seen in England's Great Charter of 1215. After a general statement on ecclesiastical liberty, the next seven rubrics dealt with wardship and inheritance, fixed inheritance taxes, required suitable guardianship for minor heirs and shielded widows from forced remarriage.

Strong though the service ethos was, all Italian, French and English knights were noble or free in the period with which this book deals. Ideologically, the Peace of God and the Crusade helped this improvement in knightly status because churchmen insisted on the soldier's dignity, and enhanced their argument by creating the military orders. In Brabant nobles never assumed the knightly title until the Temple and Hospital entered the duchy around 1175. More practically, the enfranchisement resulted from the decentralization or devolution of government. During that long process, princes, faced by restive magnates, built personal followings of quasi-servile soldiers. At the same time, they encouraged their magnates' followers to seek for themselves the liberties their masters were winning. The battle between magnates and princes gave simple soldiers opportunities to advance.

The armed militia's salaries had become hereditary and privileged. In urban republics, to compensate for expensive armour and horses, nobles were exempt from some taxes. In Arles in 1205, knights paid only the tithe on their property, others both tithe and tallage; in Pistoia they paid the usual town taxes, but their rural holdings were exempt from the hearth tax. When, moreover, their fiefs and salaries had become heritable, they tried to extend this protection to all family property, no matter how acquired. By the late twelfth century, therefore, society began to forbid alienating property to knights.

Nobles, including knights, imposed their will on the State partly because of the power of large family alliances. As a group of soldiers, nobles and knights came under the protection of their own law, the 'law of the camp' as the Romans had put it. Even later in Italian republics, litigation between military families was settled in courts of their peers. In princely and baronial courts, assessors chosen from among the litigants' peers arbitrated most lawsuits in the twelfth century, decisions being guaranteed by the relatives of the parties and often described as a 'peace' or 'pact'. Family power long upheld customs like compurgation, oaths taken by clan members asserting a member's veracity, and the judicial duel, though rare in practice, was well attuned to the spirit of the martial aristocracy. Beaumanoir's chapter on war largely concerns private war or vendetta, another mark of this group.

Family and marital alliances set the social tone of nobles and princes. Wars, like those between Plantagenets and Capetians in France or between the Welfs (Guelphs) and Weiblinger (Hohenstaufen or Ghibellines) in Germany and Italy, were partly conflicts between rival families. Poetry treated the conflict of family and State. Charlemagne was slow to proceed against Ganelon when charged with treason and Roland's death because his mighty family swore for him, and divine judgment in trial by battle was called on to settle the matter. Bernier's vassal's duty to his lord, Ralph of Cambrai, was in conflict with his love of his own family, the latter's mortal enemies.

Family size and cohesiveness varied vastly, and rested on two pillars: siblings sharing common interests and marriage linking two patrilineal families. Aristocratic clans were therefore constellations of small groups built around two patrilineal nuclei, those of the two spouses. That the system could mobilize numbers was seen in 1273 at Tournai when a patrician renounced his son before the town fathers because the youth had breached a truce. Seventy co-jurors of his lineage joined him, as did fifty-three of his wife's. The system, however, was not rigid. In *Raoul de Cambrai* two combatants withdrew because they realized they were not closely enough related to the principals.

Because of clientage, also, more than blood links counted. In places as far from each other as Lorraine and Tuscany, families formed associations partly of blood and partly of social alliance. Boncompagno of Signa's *Cedar* reports that clubs or gangs were common in urban Italy, their names reflecting aristocratic aspirations: the Falcons, the Lions, the Round Table. He was referring to the tower societies of noble or patrician lineages. A Florentine clan in 1180 linked thirty male heads of family with seven different surnames to build a tower in Por Santa Maria. The Corbolani clan of Lucca in 1287 embraced a minimum of sixteen households with an elected governing council. As in Italian skyscraper cities like San Gimignano, towers characterized the noble and patrician style.

The emancipation of the martial aristocracy was not complete in Germany where, in spite of the blows dealt the Empire during the Gregorian age, a quasi-servile knighthood dependent on the emperor or his greater ecclesiastical and secular vassals was still in place. In the mid-twelfth century to be noble meant to be free; to be a minister or soldier implied servility and sometimes peasant origins.[1] Ministers owed military and court service and also tallage and servile marriage taxes. As late as 1263 Sophia of Velturns, daughter of a great Swabian minister, was enfranchized to marry a free lord, and although her eldest son was to share her husband's freedom, subsequent ones were to be ministers. Although ministerial offices and benefices were not hereditary, some ministers, especially imperial ones, rose high. Werner of Bolanden served the Hohenstaufen from 1160 to 1190 in wars with the prince prelates of Mainz and Trier. At his peak he governed seventeen castles and towns, almost 1,100 knights owed him service and he held lands from forty-six different lords. Another great minister was the Markward of Anweiler, upon whom, in 1195, Emperor Henry VI conferred 'freedom, investing him with the duchy of Ravenna, the Romagna and the march of

Ancona'.[2] The Markward died in 1202 as regent of Sicily and guardian of the future Emperor Frederick II.

An Englishman, Gervase of Tilbury (d. after 1211), served the Empire as marshal of the kingdom of Arles in the late 1190s. He reports that Henry VI changed the German system and adopted that of the English and French, thus making knightly fiefs hereditary. Just before and after 1200 a basic change did occur in much of the Empire. In Repkow's *Saxon Mirror* (1215–35), an enfranchized minister was not noble; in the *Swabian Mirror* (1274–5), he was. The change is also seen around Namur, where in the mid twelfth century to be a noble was everything. By the mid thirteenth century the knight's title had so appreciated that, in lists of witnesses, dubbed knights preceded unknighted nobles. More, the title 'Mister', once accorded only to nobles, was given to knights from about 1220.[3] This was gradually accompanied by the acquisition of hereditary right to their fiefs and salaries, and the withering of servile restrictions.

Reinforced by French influence, the knightly title in the Rhineland stood above that of the minister. In parts of Swabia, however, ministers ranked higher because of their close connection with the Hohenstaufens, and in Austria a minister was a grand seignior. Only around 1240 did lesser knights begin to become free, and some became burghers or even yeomen farmers. Variations marked even small areas: knights were ahead in Brabant and Liège, but ministers around Namur. At Namur around 1200 only nobles and prelates had seals, symbols of jurisdiction and legal capacity. The ministerial cadres began to adopt them in the 1220s, and the first example of a knight's seal is of 1249.

The freedoms gained posed problems. Servile holdings were less divisible than free, because lords wanted viable economic entities. Partition, therefore, affected mainly free peasants, and the same was true of knights. As long as service was ministerial, subdivision was not a threat; as freedom spread, it was, but was also cushioned by economic expansion until the *rallentando* after 1300. War and 'natural' loss also helped, pruning heir groups. Of the seven sons of a castellan of Bourbourg near Guines, two entered the Church, two died accidentally and a fifth was blinded in a tournament. The two brothers who successively acquired this inheritance produced no male heirs surviving beyond 1194, when the seigniory fell to a granddaughter. Long-continued subdivision weakened families, however, and knights sometimes became farmers with tastes too elevated for their purses. In 1287 ten men and women gave homage to the bishop of Clermont Ferrand for the castle of Murat de Barrès.

To diminish the number of heirs, daughters with male siblings were given dower money for marriage or Church but no real property. The governments' desire to retain knightly militia service, as in England and France from the 1180s, also helped limit heir groups. Methods of single succession to an inheritance, sometimes primogeniture, were widely adopted in the thirteenth century. In his testament of 1202 a Gascon lord proposed that the oldest male was alone to inherit the main family property, the town and barony of Isle Jourdain. Around 1200 the great castellans in the Mâconnais began to adopt single succession, especially primogeniture, and knights imitated them later on. Nobles also pressed offspring into the clergy and careers in law and arms with ever greater insistence.

Difficulties aside, Europe's martial order had reached the point where knights were usually both noble and free, and to be knighted meant to be ennobled. Kings and princes now vied to enter knighthood. In 1248, the year of his election as emperor, William of Holland was knighted by the king of Bohemia with these words: 'I ordain you knight and joyfully accept you as a member of our college.'[4] Although knighting normally took place around the age of twenty-one, princes were often dubbed earlier – Henry III of England at the age of nine.

KNIGHTHOOD

To churchmen, the duties of the martial order were similar to those of princes, themselves warriors. Honorius addressed them: 'Soldiers! You are an arm of the Church, because you defend it against its enemies. Your duty is to aid the oppressed, refrain from rapine and fornication, repress those who impugn the Church with evil acts and resist the rebels against priesthood.'[5]

Clerks were censorious. Alan of Lille said that nowadays knights 'are not soldiers, but rather robbers and ravishers; not defenders but rather invaders'.[6] The commonplace was: burghers were usurers, nobles plunderers. And soldiers did fight for money. Bertrand of Born, enemy of Richard Coeur de Lion, poet and lord in Limousin, gloried in spring because war began again. Barons, he thought, were generous when war forced them to enlarge their households. Tournaments were training for soldiers, and could be awful: a meet between Burgundians and Englishmen at Châlons in 1274 was fought with war's ferocity. Violence was lessened by favouring single and small-group combats instead of large engagements, but they were still anathema to clerical rigorists, the first Lateran Council in 1139 having denied Christian burial to those who died in them. This law was unenforceable, however, because tourneys also gave young nobles a chance of gaining reputation and money, since victors got prizes. Having begun his career in this way, England's William the Marshal came to the deathbed, and his chaplain there intoned that, to attain heaven, what has been taken by force must be returned. The marshal said to a squire:

> Henry, the clerks are too hard on us; they shave us too closely. I took five hundred knights whose weapons, harnesses and horses I kept. If God's kingdom is closed to me for that, nothing can be done, for I can't give them back . . . . Either their argument is false or no man can be saved.'[7]

The master of the Temple attended William's agony and the archbishop of Canterbury delivered his funeral oration!

Philip of Novara said that 'good knights, by renown, valour and deeds, often attain great wealth and conquest'.[8] An Italian treatise on government has a young knight say that man's greatest glory is won by virtue in arms: 'The memory of those whom fame reports worthy in arms lives long after their passing, and, as poets' histories and eulogies in French clearly show in books long since spread throughout the world, their names are not lost to posterity.' His older opponent in the town council lamely replies that 'I'd rather be worthy in learning than in arms.'[9]

Churchmen urged knights to eschew earthly glory and seek heaven's. Philip of Novara fits his doctrine of profit and fame to the idea that, like St George, soldiers are Christ's holy martyrs, arguing that saintly fame outlasts emperors' because of the yearly feast in the ecclesiastical calendar! One clerical idea, however, appealed to soldiers. In 1128 the Templars swore: 'I will imitate the death of my Lord, because as Christ laid down his life for me, so am I prepared to lay down my life for my brethren.'[10] This brotherhood of arms was lauded by John of Salisbury – indeed, by everybody.

The bourgeois also questioned the martial order. What offended them was the nobility's pride and indifference to ordinary morality.

The speed with which gentlemen rode through the crowded streets of Italian towns provoked protest. And what about Geoffrey of Bruyères, lord of Karytaina in Morea, who, just when the Byzantines rose against the Latins in 1252, went off to Italy with the wife of the lord of Catavas, the prettiest woman in all Romania? Whatever others thought, Geoffrey's peers greeted him with cheers when he returned. Boncompagno of Signa tells why nobles fell into debt:

> Frequent hospitality for reason of courtliness, standing as guarantors for their friends' debts, gifts given in praise of war, seditious plots, lawsuits, tournaments, marriage settlements, love making, dicing . . . borrowing at usury, gluttony, drunkenness, negligence, violent contentiousness and improvidence.[11]

Rich lords at tourneys or 'courts' rivalled each other in ostentation. An exaggerated report of a meet held by Raymond VI of Toulouse at Beaucaire on the Rhone in 1174 claimed that one lord used wax candles for cooking, another drove twelve ox teams to sow the fields with 30,000 shillings, and yet another burned thirty horses. In the *Romance of the Rose*, John of Meung has the lover's army assault the castle of maiden chastity. A literary fancy? In 1214 nobles assembled in Treviso. Armed with golden crowns and jewellery, the maids and ladies defended a fortress whose walls were cloth of gold, scarlet silk and velvet. With fruit, spices, perfumes and flowers, the gentlemen began the assault. Unfortunately the banner of St Mark was knocked to the ground when the Venetians and Paduans began to brawl entering the first gate, thus fuelling the already lively animosity between the two cities.

Nobles expected to have their way and were easily angered when they did not. A French preacher reports that humble folk lavished affection on their children until their hands were suddenly put to the plough. Gentlefolk differed. They rarely saw their issue, gave them over to servants and then sent them to serve in a notable's household. When ready for war or marriage, however, they were raised on high. Although other classes also went to war, nobles experienced more of it. Giles of Rome asserted that the fear of being cut up in combat was more intense than any other. In his lawbook, Beaumanoir discusses permissible and impermissible flight, asserting that those who flee are more likely to be slain than those who stand. Contrariwise, the popular *Roman de Sidrac* observed that 'a good flight is better than a bad remaining'.[12] Joinville's description of the rout of Louis IX's first 'battle' at Mansurah in 1249 and the king's counter-attack has rarely been equalled.

To use the Roman term, the soldiery was a militia or profession. The clergy, especially the monastic, was also a militia. As society matured, other militias also appeared. Of these the most significant were the lawyers and masters of law, those whom Placentinus (d. 1192), a jurist who taught at Bologna and Montpellier, called 'a militia of unarmed soldiers, militating in letters'.[13] This echoes Justinian's *Code* and *Institutes* where majesty was said to be not only decorated by arms but also armed by laws, victorious over enemies abroad and injustice at home. These familiar texts were also enshrined in the English codes named after Glanville and Bracton. Alfonso X of Castile's jurists also used them, and his *Book of the Laws* went on to divide society's orders into 'nobles, knights, masters, citizens, artisans and labourers', adding that 'knowledge of law is another manner of knighthood'.[14]

Jurists of the 'literate' or 'robed militia' even claimed precedence over the 'armed militia'. When Azzo read in the *Code* that those devoted to letters for twenty years were accorded the ex-vicarial dignity, he said it meant that the grammarian Master John and Accursius, the professor of law, should be ranked as counts or dukes on retirement. Albert of Gandino's treatise on criminal law (1286–1301) argued that, although lawyers and judges were exempt from legal torture, knights were not, unless in actual service. Bartolo of Sassoferrato (d. 1357) blandly summarized juristic tradition in 1355: '[The *Code*] says that, as soldiers do in arms, lawyers militate in laws and are more necessary for a republic than soldiers.'[15] In Bologna, fountainhead of legal studies, a statute of 1301 provided that parades were to be headed by the city's elected officers, followed by judges and doctors, after whom trailed the knights and commonalty.

Rivals aside, professionalism was welcomed by nobles because they were career-minded. In the romance *Erec and Enide*, Christian of Troyes taught that marriage, making love, wealth and high lineage were not enough; one must also make one's way in the world. The poet borrowed the divisions of 'practical philosophy', namely self-government (ethics), the government of groups (economics) and the government of society (politics). Hence his married hero and heroine first learn self-respect or self-love, then friendship and love of others and finally love of society, at which point they are crowned king and queen.

During the twelfth century warfare became a more complex art. Crossbows, followed soon by improved ordinary bows, made horse armour and reinforcement of chain mail with plate advisable. Grasse in Provence in 1214 estimated that 'a knight and armoured horse equalled two knights without horse armour or eight sergeants.'[16] More specialized and riding heavier horses, knights still ruled the field of battle, but needed ancillary formations. A force sent to Agen in 1221 during the Albigensian Crusade consisted of twenty knights, thirty sergeants and ten crossbowmen, all mounted. A Genoese mercenary company in 1255 had three hundred knights, each with a pack animal and two squires, twenty mounted crossbowmen and a hundred archers on foot.

Increasing complexity was accompanied by growing professionalism. In the 1270s Giles of Rome likened knights to

> the masters and doctors of other sciences. Nobody should become a master in any branch of learning unless all agree he is instructed in that art, and none should be promoted to knightly dignity unless . . . competent in war's work . . . . Although foot and cavalry who are not knights wage war, knights ought to be the masters and organizers of the others in battle.[17]

A learned literature on war appeared, initially consisting mainly of versions of Vegetius's ancient *Epitomy*. True to his time, Salimbene remarked about a *podestà* of Parma that he was 'a brave knight and learned in war'.[18]

Professional competition revived definitions of nobility. Three were current: blood, wealth and virtue. In the mid 1180s, Andrew the Chaplain's lady argued the case of blood. Scarlet dye held better in English cloth than in Italian, and virtue is found more often in nobles than plebeians. Besides, being slenderer, gentlemen are more handsome, nor would God have instituted different social orders without reason. Andrew's contemporary, the Abbess Hildegard of Bingen, had earlier explained why she admitted only noblewomen. God had instituted a natural order and mankind should not try, as had Satan, to vault above his natural place. Who would stable cattle, asses, sheep and goats pell-mell together in a barn? As there is a heavenly hierarchy, so also is there an earthly one: God loves all equally, but not all are equal here below.

That most writers were jurists or clerks, whose blood often left something to be desired, denied such sentiments universal plaudits. Blood has little intellectual appeal: all, taught the *Roman de Sidrac*, are sons of Adam, and Dante laughed at the question whether Adam was or was not noble. Earlier, the chaplain Andrew had remarked that virtue had ennobled men in the past, and 'there are many deriving from these first nobles who are wholly degenerated. And, if you reverse the proposition, it's equally true.'[19] Historian of the house of Anjou, Thomas of Loches (d. 1168), explained its humble origins by observing that the Emperor Charles the Bald elevated commoners because

> there were men of old stock and many family portraits who boasted about their forefathers' deeds, not their own, and who, when given office, employed someone from the people to instruct them in their duty, so that those whom the king ordered to command others sought another commander for themselves.

Much of this comes from Sallust's *Jugurthine War*, thus showing that the arguments against nobility of blood were truly antique. Thomas also remarked that the humble origin of the Angevin line was of no moment, 'for we have often read that senators formerly lived on the land and emperors were torn from the plough', a point substantiated by scripture's shepherds Saul and David.[20]

Dante discussed Aristotle's maxim, repeated by Emperor Frederick II, that nobility was old wealth combined with virtue. He rejected the first part of the proposition because of wealth's three imperfections: 'first, the wantonness of its acquisition; second, the moral danger of its increase; and third, the harmfulness of its possession.'[21] But wealth surely meant something. In Andrew's *On Love* a plebeian suitor tells a noble lady that he makes money only to spend it, thus defending 'the nobility of my behaviour and virtue. Had I not honest profits, poverty would keep me in obscurity so that I could not perform noble acts, and thus my nobility would rest on nothing but my word, a type of courtliness and nobility no one believes in'.[22] About 1265 a Parisian Dominican saw nothing in nobility 'except that nobles are constrained by a certain need not to degenerate from the virtue of their parents'.[23]

For some, neither blood nor money counted. Since, says the Chaplain, 'virtue is more to be praised in a plebeian than in a noble', a commoner is to be preferred as a lover.[24] Dante's teacher, Brunetto Latini, states in his popular *Treasure* of 1260–6 that 'they commonly say that courtesy comes from lordship, or that its cause is riches or nobility of blood, but the wise say that the only reason a man is worthy of being a prince or lord is intrinsic virtue'.[25] To be 'of mean spirit and high lineage is like being an earthen pot covered outside with fine gold'.[26] Cino of Pistoia expressed similar ideas in his lectures on the *Code* in 1312–14: 'Whoever deserves nobility by virtue is more worthy of being called a noble than he who descends from a noble family, because no one is noble by race . . . . He is to be commended for what he has sought for himself rather than from what he has from his parents.[27] Dante himself concluded that 'nobility comes from virtue; not virtue from nobility'.[28]

In spite of these ideas, blood was popular. James of Voragine's *Golden Legend* described most saints as of high origins, enhanced, of course, by virtue. And many weaselled. The Castilian *Book of the Laws* averred that nobility derived 'first, from lineage, second, from knowledge [as of law] and, third, from excellence in arms, customs and manners'. Still, if 'lineage is a noble thing, virtue surpasses it; and whoever has both may be really called a noble, because he is rich by lineage and rounded out by virtue'.[29]

NOBILITY AND WAR

Great though knighthood and nobility were, they did not escape change. Of forty-three knightly families around 1100 near Cluny in Burgundy, six had vanished by 1200, being replaced by three new ones, one of peasant origins. The tempo then began to accelerate: by 1240 sixteen new knightly lines appeared. Seven of these were branches of old ones, two rose from being bailiffs and one from the peasantry. What goes up can also go down. By the early thirteenth century, about three-fifths of the old nobles around Namur had sunk to the level of ordinary knights. A new and higher nobility called the 'peers of the castle of Namur' appeared during the second half of the century and contained about five of the older families. To some, knighthood seemed so unprofitable that they exchanged it for economic advantage. In 1238 the chapter of St Cunibert of Cologne conceded land to one 'who does not intend to become a knight . . . . Furthermore, be it known that, if the said Otto should become one, he must sell the said property within the year but not to a church, knight or son of a knight who wishes to become one.'[30]

Subdivision of inheritances hurt some of the martial aristocracy, and others whose condition was static were affected by the increased expense of warfare caused by the specialization mentioned above. A result was that, although usually well-to-do, nobles were busy making ends meet. The poem *Siegfried Helbing* describes Austria's lesser knights. Tournaments were not for them; they wanted to increase their cows' yield of milk. Instead of drinking, they sold the wine they raised. War had best be over by harvest because these farmers had then to go home. Since knights' privileges were justified by service, however, the statutes of Fréjus in 1235 state that, if a knight spends all his time 'ploughing, digging, carting . . . or doing other agricultural labour, he should not have the knight's liberty'. Had he not assumed knighthood's duties by the age of thirty, he would have to pay the count of Provence's tallage.[31] Writing in the 1270s, Raymond Llull recommended that poor squires should forego the golden belt and spurs. They would otherwise become 'thieves' – mercenaries!

Because wealth tended to concentrate and warfare became more demanding, the character of armies was changing. Old terms for knights in southern France, such as *caballarii*, vanish early in the thirteenth century, leaving the impression that in the past some had been only light horse who swelled the formations of more heavily armed knights. A 'company' seen at Limoux in the early 1230s may represent the new style. It consisted of four knights, four mounted crossbowmen and some squires on foot, a configuration close to the later 'garnished lance'. The numbers of knights owing service from given localities clearly diminished. Simon of Montfort required only one well-accoutred knight from Verfeil in 1214, but in 1229 the count of Toulouse was owed fifteen and even thirty-three from comparable places like Fanjeaux near Carcassonne and Montégut near Albi. Such persons must have been like the 'sergeants and crossbowmen' who, after the knights, took oath to a new count of Toulouse in 1249. In brief, the numbers of those considered fully armed knights was declining. Around 1350, although the Basque provinces and maritime Brittany had many nobles, just under four per cent of the population was noble in Provence and under one and a half per cent in Clermont and Amiens in central and northern France. Western Europe seems to have evolved more rapidly than eastern. In early modern times, nobles in Poland were ten per cent and more of the population, whereas in the west they ranged from one to four per cent.

Town patricians went to war with knights' equipment. The fusion of nobles and patricians was most advanced in Italy where cities were relatively independent of princes. Since ministerial dependency was not permitted in urban republics, Italian and other towns early developed the practice of knighting any likely person. In the mid twelfth century the imperialist historian Otto of Freising complained that

> to oppress their neighbours, [the Milanese] are not ashamed of allowing young men of low condition, artisans of contemptible or mechanical arts, whom other peoples would reject like the plague from honourable and liberal pursuits, to assume the knight's belt . . . and hence far excel all other cities in wealth and power.[32]

Italians answered in the *Entry into Spain*, averring that the Lombards with Charlemagne at the siege of Pamplona were all free, all knighted without regard to birth and privileged to carry bared swords before the king.

Republican knighthood developed an almost modern quality. Although Accursius's *Ordinary Gloss* of 1220–34 repeated Roman law's prohibition of soldiers being merchants, Florentine and other merchant bankers were usually noble. In 1312–14 Cino of Pistoia sourly remarked that 'nowadays knights rarely give up mercantile pursuits or business, and not a few exercise common crafts and are ignorant of how to arm themselves'.[33] For these, Cino comments, golden spurs and honorifics are enough; they need no other privileges. Knighting became so common a recognition of civic worth that in 1322 the Florentine government ordered that no corpse could be dubbed! Patricians being like knights and knights like patricians, all knights, squires and commoners wealthy enough to 'live nobly' were to serve the republic as knights, either personally or by substitute. Knightly service was equated with a certain level of personal taxes throughout northern Italy by the mid thirteenth century. As a result, the right of knights to judgment by their peers and exemption from taxes slowly faded. A Florentine statute of 1289 defined nobles as members 'of a house where there is a knight, or where there was one within the last twenty years, or as those who, in common parlance, are normally held to be or are called notables, nobles or magnates'.[34]

As the popular parties rose in Italy, magnates were deprived not only of privileges but even of the right to hold public office. This persecution prompted four nobles of Putignono to petition Pisa to become commoners in 1322, claiming that, 'although they . . . have the name of nobles, they were nevertheless always effectually commoners and supporters of the Pisan people, and always intended to be so'.[35] Such being the case, ambitious persons no longer wanted knighthood if it implied nobility, and consequently 'popular' knighthood appeared. Bartolo of Sassoferrato (d. 1357) remarked in his commentaries on the *Code*: 'We observe here in Perugia, that if a plebeian is knighted, he becomes noble; but if in Florence, remains a commoner.'[36] The first treatise on heraldry was Bartolo's posthumously published *On Insignia and Arms*. This famous jurist was so indifferent to nobility that he blandly compared coats of arms to watermarks, trademarks and the signs of commercial companies, opining that anyone could have them.

Popular knighthood is not found outside of Italy, but the fusion of patricians and nobles was known elsewhere. The consuls of Avignon in 1243 ordered that 'according to the ancient liberty of this city, every knight and bourgeois . . . may aid their lords and friends in a vendetta'.[37] In 1303 at Toulouse, 'feudal persons, noble or non-noble', having £100 (of Tours) annually were to appear with horse and arms. Other 'nobles' having less than this were to appear as best they could.[38]

England's 'distraint' of knighthood was somewhat similar. It began in 1224, when those with fiefs worth £20 a year were ordered knighted or else pay a fine. In 1225 the king addressed 'all earls, barons, knights and freemen who are not merchants', showing that he was thinking in Roman law's terms seen above. By 1241 distraint was extended to anyone with property worth that amount, whether or not the owner was of knightly stock. When repeated in 1256, Matthew Paris, the historian of St Albans, observed that the law was enacted 'to reinforce knighthood in England as it was in Italy'.[39] Princes everywhere wanted to use the knightly militia, so much cheaper than mercenary companies, and tried to reinvigorate it. Raymond VII of Toulouse (d. 1249) knighted perhaps as many as 200 'nobles and others' in 1248 and Edward I of England (d. 1308) dubbed 300 in a ceremony in 1307. If the effort failed, they could at least help fill their treasuries by fines for non-service.

As did republics, princes found knighting or ennobling useful as an accolade for rewarding service. To a prince, nobility was won by virtuous individuals, and virtue was service to himself. What this meant for social levelling was already understood: Rudolph of Habsburg in 1276 greeted all subjects, from peasant to great noble, as 'my ministers'.[40] Since this rational absolutism meant little even where it was propounded, knighting was used to ennoble people for service. Nor was the service always military. Seen above, an architect was dubbed by Charles I of Naples and a jurist by a duke of Burgundy. Another example is a chamberlain of a count of Namur who was in office in 1289, became a squire in 1300 and a knight in 1305, obviously not grade A for campaigning.

Like republics, princes tried to monopolize knighting, but the tradition was that any knight could dub anyone. In France, with semi-independent provinces – Brittany, Flanders, England's Guienne and Gascony – royal monopoly was long in coming. In 1298 the crown confessed that in the seneschalcy of Beaucaire, from time immemorial 'bourgeois assumed the knight's belt from nobles, barons and even archbishops without the licence of the prince'.[41] But royal knighthood slowly began to win out. A lord of Isle Jourdain, whose predecessor had been dubbed by the count of Toulouse in 1248, styled himself in 1280 'knight of the illustrious king of the French'. An example of royal ennoblement is a charter of 1295: 'Because . . . our dearest father manumitted master John of Taillefontaine, clerk . . . we, approving this liberty, allow . . . him to acquire noble fiefs and assume the belt of knighthood, and, by that act . . . enjoy . . . perpetual nobility.'[42]

The mix of function and privilege characterizing the martial aristocracy had changed. Until about 1200 – and later in Germany, not to speak of Scandinavia and Slavic lands where knighthood was only being introduced – function had been accented; thereafter it was the hereditary privilege of those of knightly stock that was stressed. In 1226 the emperor wrote to the 'knights' of the Rhenish–Franconian town of Oppenheim; in 1269 he greeted the 'knights and sons of knights'; and in 1275 Rudolph of Habsburg addressed 'all knights, their sons and grandsons at Oppenheim possessing the military right', the latter phrase referring to the privileges accorded soldiers in Roman law.[43] Unknighted gentlemen from knightly lines were therefore considered nobles. Up to about 1260 around Namur non-knighted military were generally called sergeants, a term with servile connotations in that area; thereafter, they were called squires and considered noble. The result of this evolution is witnessed by a charter of 1293 emanating from Manosque in Provence adverting to questions raised between 'the knights and military persons whose names are [so-and-so] knights, and [so-and-so] squires or military on one hand, and the good men and popular persons on the other'.[44]

In France knighthood became gradually rarer, being replaced by the claim to belong to a noble line. Of the sixty nobles of forty-three families in the county of Forez near Lyons who leagued together against royal taxes in 1314-15, four were widows, twenty-nine knights (two of whom had lately been bourgeois) and twenty-seven squires, one of peasant origin. Of the squires, eleven died as such, six were knighted before the age of forty, five before fifty, four before sixty, and one in his sixties. Gone were the days when one was dubbed at twenty-one or shortly thereafter. Although though nobles still paid the 'tax of blood' in defence of prince and community, privilege was what especially typified them.

The late thirteenth century saw a recrudescence of literature defending hereditary nobility. The most famous voice was that of Raymond Llull, whose *Order of Chivalry* of 1274–5 was vastly popular. To Llull, a knight who had children by a plebeian wife honoured neither gentility nor knighthood, and a knight's wife bearing a child by a villein destroyed 'the antiquity of chivalry and the noble confraternity of noble lineage'.[45] He even asserted that commoners cannot be knighted, but soon grudgingly contradicted himself. Unlike beasts, humans are rational, he opined, and so, 'by many noble habits and deeds and by being ennobled by a prince, . . . an occasional man of new, honourable and gentle lineage is admitted into chivalry'.[46] Sure that judges should be chosen only from chivalry, he at least believed they should be trained in law as well as war.

This didactic literature added to the romances about war that usually served as soldiers' textbooks, works that Humbert of Romans likened to the clergy's scripture. Books of manners began to appear, urging gentlemen to learn music, chess and suitable sports. John of Meung recommended that they should also be literate because letters and arms go together. The first evidence of family heraldics dates from the thirteenth century, glorifying lineage with handsome banners and heraldry. During this period the flowery titles used by noblemen in modern times came into general use: in documents at least, knights were 'noble and puissant'.

With all its pomposity, so useful an impediment to totalitarian social organization was the irrational principle of noble blood's intrinsic freedom that no medieval government could bind its citizens to a common servitude. Nor did the State do so until both princes and nobles had bowed off history's stage.

From ancient times, governments could summon all citizens to arms when the fatherland was endangered, and so sonorous was this call that feudal and urban limitations on service became inane when the trumpet was sounded. The most precocious development of this idea was seen in Italy's republics whose wars, however aggressive, were all called defensive because their citizens had voted them. This totalitarian vision spread to the larger pre-national units of Latin Europe in the late thirteenth century. By the early fourteenth century all France owed service or compensatory taxes based on wealth and status, a matter examined later on.

This militia service for the 'defence of the fatherland' was not especially efficient. It was shown for England at Bannockburn against the Scots in 1314 that, to paraphrase Vegetius, multitudes of unpractised soldiers serve only to perplex and embarrass. Similar policies in France led to the log-jam of the Crusade against Catalonia–Aragon in 1284–5 and the uncontrollable mob at Courtrai in 1302 arrayed against Flanders' militias. Both of these defeats foreshadowed the disasters of the Hundred Years' War. In that later great combat, England's advantage was that her knightly militia could not be mobilized for overseas service, and the crown therefore hired the magnates' professional households and French or English mercenary companies. Although Charles of Anjou's successful intervention in the Italian war against the Hohenstaufen had been carried out with professional companies, France's defence against England was based on militia, the invasion having justified calls for the 'defence of the realm'. By virtue of numbers, militias of occasional soldiers can sometimes defeat professionals, but most especially require social solidarity, a quality lacking in France in the later fourteenth century. Impeded by chivalry, it took generations of disaster before professionalism triumphed and the militia principle atrophied in France. Until that occurred the nobility could not really be called a 'privileged order'.

NOTES AND REFERENCES

1   A *Freiherr* was the lowest free noble; a *ministerialis* (translated as 'minister') was a semi-servile soldier.
2   The *Ursberger Chronicle* in Bosl, *Reichsministerialität* I, 593.
3   *Dominus* or *messire*.
4   Gauthier, *Chevalerie*, 291.
5   *Speculum ecclesiae* , *Sermo generalis ad milites* in *PL* CLXXI, 865.
6   *Summa de arte praedicatorum* 40 in *PL* CCX, 186.
7   *Histoire de Guillaume le Maréchal* (ed. Meyer), v., 18,480 ff.
8   *Des quatres tenz d'aage d'ome* 15 (ed. Fréville), 11.

9 *Oculus pastoralis* 6, 1 in L.A. Muratori (ed.) *Antiquitates Italicae medii aevi* (Arezzo, 1776) IX, 840–2.
10 *La règle du Temple* (ed. Henri de Curzon, Paris, 1886), 63, and 1 John: 3,16; John: 15,13, etc.
11 *Boncompagnus Boncompagni* in *BuF* I, 166.
12 Langlois, *La Vie en France au moyen-âge* III, 261.
13 Fitting, *Das castrense peculium*, 551.
14 *Las siete partidas* 1, 10, 3 (Madrid, 1807), II, 90.
15 Fitting, *Das castrense peculium*, 551.
16 *Recueil des actes des comtes de Provence appartenant à la maison de Barcelone* (ed. Fernand Bênoit, Monaco and Paris, 1925) II, No. 18.
17 *De regimine principum* 3, 3, 1 (Rome, 1607), 558–9.
18 *Cronica fratris Salimbene de Adam, ordinis minorum* in *MGH SS* XXXII, 98.
19 *De amore* 1, 6 (ed. Trojel), 17–18.
20 *Gesta consulum Andegavorum* in *Chroniques des comtes d'Anjou* (ed. Halphen and Poupardin), 25 and 27. The reference to Cincinnatus is from Cicero's *De senectute* 16, 56.
21 *Convivio* 4, 1, 3.
22 *De amore* 1, 6, 2 (ed. Trojel), 46.
23 Pseudo-Thomas's *De eruditione principum* cited in Berges, *Die Fürstenspiegel*, 11n, a commonplace from St Jerome.
24 *De amore* 1, 6, 4 (ed. Trojel), 76–7.
25 *Li livres dou tresor* 2, 29 (ed. Carmody), 199.
26 *Ibid.* 2, 54 (ed. Carmody), 230.
27 Fitting, *Das castrense peculium*, 552.
28 *Convivio* 4, 1, 19.
29 *Las siete partidas* 1, 9, 6 and 1, 21, 2 (Madrid, 1807), II, 63 and 197–8.
30 Guilhermoz, *Origines de la noblesse*, 379.
31 Published in Giraud, *Essai sur l'histoire du droit français* II, 12.
32 This passage from the *Gesta Friderici* is cited everywhere, but see Salvemini, *La dignità cavalleresca*, 355.
33 Fitting, *Das castrense peculium*, 559.
34 Salvemini, *La dignità cavalleresca*, 398.
35 Cristiani, *Nobilità e popolo nel commune di Pisa*, 114–15.
36 Salvemini, *La dignità cavalleresca*, 399.
37 *Coutumes et règlements d'Avignon* (ed. Maulde), 190, No. 112.
38 Municipal Archives of Toulouse II, 41 dated January 1303.
39 *Chronica majora* in *Rolls Series* LVII, v., 560.
40 Ritter, *Ministérialité et chevalerie*, 105.
41 Gauthier, *La chevalerie*, 249.
42 Guilhermoz, *Origines de la noblesse*, 478.
43 *Ibid.*, 482.
44 *Ibid.*, 479.
45 *Livre de l'ordre de chevalerie* 7 (ed. Minervini), 176.
46 *Ibid.* 3 (ed. Minervini), 535b.

12

ECCLESIASTICS

TYPES

In his *Golden Summa* of 1251–2, Hostiensis saw the Trinity reflected in the Church's three orders: layfolk, regular and secular clergy. Clergy in the seven or eight holy orders were the core of the Church.[1] Jurists often elevated the episcopate into a ninth, paralleling the nine orders of the church militant with the nine angelic ones of the church triumphant. Theologians, however, never accepted this doctrine.

Estimates of numbers are vague. After 1300 clerks in major orders were perhaps one in ninety of England's population, and parish rectors were rare enough to be like belted knights among laymen. In Carcassonne in the early fourteenth century nine parish rectors equalled the nine university-trained physicians in this community of about 9,000 souls. This gives a distorted impression, however. By the thirteenth century, rectors had sacerdotal assistants, and cathedrals beneficed priests working with the laity. The many chapels and churches attached to hospitals, monastic houses, chapters of canons regular and the mendicant orders also had priests in service.

Tonsured persons below the grade of subdeacon were not required to be celibate. These performed many duties in cathedrals, parishes and hospitals, and although most were humble, those trained as lawyers or notaries did well. The new bishop's judge or Official, first seen in northern France about 1178, was often a layman, as were many notaries and judges posts at the papal court. Since clergy were exempt from taxes and military service, tonsure was valuable. In the late thirteenth century about a tenth of

197

Rheims' inhabitants were tonsured, busy as lawyers, notaries and beadles in the several church courts. Students in parish schools and universities also came under canon protection. Churchmen were already trying to reduce these intermediary groups: Innocent III completed the elevation of the subdiaconate into the higher orders, and psalmists were fast vanishing. The main reason for this was, as a bishop of Olmütz complained to the Council of Lyons in 1274, the multiplication of clerks beyond need.

The second principal segment of the clergy was the religious. Some were in cathedral chapters, some secular and others regular canons. If the former, they were often in lower orders, assigned a living, inhabited individual houses and had private means. Canons regular were like monks, cloistered and bound by profession to an order, especially Augustinian or Austin (founded 1059). Premonstratensian canons regular (founded 1120) had independent houses. Monks were bound by a rule and defined by celibacy, claustration and community of property. Once, monks had usually remained lay, but by this time most advanced to the priestly grade. Male religious were often divided into three groups. The first, choir monks, was composed of those who had professed; the other two were the lay brethren and oblates.

Significant in orders like the Cistercians (founded 1098), lay brethren did not live in the monks' cloister or enter holy orders; theirs was the duty of manual labour. Ideally, the lay brother fulfilled the function of Martha, sister of Mary Magdalene and Lazarus, whose labour supported Mary's contemplation. The sisters did not always get on. Disputes between monks and lay brethren were frequent where, as in the order of Grandmont (founded early twelfth century, rules in 1143), the latter administered the monastery. According to James of Vitry, the real issue was that, raising money, lay brethren wanted monks to attract lay donors by singing masses for dead donors and the Virgin, but the monks liked the quiet of the cloister. Orders mostly composed of lay brethren had no troubles. The Hospitallers (founded 1099, military brothers admitted before 1160) and the Templars (founded 1118) got on well with their priestly chaplains.

The lay brother's grade was fading at this time, perhaps because recruits came from an increasingly free world, and both Benedictines and Cistercians were replacing them by salaried domestics. Franciscan lay brethren were titled brothers or friars and, like those in holy orders, belonged to the First Order (founded 1209, given rules in 1221 and 1223), the Second being the nuns of the Clares (founded 1215) and associated layfolk the Third or Tertiaries. They also called their male Tertiaries lay brethren, although they lived in the world.

Lacking final vows or tonsure, oblates were the third group. These shaded insensibly into purely lay groups, such as teachers in the schools of monasteries or chapters, children entrusted to them for education, corrodian holders in or near the community and even old soldiers pensioned by secular patrons. Aged, leprous and sick hospital inmates, hospital and educational staffs and male and female recluses or hermits (who often lived in town) had similarities with the religious. When one adds to this minestrone layfolk who banded together to emulate the life of the religious while remaining in the world, such as Humiliati, Franciscan Tertiaries and Beguines (female) and Beghards (male), one understands why contemporaries were astonished by the variety of such groups. They obscured the line between oblates and converses – Beguines were often called both – and confused the professed religious with layfolk.

Individual religious houses were not large. At its peak around 1150 the mother house of Cluny is said to have had 300 monks as well as Europe's largest basilica. A little later, England's Cistercian Rievaulx had 140 monks and 600 lay brothers; in 1286 Bury St Edmunds had eighty monks and 122 domestics. These were big houses. An affiliate of Cluniac Moissac, the house of Lézat south of Toulouse, had a minimum of forty-two monks in the 1260s. The visitations of Odo Rigaud, archbishop of Rouen, from 1248 to 1269 show many small priories and granges housing two to five religious. Regular or secular, French cathedral chapters ran from thirteen to eighty-four canons, Beauvais having thirty-nine in 1267.

The number of houses was huge. In 1316 a Franciscan assembly at Naples estimated 1,017 male houses in Germany, France and Italy and those of St Clare's nuns at 285. Dominicans (founded 1215) were fewer, 582 male convents and 149 female being listed in 1303. Two other major mendicant orders, the Carmelites (brought to Europe from the Holy Land in 1242 and made mendicant by 1245) and the Austin Friars (Augustinian Eremites, founded 1256), and at least six smaller orders appeared before 1300, all with associated lay groups. By 1300 the Franciscans boasted 250 Tertiary societies, and a provincial council at Colmar in 1303 gathered 150 friars greeted by 300 local Beghards. In 1288 Bonvesino of Riva tells us that in Milan, 'there are fully 220 houses [like private homes] of the second order of the Humiliati of both sexes in our city and county in which a copious number of individuals lead the religious life by labouring with their hands'.[2]

To review, two great surges of the religious recast Christendom, the first occurring in the Gregorian age before this book begins, and the other around 1200. Both began with waves of enthusiasm that, though initially repressed, eventually broke free. The Premonstratensian Anselm of Havelberg (d. 1158) reported that the calumniators of the earlier new devotions asked: 'Why are there so many innovations in God's Church? Why do so many new orders rise up? Who can even count the many orders of clerks? Who is not astounded by the many types of monks?'[3]

Although Cistercians and Carthusians sometimes settled in the wilderness, the new canons regular were habitual town dwellers, and sought to reinvigorate the secular clergy, build hospitals and educational institutions. An anonymous Premonstratensian tract divided the religious: 'Wholly separated from the crowd, some lead a peaceable life in God . . . . Others, located next to men in town or in villages, are sustained by charity from the faithful and by incomes from churches and tithes.' Canons lived largely in towns: 'Some are separated as much as possible . . . from the crowd; others are placed next to men; and yet others live among men, and hence are called secular.'[4] Few occupations were as resolutely worldly as those of the Templars and Hospitallers. The later mendicants were largely urban in origin, as befitted an age when towns reached their peak, but if they began in cities, they soon spread to quite small towns.

Another similarity between the two 'reform' waves was that both lost impetus partly because, once established, the new orders joined with old ones to brake expansion. Restrictions were finally summed up by papal law prohibiting monks in the houses of old orders from leaving to join ones considered to be more 'rigorous'. Secular clerks also did not want them intruding in their parishes. The Premonstratensian cited above reported that 'I have heard priests . . . muttering that those who have left the world should remit the care of it to secular men, as though [monks] were unsuited to deal with secular business.'[5]

Cluny's and Cîteaux's monks and the canons regular nevertheless remade the secular clergy by inculcating standards of literacy and celibacy. Priesthood was also exalted by the withdrawal of the eucharistic cup from the laity and the teaching of transubstantiation with its priestly miracle of the mass. Joined to the peace of God and the Crusade, also, penitential ideas, once mainly monastic, invaded the world to create the court of conscience presided over by secular priests. In the late twelfth century, also, the schools of the canons of the cathedral, of St Victor and Mont Ste Geneviève created the university of Paris. Peter Cantor, grand chanter of Nôtre Dame, taught there and his works on ecclesiastical discipline and penitence were immensely influential. Peter's student James of Vitry, canon regular of Oignies in Brabant, was a spell-binding preacher and in contact with the new Humiliati and Franciscans. In 1216 he won papal approval for the Beguine movement, begun earlier around the Premonstratensians in the Low Countries and enlivened by his 'spiritual mother' Mary of Oignies (d. 1213), famous at Liège. Cistercian monks were chosen by the popes for missions in Greece after the Latin conquest of Byzantium in 1204. They also mounted the first preaching tours against Catharism in the Midi, and the pontiffs chose them to head the armed invasions of 1178, 1181 and 1209.

In the forefront of intellectual life until just before 1200, the monks thereafter fell behind. Robert Grosseteste, bishop of Lincoln and patron of England's Franciscans, warned the friars that, unless they studied at the university, 'it will surely happen to us as it has to other religious who' we see, alas! walking in the shadows of ignorance'.[6] Stephen of Lexington, abbot of Clairvaux, attempted to rectify this by founding St Bernard's College at Paris in 1245–6, and Cluny's Benedictines followed in 1260 with theirs.

Leadership was lost by the older orders to new ones frankly designed for work in the world. After some hesitation, the pope recognized the working class Humiliati in 1202, and thereafter the mendicant flood began. Famous for public begging (from which their name came), the mendicants were privileged by the popes. Save for the Franciscans, however, no new order was permitted to have a rule of its own, new rules being prohibited by the Lateran Council of 1215. The Dominicans erected study centres in their convents, and sent the first mendicant master, Roland of Cremona, to teach at Toulouse and Paris in 1229. They enriched the liturgy, Thomas Aquinas composing the order of service for the Corpus Christi feast in 1264. They specialized in penitence, and their jurist Raymond of Peñafort issued a basic manual of casuistry in 1234. They were also leading preachers. General of the order from 1254 to 1263, Humbert of Romans remarked that the Saviour celebrated only one mass and was not known to have heard confession; his life was spent in prayer and preaching, to the latter of which he gave most of his time. Preaching explains why Dominicans laid out their churches with a central colonnade separating women from men.

The religious, in fine, twice invaded the world and twice remade the Church. During the two interventions they had themselves changed. In the earlier age, they wanted the world to withdraw into the hermitage. Peter Damian reported that Romuald, founder of the Camaldolese monks about 1012, 'wished to convert the whole world into an hermitage and join the whole multitude of the people into the monastic order'.[7] Later on, they wanted the hermitage to invade and restructure the whole world. The abbot Joachim of Fiore (d. 1202) dreamed of a society to suit the coming age. Five oratories of monks were to inspire the faithful. An oratory of priests and clerks was to perform divine offices, visit and heal the sick and teach Latin and scripture to the young. The final and largest oratory was to be that of the married 'living the common life with their children, using wives for procreation rather than libidinousness'.[8] The married folk were to live by labour, sharing their fruits in common after providing for the clergy and monks.

Joachim proved to be a bad prophet. Sacerdotal and teaching duties almost wholly absorbed the utopian and eremitical drive of the new orders. By invading both the secular clergy and laity and having nearly converted the streets and marketplaces of the world into a monastery, however, the religious may be thought to have been victorious. The victory was self-defeating, however. If all men and women were gradually becoming monks, what future was there for the cloistered religious?

FREEDOM

Monks hoped to live like the apostles: from each according to his means and to each according to his need.[9] So essential was the common life that Peter Damian asserted: 'those only are fit for preaching who have no gain from earthly riches, and who, having nothing individually, have everything in common'.[10] The popes encouraged the creation of lay communities devoting themselves to the common life, Urban II in 1091 saying of such a group 'it is worthy of perpetual conservation because it is stamped in the form

of the primitive Church'.[11] Praise of the life apostolic was incorporated in Gratian and was thence cited by later ideologues: 'Most
unsuitably does he teach who announces the poor man Christ with
a fat belly and rubicund cheeks.'[12]

Nor should learning be misused: John of Salisbury said it was for
man's betterment and God's glory. It could corrupt, however, and
Francis of Assisi urged: 'Care not about books and knowledge, only
good works . . . . Learning puffs up but love builds!' He told a
novice wanting a psalter: 'After you get that, you'll want a breviary.
And when you have that, you'll sit in your chair like a prelate, and
say to your brother: "Fetch me my breviary!"'[13] Besides, learning is
not enough. Although sententious, Bernard of Clairvaux was right:
'Believe one who knows: you will discover some things more fully
in forests than in books. Trees and rocks will teach you what you
cannot hear from schoolteachers.'[14]

When St Paul said, '"I wish you to be without care," he was
speaking about the solicitude of house and family incumbent on
those who have wives'.[15] Freedom from care even concerned intellectual lovers. Preferring to be Abelard's 'strumpet', Héloise at first
refused to marry her middle-aged professor. Even married folk
longed for this freedom. In 1254 a well-to-do Toulousan smith
willed his bed to be kept in his house 'wherein a poor man may lie
to remit my sins'.[16] The pauper was Christ; the sins were the
angers and excesses occasioned by family and business.

Carelessness sometimes eased fear. Told of oncoming death,
Francis of Assisi called Angelo and Leo, 'and when these brothers,
full of grief, had come to him they sang with many tears the Song
of Brother Sun and those of all the other creatures the saint had
written'. Francis then added a verse: 'Be praised, our Lord, for our
Sister Bodily Death from whom no man can escape.'[17] Transcending care was sometimes strained. When the anchorite St Macarius,
James of Voragine recorded, had 'killed a flea that stung him, and
much blood came out of it, he blamed himself for having avenged
an injury, and hence remained naked for six months in the desert,
whence he returned [to die] torn by wounds and bites'.[18]

Work in the world impeded freedom, and Jerome provided the
commonplace: monks do not have the duty of teaching but rather
of grieving, of lamenting themselves and the world. 'Practical'
monks, however, knew they had to teach and serve those in the
world. Before 1141 the Cluniac Orderic Vital lauded a Norman
priory because local knights not only worked with the monks but

also received instruction, so that the convent became 'a school for the living and a refuge for the dying'.[19] Schools require book learning, as Geoffrey of Breteuil (*fl. circa* 1173) put it: 'a cloister without a library is like a fortress without an arsenal'.[20] Overriding the founder's eremitical bent, the Franciscans therefore educated themselves and built churches in which to preach. Earthly fame, moreover, tempted all, even John of Salisbury: 'Nothing appears wiser to me for a man striving for glory than the favour of honest writers.'[21]

Charity and parish care were supposed to be free, but customary fees to make them predictable had appeared. A dispute between the parish priests of Toulouse and their parishioners just before 1251 or 1255 over testaments, burial, marriage and other fees illustrates the problem, as do those among clergy over burial rights. Popular preachers like James of Vitry won plaudits by saying that the religious gave little to the poor in order to gain much for themselves, and John of Salisbury sourly remarked that the Hospitallers sucked up to the rich instead of embracing the pauper Christ. John of Flagy's *Romance of Garin the Lorrainer* comments: 'When a noble lies sick abed in great fear of death, he does not look to his brother or son, nor to his relatives . . . he gives his lands, rents and mills to St Benedict's black monks, and neither daughter nor son gets anything.'[22]

Charity's economy was a problem. With money, property or rents, layfolk bought pensions or care in old age or illness and provided education for children. Mutually profitable, over time these contracts resulted in property accumulation, something that explains anger against the wealth of the Church. Fund-raising, moreover, harassed the rich. The Dominican William of Abingdon delighted his audiences until he began to build the order's house. Henry III of England then remarked: 'Brother William, you used to speak so spiritually; now all you say is "Give, give, give!"'[23]

Attractive to some, the sparse communitarian life repelled others. Around 1200 Guiot of Provins' *Bible* discussed the religious. Cistercians in outlying granges lived well but the rest starved. The abstinence of sick Carthusians from meat was little more than suicide, and recluses or hermits were simply mad. Happy were Augustinian canons, who ate, drank and dressed well; Guiot would like to suffer with them. Moderation, even ease, in fact, was needed by celibate brotherly communities. Robert Grosseteste said:

Three things are needed for earthly health: food, sleep and play. He enjoined a penance on a certain melancholy brother, namely to drink a cup of good wine, and, when he had drunk it, although most unwillingly, said to him, 'Dear brother, if you had such a penitence frequently, you'd have a much better ordered conscience.'[24]

The ascetic urge posed problems, especially concerning priestly marriage. As canon law called it, clerical concubinage was attacked in the Gregorian age, providing an issue with which to mobilize lay support – make the teacher suffer! Although provoking change in clerical practice, observed with stunned disapproval by Muslims and Jews, old ways were hard to uproot. The distinguished Ailred, who died as abbot of Rievaulx in 1166, was the son, grandson and great-grandson of rural priests. Clerical concubinage remained customary in northern England, Scandinavia and parts of Germany, and was not infrequent in France and Spain. Of 700 priests visited by Odo Rigaud, archbishop of Rouen, twelve per cent were denounced to him for this 'fault'. In one semester of 1335, of the over 200 papal dispensations for illegitimacy to allow entry into holy orders, over seventy per cent were granted to sons of priests. Below the priestly level, clerical concubinage was even more widespread. Peter Cantor's circle at Paris proposed – quite in vain! – releasing subdeacons and deacons from the prohibition, partly because they corrupted themselves so easily by buying papal dispensations.

Medieval clerks were more free in their talk about sex than religious men today. Clement VI (d. 1352) is said to have answered objections to his relations with women by saying that he had picked up the habit in youth, and engaged in it now only on doctors' orders. To quiet the murmurs, he produced 'a small black book in which he had written the names of different . . . incontinent popes, showing from the deeds written there that they governed the Church better than others who were continent'.[25] They also described the prickings of the flesh with great fidelity. The strange 'autobiography' of the hermit Peter of Monte Morrone who became Pope Celestine V records that, for him, God's kindest miracle was to ease his conscience about wet dreams.

Living in a society where class distinctions were overlaid by functional orders, men and women chose ways of life because of the roles inherent in them. The courtliness, eruptive romance and angers of gentlefolk contrasted sharply with the bookish and sometimes maudlin emotionalism of the clergy. Few, however, were wholly fulfilled or contained by the choice of order they, their families and circumstances made for them. Francis of Assisi was the son of an ambitious cloth merchant, and his flight from business led him to seek to shine in chivalry. Defeated, he then turned to poverty's wonders, and there instilled the sacrifice, humility, freedom, psychic ostentation and self-love of the religious life into a migratory community of like souls.

Although hearty bachelors were also attracted, the Church, especially monasteries, offered a way to men who had a larger share than most of motherly qualities. A plan for a Franciscan hermitage will illustrate this:

> Two of [the hermit friars] should be mothers and they should have two sons . . . . The two mothers should imitate the life of Martha and the two sons that of Mary [Magdalene] . . . . And the brothers who are mothers should strive to remain remote from all persons and . . . guard their sons . . . so that no one may speak with them. Nor should the sons speak to anyone except their mothers.[26]

Womanly warmth among communities of men does not mean that homosexuality was general. In the 1260s four monks reported on forty-two Benedictines of the monastery of Lézat. Other than simony, retention of property, working in the fields with members of their lay families, eating meat and other occasional minor offences, almost half the inmates were reported to be or have been sexually active. Seventeen specific women, including sisters at the Fontevrault house of Longages, were named, and eleven monks were charged with having had specific children. Only two, however, were charged with homophilia. About one of these, one witness said that he rather doubted the truth of the allegations, and another that he suspected his informants were moved by a desire to harm the monk. In short, here to the south of Toulouse the 'vice of sodomy', as they described it, was decidedly ill-considered, at least when talking to the police, so to speak. On the other hand, the religious habitually practised self- and mutual flagellation. Although the lash was used by layfolk for corporal punishment, penitential whipping remained monastic until the spread of the religious vocation in the mid thirteenth century. It then appeared among the laity, an early example being the relatively large-scale flagellant movement that swept wartorn Italy in 1259.

Although otherworldly, the faith reflected the world's variety. On one hand it was monotheistic; on the other, to speak like a

Muslim, polytheistic: three divine persons, the Virgin and local saints' cults, both male and female. The faith penetrated daily living, and earthly life emulated heavenly. Eight knights and four sergeants elected the grand master of the Temple, twelve 'in honour of the twelve apostles. The twelve brothers should together elect a brother chaplain to hold the place of Christ Jesus and keep the brothers in peace . . . . And so there will be thirteen brothers.'[27] According to the theological masters appointed to examine the writings of Peter John Olivi in 1319, this Franciscan believed that, just as the Synagogue had been propagated by twelve patriarchs and the Church by twelve apostles, 'so the final Church of the remaining Jews and gentiles is to be propagated by twelve evangelical men. Whence Francis had twelve associates or sons, through whom and in whom was founded the evangelical order.'[28] The world was also a comic mirror of heaven. To Boncompagno of Signa invalidation of contract was prefigured in paradise, because, when the Lord asked, "Adam, where are you?" [Adam] straightway proposed the objection of fraud, saying: "The wife you gave me deceived me."[29]

Even though taboo, also, objects of the faith were handled crudely. When Constantinople fell in 1204, the Latins ransacked the city for relics. James of Vitry hung a finger of Mary of Oignies encased in silver on his necklace, and finally gave it 'to Pope Gregory IX of solemn memory to carry against the vice of swearing by which he was atrociously tempted'.[30] Nor were contemporaries shocked when Countess Theodora, Thomas Aquinas's sister, 'asked for the right hand of the said holy body [Thomas's] from the abbot of Fossanuova. Although fourteen years in the earth, he was unable to pull it easily off the body, and had to cut it off with a knife, and it gave off a wonderfully sweet odour to those venerating it.'[31]

The incarnation was treated in much the same fashion. In 1178 Peter Maurand, a Cathar at Toulouse, recanted and swore concerning the mass that the consecrated wafer was 'not only a symbol but also the true body and blood of our lord Jesus Christ, and actually and not only symbolically, but in very truth, is handled and broken by the hands of priests and ground by the teeth of the faithful'.[32] Peter repeated the oath exacted from Berengar of Tours in 1059 about transubstantiation, a text carried by both Gratian and Peter Lombard. This miracle was awkward, however. Because their intention is evil or lacking, the latter remarked, neither heretics nor excommunicates can confect a sacrament and an animal cannot eat the host. Thence arises a question: 'What then does a mouse take or chew?' And an answer: 'Only God knows.'[33] And why did the Lord choose this particular miracle? 'Lest the mind abhor what the eye perceives, because we are not in the habit of eating raw flesh or drinking blood . . . and lest the Christian religion be mocked by unbelievers.'[34] God was perhaps being tactful, but, according to Roger Bacon and others, Jews and Muslims both continued to charge the Christians with covert or religious cannibalism.

RIVALRIES

Secular clerks came to terms with the world in which they worked. In spite of efforts to separate God's things from Caesar's, they remained bound together, providing targets for rigorist monks and mendicants. Archetypal, the prince-archbishop of Mainz rode in full armour with bared sword borne before. A clerk from the university at Paris joked that he could believe anything save that German bishops could be saved. 'Almost all wield both swords, spiritual and material. Judging blood cases and waging wars, they care more about paying soldiers than about saving souls.'[35]

Ecclesiastical and secular careers overlapped. An example is that of the financial officer Richard Fitzneale, treasurer and presumed author of the *Exchequer Dialogue*. Richard was a second-generation crown servant who died as bishop of London in 1198 and whose father, then bishop of Ely, had bought him the treasury office in 1169. In today's view, the mixture of war and clergy is far more shocking. True of institutions, such as the military orders, the mixture was also seen in individual careers. An Englishman, Gervase of Tilbury, was raised in Italy, studied and perhaps taught at Bologna and served as a chancery officer in England, Sicily, and for the archbishop of Rheims before becoming military commander of the kingdom of Arles for Emperor Otto IV (d. 1218). Although he married in Provence, he may have retired as a secular canon in England. In 1215 France's army at Bouvines was marshalled by Garin, one-time canon and Hospitaller, then bishop of Senlis and later chancellor of France. A Poitevin, Peter of Roches (d. 1238), began as a knight under King Richard, entered orders to become bishop of Winchester in 1205 and in 1213 was England's chief justiciar. Politically active until 1235, he was also an excellent soldier in England, Wales, the Holy Land and, in his last years, the papal states. Not surprisingly, the mores of the martial aristocracy pene-trated the clergy. In 1298 the chapter of the Church of St John the Evangelist at Liège allowed members to serve in arms to protect family interests.

Secular churchmen sometimes suffered at the hands of the regu-lars. In the early fourteenth century the mendicants held up the theological degree at Paris of a Picard parish rector hostile to them. In exchange for permitting friars into his parish, the Dominican master Hannibal of Ceccano finally let him get his licentiate, and in the festive dinner congratulated him on his advanced age: 'Indeed, for a long time now has our bachelor expiated here in Paris a sin committed in Picardy!'[36] Even the cardinals sometimes evoke sym-pathy when confronting the friars. When Pope Nicholas IV (d. 1292) asked the prior general of the Austin friars for a penitentiary, he produced Augustine, a former jurist and chancellor of King Manfred of Sicily. Augustine had joined the order after the defeat and death of his Hohenstaufen prince in 1266 and had subsequently re-established himself by spectacular moral rigour and self-abnega-tion. When the general led him before the pope and cardinals in consistory, the latter, 'seeing him despicable in dress and austere and rigid in visage, exclaimed to the general, "What woods did you drag him out of?"[37] Nor were the religious humble. Convinced of their superiority, they often forgot the injunction: 'Nothing so pleases God in a monk as obedience, and one obedience is worth more than all the virtues.'[38]

Regulars also fought among themselves, sometimes harmlessly, sometimes viciously. The Franciscan Salimbene even maintained that Dominic of Caleruega (d. 1221), the founder of the Domini-cans, was a fake saint. He reported that the Dominican preacher John Schio of Vicenza (d. 1260) once threatened his brethren with: 'I have exalted your Dominic, who' you kept hidden twelve years underground, and . . . I'll vilify your saint and tell everybody what you're doing.'[39] Thinking of Francis's canonization of 1228, he also made the cardinal promoter of Dominic's in 1234 say: 'Since the Franciscans have a saint, make sure you have one too, even if you make him of straw.'[40]

This partly reflected conflicts over ideals. Although Dominic himself shared much with Francis, his preachers soon advanced in the hierarchy. Eremitic, Francis opposed building churches and was reluctant to encourage his brethren to preach or hear confession. Nor did he want Franciscans to be prelates, in spite of a plea by

Hugolino, cardinal of Ostia, later Pope Gregory IX: 'In the primitive Church, pastors and prelates were poor and fervent in love and not in cupidity. Why then do we not make your brethren bishops and prelates whose words and deeds would influence others?'[41] Francis favoured leading by example instead of by commanding. The saint lost the argument, however: only two in number in 1245, fifty-six Franciscan bishops attended the Council of Vienne in 1311.

Orders were themselves rent by disputes. In the Franciscan, the lay friars fell out with those in holy orders, and the crisis came to a head during the generalate of Elias (d. 1253) from 1232. A layman like the founder, Elias wanted the lay friars to run the order but was defeated by the clerical friars and replaced by the pope in 1239. In his *On Prelates*, Salimbene describes the general's 'tyranny', repeating stories against the lay brethren. A priestly friar, taking his turn at kitchen duty, was asked to perform the mass for passing travellers. He replied: 'Go sing the mass yourselves! I'm cooking . . . !'[42] The slow exclusion of the lay friars from the First Order changed the Franciscans' basic character: Francis had wanted the friars to work with their hands.

Because of those they admitted, the two orders appealed to different audiences. Far less numerous, Dominicans were selective and excluded those without Latin, for example, because, as Humbert of Romans said, they

> incur temptation when they see that, in preaching, giving advice and similar duties, they cannot do what their colleagues do. The Law therefore ordained: 'You shall not plough with an ox and an ass together,' because, owing to his weakness, an ass cannot do what an ox can, and is upset when yoked to him.[43]

Even after the defeat of the lay friars, Franciscans were more open. According to Salimbene, they were 'fishers of men' whereas Dominicans were 'hunters', richer, more urban and noble and, as will be seen, more inquisitorial.

LAYMEN

Lay institutions were imperfect. Giles of Rome, for example, said that most people married, and that those who do not, do not 'either because they wish to fornicate more freely and hence choose a quasi-bestial life below that of men, or because they wish to study truth and divine works and hence lead a life superior to that of men, that of a quasi-God'.[44] To Giles, the clergy were the celibate quasi-gods. He also argued that 'if men . . . were not prone to evil, their possessions would be in common because the more property is in community, the more divine it is . . . . Things being as they are, however, and men being too imperfect, the world's inhabitants need private property.'[45] To Giles, the regular clergy – and only they – were those who held property in common. As seen above, however, other churchmen believed that active and believing lay-persons were as 'religious' as the formally professed.

That aside, churchmen were convinced that they were especially fit to educate humanity to attain heaven. Penitential and confessional practices and Church courts claimed jurisdiction over 'moral cases' in the lay world. A Council of Toulouse in 1229 ordered that last wills be drafted with clergy in attendance to discourage heresy, encourage restitution for usury and require charitable donations. Endowed commemoratory feasts and masses helped finance parish schools and charity. These were amplified by the indulgence, a remission of the penalties for sin won by good works. This institution grew up in conjunction with the Crusade but soon went beyond it, being sold for any good cause. When Maastricht planned to replace a collapsed bridge, her magistrates turned to Rome, and at Orvieto in 1284, forty-day indulgences were sold to help out. For a time, the laity were dazzled by this 'sweet and sour' mixture of coercion and attraction.

Even soldiers had a role to play in this heaven-bent economy. Defence of family and fatherland was enjoined on them, even in Lent, lest, said Bartholomew of Exeter, they tempt God by unpreparedness. Churchmen, however, also condemned them. John of Salisbury remarked in the *Policraticus* that there had hardly ever been a just war. Bernard of Clairvaux said that soldiers were nothing but murderers seeking booty, even converting self-defence into self-indulgence. 'There is one who slays a man not with zeal for vengeance nor pride in conquest, but only as a means to escape. But I would not call even this a good victory, since of the two evils, it is easier to die in body than in soul.' Not that Bernard was pacific. He cheered crusading Templars on to battle with a perfervid prose appropriate to one whose lance was his pen.

How gloriously the victors return from battle! How blessed are the martyrs who die in battle! Rejoice, stout champion, if you live and conquer in the Lord, but exult and glory even more if you die and join Him! . . . . If those who die in the Lord are blessed, how much more are those who die for Him?[46]

Families were often of two minds. Peter the Hermit of Monte Morrone (Celestine V), was the youngest of seven remaining sons of twelve born to his farming family. One was already a monk, but his mother wanted Peter to be a clerk also. His brothers opposed it, arguing 'one who does not work is enough'.[47] Thomas Aquinas's aristocratic family put him in the clergy, but wanted him at hand in Montecassino. When, around fifteen, he joined the Dominicans, the friars intended to take him to Paris 'so that he should be removed from his relatives'. His mother had him kidnapped and forced to stay at home for over a year.[48] Salimbene of Parma's entry into the Franciscans reflected adolescent revolt. He never forgave his mother for saving his sisters first in an earthquake. 'I did not love her so much after that,' he reports, 'because she ought to have cared for me, a boy, more than for the girls.'[49] He entered the order at fifteen under the influence of his older brother Guy, who had left the world as a judge and married man. Apart from an illegitimate brother who went away to Toulouse, Salimbene was the last male, and his father fought him bitterly. A Ghibelline, he even enlisted the help of the emperor, once crying out against the brethren: 'Don't believe these piss-in-skirts!'[50] A Guelf, the youth replied to his parents' final overtures by comparing himself to the harlot Jerusalem – 'My father was an Amorite and my mother an Hittite' – but forbore from continuing: 'No eye pitied me . . . but I was cast out in the open field, to the loathing of my person, on the day I was born.'[51] Although proud of his blood, Salimbene enjoyed his parents' defeat: 'I, brother Salimbene, and brother Guy destroyed our family both male and female by entering the order that we might build it in heaven.'[52]

Taking young rebels from their families, monks were harsh. Both Bernard of Clairvaux and the Franciscan radical Angelo of Clareno (d. 1337) repeated a passage written by Jerome:

'if your mother's torn clothes . . . show the breasts that fed you and your father lies prostrate on the threshold, push over him, and, with dry eyes, fly off to the banner of the cross . . . .' For [continued the Franciscan] their own misery and the judgment they will incur for their sins does not suffice for your parents, because, just as they bear and raise us in sin, so do they love us to remain in sin to have us with them in hell's torments![53]

If monks often hurt layfolk, the laity often exploited the cloister. At Ardres near Boulogne in 1161 the abbot was appalled to find that his Benedictines were mostly lame, blind, deformed or illiterate. They were also almost all noble, showing that the house was a dump for the aristocracy. Boncompagno's manual of love letters has one addressed to a nun. 'The voice of the turtle or rather of the cuckoo has been heard in our land, saying that you have decided to put off the honour of this world and receive the monastic garb to live a cloistered life together with hunchbacks, lame, hooknosed and squinting women.'[54] Families also forced the old to enter religion. A preacher at Tortosa in the thirteenth century tells that 'we many times see that sons make their fathers monks or hermits because they are annoyed at their living so long and want their inheritances'.[55]

Lay lordship of churches was now rare, but patronage still very much alive. In 1207 Philip Augustus of France ordered conflicts over secular patrons' presentations of candidates for rural parishes in Normandy settled by four priests and four knights. Lay influence also saw to it that prelates came largely from the well-to-do. Of about 314 German bishops in the thirteenth century, only six per cent were of burgher or peasant origin. Although it could no longer be said, as earlier in Cluny, that, save as a converse, 'no son of a villein will ever be in my cloister', the rich and noble were advantaged.[56] Acquiring office by family influence, clerks owed favours. In his archiepiscopal inspection Odo Rigaud turned up an abbot who had dowered and married off his nieces and sent a nephew through the university, giving him a copy of the corpus of Roman law.

Privilege, however, was vigorously, if sometimes inefficaciously, attacked. Peter Cantor called class 'prejudice' simony. A gloss on John of Garlande's *Scholars' Behaviour* of 1241 notes that 'nobles in spirit and word ought be preferred to nobles of family'.[57] The Dominican Hugh of St Cher (d. 1263) castigated his order's bias which allowed gentlemen novices to enter before the canonical age of fifteen. The medical doctor Arnold of Villanova (d. 1311–13) found class prejudice a vice threatening the Church, even asserting that 'those born of vile adulteries, if decorated by mores and cleanliness of life, are more noble than others, even to the degree that their parents gave a clearer example of vileness'.[58] In 1232, Gregory IX was informed that the chapter of Strasbourg refused to admit anyone not noble on both sides of his parentage. He disallowed the practice because 'purity of life and nobility of virtue, not lineage, make a pleasing and suitable servitor of God. God chose for [his Church] not many noble or powerful according to the flesh but instead those who were non-noble and poor, for God is no respecter of persons'.[59]

·Even those who loved the Church were not disinterested. When Francis of Assisi was near death at Nocera, news of his condition reached home. 'Certain knights hastened to that place to bring him back to Assisi, fearing that he would die there and others would have his most holy body.'[60] Pious confraternities, Boncompagno of Signa wrote, were actuated by more than piety.

> Inspired by charity, confraternities are created . . . for which simple statutes are written, telling how much wine or grain each member is to contribute. 'Inspired by charity', I say, because folk join such confraternities so's to . . . swell their bellies. In the diocese of Florence, a rustic fraternity exists for the utility of the church. As is usual in such fraternities, the rectors arrange no mean banquets for the members and, after them, render accounts. A rector once rose and said: 'Blessed be the Lord who has performed a miracle in and through us, because nothing of that which we have given was lacking to pay the expenses and nothing remains save a ha'penny!'

for the church. Whence, says Boncompagno, comes the Tuscan proverb: 'May what happened to the parishioners of St Hilary's church happen to us.'[61]

Although seemingly influencing everything and seen everywhere in secular society, moreover, the Church barely touched much of lay life. If current ideas of love borrowed much of their intensity from religious and especially monastic thought, churchmen cut pitiful figures in love poetry. The most religious of all poems, *Tristan and Iseult*, argues that true love exists only in heaven, not on earth. The God who loves true lovers, moreover, even helps the lovers cheat the queen's husband. The institutional Church is represented only by an old hermit whose hopeless duty is to make the lovers give up love, re-enter society and resume their normal careers. Another example is seen in *Aucassin and Nicolete*. When told that he is buying hell with his unsuitable love, Aucassin avers he'd as soon go there. Hell holds the lovesome, beautiful and brave; heaven a few old Enochs and Elijahs, miserable priests, the decrepit and the sick.

In conclusion, medieval men and women treated their beliefs as men usually do. They built their Church and applauded its law, yet played ˉvith its rules to fit them to their taste. In the age treated here, however, the world seemed so bright that men took only occasional exception to what they had inherited and re-created. Their adherence may be measured: after fortification, churches and cloisters received the largest investment of money and energy.

The beauty of these buildings was not all gain. Fulk, parish priest of Neuilly, was a great preacher, and early determined to replace his church at Neuilly with a sumptuous edifice. But, for all his talk about voluntary poverty, against usury and his plan to finance the poor to go on crusade, his career fell apart because men saw where the money was going, 'and by the hidden judgment of God his authority and preaching began to diminish remarkably'.[62] Shortly beforehand, Fulk's teacher Peter Cantor tells of Bernard of Clairvaux, weeping because he saw

> the thatch-roofed shepherds' huts . . . in which the early Cistercians had lived [now converted] into star-strewn palaces. For this disease of building, these monks . . . are often punished . . . . For protection, even their farms are castellated and, lest they lose them, they often hide the truth and leave unmentioned God's justice, fearing to grumble against princes. For this reason they have lost their freedom of which 'tis said: 'An empty-handed traveller will sing before a thief.' [This have they lost] for the riches of their farms and fields, permitting dormitories and refectories to be built for them by plunderers and usurers as a sign and eternal memorial of their avarice.[63]

Caesarius of Heisterbach says that when a rich Parisian usurer came to repent, Peter Cantor told him to restore his ill-gotten gains to the poor or those from whom he had taken them. His bishop, Maurice of Sully, who died in 1196 with the choir and nave of Nôtre Dame of Paris completed, had wanted the money put towards his cathedral. Who was right?

NOTES AND REFERENCES

1   Major orders were priests, deacons and subdeacons; minor ones acolytes, exorcists, readers, porters and psalmists.

2   *De magnalibus urbis Mediolani* 3, 7 in Francesco Novati (ed.), *Bullettino dell'istituto storici italiano* XX (1898), 81–2.

3   *Liber de una forma credendi et multiformitate vivendi a tempore Abel, justi usque ad novissimum electum* in *Dialogi* 1, 1 in *PL* CLXXXVIII, 1141.

4   *Liber de diversis ordinibus et professionibus* 2 and 5 in *PL* CCXIII, 814 and 827.

5   *Ibid.*, 2 *in PL* CCXIII, 836.

6   Thomas of Eccleston, *De adventu fratrum minorum in Angliam* 15 (ed. A.G. Little, Manchester, 1951), 91.

7   *Vita beati Romualdi* in Giovanni Tabacco (ed.), *Istituto storico Italiano per il Medio evo: 'Fonti per la storia d'Italia'* XCIV (1957), 78.

8   *Dispositio novi ordinis pertinens ad tercium statum ad instar superne Jerusalem* in Grundmann, *Neue Forschungen über Joachim von Fiore*, 120–1.

9   1 Corinthians 7: 32–3 and Acts 4: 32–7.

10 *Contra clericos regulares proprietarios* 5 in *PL* CXLV, 490.

11 Letter 56 in *PL* CLI, 336.

12 Jordan of Saxony, *Liber vitas fratrum* 3, 8 (eds Rudolph Arbesmann and Winfred Humpfner, New York, 1943), 346, adapted from Gratian's *Decretum* 1, 35, 4 in *CICan* I, 131, taken from Jerome.

13 *Speculum perfectionis* 4, 7 and 9 in Paul Sabatier (ed.), *Le Speculum Perfectionis ou Mémoires de Frère Léon* (Manchester, 1931), II, 13–14, stories dated about 1311–12, and also 1 Corinthians 8:1.

14 Letter 106 to Henry Murdach in *PL* CLXXXII, 242.

15 Jordan of Saxony, *Liber vitas fratrum* 3, 8 (eds Arbesmann and Humpfner), 345.

16 My 'Charity and Social Work in Toulouse', *Traditio* XXII (1966), 209–10n.

17 *Speculum perfectionis* 12, 123 (ed. Sabatier), I, 345–6.

18 *Legenda aurea vulgo Historia Lombardica dicta* (ed. Th. Graesse, Bratislava, 1890), 102.

19 *Historia ecclesiastica* 2, 5, 22 in *PL* CLXXXVIII, 447.

20 Philippe Delhaye, 'L'organisation scolaire', *Traditio* V (1947), 237.

21 *Policraticus* 8, 9 (ed. C.C.J. Webb, Oxford, 1909), II, 280.

22 Schreiber, 'Cluny und die Eigenirche' in *Gemeinschaften des Mittelalters*, 117n.

23 Thomas of Eccleston, *De adventu fratrum minorum in Angliam* 10 (ed. Little), 46.

24 *Ibid.* 15 (ed. Little) 92.

25 From the chronicle of Melas cited by Haller, *Vier Kapitel zur Geschichte des ausgehenden Mittelalters* I, 121.

26 Heinrich Boehmer (ed.), 'Analekten zur Geschichte des Franz von Assisi' in *Sammlung ausgewählter kirchen- und dogmengeschichtlicher Quellenschriften* IV (Tübingen, 1961), 46.

27 *La règle du Temple* (ed. Curzon), 210.

28 In Etienne Baluze *Miscellanea sacra* (Lucca, 1761) II, 271b.

29 *Rhetorica novissima* 1, 14 in *BIMA* II, 254a.

30 *Les lettres de Jacques de Vitry* (ed. R.B.C. Huygens, Leiden, 1960), 1n and 72.

31 A life added to James of Voragine's *Legenda aurea* (ed. Graesse), 919, reflecting Chapter 11 of William of Tocco's life in *AA.SS.* 1 March, 678A–B.

32 My 'Une famille Cathar: Les Maurands', *Annales: ESC* (1974), 1222–3.

33 *Libri IV sententiarum* 4, 13 in *PL* CXCII, 868.

34 *Ibid*. 4, 10 in *PL* CXCII, 863.

35 Caesarius of Heisterbach, *Dialogus miraculorum* 2, 27 (ed. Strange), I, 9.

36 Jordan of Saxony, *Liber vitas fratrum* 2, 6 (eds Arbesmann and Humpfner), 110–11. Hannibal Gaetani, archdeacon of Arras and university master, became archbishop of Naples in 1326 and cardinal in 1327.

37 *Ibid*. 2, 7; *ibid*. 117. Prior general from 1298 to 1300, Matthew of Termini (d. 1309) took the name Augustine.

38 *Ibid* 2, 2; *ibid*. 78. Jordan cited Hugh of St Victor, who in turn used pseudo-Augustine *Sermo de obedientia et humilitate.*

39 *Cronica* in *MGH SS* XXXII, 77.

40 *Ibid*. 72.

41 *Speculum perfectionis* 3, 43 (ed. Sabatier), I, 109–10.

42 *Cronica* in *MGH SS* XXXII, 103.

43 *Expositio regulae B. Augustini* 144 (ed. Berthier), I, 472, and Deuteronomy 22:10.

44 *De regimine principum* 2, 1, 7 (Rome, 1607), 240.

45 *Ibid*. 2, 3, 6 on p. 361.

46 *De laude novae militiae ad milites Templi* 1, 1 and 2 in *Sancti Bernardi opera* (eds Jean Leclercq and H.M. Rochais, Rome, 1963), 214–15, and Apocalypse 14:13.

47 *Tractatus de vita sua* in Arsenio Frugoni (ed.), *Celestiana* (Rome, 1954), 57.

48 James of Voragine, *Legenda aurea* (ed. Graesse), 918–19.

49 *Cronica* in *MGH SS* XXXII, 34.

50 *Ibid*. 40.

51 Adapted from Ezekiel 16:3–5, the text in Salimbene's mind.

52 *Cronica* in *MGH SS* XXXII, 56.

53 Clareno's Letter 11 in Florence, Bibl. Nazionale, Codex Magliabecchi XXXIX, 75, 31r. Bernard's is Letter 322 in *PL* 182, 527d–8a.

54 *Rota veneris* (ed. Friedrich Baethgen, Rome, 1927), 20. Song of Solomon 2,12.

55 M. Zink, 'Le traitement des "sources exemplaires" dans les sermons occitans, catalans, piémontais du XIIIe siècle' in *Cahiers de Fanjeaux* 11 (1976), 177.

56 Discussed in Schreiber, 'Cluny und die Eigenkirche' in *Gemeinschaften des Mittelalters*, 83n.

57 *Morale scolarium* 10 (ed. Paetow), 208.

58 *Apologia de versutiis atque perversitatibus pseudotheologorum et religiosorum ad Magistrum Jacob Albi* in Heinrich Finke, *Aus dem Tagen Bonifaz VIII* clxv, p. 24.

59 *Venerabilis frater* in *Liber extra* 3, 5, 37 in *CICan* II, 480–1.

60 *Speculum perfectionis* 1, 22 (ed. Sabatier), I, 57; also in Celano's and Bonaventura's lives.

61   *Cedrus* in *BuF* I, 125.
62   James of Vitry, *Historia occidentalis* 8 (ed. Hinnebusch), 101.
63   *Verbum abbreviatum* 86 in *PL* CCV, 257, quoting from Juvenal's *Satires* 10, 22.

PART FOUR
Government

13

THE CHURCH

GOVERNMENT AND WAR

The Church was Latin Europe's symbol of identity. In 1301 Boniface VIII called Rome 'the common court of all the nations of the Christian people'.[1] Even Peter Dubois, Boniface's enemy, seeking European unity under the French king, chose the pope as Europe's ultimate arbitrator.

Churchmen regarded Christendom as governed by princes or magistrates submissive to the pope. In 1198 Innocent III stated: 'We do not deny that the emperor is superior in temporal matters to those who receive temporal things from him, but the pope is superior in spiritual matters, which, as the soul is superior to the body, are more worthy than temporal ones.'[2] Secular might advanced humankind's earthly good. Higher were eternal life and supernal virtue, attainable only by God's grace through the Church. So highly were sacerdotal functions esteemed that the great Hostiensis did not blush to state that the sacerdotal dignity was 7,644.5 times greater than the royal, paralleling the difference in the brightness of the sun and moon stated in Ptolemy's *Almagest*.

Lay governments were to serve the Church. Writing in 1301, Giles of Rome avowed that, because the Church could not shed blood, the State must act for it, but in so doing, gained no power of its own. Secular might was like a smith's tongs. Although the tongs touched hot iron, which the smith could not, the smith, symbol of spiritual power, moved them. Suger, abbot of Saint-Denis, urged the kings of France and England to cast themselves at the pontiff's feet, and the emperor to serve as groom for this prince of princes. To John of Salisbury, companion in exile of Thomas

Becket, 'all law not bearing the imprint of divine law is . . . inane, and princely enactments not conforming to Church discipline must be considered harmful'.[3] Around 1160 a canonist remarked that the pope 'is the true emperor, and the emperor is his vicar'.[4]

A source of this power was Constantine's Donation. In 1207 Gerald of Wales congratulated the emperor because his gift of majesty was worth more than one of property. But the donation was awkward. Had the emperor really given the Empire to the pope? The civilian Accursius's ordinary gloss (about 1250) observed that, if so, Constantine gave what was not his to give. He was the Empire's administrator, called 'august' from the Latin 'to increase', but the donation had hardly done that. Rising against papal rule in 1152, the Romans wrote to the emperor: 'This lie and heretical fable in which Constantine is alleged to have simoniacally given the Empire to [Pope] Sylvester is so thoroughly exposed in Rome that common workmen and washerwomen silence even the most learned about it.'[5] Besides, he who gives is greater than he who receives. Around 1211 Gervase of Tilbury said that God founded the Empire and Constantine the pope's glory. The donation was therefore supplemented from history: had not the popes transferred the Empire from the schismatic Greeks to the Franks at Charlemagne's crowning? Albert Behaim, archdeacon of Passau, went on to ask in 1240 whether they could not transfer it again if Germany's princes proved delinquent.

Scripture was better than history: the pope had received all power from Christ through St Peter. This magic allowed Gregory VII to ask a council at Rome in 1080: 'Act now, I beg, fathers. . . and let the world know that, if you can bind and loose in heaven, here on earth you can remove from anyone and grant to anyone . . . empires, kingdoms, principates, duchies, marquisates, counties, indeed all men's possessions.'[6] Congratulating John of England because he held his realm of Rome, Innocent III remarked in 1213:

> The king of kings and lord of lords Christ Jesus . . . has so established the kingdom and the priesthood in the Church that the kingdom is priestly and the priesthood royal . . . so that, as body and soul, both kingdom and priesthood should be unified in the single person of the vicar of Christ to the great advantage and augmentation of both.[7]

He also pithily summed up the subordination of the material sword to the spiritual by telling an archbishop of Ravenna in 1198 that 'ecclesiastical liberty is never better served than when the

Roman Church obtains full power in both temporal and spiritual matters'.[8]

Popes wrote to princes as to children. A form letter for a newly elected German king reads: 'Mothers derive great joy from their sons' excellence and nothing so delights parents as the wisdom and probity of their offspring.'[9] Boniface VIII importuned Philip IV of France in 1301: 'Hearken, dearest son, to the precepts of your father and bend the ear of your heart to the teaching of the master who, here on earth, stands in place of Him who alone is master and lord.'[10] Knowing that the pope was addressed as 'prince of princes', Boncompagno of Signa told lawyers pleading in consistory to begin with 'I have risen to speak before the father of fathers, who obtains the plenitude of power on earth in place of Simon Peter' or 'before him . . . who yokes the necks of kings and emperors, crowning the worthy and deposing the unworthy'.[11]

Secular princes were thought to hold of the pope. At a diet of Besançon in 1157 two cardinals, irked by imperial support of the see of Hamburg–Bremen against Scandinavia's Lund, asked that, if the emperor did not hold the Empire from the pope, from whom did he? One of the two was Roland Bandinelli, the later Alexander III and, for five years previously, chancellor of the Holy See. The jurist Roffredo of Benevento (d. *circa* 1243) wrote that 'vassals are those who receive anything from anyone in fief, as the emperor has the kingdom of Sicily from the pope, and many say the same about the Empire', an opinion stated as fact by the papalist Alvarez Pelayo in 1327.[12] Such views were widespread. Thomas Aquinas contrasted Roman times when the emperors persecuted the Church with the present when they defended it. Now, he said, it befits kings to be Church vassals. His secretary, Ptolemy of Lucca (d. 1327), observed that the emperor received the Empire 'from the Church under oath like a vassal getting a fief, which is why the Church can depose him more easily than other princes'.[13]

On Europe's frontiers, kings were papal vassals. Papal suzerainty was momentarily acknowledged in Scandinavia, Hungary, Poland, Bohemia and Bulgaria, and the British Isles were all at one time or other under papal lordship. Adrian IV may even have given Ireland to England in 1155 to propagate a 'reformed' religion, and in return Rome got one penny annually from each hearth, a tax reminiscent of the Peter's pence revived when England was conquered in 1066. To repulse a French invasion, John placed his realm under Roman protection in 1213, granting a modest tax of which Ireland paid a third. If papal suzerainty ended with Edward I, Peter's pence lasted until Henry VIII.

The Norman kingdom of Apulia–Sicily had been held of Rome since the mid 1050s. Aided by French immigration, the popes intervened in Iberia, taking Portugal in 1179, Aragon and even Leon under their suzerainty. These nations used the papal link to raise Crusades against Islam and balance the might of Castile–Leon. In 1198 the pope was titled suzerain of Jerusalem, Cyprus and Armenia, and in 1217 Peter of Courtenay, the second Latin emperor of Constantinople, was crowned at Rome. In 1217–21 a crusade against Egypt, the Muslim strategic base, was actually commanded by a cardinal.

Secular states often resisted: excommunicated, Frederick II crusaded and took both Jerusalem and Cyprus in 1228–9. With the resounding defeat of the Hohenstaufen, however, even imperialists like Alexander of Roes admitted that at Lyons in 1274 'not only did the Christian people and ecclesiastical prelates assemble at the feet of the Roman pontiff, but even the kings of the world, together with the Jews, Greeks and Tatars, confessed that world monarchy [belonged] to the Roman priest'.[14] The rabbi Todros son of Isaac casually referred to the pope as the 'king of nations'.

The pope had his war, the Crusade. The word 'war' was usually avoided, although one pope, Clement III (d. 1191), used it. Bernard of Clairvaux even liked it, and the jurist Hostiensis described Crusades as 'Roman wars' because Rome's Syria, Palestine and Spain had been 'usurped' by Christ's enemies. And crusaders were not soldiers, simply penitent pilgrims wearing the cross. This led to curious ideas: crusaders slain in battle were likened to Bethlehem's Holy Innocents slaughtered on the order of Herod the Great. Not all these 'innocents', however, were voluntary. Heretics were condemned to crusade, and many serving in Spain against Islam and the 'crusades' against the Hohenstaufen and Catalans in southern Italy were even criminals. If some were coerced, others were bought. Crusade indulgences had expanded in conjunction with holy war, but soon went beyond gratifying soldiers: when Majorca was taken from Islam in 1228, Christian settlers were granted them.

Hard on non-Christians, Crusades helped limit warfare at home. There, wars were to be just, defined, that is, by a good cause like self-defence, observance of formalities and moderation. As the war between the emperor and the popes and their allies grew in violence, however, domestic combats became more violent. Describing the Guelf Crusade against Ezzelino of Romano (1256–9), Rolandino of Padua said of the past: 'Then were wars, if one may say so, good wars . . . . A captured man was not forthwith put to death or loaded with chains, nor condemned to be horribly mutilated in his members, but was instead sent where he wished honourably and with praise. But today'[15] brutality and fratricide rule. Ideology embittered the Hohenstaufen wars, and prompted the unprecedented execution of Conradin, the last Hohenstaufen of the male line, by the pope's French allies in 1268.

Once taken, a crusader's oath was irrevocable. Forced to take the cross in order to be crowned in 1220, Frederick II was excommunicated in 1227 for non-fulfilment while trying to cement his south Italian realm. Popes also controlled marriage and divorce, vital because dynastic marriage affected interstate policy. Unimportant until Rome defeated the old state churches, marital control then became real, confounding princes used to subservient local prelates appointed by themselves. When Philip Augustus of France dissolved his marriage to Ingeborg of Denmark and tried to ally with the Hohenstaufen, a local council at Compiègne annulled the marriage. Times had changed, however, and from 1193 to 1200 the pope fought Philip to his knees.

Enforcement mechanisms underwent development. Personal excommunication severed the communion of a prince with his subjects, thereby dissolving their allegiance. Interdicts evolved by which all but last sacraments were withdrawn from subjects whose indifference to 'spiritual' causes led them to live easy under recalcitrant leaders. Although group interdict had long been known, whole peoples were not touched until Alexander III and Innocent III won great triumphs using it against France in 1200 and England in 1208. Later, stronger stuff was needed, and at the first Council of Lyons in 1245 Innocent IV both anathematized Frederick II as a heretic and launched a Crusade against him. After this fulmination, one that harked back to Europe's civil wars of the Gregorian age, no new weapons were found in the papal arsenal.

POPES, PRINCES AND EMPERORS

Writing between 1149 and 1152, Bernard of Clairvaux minted arguments much repeated thereafter. Like most churchmen, he asserted the supremacy of the pope's spiritual power and right to use secular coercion. Had the material sword not pertained to the Church, 'the Lord would not have replied "It is enough" to those who said "Look, here are two swords," but rather, "It is too much." Therefore both spiritual and material swords are the Church's, but the latter is to be wielded for it and the former by it.'[16] But the pope's power should not encourage him to wear a crown or ride a white charger surrounded by soldiers, imitating Constantine instead of Peter. Bernard told the pope: 'You err if . . . you think your apostolic power to be the only one instituted by God. If you do, you disagree with him who says, "There is no power but of God. . . ." Although said mainly for you, he did not say it for you alone.'[17] All was permitted the pope, Bernard taught, but not all was expedient.

To clerks still attached to Europe's faded state churches, princes were God's vicars, a title the popes monopolized by 1200. During the Gregorian fury, proponents of princely authority borrowed late Roman teaching. A monk of Farfa, Gregory of Catina, wrote about 1111 that God alone judged the Empire, which preceded the priesthood. Christ never gave the Church temporal power; Constantine did that, and his action was inane. The Lord had recognized the imperial authority vested in Pontius Pilate. Based on such sources, Jordan of Osnabrück and Alexander of Roes commented in the 1280s that, if the pope's was a royal priesthood, the emperor's was a priestly kingship. Although the pope transferred the Empire from the Greeks to the Germans, this was no human initiative, being instead heaven's unalterable design: 'Before it happened, the deity foreknew that the Roman Empire must be transferred to the Germans,' to remain in their hands until the Antichrist's coming. 'Christ Jesus deigned to honour the Roman Empire in the days of his flesh . . . honouring Caesar or the Roman king when entering the world, living in it and departing from it.'[18] The Saviour's coming signalled Rome's era of universal peace. He submitted to the census, paid tribute, and admitted Pilate's jurisdiction over his body, thereby confirming the emperor's material sword. These arguments were summed up anew by Dante Alighieri in the early fourteenth century.

Because effective censure depends on popular cooperation, papal resistance to these ideas reflected the Church's alliance with Europe's aristocracies. What there was of political liberty within any monarchy at this time was because its subjects had two monarchs –

a secular prince and the pope – and shifted allegiance from one to the other as circumstance dictated, thus destroying the pretensions to absolutism of both. With inadvertent accuracy, John Quidort of Paris (d. 1308) described this state of affairs:

> When a king sins in temporal matters, the judgment of which does not pertain to the Church, [the pope] has no right to correct him in the first instance, for this right instead belongs to the barons and peers of the kingdom. If they are unable . . . to do that, however, they may invoke help from the Church which, as an aid to law, may warn the prince,

excommunicating him so that the people can replace him.[19]

Overthrowing tyrants was urged by Manegold of Lautenbach in the Gregorian age and more discreetly by John of Salisbury later on. Manegold (d. *circa* 1103) proposed that princes who breach their contract with the people may be removed. For John, tyranny was to attack ecclesiastical freedom, but he and others reminded their audiences that all were affected. Popes, in fact, responded with alacrity to complaints about tyrannical princes. Condemning Frederick II in 1245, Innocent IV not only adverted to this prince's heresy, but also to the misery of his realms, claiming that the best citizens had been driven out and the rest reduced to indigence and slavery.

Being itself electoral, the papacy favoured elected over hereditary monarchy. The priests of Alexandria, Jerome said, elected their bishops, 'even as the army raises the emperor or deacons choose one of themselves . . . and call him archdeacon'.[20] This seemed a satisfactory way of aligning the interests of the 'people' with those of the supreme pontiff, and Innocent IV was emboldened to say: 'The pope has the Empire from God, and the emperor from the people.'[21]

A weakness of this position was that the divine origin of the office and the election of the officer by the people could also be combined to exclude the pope. Cino of Pistoia wrote: 'Nor is it absurd that [the Empire] should derive from both God and the people. The emperor is from the people but the Empire, called divine, from God.'[22] Cino was not being inventive. Writing around 1302–3 with the French monarchy in mind, John of Paris said the same about royal power, and also used the argument to undermine the historical base of the papal claim, namely, the transfer of the Empire from the Greeks to the Franks. This was done not by the pope alone, he asserted, but also by the Roman people, 'for a reasonable and necessary cause, namely, defence against infidels and pagans, since no other seemed able to defend them; which action was legal because a people makes the king and an army the emperor'. John also justified hereditary monarchy, saying that royal authority derived not from 'a pope but from God and the people electing the king either in person or in dynasty'.[23]

The popes were never wholly able to impose their will, even in the Empire. That Rome won there cannot be doubted: the electoral tradition of other western monarchies faded in this period; the reverse was true in the Empire. Other states increased; the Empire slowly weakened. But the victory was incomplete. Viewing a German king's election as an episcopal one, the popes tried to intervene if disputes erupted. Partial successes were enjoyed in the conflict between the Welf Otto IV and the Hohenstaufen Philip of Swabia in 1199 and again during the Great Interregnum in 1263, when the electors fell out over Richard of Cornwall and Alfonso of Castile. In 1202 Innocent III claimed the right to refuse to crown as emperor an insufficient German king or emperor-elect. 'If the princes . . . elected as king a sacrilegious person, an excommunicate, a tyrant or fool, a heretic or pagan, should we then unction, consecrate or crown a man of that kind? Certainly not!'[24]

Electoral monarchy was, Germans said, a mark of German natural freedom. Not a few, also, preferred a weak imperial government, but none accepted the rest of the papal programme. Eike of Repkow's *Saxon Mirror* refused to exclude excommunicates from imperial election, because it opened the door to papal intervention, and the electors were certain that their vote alone made the Roman king and that he could rule without papal coronation. This doctrine grew from the Hohenstaufen Declaration of Speyer in 1199 through Lewis of Bavaria's edict *Licet juris* in 1338 to full acceptance in the Golden Bull of 1356.

To defeat the Empire, the popes reinforced Europe's other princes, who anyway disliked Frederick Barbarossa's remark that they were mere kinglets. Some peoples subscribed to the fiction that, like Rome, they were founded by the Trojans. Having never been part of the Carolingian 'reconstruction' of the Roman Empire, England and Castile asserted freedom from imperial sovereignty, and there the germ of the notion that each king was emperor in his own kingdom made its appearance. Castile recalled Visigothic declarations of independence from Rome. Geoffrey of Monmouth in 1147 tells of a fictional English king who requested Roman law from an imaginary pope. The pontiff refused, saying: 'You are

God's vicar in your kingdom. The royal psalmist [said] "Give the king thy judgment, O God," etc. He did not say, "the judgment or justice of Caesar".'[25]

Areas once under Carolingian sway went about it differently. During the twelfth century France's Capetian kings claimed to be Charlemagne's heirs, true rulers of the Franks. Germans like Alexander of Roes replied by saying that the French were mere by-blows of Frankish soldiers and Gallic women. The popes rescued the French by first applying to them, in the letter *Per venerabilem* of 1213, the idea that kings justly recognize no superiors. This became a commonplace, as in the later Castilian code: 'Kings are vicars of God each in his kingdom placed above his people to maintain them in justice and truth as far as temporal things are concerned, just as the emperor is in his Empire.'[26] This doctrine helped the popes prevent the united front of secular princes the Hohenstaufen promoted.

Dividing in order to rule, papal action and ideology were partly determined by expediency. In 1310 a hostile witness charged the dead Boniface VIII with having said: 'If between the kings and princes of the world there is no discord, the Roman pope cannot be pope; but if there is, then he is, because each one fears him for fear of the other, and he can rule them and do what he wants.'[27] Boniface himself came close to this in 1296 when he asked the French king, then at war with England and at loggerheads with the Empire, what would happen if he so offended the papacy that Rome joined his enemies. More significantly, local society lent strength to papal leadership. Action by substantial elements of the English nobility and Church against 'tyranny' made John Lackland capitulate to Innocent III in 1213. A similar combination of powers let Innocent IV, acting as suzerain of Portugal, depose Sancho II and crown his brother Alfonso in 1245.

This support was sometimes lacking. An example is the Albigensian Crusade of 1209, which began as a papal war. From 1210 on, Rome recouped its investment by a hearth tax of three pence in the conquered territory, and in 1215 the pope dictated a settlement. A popular uprising against the crusaders then forced the popes to beg Capetian intervention in 1226. After the royal victory in 1229, the popes were effectively excluded from the Midi. Another example is the revolt of Sicily against the Angevin French in 1282. Once a papal fief, Catalonia–Aragon implemented this attack on the pope's French allies, and tied Sicily to their growing Mediterranean Empire.

LOCAL CHURCHES

Church freedom was the right of the clergy to be judged by those of their own order, to choose their own officers and to be exempt from secular taxation. To achieve this was not easy. The further from France or Italy, the more primitive the nature of the Church. In Scandinavia, for example, Carolingian-style state churches were still the order of the day. Courts Christian were not separate from secular tribunals, and canon jurisdiction over laymen was undeveloped. As late as 1247 the right of clergy to trial in their own courts hardly existed in Sweden. Sverre of Norway (d. 1202) was deposed by papal order and the land laid under interdict, but the king mobilized his bishops in 1199 to support his appointment of prelates. Even in Europe's heart, the old state Church was never forgotten. In 1247 France's bishops reminded the pope that Charlemagne once chose supreme pontiffs and France's kings conferred bishoprics.

In principle, clerks were exempt from lay taxes. In practice, since prelates held baronies and counties, they usually, like other vassals, owed both service and taxes. Most princes retained powers over local churches, among them *regalia*, the revenues of a vacant see. German and Spanish princes were often given shares of the tithe to protect Europe's frontiers. The customs of Milan in 1216 noted that 'although by canon law, laymen cannot possess [tithes], custom generally allows them to acquire and collect them'.[28] Even when tithes were 'returned', lay collectors often took the cream.

More threatening were taxes on real and other property. The first significant legislation, that of Alexander III in the third Lateran Council of 1179, was directed against Italy's city republics. Charged with imitating Pharaoh's plundering of the Jews, towns were told that such taxes were forbidden 'unless the bishop and clergy perceive so great a need . . . that, without coercion and for common purposes . . . when lay resources do not suffice, they esteem that the churches ought to lend aid'.[29] So open to pressure were local clerks, however, that Innocent III made such grants contingent on papal approval in 1216. In 1260 Alexander IV (d. 1261) applied the same legislation to French and other towns, and also forbade taxes on ecclesiastical acquisitions that were becoming common. The capstone was Boniface VIII's bull *Clericis laicos* of 1296, extending the prohibition to all monarchies. Strong opposition obliged the pope to suspend the bull in 1297 and fall back on Alexander III's position.

After this capitulation, 'voluntary gifts' to local governments became common. Nor could it have been otherwise. Italy's republics against which papal law was first directed were Rome's allies in the war against the Hohenstaufen, and had come to rely on these taxes. France, as another of Rome's allies, was also granted clerical taxes from the days of the Albigensian Crusade and by 1300 was used to this income. The crown could count on about £260,000 (of Tours) from the French clergy's tenth. The revenue from the tallage raised on all properties other than military fiefs gave only a slightly larger sum, about £315,000. In short, as with Jews, the State found it easier to tax the Church than its citizens.

Benefit of clergy, the right of clerks to be tried by their peers, members of their own order, expressed a Roman idea: 'Accusers plead their suits in defendants' courts.'[30] This worked well in civil cases but not in criminal ones, and it was there that the Church took its stand. A letter of Lucius III in 1181 stated that 'especially in criminal cases, [clerks] may never be condemned by other than ecclesiastical judges'.[31] Criminal clerks were therefore a main issue in the long battle from 1164 until 1170–2 between Henry II of England and Thomas Becket (d. 1170). The king was willing to let trials be conducted in a church forum, but insisted on his right to punish guilty clerks. Becket argued that this not only invaded clerical immunity but also offended God, who did not wish men punished twice, degraded, that is, from orders by the Church and then executed by the State. Becket's position is hard to understand unless one recalls that clerks hoped to relive the freedom of the apostolic community, and that canon courts were gentler than secular. From John of Salisbury to Peter Cantor, clerical leaders attacked violent secular punishments. Bad in itself, execution was not to be inflicted on clerks, for whom imprisonment amply sufficed.

Churchmen never got their way, partly because some 'crimes' also threatened them. In 1222 Stephen Langton, archbishop of Canterbury, usually an exponent of Peter Cantor's views, stripped a deacon of orders for judaizing and gave him to the crown for punishment – he was burned! – thus obeying a papal decretal of 1184.

The clergy also bowed to enraged public opinion. In Padua in 1301 a clerk found guilty of theft, murder and rape by secular judges, but exempt from execution, was put in a cage hung from the top of the Red Tower, expiring after a fortnight. Political cases were also very chancy. The arrest of Bernard Saisset, bishop of Pamiers, in 1301 for treason precipitated the final struggle between Boniface VIII and Philip IV of France, which the former lost.

Churchmen won part of what they wanted by surrendering activities judicable in secular tribunals. Their course was necessarily tortuous. On one hand, except for Pascal II's abortive agreement with the emperor at Sutri in 1111 and in spite of 'moral' ambivalence, the popes refused to surrender secular jurisdictions whose clerical lords were judicable by lay authority. On the other, they legislated against clerks' exercising secular offices, a paradox because the Church was at the same time regulating the world 'for reason of sin'. By 1215 clerks were prohibited from serving as lawyers, judges and public notaries for civil persons and governments. In 1198 Innocent III wrote to Richard Coeur de Lion about Hubert Walter, archbishop of Canterbury and England's chief justiciar, telling the king that 'for the sake of his soul, he should not permit the said archbishop to exercise secular administration any longer nor should he again admit the archbishop or any bishop or priest into secular government'.[32]

This law advertises Rome's inadvertent Italian myopia. It suited Italy's urban regions where lay education and professionalism were advanced, but few other places. In the north, lay society did not yet have large enough professional cadres from which to draw state servants, and weak public finance obliged lay power to rely on clerical benefices to pay its officers. In England, for example, the twelve members of the king's court of 1195 included the chief justiciar named above, three other prelates, three archdeacons and another clerk who later became bishop of London. One is not surprised that, after Hubert's obedient resignation in 1198, he soon resumed office, holding it until his death in 1205. Still, things were changing north of the Alps. As early as 1259, the composition of the *parlement* of Paris, royal France's highest court, was nearly half lay, and if, in 1272, England's king's bench was nearly wholly clerical, it too was half lay by 1307. Hardly begun, secularization was the order of the day.

Lay government's use of clerical personnel and benefices partly explains the importance of appointments. During the period treated here, however, the Church, heir of the Gregorians, increased the freedom of clerical elections. This was especially marked in the Empire, where the struggle between the Welfs and the Hohenstaufen cost the emperors almost all left them after the Treaty of Worms in 1122. From 1201 to Speyer in 1209 Otto IV Welf surrendered taxes and rights to collect income from vacant sees and to appoint to clerical benefices during a vacancy. His representatives were withdrawn from episcopal elections and lost the power to intervene in disputed ones. His rival Frederick II confirmed these losses by the Golden Bull of Eger in 1213. Although not implemented until after Frederick's death in 1250, Eger was decisive; after it, popes and local princes had more to do with German bishops than emperors.

England's princes retained much even after Becket. The biographer of William the Marshal reports that in 1194 Richard Coeur de Lion ordered the archbishop of Rouen to give the marshal's brother the see of Exeter. Still, when John Lackland fought Innocent III from 1208 to 1213, the bishops, usually royalist in the past, sided with Rome, only two of seventeen prelates remaining at home with John. When the dust settled, the king admitted the pope's right to settle disputed elections. In 1208 when two candidates were elected to Canterbury, Stephen Langton, inimical to the crown and teaching at Paris, was provided by the pope and occupied the see in 1213.

If secular power diminished, much was retained. Prelates holding fiefs always needed princely consent, and lay patrons of churches and monasteries helped provide persons for offices and livings. The laity as a whole had rights. In Gregorian times lay participation (other than princely) had ended in episcopal elections, but, paralleling the economic corporatism seen earlier, town and village parish associations appeared. In Venice from *circa* 1150 and Florence from the 1180s parishioners elected laymen to regulate building and charity in their churches. Parishioners wanted a voice in setting burial and marriage costs. In 1296 those of a parish in Toulouse accepted an arbitral settlement between themselves and the parish priest, which, after regulating fees, provided that changes were to require 'the assent of all parishioners or of two-thirds of this body'.[33]

Parish organizations also became collective patrons, presenting candidates to bishops or choosing among those they nominated. Rolandino Passaggeri provides a model letter showing how parishioners, after inquiry and invocation of the Holy Spirit, 'unanimously and in full accord and consent agreed on Dom Peter . . . among others nominated . . . electing him priest and rector of the said church'.[34] Parish election of rectors was widespread in northern and central Italy and in towns of south central and eastern Germany. About 1311 William Durand the Younger remarked that 'a bishop should not be installed without the testimony of the clergy nor [a parish priest] without that of the people'.[35]

Laymen were never loath to reinforce the 'moral' fabric of the Church. This was sometimes political. Although few rallied to him, at Pavia in 1160 and again at Avignon in 1162 Frederick I Barbarossa summoned councils to heal the schism caused by the disputed papal election of 1159. It was also sometimes 'moral' propaganda. Louis IX of France eradicated blasphemy so enthusiastically that he was censured by Clement IV (d. 1268). Princes often inspected 'their' clergy. In 1234 Otto I, duke of Brunswick, removed all young nuns from the double monastery of Nordheim and, by prohibiting replacement, converted it into a male house. Ottokar II, king of Bohemia, deputized a parish priest and a layman to visit monasteries in the diocese of Passau in 1259.

Confronting lay power, churchmen were necessarily opportunist, popes, for example, never being able to act everywhere at once. Their prime target was the emperor, and hence other princes escaped their ire. Threatened by the Hohenstaufen, the disputed papal election of 1159 and by Frederick I's proposed arbitration at Pavia in 1160, Alexander III fled to France, seeking help from Henry II of England. In 1161 he canonized Edward the Confessor, thus confirming the Plantagenet house on England's throne, a gesture countered by the imperialist Pope Pascal III's canonization of Charlemagne in 1165. In the 1160s, Alexander muted Becket in the conflict with Henry II, and the archbishop's assassination in 1170 was well timed. Not only did the king's domestic troubles increase during the 1170s, but the Hohenstaufens also weakened. The pope came to an agreement with Henry in 1172, canonized Becket the next year, and turned to devote his attention to the Empire, where the emperor's defeat at Legnano in 1176 led to a temporary settlement. Alexander had dragged his feet in England in order to gain footing in Italy, but the settlement upset Anglicans favouring church freedom.

Local churchmen complained ever louder in the thirteenth century as the popes mobilized everything to defeat Italy's Ghibellines.

William Durand the Younger protested that they were surrendering the clergy to English, Aragonese and especially French kings. As England and France gravitated towards war over Flanders and Guienne in the 1290s, clerical taxes became crucial and Boniface VIII tried to recover them. His bull *Clericis laicos* of 1296 was a reason why Robert Winchelsea, archbishop of Canterbury, stood so firmly against King Edward I, but French power made him compromise. In 1297 he permitted Philip IV the Fair to collect clerical taxes without papal consent in case of dire need, a switch that neatly cut off the limb on to which Winchelsea had ventured.

William Durand also complained about appointments. In the appeasement of 1297 Boniface granted Philip the right to provide one canon in every collegiate church of France and the provinces of Lyons and Viviers. This favour reflected how monarchy, whether of popes or of princes, was triumphing over electoral traditions. An example is seen in the Neapolitan kingdom of Charles II. In 1302 a Catalan ambassador reported that Boniface was angered when the Angevin refused to appoint a family member to a church office, and had remarked: 'if you look at the matter carefully, Father, I've given your family enough'. Furious, the pope said: 'Don't you know I can take your kingdom from you?' But he couldn't.[36]

CHURCH GOVERNMENT

Around 1348 the jurist Lucas of Penna rightly said that the Church was a state, and it was the best organized one in Latin Europe. Its territories had long been divided into archiepiscopal provinces and episcopal dioceses. The diocese was usually split into archdeaconates, areas placed under a senior priest, sometimes titled rural deans. Below were the parishes, headed by rectors.

Size varied widely: in the diocese of Lincoln the archdeaconate of Stow consisted of four rural deaneries, that of Lincoln itself of twenty-three. There were poor and rich bishops: Rochester had about a fifth of the income of the bishop of Winchester. History explains the variations: Italy's ancient dioceses were smaller than those created later in northern Europe. The bishop of Cavaillon in Provence ruled a territory scarcely as big as a northern parish, enjoying hardly a hundredth of the bishop of Winchester's revenue. The petty size of Italy's dioceses explains why many papal courtiers had episcopal grade and why a wealthy prince-bishop from the north, like Anthony Bek of Durham, seemed of a different scale to the Romans in 1302.

Administrative changes created new offices, emptying old ones of authority. Archdeacons had been interposed between bishops and their clergy, but from the 1170s were replaced by a new episcopal judge, the Official, who, by Boniface VIII's decretals published in 1298, had become the second personage of the diocese. Structures also changed: from 1316 to 1334 John XXII created ten new dioceses and one archdiocese.

Powerful primates were protected by local interests. Toledo's primacy evoked in Castilian minds Iberia unified as in Visigothic days. Milanese and Palermitan pretences to freedom from Rome were used by the emperors against the papacy. The momentary subordination of the see of Lund to that of Bremen in 1133 reflected German expansion into Scandinavia. Because York was 'royalist' and Canterbury 'Gregorian', the former's vain struggle for equality with the latter epitomizes the defeat of England's royal church. The papacy recognized still larger entities, the nations. National identity surfaced at the council of Vienne in 1311–12 where the clergy from France, Spain, the British Isles, Germany, Scandinavia and Italy sat separately in preliminary discussions. Showing who led the Church, ten rolls of these records are French, nine Italian, five Spanish, four German, one English and one Scandinavian. A papal letter of 1335 imitated antiquity by dividing Europe into four nations: France, Germany (including Scandinavia and the British Isles), Italy and Spain.

Jurists said the pope's plenitude of power was analogous, though superior, to that of the emperor. The papacy adopted secular insignia: the umbrella of the east sent by Venice in the 1170s and the superimposed coronets that, by the early fourteenth century, made up the triple-tiered tiara. Ceremonials were borrowed from the emperors, and in 1161–2 Gerhoh of Reichersberg caustically remarked that the 'Roman court' had previously been called the 'Roman Church'.

Meeting in consistory, the pope and cardinals had replaced the old episcopal synod of the Roman clergy and become Christendom's highest court, wherein were promulgated the decretals. At first numbering about twelve but rising to over twenty in the early fourteenth century, these cardinal bishops, priests and deacons formed a true college by the end of Alexander III's reign in 1181.

They were raised above the rest of the clergy, a process completed by 1245, when they were gratified with the red hat. The most important legatine missions were normally entrusted to them, but since papal legates had precedence over all clergy, lesser affairs were given others. Papal judicial functions had so expanded by the mid thirteenth century that auditor judges hearing cases below the episcopal grade constituted a tribunal later called the *Rota*. The consistory and *Rota* brought to Rome cases reserved to the Holy See and appeals from sentences issued locally. The secretariat was under a chancellor, a powerful officer invariably a cardinal until 1216 when replaced by a vice-chancellor, never a cardinal. Finances were entrusted mainly to the chamberlain. Curial personnel totalled about four hundred in the late thirteenth century, not including servants and soldiers. For postal service the popes used passing clergy and the couriers of Italy's merchant bankers.

Papal letters or decretals contained decisions taken in consistory, which were enrolled as precedents. Some protested that popes should legislate only in council with clergy other than Roman participating. And indeed, much law was issued in the general councils summoned by the popes. These, beginning with the first Lateran in 1123 and ending with Vienne in 1311–12, illustrate the papacy's triumph over the Empire, whose rulers had been wont to call councils in the past. From the third Lateran Council of 1179 to Vienne, a general council met on an average of once every thirty-three years. At the fourth Lateran Council of 1215, metropolitans, bishops, mitred abbots, provosts of cathedral chapters and even university masters of theology and law participated. Nor were general councils the only assemblies where laws were written. By 1215 every unit from the rural deanery to the archbishop's province was urged to hold yearly convocations, and statute books from some are extant. Above these were larger regional councils, the Scottish and English Churches, for example. After the Capetian conquest of Normandy the provinces that, together with the University of Paris, constituted the kernel of the Gallican church were Rheims, Sens and Rouen, joined occasionally by Bourges and Tours. The meetings of national synods, and some provincial ones like Canterbury and York, often coincided with lay parliaments summoned by princes.

Except for mitred abbots, the regular clergy did not attend councils but instead sought exemption from episcopal authority and looked to the papacy. Cistercians, for example, were not visited by bishops and, together with Templars and Hospitallers, were exempt from crusade taxes. The later mendicants also won exemption from episcopal control, and were busy in the lay apostolate in spite of secular opposition. Exemptions contributed much to the centralization of authority, making Rome the arbiter of the battles between regular and secular clergy.

More and more power accrued to Rome. By 1153 canonization had become a papal monopoly and, by 1215, the authentication of relics. During the twelfth century prelates were obliged to visit Rome, and local elections scrutinized, disputed ones invalidated and rival candidates replaced by papal appointees. The thirteenth century saw the reservation of certain posts by Rome, and by 1215 the papal right to provide was admitted everywhere. In 1265 Clement IV claimed an unequivocal right over all Church posts but actually reserved only the provisioning of benefices falling vacant when incumbents were serving at, or visiting, the Holy See. Thereafter papal intervention increased. Of the sixteen promoted to the episcopal grade in France from 1295 to 1301, only one was elected by a cathedral chapter as of old; popes chose the others. In 1311 the bishop of Angers noted that, of the thirty-five prebends vacated in his diocese since 1291, he had conferred only five; the rest were Rome's providees. Provisions and reservations provoked enmity because they overrode local interest and, at the cost of absenteeism, enabled the popes to finance their court personnel, favouring Italians and others wedded to their cause. The system had local advocates, however. The educated favoured it because without it graduates could not penetrate the serried ranks of the local clergy. Nor, in spite of polemics, was it always vicious. Laws regulating the provision of vicars made pluralism into a form of rural taxation designed to subvent urban clergy, university teachers and curial officers.

Papal taxation also grew. Providees or those elected, for example, paid fees for confirmation, the amounts varying according to the wealth of the benefice and the litigation involved. Fees usually included common services (about a third of the first year's revenue of a benefice), minor services (fees for curial personnel) and a private audience with the pontiff. Wealthy prelates paid heavily. In 1302 an abbot of St Albans confirmed his election at Rome at a cost of just above 10,000 florins. He borrowed the sum from Italian moneylenders, and consequently had to buy a dispensation for conniving at usury. Although some were exempt, metropolitans and some abbots were required to visit Rome at specific intervals, an obligation that could be commuted to sending a deputy and fixed payment. In 1300 Rouen and Rheims each paid 2,000 florins every second year, Canterbury 1,500 and York 600 every third year.

After 1199 a papal tithe on ecclesiastical benefices and installations was instituted. Initially designed only to subvent the Crusade, it speedily grew. In 1199 it was a fortieth, and in 1215 the Lateran Council authorized a twentieth for three years. In the period from 1247 to 1274 a tenth was raised no less than twenty-one times. Moreover, because the crusade was 'internalizing', receipts were increasingly used at home. During the nine years of his pontificate, Boniface VIII encashed about 1,800,000 florins, a sum spent largely against Catalonian or Aragonese Sicily and rebels in the papal states. Secular states were already cutting heavily into this revenue, however, so this figure does not record what they took. Regularity made the papal tithe Europe's most advanced tax except for those in urban republics.

Local churchmen complained about growing central government, even about general councils. A bishop of Chartres is said to have exhorted the Lateran Council of 1179 to issue no new law: 'let us rather . . . strive that evangelical teaching be observed, which now only few obey'.[37] Writing around 1150, Bernard of Clairvaux bewailed the frequency of appeals to Rome, attributing their increase to curial avarice. Many deplored papal dispensations permitting a single clerk to hold several benefices. Peter Cantor attacked papal exemptions, whereby abbots were freed from their bishops or bishops from their metropolitans. He said that even the celebrated rivals Bernard of Clairvaux and Gilbert of La Porrée (d. 1154), bishop of Poitiers, agreed on this matter. The latter said that exempt abbots were schismatics, and Bernard complained to the pope that, by granting exemptions, 'you prove you have the plenitude of power, but perchance not that of justice. You do this because you can, but the question is whether you ought,' and pictured the Church as a disordered body with fingers attached to its head.[38] William Durand the Younger directed criticism against papal reservations and provisions, citing ancient canons against such practices: 'Bishops from other cities ought not be elected, nor foreign clerks preferred to those raised in their own churches.'[39]

Bernard's *On Reflection* set the critical tone: the apostle Peter gave Rome what the Lord gave him, 'solicitude . . . over the churches. Did he give domination? Hear him! "Not ruling over the clergy, he says, but being examples to the flock" . . . . Domination is clearly forbidden.'[40] He concluded that

> your power is therefore not the only one derived from God. So also is that of the middling and the lesser . . . . Above all, reflect that the holy Roman Church . . . is not the mistress but the mother of the churches. You are not lord of the bishops but rather one of them.[41]

Resistance to papal centralization grew, slowly, a reason being that local excesses were greater than those of Rome. Before his election to the see of Durham in 1283 Anthony Bek was a pluralist, holding five benefices in addition to his archdeaconate. The motives behind antipapal diatribes were sometimes frankly stated. The protest of the Gallican Church in 1247 stated that papal provisions were prejudicial 'to the lord king and the nobles of the kingdom, whose sons and friends were accustomed to be promoted in the churches'.[42] Local churches, in fact, often needed papal action to resist the 'armed prayers' of princes and nobles.

Criticism was also muted because Rome grew as did clerical liberty. Besides, the Church was a monarchy. Fearing to offend, Peter Cantor worried:

> Am I not allowed to ask the lord pope, 'Why do you do that?' It is only sacrilegious to contradict . . . [him]. True, I do not see the solution of these problems . . . but I know that divisions and exemptions of this kind in the Church do not derive from its canons, old or new, but rather from the special authority of the apostolic see that God will not permit to err.[43]

The result is that Caesar governs everything and his proconsuls nothing.

Lacking solutions, Peter and others blamed the pope and his court, especially the latter, for the Church's problems. They had made, as the Saviour said in the Temple, 'my house, the house of prayer, into a den of thieves and a house of commerce'.[44] William the Marshal's biographer used the theme of Roman corruption to good effect. When France's 'sly' king wanted to rob 'honest' England at Rome, he sent the necessary relics: money for greasing palms. John of Salisbury told Pope Adrian IV that everyone knew the Roman court was, not the mother, but the plundering step-mother of the Church. In reply, Adrian told a story: a body's limbs once complained that the stomach ate what their labour brought in. True, he added, but limbs wither without nourishment.

Rome's eminence left it exposed. In the pre-Gregorian days of the state Churches, 'reformers' attacked the vices of particular prelates and parts of the Church but rarely the whole as subsumed in its head. In this age, as a general is blamed for an army's defeats, so was Rome for Christendom's failures. Until after 1300, however, occasional failures were more than compensated for by great victories.

NOTES AND REFERENCES

1   *Rem non novam* in *Extravagantes communes* 2, 3, 1 in *CICan* II, 1256.

2   *Solitae* in *Liber extra* 1, 33, 6 in *CICan* II, 197.

3   *Policraticus* 4, 3 and 6 (ed. Webb), I, 239 and 251.

4   *The Summa Parisiensis on the Decretum Gratiani* (ed. T.P. McLaughlin, Toronto, 1952), 108.

5   Wenzel's letter cited in G.W. Greenaway, *Arnold of Brescia* (Cambridge, 1931), 136.

6   *Registrum* 7, 14a in Ph. Jaffé *(ed.) Bibliotheca rerum Germanicarum – Monumenta Gregoriana* (Aalen, 1965, rprt) II, 404.

7   Letter no. 131 in *PL* CCXVI, 923–4, and Genesis 14:18, Ps. 110:4, Exodus 19:6 and 1 Peter 2:9.

8   Letter no. 27 in *PL* CCXIV, 21.

9   *Baumgartenberg Formularius de modo prosandi* in *BuF* II, 807.

10 Pierre Dupuy, *Histoire du différend d'entre le pape Boniface VIII et Philippe le Bel* (Paris, 1655, rprt), 48.

11 *Rhetorica novissima* 5 in *BIMA* II, 262b.

12 E. H. Kantorowicz, *Friedrich II – Ergänzungband* (Berlin, 1931, rprt), 26.

13 *Determinatio compendiosa de iurisdictione imperii* 30 in *MGH FIG in usum scholarum* 60.

14 *Notitia seculi* 8 in *Alexander von Roes Schriften, MGH Staatschriften* 154.

15 *Cronica . . . marchie Trivixiane* in Muratori (ed.), *RIS* (1905 edn) VIII, i, 22.

16 *De consideratione* 4, 3 in *Sancti Bernardi opera* III, 454, and John 18:11 and Luke 22:38.

17 *Ibid*. 3, 4 in *ibid*. III, 444 and Romans 13:1–2.

18 Alexander of Roes, *Memoriale* 4 and 36 in *MGH Staatsschriften* I, i, 94–5 and 147.

19 *De regia potestate et papali* 13 (ed. Fritz Bleienstein, Stuttgart, 1969), 138–9.

20 Gratian, *Decretum* 1, 93, 24 in *CICan* I, 328.

21 Kantorowicz, *The King's Two Bodies*, 298n.

22 *Ibid*., 322n.

23   *De potestate regia et papali* 10 and 15 (ed. Bleienstein), 113 and 150–1, cited in reverse order.

24   *Venerabilem* in *Liber extra* 1, 6, 34 in *CICan* II, 80. The bull in 1263 was *Qui coelum.*

25   From the *Leges Anglorum* of *c.* 1200, a London version of the *Leges Edwardi Confessoris* in Felix Lieberman (ed.), *Gesetze der Angelsachsen* (Halle, 1901), 636; Psalm 71:1 (72:1).

26   *Las siete partidas* 2, 1, 5 (Madrid, 1807), II, 7.

27   Dupuy, *Histoire du différend,* 335.

28   *Liber consuetudinum Mediolani* 22, 2 (ed. Enrico Besta, Milan, 1949), 115.

29   *Liber extra* 3, 49, 4 in *CICan* II, 655.

30   *Code* 3, 19, 3.

31   *Liber extra* 2, 1, 8 in *CICan* II, 241.

32   Hashagen, *Staat und Kirche vor der Reformation,* 207.

33   R.C. Julien, *Histoire de la paroisse N.-D. la Dalbade* (Toulouse, 1891), 138 and 151.

34   *Summa artis notariae* 1, 5 (Venice, 1583), I, 126r–v.

35   *De modo generali concilii celebrandi* 2, 15, 2 and 35, 3 in *TUJ* XIII, 161ra and 165ra.

36   Lawrence Martini's diary for the bishop of Valencia from January to March 1302 in Finke, *Aus dem Tage Bonifaz VIII,* xlv.

37   *Verbum abbreviatum* 31 in *PL* CCV, 116.

38   *De consideratione* 3, 2 in *Sancti Bernardi opera* III, 442.

39   *De modo generali concilii celebrandi* 2, 15, 2 in *TUJ* XIII, 161ra.

40   *De consideratione* 2, 6 in *Sancti Bernardi opera* III, 418, and 1 Peter 5:3.

41   *Ibid.* 3, 4 and 4, 7 in *ibid.* III, 444 and 465–6.

42   *Gravamina ecclesie Gallicane* in the '*additamenta*' of Matthew Paris, *Chronica majora* in *Rolls Series* LVII, vi, 105, dated by Barraclough, *Papal Provisions* 11.

43   *Verbum abbreviatum* 44 in *PL* CCV, 139.

44   *Ibid.* 36 in *PL* CCV, 123; Matthew 21:13.

14

THE GREATER MONARCHIES

THE EMPIRE

All Latin Europe's states were beginning to centralize, with one exception. In the late eleventh century the Empire, once the greatest state, reaching into northern and central Italy, France and the Low Countries, began to fall apart.

This was hard to believe around 1150. After the Gregorian wars from the 1070s into the 1120s, when many of the later German princely lines appeared, a period of pacification and renewal began before the death of Henry V in 1125 and continued through the crowning of the Hohenstaufen Frederick I Barbarossa in 1152. Pacification was aided by Germany's churches, now somewhat freed from imperial control and fearing domination by local princely houses. Smaller Italian towns also resisted greater ones, like Milan, that grew at their expense. The need to stop unremitting civil war by means of regional peace ordinances likewise played a role.

The Hohenstaufens tried to tighten controls. Barbarossa proposed at Würzburg in 1196 replacing the elective monarchy by dynastic succession. In Italy the diet of Roncaglia in 1158 asserted the Empire's right to tax and govern the towns by *podestàs*. In Germany he forced even great princes to surrender freehold offices and receive them back in vassalage. The ministerial system of quasi-servile knights was improved along major arteries of communication, and the monarch allied with townsmen against local princes and with the ministers against the nobility. The greater magnates who had profited from the Gregorian breakdown nevertheless retained most of their gains. When, in 1138, they elected Conrad III Hohenstaufen, they passed over the Welf Henry the Proud, whose Saxon, Bavarian and Tuscan domains would have built a solid royal power. The ensuing combat of the Welfs and Hohenstaufen ensured the monarchy's failure.

In Germany a Rhenish prince-bishop and Saxon notables defeated the emperor's dynastic attempt at Würzburg. In Italy the imperial renewal and attempt to profit from Italy's commercial and industrial growth announced at Roncaglia in 1158 failed at Legnano in 1176, and the judgment of that battlefield was confirmed by the Peace of Constance in 1183. After helping Frederick I defeat Henry the Lion in 1180, the Saxon magnates distributed the powers taken from the Welf and set a precedent forbidding the emperor to hold great fiefs for more than a year. Lack of means led to alienation of imperial rights. In 1162 Pisa bought control of its county and Florence gained self-government by 1187.

The marriage of Henry VI Hohenstaufen in 1194 to Constance of Sicily, heiress of the Norman kings of south Italy, threatened Rome with Germano-Italian unification.[1] After Henry's death in 1197, this effort collapsed in another war between Welfs and Hohenstaufen, popes and emperors, north and south Italy and north and south Germany. Innocent III helped wreck the rule of the Hohenstaufen Philip of Swabia. In 1199 he appealed to the German conviction that their electoral monarchy proved them naturally free in these words: 'we oppose [Philip] lest, if a brother should immediately succeed a brother just as a son a father, the Empire would seem . . . not to be conferred by election but by [dynastic] succession. Hence what ought to be free would appear to be hereditary.'[2] After Philip's death in 1208, his Welf rival Otto IV adopted the Hohenstaufen programme of uniting the Empire with south Italy and Sicily, but his defeat by the French at Bouvines in 1214 reinforced the popularity of his Hohenstaufen enemy, Frederick II. Thereafter this new prince, called the 'Apulian boy', worked to unify north and south Italy and join it to the Empire, and for a time seemed about to defeat the popes and their allied city republics.

At the Council of Lyons in 1245 Innocent IV wove the alliance of Italy's republics, dissident German princes and French invaders that brought down the Hohenstaufen. Frederick died in 1250; the Capetian Angevins invaded south Italy in 1265, replacing the Hohenstaufen after the execution of Conradin in 1268. Catalan intervention under Peter III of Aragon (d. 1286) in Sicily's rebellion of 1282 finally destroyed south Italian unity.

The Hohenstaufens were failing before Frederick II's death in 1250. In Germany the exclusion of lesser magnates from the electoral college was gradually reinforcing the power of the greater princes. In the *Saxon Mirror* the Wittelsbach Rhenish count palatine, the duke of Saxony, the margrave of Brandenburg and the king of Bohemia (who first voted in 1237) together with the ecclesiastical princes of Mainz, Trier and Cologne, voted first, while the lesser magnates were reduced to waiting in the wings: 'He whom the [great magnates] have unanimously chosen, the lesser ones will name to be king.'[3] Earlier in 1199 at the election of Philip of Swabia twenty-six magnates voted, a vote confirmed by twenty-four others. By 1256, sign of a failing monarchy, the electors chose foreigners. Frederick's effort to unify Italy by placing its provinces under imperial vicars had also failed. So independent had even the Empire's allies become that in 1256 Pisa supported Alfonso of Castile's candidacy for the kingship of the Romans, rejecting the electors' vote for Richard of Cornwall by objecting that the whole Roman people elected the head of state.

A reason for this defeat was that the Empire's expansionary urges went in disparate directions. In Germany, guided by the flow of her rivers towards the North and Baltic Seas and by the eastward-leading reaches of her great plain, growth went north and east. In this period, as Germans turned toward Slav, Finn and Scandinavian, their intervention in France and Italy lost its earlier strength. In Italy northern towns pushed towards south Italy and the Mediterranean, and towards the north they looked up the Rhone valley, the major trade route until 1300. Imperial policies meant little to Italy's greater urban centres. What the schism between the concerns of north and east Germans and the imperialist ideas of south Germans and some Italians meant is shown by what happened at the battle of Legnano in 1176. The emperor was defeated partly because the Welf Henry the Lion refused support.

The Empire's failing was accompanied by a shift of its centre. In 1281 Alexander of Roes lamented that the Franks and Saxons had surrendered leadership to the 'weak' Swabian Alemanni. He was at least looking in the right direction. If Germans in north and east had little interest in France and Italy, those of Swabia and Austria had much. The need to control the popes who, as in the Gregorian age, helped local German princes and Italian towns to gain independence made the Swabian Hohenstaufen look south. To rule at home they had to have the resources of Italy's cities. By the thirteenth century the Empire had shifted still farther south. Under Frederick II, although Germany continued to play a big role, the base of imperial power lay in south Italy. The results were unhappy. The Empire had mortgaged wealth in undeveloped Germany to acquire rights in more expensive Italy, selling cheap to buy dear.

This costly policy resulted in the wholesale loss of imperial rights along the western frontiers and north of the Alps. In the late twelfth century imperial ministers were being freed or given hereditary rights, a policy pursued with abandon by Otto IV. As noted above, in 1213 and 1220 the emperor surrendered controls over the election of German bishops. The greater secular imperial fiefs – Austria in 1156 and Bavaria in 1180 – were becoming hereditary, and fiscal resources and jurisdictions were alienated to local princes. A final attempt to arrest this course was crushed by Frederick II's defeat of his own son Henry VII in 1232. By Conrad IV's death in 1254, Italian expeditions were financed by massive sales of rights in Germany, and the exercise of most imperial rights was limited to the moment when the emperor appeared in person to exercise them. The prince being absent, the citizens of Bern elected their imperial governors in 1268, 1271 and again in 1291, just like, they said, Roman citizens. In 1290 Besançon asked the pope to confirm the election of Rudolph of Habsburg as German king before accepting him. Meanwhile, French pressure dissolved the political structure of the Lorraines and the Rhineland and profoundly influenced Franconia, Thuringia and Swabia. The left bank of the Rhone and territories along the Rhine gradually fell to France, Provence going to the Capetian Charles of Anjou in 1245.

The Empire went into receivership. A modest Dutch princeling was elected in 1245 and was replaced by a brother of the king of England and a king of Castile in the disputed election of 1257, neither of whom played a role in Germany. By the time Rudolph of Habsburg acceded in 1273, the treasury was empty, and, as Humbert of Romans remarked, the Empire was reduced 'almost to nothing'. Alexander of Roes lamented in 1285 that the papal peacock and the French cock had brought down the imperial eagle. The rabbi Meir son of Baruch of Rothenburg remarked that 'now every prince is like a king in his land and nobody dares to tell him what to do'.[4] In 1274 Humbert of Romans recommended that
the German king should no longer be elected but instead succeed by dynasty, to

be thereafter content with his kingdom . . . . Italy should have one or two kings
bound by laws and statutes based on the consent of the towns and prelates, one
in Tuscany and the other in Lombardy. These should accede by succession but
could . . . be deposed by the apostolic see.[5]

In 1280 Nicholas III may have suggested to Rudolph of Habsburg
that the Empire be split into four independent monarchies: Germany, Arles, Tuscany and Lombardy.

In fine, to see evidence of the growth of the State, one has to
turn from the fading Empire to the German and Italian princely
states and urban republics. Not that the Empire was wholly dead by
1300, however. Revivals were seen after that date and, to Dante
and others, the memory of Hohenstaufen greatness left a legacy of
hope for a universal State.

The collapse of the Empire has been seen as a tragedy, but its
subjects did not view it so. Italy was rent by wars in the thirteenth
century, but rose to lead Europe's economy, an Italian papacy ruling the Latin and even the Greek communion. The lawyers remarked that the Peace of Constance in 1183 freed Italy's city
republics from any temporal superior on earth. Alberic of Rosate of
Bergamo opined that, in strict law, only Lombard cities, who had
won it at Constance, possessed the right to tax, but added that 'in
fact, all [Italy's] cities have usurped this right'.[6] In Germany the
Hohenstaufen defeat of the Welf Henry the Lion in 1180 split the
Saxon duchy among local magnates, busy building expanding frontier states. The rulers of Holstein, Meissen and Brandenburg raced
to open land for settlement. In 1212 Bohemia became a kingdom,
and in 1220 the Teutonic knights allied with others to subject the
Baltic's shores. German town liberty grew, and leagues of all kinds
linked towns, princes, rural magnates and even counties. In areas
like Westphalia, nominally ruled by a powerless duke, the archbishop of Cologne, townsmen and rural nobles banded together to
maintain the peace.

It is then worth reasserting that, although modern historians
raised in the age of the nation-state thought that the imperial failure
was detrimental for both Germany and Italy in the long run, the
late twelfth and thirteenth centuries instead constituted a happy age
of regional and urban liberty marked by great economic, social and
intellectual inventiveness.

ENGLAND

England provided the best contrast with the Empire. Although other centralized governments existed, England was the only one where the lineaments of a nation-state could be seen before 1300.

William I of Normandy took over Saxon unitary institutions, the shires and courts in the subdivisions called 'hundreds'. The conquest of 1066 also gave the crown greater resources with which to remunerate servitors than found elsewhere. Nor was the invasion a single event. Although the penetration of foreign institutions and population into England gradually lessened, a second invasion ran from about 1135 to 1154, ending with the accession of the Plantagenet Henry II of Anjou. A later one in 1216–17, that of the Capetians, was repulsed. Early and late, noteworthy leaders of disruptive baronial factions, like King Stephen of Blois (d. 1154) and Simon of Montfort (d. 1265), came from France, but invasion usually enhanced centralization.

England's monarchs were Frenchmen and from Henry II to John spent most of their time in France, meanwhile exploiting their island kingdom. Royal justice, in fact, was unusually exploitative: until 1278 even accidental killing involved hanging and confiscation of property unless bought off. Besides, the conquest encouraged French feelings of superiority. The *Exchequer Dialogue* states that, after the conquest, English communities were fined when Normans or French were assassinated. By the time the *Dialogue* appeared in 1174–83, the races had so fused that the fine was collected for the murder of any freeman, but until 1340, could be avoided by the 'proof of Englishry', if, that is, the murdered man was a serf. One sees why Gerald of Wales called England the home of tyranny.

The monarchy used any tool that came to hand. The Norman connection enabled England to recruit administrators from as far away as Sicily. Although French settlement slowed, Savoyards helped build the offices of the royal court during the reign of Henry III from 1216 to 1272. The Bolognese son of the great Accursius, Francis Accursius, served Edward I from 1273 to 1281. More than France or Germany, England was open to the influence of Italy's schools of Roman law, a subject treated later.

England nevertheless shared much with continental states. Her Church sought freedom and usually had its way up to the early thirteenth century. Her aristocracy was restive, building centres of local power, private castles and seizing once-royal courts and offices. In the early twelfth century about a hundred families possessed palatine counties, monastic advocacies and county administrations in hereditary right. England's frontier barons continuously disturbed the monarchy, and the Anglo-French of Ireland and southern Scotland often intervened in England. Palatine counties, those of the prince-bishop of Durham and the earl of Chester, were like little kingdoms. As in Normandy, county or shire administration tended to become hereditary. The magnate Geoffrey of Mandeville (d. 1141) gained hereditary right to the shrievalties of London, Essex, Middlesex and Hertfordshire, a veritable principality close to the monarchy's heart. At the accession of Henry II in 1154, England seemed about to undergo the decentralization seen on the continent.

This did not happen; the reigns of Henry II and his sons brought centralization. That Richard was rarely in England and John was weakened by the loss of his French domains did not halt the process. This was partly because England's Church rarely led magnate opposition successfully, a reason being Rome's need for England's friendship while battling the Empire. As seen above, Alexander III dragged his feet at the time of Becket's combat with Henry II over clerical immunity. Initially hard on John because he allied against the French with Emperor Otto IV Welf, then threatening Rome, Innocent III had moved Langton from Paris to Canterbury. John capitulated in 1213, admitting the suzerainty of the pope over England and Ireland. Langton and his bishops fought on until 1215, but were defeated when Innocent released his royal vassal from his oath to the Great Charter, suspending Langton for failing to excommunicate baronial leaders. A similar conflict between pope and local Church occurred during Robert of Winchelsea's (d. 1313) tenure as archbishop. In 1296 Winchelsea obeyed papal law prohibiting lay taxation of clergy even after the pope had withdrawn it. The latter then suspended the primate and aided the king. In return, Italians were provided with English posts and the payment of common services was extended to all England's prelates.

Emerging from those coming to England during and after the conquest, the barons were both the king's principal servitors and opponents. Since they won hereditary title to their fiefs by the early twelfth century, the desire of knights (lesser nobles or gentry) to enjoy similar tenures led to an alliance between the latter and the crown. From the assize of Clarendon in 1166 onwards, royal writs provided knights with ways of appealing from baronial courts to the crown to protect their 'rights' or interests, and royal inquests gave them juries of their peers. Prompted by the future King Edward I, knights supported the provisions of Westminster in 1259 which repeated the earlier provisions of Oxford requiring sheriffs to be chosen from the knights of the county where they served. Knights and the rest of what was soon termed the 'Commons' began to think of themselves as representing the whole realm.

The Commons also included the representatives of cities and boroughs. As the barons attacked Henry II's centralism, his successors Richard and John made money and friends by granting townsmen rights. By 1216 seventy cities and boroughs had gained them, and the care with which London was treated in the Great Charter shows that the barons knew how significant they were. Still, one cannot separate the interests of many boroughs – really villages – from those of the barons who often promoted their growth. Of about 160-odd new towns founded in England from 1066 to 1370, about forty per cent of them being planted between 1151 and 1250, only twelve per cent were royal foundations and seventy-eight seigniorial, either ecclesiastical or lay. When this figure is considered together with the baronial attack on royal forestry restrictions, villages, small towns and many knights plainly gained as much from the barons as from the crown.

Arbitration of conflicts created a community. In 1205 John promulgated a sworn commune to defend the realm's peace. The obverse of this was the prince's demand for service, especially fiscal. As early as 1166 Henry II collected scutage in lieu of military service from knights' fiefs held of his tenants in chief. The Saladin tithe of 1188 taxed everyone, although, being for a Crusade, did not set a precedent. The wars with the Capetians prompted Richard to demand an aid of five shillings from each hide in 1198. By 1207 John's feudal aid required a shilling on every mark of rent and personal property from everyone no matter from whom he held his land. Together with custom duties, these taxes illustrate England's precocious centralization.

Like the papacy or the Norman and Hohenstaufen realm in south Italy, English unity built a real central government, most of whose principal bureaux were established in the reign of Henry II. The realm's second person was the chief justiciar, an officer analogous to an Islamic vizier, especially significant under an absentee monarch like Richard, and the courts he supervised began to specialize in the early thirteenth century. That of Common Pleas, sitting in Westminster, dealt with suits between private litigants; that of the King's Bench dealt with criminal cases, royal rights and, by the 1260s, investigated failures in the magnates' courts. Besides these offices were the treasury, chancery and exchequer, the latter a semi-judicial body. As in France and most other monarchies, these offices were usually farmed out or were directly venal. Churchmen often bought them, especially the monarchy's central offices, as has been seen in the case of Richard Fitzneale, royal treasurer, frequent judge and bishop of London.

On the local level, viscounts or sheriffs ceased being hereditary and were recruited annually from among local knights. To police the shires, justices were despatched from the king's court from about 1166. Initially both investigative and judicial, analogous judge-visitors had been seen before in England and on the continent in Carolingian days. These justices pursued crime without waiting for accusations by a harmed party. This active prosecution both weakened local independence and also was profitable, which explains the sour comment by Becket's partisan, John of Salisbury, about justices in eyre: 'And indeed the verb "to err" . . . fits those who wander from the path of equity to follow avarice and rob the people.'[7]

Had not the gentry supported them, these offices would have had no future. At the assize of Clarendon in 1166 the discovery of crime was put into the hands of four to twelve knights or other worthies, a method that evolved into the jury after the Church's prohibition of ordeals in 1215. A typical example is in the code attributed to Glanville: 'Testate or intestate, a usurer's property is the king's . . . . If someone dies in this crime . . . it is to be investigated and proved by twelve legal men of the neighbourhood.'[8] In 1194 and 1195 three shire knights and a clerk assembled the crown's pleas for judgment by justices in eyre, and local knights pursued infractors of the peace in each county.

The barons fought to curb the crown's growth. Henry II's later years were embittered by rebellions, and a revolt coupled with French invasion battered John and disturbed the first years of Henry III's reign. The barons rose again in the 1250s initiating civil wars ending around 1267. A renewed time of troubles began late in Edward I's reign, leading to the Confirmation of Charters in 1297 and culminating in the 'tyrannicide' of Edward II in 1327. The magnates, however, never acted as one. In 1215, for example, central

England's baronial families and those of the Welsh marches were not as exercised as the northerners, and only about forty-five barons holding thirty-nine baronies out of a total of 197 forced John to bow at Runnymede in 1215. Although the barons won much, it was costly and families wore themselves out in the struggle. In the early fourteenth century only seven of the once twenty-three leading families still remained powerful.

Attempts to control monarchy often led to political decentralization, to splitting unified bodies into independent entities, as in France where counties had been subdivided into castellanies or baronies. Some of this was seen in England. As royal government invaded seigniorial courts, it itself partly fell into the hands of local magnates. In Wiltshire, for example, about two-thirds of the hundred courts in 1194 were the crown's; by 1275 slightly less than a third were. Decentralization, however, was not the main path England's barons trod.

Instead of eradicating the crown's central offices, they tried to run them. As shall be seen below, they created councils to control royal officers and even appoint them. Balanced between crown and magnates, royal judges became more independent. Whereas the early *Exchequer Dialogue* echoed the sentiment that kings were above the law, the later compilation named after Bracton repeated the equally hoary notion that they were under it. Worried by this, the king abolished the chief justiciarship for good after 1268, and his new offices grew out of his personal household. A wardrobe keeper, Peter of Rievaulx, helped remove Hubert de Burgh, the last real chief justiciar, in 1232.

Like judges, barons began to think of themselves as men sworn to uphold the crown but not necessarily an unsuitable prince. Against Edward II in 1308, they stated:

> Our homage and oath of allegiance . . . bind us more by reason of the crown than by reason of the king's person . . . . Whence, if the king does not behave reasonably . . . his liege men, by the oath taken to the crown, are justly bound . . . to repair it, otherwise their oath is violated.[9]

At the time of Simon of Montfort some argued that the earls were the king's associates in government, concluding that he who has such associates has a master. This participation had advantages for the crown, if not for the monarch who wore it. Owing to the growth of parliament, the national tax limned in the reign of John had become relatively permanent, far more so than in France.

Led by the baronial aristocracy, the well-to-do in parliament failed to grant the monarchy sufficient subsidies to meet domestic and foreign responsibilities, forcing it to rely on external resources. Italian merchant bankers helped carry the burden until the economic crises of the early fourteenth century. Edward I's debts to the Riccardi of Lucca alone aggregated £392,000 from 1272 to 1294, while the crown's ordinary revenue in 1318 was about £30,000 yearly. With customs dues on the export of wine and raw wool, the monarchy still exploited the three-cornered trade between Guienne, England and Flanders, and in 1318 drew slightly more revenue from Guienne than from England. As long as the king was starved fiscally at home, ties with Flanders and Guienne meant everything to him. From the late thirteenth century onwards, increasing involvement abroad prompted an emigration of the crown from England to the continent that led to the later Hundred Years' War. A people wanting centralization may not wish to pay the price.

FRANCE

Perhaps prompted by the spread of both heredity and primogeniture among their barons, both England's and France's once elective monarchies became hereditary and primogenitous. While election was alive, France's kings associated the eldest heir or designated the chosen successor during the life of the incumbent. The system worked there but not in England, where the designation (1155) and association in kingship (1170) of his son Henry by Henry II failed because the young king allied with his father's enemies. Henry III at his accession in 1216 was England's first king not designated by his predecessor; and France's was Louis VIII in 1223. The first to assume government immediately on a predecessor's death were France's Philip III in 1270 and England's Edward I in 1272. France still suffered minorities (five years in the eleventh century and ten years after Louis IX's accession in 1226) but, unlike those in the Empire, they passed easily. Popular support enabled the regent, Blanche of Castile, to give her son Louis IX a stronger government when he took over in 1235 than had been hers when her husband died.

The strength of the Capetian house was its weakness: the small size of the royal domain. Louis VI had put some order into the Isle de France and his son, Louis VII, had married France's greatest heiress, Eleanor of Aquitaine, seemingly starting the monarchy on the way to success. Louis's divorce in 1152 and Eleanor's subsequent marriage to Henry II of England, however, reduced the Capetians to their nadir. Not only were Brittany, Champagne, Flanders and the Midi all but independent, but Henry held Guienne, Anjou, Poitou, Touraine, Maine and Normandy. Even France's Church was more Plantagenet than Capetian. Of the seventy-seven prelates in the kingdom, twenty-seven were Plantagenet nominees and twenty-six Capetian. Louis knew where he stood:

> Byzantium's emperor and Sicily's king may boast about their gold and silk cloth, but they have no men who can do more than talk, men incapable of war. The Roman emperor or, as they say, the emperor of the Germans, has men apt in arms and warlike horses, but no gold, silk or other wealth . . . . Now your king, the king of England, lacks nothing and possesses men, horses, gold, silk, jewels, fruits and wild beasts. We in France have nothing except bread, wine and joy.[10]

Capetians were hard masters of their own churches, towns and baronage, but luckily did not have too big a church, too many towns or too large a baronage in their domains. Louis VII won over France's churches by confirming the liberties of clergy and monasteries ruled by other French princes. Although Philip II Augustus fought Innocent III over his divorce from Ingeborg of Denmark, pope and king made peace between 1200 and 1213 when the Capetian emerged as the enemy not only of the Plantagenet John, but also of the threatening Otto IV Welf, whose army was beaten at Bouvines in 1215. Thereafter, although Philip was slow to join the Albigensian Crusade and Louis IX refused aid against the Hohenstaufen, the Capetians became the papacy's principal ally in Italy and Germany. The Rhone valley was also the popes' refuge when Italy became too hot for them.

The Capetians' ears always heard the complaints of the subjects of France's other princes. In Plantagenet domains they supported the baronage. In Burgundy, where barons ruled, they favoured the knights. They encouraged towns like Rheims, Soissons and Dijon to gain freedom at the expense of their lords. Sometimes, as in the region around Laon, the king buttressed villagers seeking liberty. In short, Louis VII and Philip II profited by giving away what was not theirs to give, and by the accession of Louis IX in 1226 the monarchy had come to be viewed as a fountain from which freedom flowed. Resident in Paris on and off from 1165 to 1180, Gerald of Wales polemically compared England's tyranny with France's pacific bliss, saying that Normandy fell into French hands so easily because

> at the time of the dukes, before the kings [of England] had oppressed the Normans as they did the English with . . . insular tyranny, [the Normans] were . . . strong in liberty, undaunted in arms to repel injury. When the necks of the nobles were bowed by the oppression of these tyrants, how could they rise with daring arms and spirits to resist France's freemen? Nothing so excites and raises the hearts of men to virtue as does the joy of liberty; and nothing so depresses . . . them as the oppression of servitude.[11]

Aided by the subjects of other princely houses, Capetian power expanded with great rapidity. Shortly after 1200, campaigns with little fighting cost the Plantagenets Normandy, Anjou and Poitou, leaving only Gascony or Guienne in their hands in 1226. After Bouvines in 1215 royal garrisons were invited into Flanders, whose barons and towns swore loyalty in 1226. Campaigns by Louis VIII made Languedoc prostrate by 1229 when all but Toulouse and Foix was surrendered to the crown. By 1245 Charles of Anjou, a Capetian cadet, had taken the imperial territory of Provence, and at the same time the nominally independent county of Champagne was all but run from Paris. This spurt of growth meant much: the crown's income nearly doubled from 1180 to 1223, and by Louis IX's death in 1270 France was Europe's richest state. More, the once troublesome nobles of the the old royal domain had found Empire by becoming the officialdom of an expanding monarchy.

The Capetians initially rested lightly on the lands under their rule. Unlike England, government was based on the rural or urban seigniory. Beaumanoir tells readers that 'where the king is not named, "sovereign" refers to those who hold in barony, for each baron is sovereign in his barony', and, anent towns, he says that 'at no time does one strike or push communes as one does a minor child'.[12] In these particularistic entities, in fact, much of the State's development took place. In towns, for example, the first professional lawyers and notaries were seen, initially in a Midi influenced by Italian law-schools but, around 1300, in France itself. Professional political leadership also spread north. Like a *podestà*, the burgher John of Champbaudun began as royal provost of Crépy in Valois in 1246, moved to Paris, and was then successively elected mayor of Montreuil, Compiègne and again Crépy.

The crown penetrated these local entities carefully. The author of *The Book of Justice and Pleas* of around 1259 required a two-thirds majority to elect a royal officer town mayor. Whereas in England almost all new towns were founded by lords or the crown alone, in France sharing was the order of the day. In Gascony forty-three per cent of the new towns and villages founded from about 1250 to 1350 were planted by seigniors aided by princes, such as the count of Toulouse and the kings of France and England. The 'conquest' of the Dauphiny between 1274 and 1333 consisted of the crown's acquisition of two large baronies, sharing in founding two new towns and purchasing part of the lordships of Gévaudan and Viviers from their bishops.

The monarchy often waited for local society to invite it. Because of conflicts between the humble and the wealthy and the pressures of growing centralization, many towns were in financial difficulty after 1250. The humble preferred graduated taxes based on property or income, whereas the rich preferred sale taxes. Besides, the reluctance of the rich to share government with the people resulted in undeveloped taxes and finance based largely on loans or sales of communal property. Appeals to the crown led to auditing: thirty-five northern towns in 1254, and by 1262 all books were opened. The crown claimed impartiality, but this quality militated against the patricians, under whom the towns had gained liberty. Beaumanoir viewed it thus: 'We have seen many struggles in the good towns, of the poor against the rich . . . and the rich seek to put all the expense on the poor . . . . [Governors must therefore] assess the tallage in the towns by loyal inquiry, on the rich as well as the poor, from each according to his means.' To effect this, moreover, required changes in government because 'we see many good towns in which poor and middling folk hold no offices, so that the rich have them all and are feared for wealth or lineage'.[13] Initially, the crown was supported by the people against the patricians.

France was still profoundly decentralized; private war, for example, was a far graver problem than in England. Blanche of Castile outlawed it in the royal domain, but Louis IX's attempt in 1258 to extend this to the kingdom evoked wide protest. Provinces like Brittany paid no heed at all and the crown was obliged to grant exemptions. In 1278, for example, the count of Foix refused to obey the royal seneschal of Toulouse because he had royal letters authorizing him to make war.

What happened on the national level in England happened in France on the local. Provincial annual assizes performed judicial and even legislative functions. In the 1250s the assembly of Agen consisted of town representatives and four persons speaking for the nobility. In 1254 the crown ordered a convocation of prelates, barons, knights and two town proctors to embargo the export of wine from the seneschalcy of Beaucaire. As will be seen, unlike the common law of England, provincial customary law was the basis of French law. It will be recalled that Henry II of England tried to divide his continental domains among his sons. The Capetians did the same, as at the death of Louis VIII in 1226, when the realm was divided into royal France and the appanages of Poitou and Anjou, to the former being added the county of Toulouse in 1249. Luckily, these grants escheated to the crown by 1300.

In basic respects France's institutions evolved like those of England. The crown tried in 1263 to monopolize minting money. Baronial mintings were known in England, but France admitted no less than thirty-odd baronial mints even after this effort. Still, the spread of the royal coinage of Tours throughout the areas conquered by the Capetians shows the crown's gains. As in England, also, the monarchy tried to bring business into its courts. The elder William Durand (d. 1296) claimed that, although many held of barons and not of the king, 'nevertheless all men in the kingdom of France are under the power and principate of the king, who has jurisdiction over all of them'.[14] The jurists usually described two categories of cases: those reserved to the crown, such as treason, and appeals from other courts because of faulty judgment or procedure. A litigant, for example, could appeal from trial by battle, a proof forbidden by an ordinance of 1258 favouring witnesses and documents.

Another similarity with England was the crown's attempt in 1181 to require service from all inhabitants, whether or not vassals. Here the monarchy disinterred a Carolingian tradition, namely that the defence of the fatherland required service from everyone. A protest by the marshal of Mirepoix in 1272 in the *parlement* of Paris against such service was of no avail. The later Capetians and early Valois therefore tried to force those not serving to pay compensatory taxes. By the 1290s the government collected sales taxes and tallage in lieu of service. In spite of feudal and provincial reaction in the early fourteenth century, this idea was so useful that every war was said to be in defence of the fatherland.

From the mid twelfth century, when local administration was entrusted to hereditary provosts or offices farmed out to towns such as Paris, the change toward centralized control was spectacular. Similar to Plantagenet itinerant justices, non-hereditary bailiffs were sent to investigate local administration from 1190, and became France's provincial governors in the course of the early thirteenth century. As other regions from Poitou to the Midi were absorbed, similar functions were given to officers called seneschals in imitation of the Plantagenets. From 1229 these governors had judges associated with them who, by 1270, had become almost independent of their chiefs. The investigative functions were now carried on by other officers, clerical and lay inquisitors sent out from court to report on the provinces from 1247.

France's governors were more highly paid than comparable officers in England, and family traditions were seen. Son of a provincial governor, Philip of Rémi, lord of Beaumanoir, held governorships in the Beauvaisis, Poitou, Saintonge, Vermandois, Touraine and Senlis. These recruits from the aristocracy of the old domain were more than royal servants. Beaumanoir believed he could judge his king's actions, refusing to record a royal edict in his book because it contravened public interest. A governor must obey his king's commands, he says, save for those

> for which he may lose his soul because the obedience he owes is to be understood as doing right and maintaining loyal justice. Nor will he be excused before God if he wrongs his own conscience . . . . It is better for an officer to leave the service than . . . wound his conscience.[15]

Although governorships and high judgeships were not, many French offices were farmed in the same way as the shrievalty in England. The republican Brunetto Latini railed against the practice, calling it characteristic of monarchy's corruption. Even those excusing it, like Thomas Aquinas, told princes to do it only 'if . . . those [buying offices] are suitable and if the offices are not sold at so high a price that [the investment] cannot be recovered without burdening your subjects'.[16] All was certainly not bliss, and Louis IX's inquirers record many complaints. In the seneschalcy of Beaucaire, a free farmer named Durand was harassed by a local bailiff and decided, as was his right, to leave. Intercepted by this officer at the gate, he said: 'I'm leaving because I can't live in peace with you who bedevil me night and day.' The officer exploded: 'Would it not be excellent if your and your brother's mouths were stuffed *de merda* so that you couldn't bellow or breathe *nisi per anum*,' and, sweeping a cowflop off the ground, he suited the action to the word at the expense of the open-mouthed rustic.[17]

Later than England's, but more rapidly, the king's court also grew. Although the 'men of the accounts' began to exercise fiscal judicial powers from about 1285, the treasury was entrusted to the Templars of Paris until 1295. By 1306 this exchequer had sixteen members, more than England's counterpart. By the mid thirteenth century the mixed ecclesiastical and lay tribunal called *parlement* had become resident at Paris. In 1296 there were fifty-one judges, by 1319 sixty-nine, far more than the four or five justices of the Common Pleas and the three on the King's Bench across the Channel. The Chamber of Inquiries, the part of the court investigating cases appealed from lesser courts, was just under sixty per cent of the whole in 1319.

For a time France was a happy monarchy, a reason why Louis IX was canonized in 1297, but the honeymoon was ending. Like England earlier, French society needed the crown's arbitrative and centralizing functions but did not want to pay for them. By the time of Philip IV the Fair the air resounded with complaints about maladministration and illicit taxes. John of Joinville's 1309 biography of the sainted Louis IX was aimed partly at Philip's monarchy. The king, said Joinville and Peter Dubois, should live of his own, but the old domain and tax structure were insufficient to finance the services demanded of the State. Far richer, the crown was also poorer than before. In 1203 its income is estimated at £179,000 (of Paris) and its expenses at £95,000. In 1292 it took in £589,000 and spent £687,000. The hand-to-mouth financing of the later age of crisis had begun.

The monarchy began to kill geese laying golden eggs. Repeated expropriations of the Jews and of the Lombards are examples. The Templars, like Lombards, creditors of the monarchy, were attacked and their properties held by the crown from 1307 to 1313. The crown tried to float forced loans, and in 1295 began to debase the coinage stabilized by Louis IX. Even the urge towards freedom was exploited by a hungry government, and, as seen earlier, farmers were forced to buy freedom at cost of land and movables.

If the reaction against the monarchy by provincial aristocracies and free towns awaited the accession of the Valois dynasty in 1328, the signs were already ominous. Royal taxation succeeded only because local powers shared in the proceeds. In 1296 the princes of large fiefs like Flanders and Burgundy were given half the subvention raised, 100-odd great barons got a third and lesser seigniors a quarter. Provinces were also beginning to mobilize against centralization. Languedoc's *parlement* of Toulouse emerged between 1278 and 1303. In 1302 the lords and towns of the Auvergne applauded the attack on the Roman Church but demanded in exchange confirmation of local customs and local recruiting for all royal officers. The reaction against the monarchy was expressed partly in an estates or parliament similar to that in England. More typical of France, however, was provincial separatism, which was to revive the appanage with far more detrimental effect than before and invite English intervention into French affairs during the Hundred Years' War.

NOTES AND REFERENCES

1 South Italy was a dynastic union of the Kingdom of Sicily, Duchy of Apulia and Principality of Capua.

2 Letter No. 29 in *PL* CCXVI, 1025.

3 *Sachsenspiegel* 3, 57 (ed. Gärtnern, Leipzig, 1732), 449.

4 In Baron, *A Social and Religious History of the Jews* VIII, 152.

5 Hauck, *Kirchengeschichte Deutschlands* V, i, 49n.

6 *De statutis* 3, 19 in *TUJ* II, 57va.

7 *Policraticus* 5, 15 (ed. Webb), I, 344.

8 *De legibus et consuetudinibus regni Angliae* 7, 16 (ed. Woodbine), 112.

9 Kantorowicz, *The King's Two Bodies*, 365n.

10 Walter Map, *De nugis curialium* 5, 5 (ed. M.R. James, Oxford, 1914), 225, and in Gerald of Wales, *De principis instructione* 3, 30 in *Rolls Series* XXI, viii, 317–18.

11 *De principis instructione* 3, 12 in *Rolls Series* XXI, viii, 255.

12 *Coutumes de Beauvaisis* 34, 1043 and 1524 (ed. Salmon), II, 23 and 270.

13 *Ibid.*, 1520, 1522 and 1525 (ed. Salmon), II, 267, 269 and 271.

14 His *Speculum juris* cited in Lot and Fawtier, *Histoire des institutions françaises* II, 220.

15 *Coutumes de Beauvaisis* 1, 18 (ed. Salmon), I, 22.

16 *De regimine Judeorum* 5 in Spiazzi (ed.), *Opuscula philosophica*, 250b.

17 Michel, *L'administration royale dans la sénéchausée de Beaucaire*, 88.

15

MONARCHS, SENATES AND ASSEMBLIES

POPES, CARDINALS AND COUNCILS

Churchmen wanted to govern themselves, and the regular clergy
provided models. Whereas Benedictines, including Cluny, were
monarchical, newer orders were conciliar. The constitution issued
by Stephen Harding in 1119 for the Cistercians was a step in this
direction, proposing an annual general chapter of elected abbots to
issue statutes and judge cases. The Cistercian rule formed the basis
of those of the Templars and most military orders, and influenced
those of the regular canons. In the fourth Lateran Council of 1215
similar assemblies meeting triennially in each province or kingdom
were imposed on the Benedictines.

Conciliar government, however, culminated in the mendicants.
The Franciscans were socially democratic, initially gave lay brethren
a great voice and were always relatively open in recruitment. Unstable, they were a democracy with overtones of tyranny. The
Franciscan revolt against the long reign of the Minister General
Elias of Cortona from 1226 to his deposition in 1239 inspired Salimbene of Parma to propose abolishing lifetime office, arguing that
'the frequent change of prelates is the preservation of the regular
orders'.[1] Elitist but also homogeneous, the Dominicans were the
best clerical republicans. Building from 1220, they distinguished
three levels: convent, province and order. In convents, members
elected priors and voted on laws and actions. Provincial priors were
elected by, and responsible to, annual assemblies of conventual
priors and another group chosen by the houses, the 'diffinitors'. On
the highest level, an annual chapter general, composed of provincial

priors every third year and at other times of provincial diffinitors, elected and controlled the master general of the order. Excluding the general, whose tenure was lifetime, all officers were elected for limited terms and all, including the general, could be retired by an assembly. Not being administrative officers, diffinitors preserved the health of this republic. Not that debate was lacking, however. Hugh of St Cher spoke out in 1257 against the annual change of officers; Humbert of Romans pleaded at Lyons in 1274 to make the removal of tyrannical or incompetent ones easy.

The papacy was a monarchy. Being an elected monarch, the only issue was removal. Resignation became an issue when Celestine V stepped down in 1294. As for deposition, most canonists agreed that a heretical or wholly incompetent pope could be deprived of office. It had also long been recognized that, since the world is larger than Rome, an assembly, not to speak of the whole Christian people, was superior to any one officer, no matter how high. The problem was to find the agency that could control this elected monarch.

There were two such agencies, the cardinals and a general council. The former had already claimed the right of removing popes in the battles with Gregory VII, justifying that act with historical examples. Still, although cardinals often created rival popes or sabotaged a pope's programme, the notion of deposing them was little developed until the late thirteenth century. The Dominican John of Paris then declared any college superior to its elected head, asserting that 'I believe the college of cardinals suffices for a deposition because their consensus, standing for the whole of the Church, elects the pope, and it therefore seems likely that it could depose him.'[2] This position, however, won little favour even in the Sacred College.

Although monarchs, popes needed the consent of their senate. In 1234 Gregory IX ordained that 'there will be no alienation of the papal patrimony without the common advice and consent of the brethren. Each one of these also possesses the faculty of freely opposing his veto for a legitimate reason.'[3] In 1262 Urban IV rescinded his predecessor's recognition of Richard of Cornwall as emperor-to-be because he had acted without the consent of the cardinals. Unlike popes, however, cardinals had small followings and many believed that Rome's 'vices' were not attributable to the pope but instead to his courtiers.

Cardinals were also unable to find a foolproof way of electing popes. Of the thirty-five popes and 'antipopes' elected from 1145 to 1334 no more than eight were from outside their college; testimony, one might think, to this group's solidarity. Europe's conflicts, however, found ways to penetrate this body. Although its right to elect popes was established in the late eleventh century, there were recurrent disputed elections and schisms until the two-thirds majority in papal elections was imposed by the Lateran Council of 1179. During Alexander III's twenty-two-year reign, no less than four 'imperialist' popes reigned, one of whom served for ten years.

After that, the problem was to obtain the required majority. Vacancies were frequent, totalling from 1241 to 1305 about ten years, one being just under three years. To correct this, the conclave was borrowed from Italian urban elections in 1216. Used intermittently until made obligatory at the Council of Lyons in 1274, the electors were locked up until they decided on a pope. Even this method did not obviate vacancies, however, because cardinals postponed elections until forced into conclave. At the time of the Council of Vienne, William Durand the Younger proposed that, if the see were vacant for more than three months, the cardinals' power should devolve on a general council. Although nothing came of this until 1417, John of Paris also believed that general councils were the ultimate recourse.

Although Rome's general councils signalled her victory, they also focused local church opposition to papal centralization. The struggle with the Hohenstaufen made the papacy bow to the prelates in the general councils of Lyons in 1245 and 1274 and Vienne in 1311. At Vienne complaints against aspects of papal centralism make up much of the extant record. At issue were the mendicants, allies of centralism with papal privileges to preach and hear confessions. In the first half of the thirteenth century the popes generally supported them. At First Lyons, Innocent IV reversed this policy, and at Second Lyons and Vienne the prelates got their way. Legislation against expanding or founding new orders was there accepted by the popes.

At the time of Vienne, William Durand the Younger wrote a tract on conciliar 'reform'. Himself a bishop of Mende, he expressed episcopal opposition to papal centralism and the mendicants, and recommended a conciliar 'constitutional monarchy'. Counsel, William says, is salubrious for governments. To change earlier law, a pope or secular prince should act only with the express consent of the cardinals or an equivalent secular group. Indeed, no prince should dispense from old law without conciliar consent 'since, according to the rule of both laws, what touches all should be approved by all'.[4] William also proposed a system of local councils similar to that already encouraged by papal legislation, but added 'that the pope should issue no general laws from now on unless a general council has been convoked, which body should be called every ten years'.[5]

Nor was William wild. Although guardedly, canonists often held that councils were superior to popes. The canonist Alan taught in Bologna that 'in a question concerning the faith a synod is superior to a pope . . . . Hence for [heresy] a synod can condemn and judge a pope.'[6] Using similar arguments, John of Paris proposed that a defective or heretical pope may 'be warned to step down, and, if he does not wish to, can be removed, a general council having been summoned and he called before it. If found violently pertinacious, he can be removed by the advocate of the secular arm.'[7] As shall be touched on at the end of this book, ideas like these were used to attack Boniface VIII and John XXII.

Conciliarism nevertheless faltered in the early fourteenth century. Although Boniface was defeated, the monarchical principle triumphed in the Church, and no general councils were called after Vienne. Conciliarism, however, was not dead. If no more general councils were summoned, those of the regional and national churches continued to meet. Wedded now to the developing State, these councils provided the training grounds from which the conciliar fathers of the fifteenth century came.

SECULAR PRINCES AND PARLIAMENTS

As was true in the early Middle Ages, all large states were monarchies. One wonders why. It may be that, as stated earlier, medieval political freedom was found in the space between two mutually antagonistic governments, the Church and State, whose rivalry limited their implicit totalitarianisms. Ecclesiastical power may have made it unnecessary for men to seek freedom by replacing monarchies with republics, a replacement that began only after the Reformation when the Church was gradually subordinated to the State. The problem, therefore, was not to do away with monarchy, but instead to control it.

Early ages had left a rich political tradition. Monarchy was often elective and law often issued by a prince with the express consent of the 'people', as at Ptres in 864. In the tenth century Hincmar of Rheims opined that monarchies were not necessarily divinely founded. Princes had been elected and removed by citizens and soldiers, and, following Augustine, this metropolitan said they were under the law and not above it. During the Gregorian revolution, Manegold of Lautenbach argued that kings and dukes held offices not dynastic possessions, maintaining that they could be removed if they broke their contract with the people. Revolution's child, he likened princes to hired swineherds dismissible for cause.

During the twelfth century these traditions were enriched by canon and Roman law. Culminating in the translation of Aristotle's *Politics* in 1260, the scholastics added further knowledge. Some, like Brunetto Latini and Roger Bacon, worshipped the ancients Seneca and Cicero. Europe's expansion, moreover, widened Latin horizons. Continuing Aquinas's *On the Rule of Princes* around 1305, Ptolemy of Lucca compared different kinds of government. Divine in origin, the papacy was a type of monarchy; secular monarchy was either electoral and universal, like the Empire, or hereditary and local, like France. Because Aristotle had treated Carthage as well as Greek republics, Ptolemy described Egypt's Mamluk government, its imported slave élite and rejection of tyrants.

In monarchy the people delegated their powers to a man for life, but should he be elected or succeed dynastically? As seen above, ecclesiastics generally favoured election, especially for the office of emperor. Germans also supported electoral monarchy, contrasting their 'natural' liberty with French servility. Gervase of Tilbury spotted another vice of hereditary monarchy, namely that princes' subordinates tend also to be hereditary. He praised Tiberius Caesar for teaching officers that good shepherds shear their sheep but do not flay them, adding:

> Surely the Roman republic was more wisely ruled when the government was obtained by election and not by succession, and its provincial governors acted in a more restrained manner when they ruled for a term . . . . But now family succession calls to government immature infants, inconstant, harsh, impious fellows, authors of all sorts of levity, who do not believe themselves to rule as a duty imposed by God, but rather as a right owed them by nature.[8]

The Empire aside, however, electoral monarchies generally failed and hereditary kingship was normal. The problem was therefore how to organize and control this institution. Writing on prelatry, Salimbene of Parma employed Gregory I's familiar passage derived from Roman law: 'Man by nature rules brute animals, but not other men . . . . He is to be feared by animals but not by men, because it is a crime against nature to wish to be feared by an equal.'[9] Natural equality suggested government based on contract, and Rufinus, a Bolognese canonist who became archbishop of Sorrento in 1150, therefore wrote: 'When a king is instituted, a certain tacit pact is initiated between him and the people, so that the king governs the people and the people honours the king with traditional tribute and services.'[10]

Princes were to defend the faith and serve the commonweal. If tyrannical, seeking only personal gain, they rob their subjects of life, liberty, position and property, thus precipitating a withdrawal of obedience pithily described by Jerome long before: 'Why should I,' said a senator to the Emperor Domitian, 'treat you as a prince when you don't treat me as a senator?'[11] John of Salisbury went further, declaring that it is licit, even glorious, to kill tyrants. Thomas Aquinas said that revolt against tyrants was seditious only when 'the government is so inordinately disturbed that the multitude suffers more from the ensuing disturbances than from the tyrant's government. A tyrant who sows discord and sedition among his people that he may safely rule them is really more seditious.'[12] Speaking of Caesar's assassination, he went on:

> Cicero is talking about an occasion when someone violently seizes the government when the subjects do not want it or when they agree to it only because they are coerced, and when there is no recourse to a superior . . . then whoever kills a tyrant to liberate the fatherland is to be praised and receive the reward.[13]

There were better ways of limiting princely power than tyrannicide. One was Roman law's trial by a man's peers in his own court, a class idea applicable to judicial relations between prince and subject. That a prince should not judge his own case was embodied in England's Great Charter of 1215 and was common on the continent. The French *Establishments of St Louis*, a compilation of customary law of 1272–3, for example, admitted a noble's right to be judged by his peers when sued by the king in a royal court.

More suited to the grander stage of politics, another way was to expand old royal or princely courts into assemblies representing society's powerful elements. In Benavente in 1202, the king of Leon reported that 'the case both of my party and that of the knights and others having been heard, judgment was rendered between me and them' by the prelates, vassals and town representatives there assembled.[14] High judges were made to undergo annual judicial reviews. From 1265 the king of Aragon chose a chief justiciar from among the lesser nobles to try cases between the crown and its subjects, an officer to be removed only by a vote of the parliament. By the Golden Bull of 1222 in Hungary, the lesser nobles assembled annually to review the actions and decisions of the king and his chief justiciar, the Count Palatine. Princely objections to such examination led to threats to withdraw allegiance, examples being the final chapter of England's Great Charter or the thirty-first of the Golden Bull seen above.

The same courts or assemblies also issued new law promulgated by the prince. Centralizing their realms, princes wanted to address their subjects. Meeting his notables at Ariano, Roger II of Naples and Sicily (d. 1154) ordered: 'we therefore wish you to receive faithfully and obey expeditiously the commands we have caused to be shown to the present assembly'.[15] What subjects wanted often differed from what princes wanted to hear, and the latter sometimes recognized it. At Foggia in 1225 and 1234 Frederick II invited assemblymen to submit complaints against royal government.

The issue was whose will was superior, that of the prince or that of the 'people'. William Durand the Younger thought a prince was merely a person like Scipio in the Roman republic, who, although individually superior, was not as powerful as the whole people. Rome's *Royal Law*, on the other hand, asserted that, once surrendered, the people's power was forever the prince's, and that what he pleased to find in his heart had the force of law, a free product of his will.[16] Jurists disagreed about this, as Cino of Pistoia remarked about Bolognese professors: 'John [Bassiani, d. 1197] said that today the Roman people cannot make law . . . . Hugolino [d. *circa* 1233] said the opposite. The ordinary gloss approves John's opinion . . . . Certain moderns hold with Hugolino . . . . Now, choose which opinion pleases you, because I don't care.'[17] Other jurists expatiated on another passage in which the prince confessed himself bound by law.[18] And if the *Royal Law* held that was not so, it was usually admitted, as by Frederick II Hohenstaufen to the Romans in 1238, that princes were bound by reason, law's mother.

Consultation was what subjects wanted. In practice, the group of counsellors was often a small body, a consistory as in late Rome or the papacy. Writing on day-to-day actions of governments William Durand the Younger remarks that 'it is wise for the republic and its administrators to limit their power reasonably, so that, without the counsel of the lord cardinals, the lord popes and, without the counsel of other prudent men, kings and princes' should not use their plenitude of power to abrogate old law or issue new.[19] In the first book of the Castilian *Book of the Laws* the prince is forbidden to issue new law without the consent of the 'people'. At Barcelona in 1283 the prince confessed that 'if we or our successors wish to issue a general constitution or statute in Catalonia, we will do so with the approbation of the prelates, barons, knights and citizens . . . the larger and sounder part of those summoned'.[20]

Subjects also wanted to be consulted about new law, war and peace, new taxes and ordinances dealing with their service and status. Alfonso IX of Leon swore at his accession in 1188 not to make war or peace or hear important suits without the consent of his bishops, nobles and worthy townsfolk. Avid exponents of councils for other princes, the popes had a keen eye in these matters. In 1267 Clement IV castigated the king of Naples and Sicily for raising taxes without the assent of the prelates, barons and notable inhabitants of his cities and towns. Commenting on the *Decretals of Gregory IX*, Innocent IV maintained that a prince should not debase coinage without the consent of the major part of his people. In 1228 the patriarch of Aquileia, prince of the March of Friuli, referred to fortifications, public works and roads constructed on the advice of his assembly of prelates, nobles, ministers (knights) and town citizens. When a dynasty became extinct, the change to a new house came under the purview of the magnates or the 'people'. The ministers of Styria (there, the great nobles) won the right by 1300 of choosing the local prince if the dynasty ran out. All such assemblies treated new law. An assembly at Worms before the issue of the Statute in favour of the Princes of 1231–2 was asked the following question:

'Whether any territorial prince can issue constitutions or new laws without the consent of the better or more important people of his land?' With the princes' consent, this question was so answered 'that neither princes nor anyone else can make constitutions or new laws unless the better and more important people of the land have first agreed'.[21]

Since everyone could not attend, representatives' actions came to bind those at home by about 1250. Within assemblies, also, although majorities usually ruled as in the Catalan case of 1283 seen above, documents mention not only the 'larger' but also the 'sounder' part. Given the significance of monarchy at this time, the term 'sounder' was also used to limit majorities, when, for example, a prelate or prince overrode the choice of a body of electors. Majorities could be transcended in yet another way. In a law of 1234 adverted to above, Gregory IX not only envisaged that certain matters required the advice or consent of the Sacred College, but went on to state that each cardinal 'also possesses the faculty of freely opposing his veto for a legitimate reason'.[22] Such veto rights seem to have been exercised only in small bodies at this time, but were to be adopted in large late-medieval assemblies, such as the Estates of the Netherlands or Poland.

Prelates and great magnates had always been members of princes' courts and naturally took part in the new assemblies. Sometimes, as in Castile and France, all gentlefolk, baronial and knightly, formed one body, but elsewhere the lesser nobility were separated from the greater, presumably because the latter had always attended the prince's court. The author of the *Way of Holding Parliaments* in the early fourteenth century felt that the knights (two per shire by that time) and the representatives of the boroughs and lesser clergy represented the community of England, whereas the barons and prelates were there only for their own persons, that is, as little princes with great jurisdictions. At the assembly of Barbastro in 1192, Catalonia's knights constituted a separate 'arm', distinct from the magnates and town citizens, something also seen in Aragon and Friuli in Italy. In Aragon the clergy did not constitute an 'arm' until the fourteenth century. There, as in England, the lesser clergy usually met apart in their own synods, while the prelates met with the general assembly. Urban representation varied. In England the two representatives for each borough appeared for the first time in 1265. In Frederick II's parliaments of Foggia the cities and fortified villages each sent two in 1232, and in 1240 each city sent two and each village one. Decentralized France started late and tried to crowd everybody into its early estates, which in 1307–8 contained prelates, nobles and representatives of no less than 558 towns and villages in northern France.

Humbert of Romans reported that kings normally held 'great courts' several times yearly to handle business requiring broad advice, hear the crown's fiscal accounts and issue necessary edicts. Paralleling princely courts, town assemblies often met four times yearly, but this was impractical for larger political units. In Catalonia an assembly at Barcelona in 1283 decreed an annual great assembly, but a later meeting at Lerida in 1301 determined that once every third year would be enough, save in case of public need. Enforcing decisions taken in parliament required nominating councillors to sit with the prince in between times. Even before England had a parliament, twenty-five notables (of whom four were to remain permanently beside the king) were elected by the barons at Runnymede to check on the implementation of the Great Charter. In the baronial wars from 1258 to 1265 more elaborate arrangements were made. Interlocking councils of four, twelve and fifteen members, chosen partly by the king and partly by the barons, policed the working of the 'reforms' and the issuance of new law. The chief officers of state – the treasurer, chancellor and chief justiciar – were to be chosen jointly by king and barons. These radical arrangements did not last, but they show the way the wind was blowing. In 1287 the king of Aragon conceded that the parliament of Saragossa should meet yearly and that it, together with the proctors of that town, should elect commissioners 'with whose council we and our successors will govern and administer the realms of Aragon, Valencia and Ribagorza'.[23] At war with Venice over Trieste in 1283, the patriarch of Aquileia called his parliament of prelates, nobles, ministers and townsfolk together to choose twenty-four members, six from each group, and bound himself to carry out whatever they determined.

The trend towards parliaments was most successful in the smaller or less populous realms of Latin Europe. In France provincial assizes and assemblies like those of Agen were more systematized than the 'national' one which had hardly begun before 1290. In Italy particular realms, like Friuli and the Catalan kingdom of Sicily after 1282, were the centres of conciliarism. In Brunswick–Lüneburg, Pomerania, Bohemia and the Austro-Swiss mountains assemblies of clergy, nobility and townsfolk appear in the 1280s and 1290s, but elsewhere German conciliarism moved slowly. Towns and rural lords there often limited regional princes by claiming to hold directly of the emperor. Like those of Iberia's smaller states, lightly populated England's parliament regularly issued legislation, such as, for example, the Statute of Westminster of 1275, granted taxes and investigated subjects' complaints.

In 1300 no one could have guessed that the parliamentary trend would weaken, but thereafter, during Latin Europe's age of crisis, it

did. Foreign war and internal social war required strong governments trammelling people's rights in order to mobilize, police and
pacify society. What was then needed was a separate estate, the
estate royal, coercively to arbitrate social conflict. Created by the
'people', the princely estate's advantage was that it loved only itself
and no other group, class or part of society. Except for a final effort
in the fifteenth century, and except in England, parts of Spain,
south Italy and southern and eastern Germany where assemblies
continued to limit monarchies or principates, the parliamentary or
conciliar trend weakened everywhere.

Unaware of what the future was to bring, most Latins around
1300 would have applauded the sentiment of Marsiglio of Padua
when he wrote that, unlike the monarchical tyrannies of the 'servile' peoples of the east, 'royal monarchy is a temperate form of
government in which the ruler is a single man deferring to the
common good and to the will or consensus of his subjects'.[24] For a
time, regional and even quasi-national assemblies seemed a good
way of providing such a consensus. Even Giles of Rome, scholasti-
cism's most widely read monarchist, could not imagine a prince
without a council. Although it is generally useful 'for a son to succeed his father, if there is any defect in the royal child to whom the
royal charge should come, it can be supplied by wise and good men
whom the king should join to himself in a kind of society as his
hands and eyes'.[25] Besides, as he had to confess, since one person
cannot know as much as many, a prince must associate others with
himself in a partnership, thus becoming 'one man with many eyes,
many hands and many feet'.[26]

NOTES AND REFERENCES

1   *De prelato* in his *Chronicon* in *MGH SS* XXXII, 156.
2   *De potestate regia et papali* 24 (ed. Bleienstein), 201–2.
3   Bresslau, *Handbuch der Urkundenlehre* II, 58n.
4   *De modo generalis concilli celebrandi* 1, 4, 4 in *TUJ* XIII, 155va, and *Code* 5,
    59, 5, 2 and *Sexti decretalium* 5, *de regulis juris* 29 in *CICan* II, 1122.
5   *De modo* 1, 4, 4 in *TUJ* XIII, 176va.
6   Tierney, *Foundations of the Conciliar Theory*, 67n.
7   *De potestate regia et papali* 22 (ed. Bleienstein), 192–3.
8   Published by G.C. Leibnitz, *Scriptores rerum Brusvicensium* (Hannover,
    1707), 902.

9   *Cronicon* in *MGH SS* XXXII, 120.

10   *De bono pacis* 2, 9 in *PL* CL, 1617c.

11   *Decretum* 1, 95, 7 in *CICan* I, 334.

12   *Summa theologiae* II-II, 42, 2 *ad* 3.

13   *Commentarium in quatuor libros sententiarum Magistri Petri Lombardi* 2, 44, 2, 2 and 5 cited in A. Passerin d'Entrèves, *Scritti politici* (Bologna, 1946), 93–4.

14   Juan Beneyto Perez, *Testos politicos españoles de la baja edad media* (Madrid, 1944), 202, No. 532.

15   Cortese, *La norma giuridica* II, 235n.

16   The *lex regia* is in *Digest* 1, 4, 1, 1, *Code* 1, 17, 1, 7 and *Institutes* 1, 2, 5.

17   Cortese, *La norma giuridica* II, 130.

18   The *lex digna* in *Code* 1, 14, 4.

19   *De modo generali concilii celebrandi* 1, 4, 4 in *TUJ* XIII, 155va.

20   Perez, *Testos politicos españoles*, 304, No. 542.

21   *MGH Legum sectio IV* II, 420, No. 305.

22   Bresslau, *Handbuch der Urkundenlehre* II, 58n.

23   Perez, *Testos politicos españoles*, 249, No. 453.

24   *Defensor pacis* 1, 5 in *MGH SS in usum scholarum* 1, 35.

25   *De regimine principum* 3, 2, 5 (Rome, 1607), 237.

26   *De regimine principum* 3, 2, 4 (Rome, 1607), 460; see also 3, 2, 4 and 3, 2, 17.

16

PRINCES, VILLAGES AND TOWNS

COMMUNITIES AND DEFENCE

Profitable and beautiful, towns were loved by princes. Convinced that spiritual advancement required material foundation, a bishop of Meissen waxed poetic when founding a town in 1154:

> Although, with Mary, one must choose the good or, rather, the better part of intimate quiet in the sweetness of the contemplative life, we are nevertheless generally obliged, with Martha, to be busy in the bitterness of the active life . . . . For the tabernacle of the covenant and the ark of the Lord's witness would not shine with such brilliance were they not protected from storm and rain with goat's hair and rams' skins died red and blue. Whence the Church of God is not only to provide the Lord's flock with a good teacher in things spiritual and eternal, but also sagaciously to succour it as a provident shepherd in things carnal and temporal.[1]

Since a town was also often the 'origin and head' of a province, as an archbishop of Magdeburg said when founding Jterbog in 1174, there was political advantage in granting town liberties. Under Henry II, Rouen was given a measure of self-government. In 1199 and thereafter her law was given towns in Poitou and Guienne, and these were among the few stoutly loyal to the Plantagenets during the Capetian conquests in the early thirteenth century.

Town seals often had walls and towers engraved on them because all were fortified, and walling was a major preoccupation of town fathers. The third wall around Florence contained no less than fifteen gates and seventy-three towers. Keeping up with population was a problem, and Ghent's walls were enlarged five times between 1160 and 1300. Curiously, the same was true of villages. Those too small or poor to have their own walls often clustered for protection below a seigniorial castle, but many were also fortified, as is shown by the frequency of the suffix 'burg' in French and German village names. In Florence's dependent rural county, there were about eleven fortified villages in 1100; by 1200 there were 205. Since Tuscany was more pacific by 1200 than a century earlier, these figures show that walls were not constructed because society was especially given over to war. Again, although few villages could stand a siege, what their walls meant for rural security is obvious. Urban and village fortification and seigniorial castles were the material counterparts of the institutional restraints on war that gave defence an advantage over offence in this time.

The Church tried to slow war at home in order to project it abroad in the Crusades. The growing freedom of the nobility, townsfolk and even villagers also limited service owed to princes, and hence impeded using the militia for offensive wars. These limitations were reinforced by the community solidarity common in this time of increasing liberty and beneficent economic circumstances. That the cohesion necessary for defence was never complete or the militia always efficacious is obvious, and that they were weakening around 1300 has already been shown, but for a time local society joined the Church to limit war.

Liberty cannot exist without a capacity to defend oneself, and the possession of this capacity by both town and countryside reflected the decentralized political structure of this age. Decentralization helps explain why monarchy was so general. Kings and emperors were distant, and real and intense political life took place in town and village. Europe's monarchies were to be limited or destroyed in modern times partly because the seigniory and the free town had all but vanished.

VILLAGE AND TOWN

No sharp distinction between town and village existed. Settlers of unoccupied land were not infrequently called 'burghers' because they inhabited burgs, a term originally meaning fortified enclosures. Although this use died out around 1200, well-to-do villagers still often used it to set themselves apart from lesser inhabitants. The urban distinction between workers and bourgeois also appeared in villages. In Switzerland and Savoy the neighbours called to enunciate local custom and judge cases were not only called 'worthy' and 'the better and more ancient parishioners' but also, emulating Rome's ancient law, 'honest' or 'honoured men'. Not that these distinctions were always rigid, however. The customs of Villefranche in the Lauragais in 1280 considered adultery was proved when the male 'was taken naked with a naked woman or clothed with a clothed woman but lying on the ground by any inhabitant . . . having with him two consuls or other worthy men, or indeed any two others, whencesoever they may come, worthy of trust'.[2]

Villagers liked to think they had urban institutions, as two charters of 1159 issued by the archbishop of Magdeburg illustrate. In the village of Pechau, settlers were promised the 'burghers' law' which was, in fact, Flemish law, the usual north German settlers' law. In the village of Grosswusterwitz they had the same, but there called it the town law of Schartau, and moreover their market was organized according to Magdeburg law. Titles of office, like mayor and *scabini*, had long been shared by village and town, and villages emulated new town styles as well. One was the term 'consul' (to be defined below) used for elected governors of towns in Italy, southern France and parts of Spain. By the later thirteenth century almost all north Italian villages had consulates. In the Lauragais south of Toulouse, a city with a consulate from 1189, about nine villages used this elevated style in 1256. Sixteen years later, just under a hundred small towns and villages did. This was not so everywhere: the manualist of Baumgartenberg remarked that 'because there are no consuls in cities, fortified villages or open ones in our country, we [Austrians] do not have the habit of writing them'.[3]

Like towns, some village boards combined knights and commoners. In 1282 the consuls of Cordes near Albi were half knights and half 'good men'. Where lordships were subdivided over time, the lords themselves were reduced to being scarcely more than yeoman farmers. Just after 1150 seven lords, sons of four fathers, held the lordship of Montferrier near Montpellier; in 1207 no less than thirty-five co-seigniors divided the large barony of Mirepoix at the foot of the Pyrenees. Lordly rights were also often held by patrician townsfolk, an example being the Sienese lords of Cerrato, who in 1216 promised its inhabitants that 'we will choose one of us rector who will govern the castle, inhabit it three days each month and there decide the suits brought to the castle's court'.[4] Like towns, also, villages allied together. In the early fourteenth century the thirteen villages of the bailiwick of Mas Saintes Puelles near Carcassonne customarily acted as one unit in law. In a charter of 1314 the hamlet of Aigne in the same region joined the large village of Cintegabelle to elect one of the eight consuls governing the joint community. The best-known example is the Swiss alliance of the small towns and villages of Uri, Schwyz and Unterwald in 1291. Renewed in 1315, it lasted for centuries.

Villager and townsman differed in the degree of liberty attained. In theory, every 'university' or whole could make law, but Italian commentaries show that this freedom was in fact limited by lords or larger communities. Most village customs merely tried to limit taxation, military or labour service, rents and fines for justice, and sometimes allowed inhabitants the freedom of moving away. Villagers nevertheless usually participated in judging civil cases and sometimes had jurisdiction over them, especially in newly founded centres. More rarely, as in parts of Italy, Swabia and southern France, their consulates won the right to try criminals, whose punishment involved death, confiscation of property and heavy fines, although the costs and fines were usually shared by their lords. Rare were the rights accorded to Villefranche in the Lauragais in 1280 where the consuls had full jurisdiction over theft, homicide, adultery and other crimes. Tax control was also unusual, but villagers frequently regulated collection and shared the amount raised.

Rural consuls in Italy and France were elected, sometimes by all freemen, sometimes through co-optation by an outgoing consulate, thus building village oligarchies. The law of Beaumont in Argonne of 1182 – it eventually spread to 500 towns and villages – gave inhabitants the right to elect officers directing justice and finance. In most south French or Gascon new foundations, the community presented a slate to the lord, who chose the four or so consuls for the year. In Pasignano, a village outside Florence owned by the Cistercians, the monks chose half the magistrates and the inhabitants the rest. This did not assure subservience because one of the consuls in 1173 was the village's largest landed proprietor, a contentious man busy suing the abbot. Sometimes, as at Vidigulfo near Milan in 1254, consuls were elected by the people and merely confirmed by the lords: 'the inhabitants of this place may choose the consuls, smiths, guards of the fields and swineherds; and the aforesaid lords . . . shall invest and confirm them'.[5]

Areas where villagers had freedom were often those needing settlers, like Germany east of the Elbe. Again, in parts of France, Italy
and southern and western Germany, seigniorial and urban particularism made it necessary for lords to buy their subjects' loyalty.
England had a 'new-town' movement as vigorous as the Gascon
one, but substantial political liberties were rarely accorded to settlers
there. Gascons won them probably because, if blocked by the officers of the king of England, they could switch loyalty to those of
the king of France, and vice-versa.

At best, however, village liberties, especially political ones, were
restricted. Save for relatively primitive areas like Scandinavia, Frisia
and Schleswig, the lands of the Baltic Slavs and occasional mountain
areas where seigniorial and urban institutions had barely penetrated,
villagers were everywhere affiliated with a lord or a town. A charter
of 1172 records the subjection of some Swabians to the emperor:

> The inhabitants have unanimously subjected their town of Bernheim, which
> they have possessed up to now free of all lordship, to our power, on these
> terms, namely that they and all their posterity will pay the Empire twenty-five
> measures of wheat each year in order . . . to be free from all tyranny under the
> protection of our imperial highness.[6]

In an age when the ideal political unit was the barony or free
town, villages lacked sufficient industry and commerce to stand
alone, but large towns or substantial baronies that united many villages could. Updating Aristotle, Ptolemy of Lucca opined that monarchy was best for large areas with discordant interests and
traditions, and that the republican form was ideal for substantial
cities. Small communities, however, lacked what cities had, namely,
'the community of the multitude, without which a man cannot live
decently; and this is much more true of a city than of a village,
because cities have many arts and crafts providing a sufficiency for
human life'.[7] To crafts and trades may be added legal, scribal, political and military training beyond that of a farmer tilling the fields.
The result was that patricians and nobles not only served those
functions themselves and trained their sons in them, but also taxed
the villages to pay for soldiers, lawyers, bailiffs, clergy and other
specialists. Farmers surely wanted freedom and political rights; yet,
considering the time at their disposal and the size of the economic
units characteristic of the age, it was more profitable for them to
buy these functions from seigniors or townsfolk. The characteristic

village political form was therefore the intimate monarchy of the rural seigniory.

Urban or rural, the rulers of these farmers often confused their sometimes brutally exercised prerogatives with the liberties of 'their subject people'. Possessing 'sovereign' fiefs as Beaumanoir called them, great baronial families were convinced they possessed by divine right, and their subjects made this boast meaningful. Rustics often favoured the independence of the little states in which they lived because they sheltered them from the economic power of great towns and the taxes and services demanded by great monarchs.

The provision of the services thought necessary by Ptolemy of Lucca for true self-government may be tested by examining small towns, those between city and village. Isle Jourdain in Gascony near Toulouse in 1210 had a stone bridge, a leprosery and two hospitals, one named after its lay founder, just as was customary in its greater neighbour. Before 1200 lay public notaries were instrumenting within its walls, between a quarter and a half a century after they were seen in Toulouse and a slightly shorter length of time before nearby villages boasted the same. In 1230 or 1232 the community elected thirteen worthies to serve as its consulate, a body having, 'with the consent of the university, full and free power of changing, tempering and deleting heavy and onerous customs, written or not, and the right of making and instituting by itself . . . new customs to advance the common utility of the whole university'.[8] These republican rights were lost by 1275, when the lord or his vicar and the outgoing consulate together nominated forty worthies, from whom seven consuls were chosen by lot.

Monarchy, in short, was seen in rural and small town political life, and so also was oligarchy and even democracy.

TOWN AND CITY

To Ptolemy of Lucca the natural urban political form was a collective lordship or republic. He observed 'that in every region, whether Germany, Scythia or France, cities are republics, but [other than in Italy] are bound by laws under the power of a king or emperor'.[9] He was surely right about the general principle. Areas marked by urban self-government lay along the frontiers of the principal power blocs. The most important of these were the western and southern marches of the fading Empire, extending from the North Sea through the Lorraines and Burgundies and down the Rhone to Provence, thence traversing northern and central Italy. Of these, northern and central Italy's cities were the most free, some winning independence in 1183 at the treaty of Constance, others during the Hohenstaufen collapse in the mid-thirteenth century. Other areas notable for liberty were the Lorraines, the Burgundies and adjacent regions in the Empire along the Rhine valley and its confluents. As the Hohenstaufen fell, towns in Swabia, modern Switzerland and along the upper Rhine and Danube advanced greatly. So also did communities in imperial Provence and on the Rhone until 1250 when Capetian power began to penetrate there.

Cities also profited when local ruling houses were harmed by greater ones. An example was Flanders, a French province. Her towns were almost as free as Italian ones, because, after Philip of Alsace (d. 1191), the French crown intervened to ruin the counts by the time of Guy of Dampierre (d. 1305). With the region's tallest belfry, adjacent Tournai, freed from its bishop in 1188 with French aid, was almost an Italian-style republic. Toulouse and other towns of the Midi did well as long as the local house of St Gilles was being squeezed by the Catalans and the French, both Plantagenet and Capetian. After the Capetian triumph by 1229, town freedom slowly withered. Flanders and northern and central Italy had the additional advantage of great industrial and commercial power. Since these regions imported food and raw materials, however, their industry would not have sufficed had not Europe been politically decentralized.

To have freedom is to vaunt it. From 1212 onwards, Marseilles was led by the rich Confraternity of the Holy Spirit. This body acquired the lordship of the town's various parts; 1214 saw a town seal, in 1218 the town won the right to mint its own coinage, and in 1220 the counts of Provence recognized the community's right to self-government. Thereafter political leadership was entrusted to an elected *podestà* or head of state. The period from 1220 to 1230 was Marseilles' age of self-government, and a preamble dated 1218 to a public act read: 'With God's aid, we have gained the liberty of our city, decorated our republic and increased its profit and right . . . . . Wherefore, God alone governing our city of Marseilles, we, wishing to provide for its profit in the future,' form an alliance with the town of Nice.[10] The legend on the Venetian ducat said much the same: 'Be this duchy, which you rule, given to You, O Christ!' To be ruled by the deity is to be ruled by no earthly power.

Town alliances advanced urban independence. In Italy leagues date from the later eleventh century, but the great one was that formed by Lombard cities after Frederick I destroyed Milan in 1161. In 1167 and 1168 ten major towns (including a new Milan) in Lombardy and the Romagna joined with lesser allies to defeat the Empire, and Barbarossa capitulated at Constance in 1183. Thereafter, although leagues were common enough in Italy (Milan headed one of seventeen cities in 1226), oath associations were replaced by something like a modern system of interlocking alliances. During the thirteenth century Germany became famous for leagues, a manifestation of that realm's decentralization. From 1226 onwards Frederick II, who wanted peace at any price in Germany and supported local princes, tried to ban them by condemning seven Franconian towns fighting the prince-archbishop of Mainz. The Empire's weakening made such efforts nugatory. Leagues, such as the Rhenish Peace Confederation founded in 1254 by Mainz, Cologne, Worms, Speyer, Basel and other communities, made political decentralization tolerable. Eventually comprising about a hundred towns as far afield as Zürich and Bremen, seven ecclesiastical princes, the Count Palatine of the Rhine and many lesser lords, this league called for parliaments to meet four times yearly at Cologne, Mainz, Worms and Strasbourg. Another and more durable association was that of Germany's seaports and allied towns. Eventually known as the Hanseatic League, it began in 1210 when Lübeck and Hamburg granted each other's burghers joint citizenship. Together with local seigniors, this league smashed Danish Baltic power in 1227, thus beginning German penetration of Scandinavia. By 1285 the king of Norway observed that the thirteen cities extending from Bremen, Hamburg and Lübeck to Wisby, Riga and Revel constituted a 'university'. A large town like Cologne was a member of several leagues, allied to Franconian and other Rhenish towns, to those of the Netherlands and to Bremen and Hamburg on the North Sea.

Elected boards possessing judicial and executive powers characterized towns. In Italy, numbering anywhere from four to twenty-four, members were initially called consuls. The word 'consul' was borrowed from princes, the counts of Toulouse, for example, and the dukes of Benevento who, in turn, found in it a reminiscence of

Rome's consuls. Consuls were widespread in Lombardy by 1100 and were seen at Florence first in 1138. The institution spread throughout southern France and penetrated into Germany, even far to the north. The members of Lbeck's governing board were called consuls in a charter of 1188, and the same was true in Utrecht in 1192. The further from Italy, however, the more this was mere fashion: Lübeck's consuls were ordinary town councillors.

Another office invented in Italy was that of the *podestà*. Originally an office (*potestas* = power) attributed to imperial governors, it became elective after the Peace of Constance as towns became independent both of the Empire and of local lords. The elected *podestà* was accorded the honours given princes and, acclaimed by parades when entering town, was seated on the 'throne of glory'. Initially chosen from a town's own inhabitants, as in Pisa in 1190, such officers were later recruited from other communities, as in Pisa in 1208. The main motive for electing foreigners was fear of monarchy, the institution that had just been replaced. Foreign *podestà*s were forbidden to marry within a town or dine privately there, and were prohibited from summoning general assemblies, lest tyranny be established by working on the passions of the many. Strictly limited by community law and elected town councils, the *podestà* underwent public examination at his term's expiration.

Elected for a year or six months, a *podestà* was a salaried officer who brought with him jurists, notaries and soldiers. Invariably nobles in order to command the militia, they were also professional. In four decades of the thirteenth century, twenty such officers are known to have served in at least six towns each. Writing in 1282, Bonvesino of Riva praised William of Pusterla, a fellow citizen of Milan, because he had been elected magistrate sixteen times in nine cities from 1190 to 1224, no less than four times in Bologna. 'When [William was] *podestà* of Bologna, there, among the jurisconsults, these latter, seeing a man without Latin to be so wise, called him antonomastically the "Wise Layman".'[11] The Franciscan Salimbene showed the respect accorded these officers by complaining that Elias, then general of his order, failed to rise when receiving Gerald of Corrigia, *podestà* of Parma, accompanied by his sons, themselves occupants of many similar offices. Manuals on city government soon appeared.

Except in Provence and southern Germany, Italian-style podestarial office rarely spread beyond the peninsula, other officers heading towns in the north. The professional mayor was one of these. The difference between the *podestà* and the mayor was that the latter was usually a royal officer elected to serve in this capacity, a reflection of town subordination to princes. In the laws of Rouen that spread through Plantagenet domains, the mayor was chosen by the king from a slate of three presented him by the electoral body or the citizens. Another partial analogue to the *podestà* was the burgomaster (president of a town council) seen as early as 1224 in Strasbourg but widely spread only around 1300. Their office differed from that of the *podestà* in that they were natives of the towns where they served their yearly terms and usually not professional. Well before 1300 Italy's towns boasted professional associations of judges, lawyers and notaries, something hardly equalled elsewhere in Europe save in the courts of kings.

Ideally, northern towns were capitals of provinces, housing merchants and artisans and the old service cadres that were slowly becoming knightly. Save for a few late foundations, like Freiburg in the Breisgau (1120) and Lübeck (1157–8), from which ministers or knights were expressly excluded, such groups generally lived in or near towns and initially took part in their political life. Until 1112, for example, ministers led communal activity in Cologne. In Mantes on the Seine as late as 1150 a common council of knights and burghers was formed to maintain peace and protect the poor. This old pattern changed where princely power was fairly strong, and changed in two ways: either the knightly or ministerial aristocracy was excluded from active participation in town politics, or town and countryside were separated. In northern and central Italy the fading Empire did not prevent knightly participation, and this was also true in Languedoc and Provence until after the 1230s. The participation of knights or ministerial groups was known in Germany as far north as Alsace and Franconia. Cities like Mainz, Worms, Strasbourg and Zürich had active knightly aristocracies, the town council of Worms, for example, being composed of twelve ministers and twenty-eight burghers in 1198. Elsewhere, as in Cologne and Regensburg, not a few ministerial families, faced with the choice of being knights outside the community or burghers within, simply became burghers, helping to shape a patriciate.

The effect on a town's political structure of the exclusion of knightly elements was unmistakable. It sometimes created double towns. In a Capetian charter to St Quentin in 1195, for example, knights and some clergy were assigned their own court, that of the count. The viscount's court, on the other hand, was to handle the burghers' cases, who in 1215 won the right to elect its judges. The mayor and sworn men of his council exercised the general right of government, other than judicial, over the burghers. A similar pattern may be seen in Liège, where the old town nucleus or 'city' remained in the hands of the archbishop-prince, his knights and their councillors who also exercised criminal justice throughout the town. The 'Port' or new town was ruled by its burghers whose sworn men judged civil cases.

A corollary of division within a town was the separation of town from countryside. In Flanders, for example, councillors often split into two bodies, a town board presided over by the count's bailiff and another that served as the count's court for the countryside. Beginning in 1194 in Arras in Artois and spreading to Flanders in 1209, councillors of the town board were elected yearly by the burghers. Although large Flemish towns dominated the countryside by 1300, such jurisdictional divisions rarely vanished and were sometimes reinforced in later ages. In Italy towns often ruled whole provinces. Little north of the Alps equalled this, although towns had similar ambitions. From 1202 to 1204, for example, the consuls of Toulouse led expeditions against twenty-three rural seigniors and communities. Although at first successful, the effort was beaten back by the Albigensian Crusade and the subsequent reimposition of princely control. Most northern town jurisdictions, however, extended beyond their walls. Seen above, even modest Provins in Champagne had eight outlying villages, whose inhabitants voted in town.

In Germany, moreover, towns used their link with the Empire to win freedom from the territorial princely states that were just beginning to form. The idea of the later 'imperial free city' was already expressed when Lübeck was described as a 'free city' and an 'imperial place' in 1226. Vienna won similar status in 1237, the emperor recording that 'we have received this city and its citizens into our protection; nor shall they ever be removed from our power or that of the Empire'.[12] Cities of this kind in Germany had extensive rural circumscriptions, especially in Swabia, Burgundy and Lorraine. Metz eventually ruled 150 villages. Great though these towns were, however, they did not equal Italy's republics, whose citizens were inordinately proud of their institutions. Remigio de'Girolami catalogued God's seven gifts to his native Florence: 'the abundance of money, the nobility of the money itself, the multitude of the people, the civility in style of life, the woollens industry, the armaments industry and the command of the country-side in the county or district'.[13]

Although small, these republics were powerful. Although England's crown had done better in the Welsh wars of the late thirteenth century, it assembled 3,000 knights and over 25,000 foot for a campaign in Scotland in 1298. In 1325 the republic of Florence fielded 2,000 knights (three-quarters professional) and 15,000 foot for a war with the great soldier Castruccio Castracani, lord of Lucca.

In conclusion, although Europe's larger states and rural and urban seigniories were monarchies large and small, republican and even democratic elements were to be seen in town and village constitutions.

NOTES AND REFERENCES

1   Kötzschke, *Quellen zur Geschichte der ostdeutschen Kolonisation* 25, No. 10, and Luke 10:35–42 and Exodus 25:4–5.

2   Ramière de Fortanier, *Chartes de franchises du Lauragais*, 706.

3   *Formularius de modo prosandi* in BuF II, 741.

4   Plesner, *L'émigration de la campagne à la ville libre de Florence au XIIIme siècle*, 56n.

5   Leicht, *Storia del diritto Italiano – le Fonti*, 334.

6   Gierke, *Das deutsche Genossenschaftsrecht* I, 204n.

7   *De regimine principum* 4, 2 in Spiazzi (ed.), *Opuscula philosophica*, 325a.

8   My 'Village, Town and City in the Region of Toulouse' in J.A. Raftis (ed.), *Pathways to Medieval Peasants* (Toronto, 1981), 165, n. 79.

9   *De regimine principum* 4, 1 in Spiazzi (ed.), *Opuscula philosophica*, 326b.

10   L. Méry and F. Guindon, *Histoire analytique et chronologique des actes et des délibérations des corps et du conseil de la municipalité de Marseille* (Aix, 1873) I, 272.

11   *De magnalibus urbis Mediolani* 19 in Novati (ed.), *Bullettino dell'Istituto Storico Italiano* XX (1898), 147–8.

12   Planitz, *Die deutsche Stadt im Mittelalter*, 418n.

13   His *De bono communi* in Davis, 'An Early Florentine Political Theorist: Fra Remigio de'Girolami' in *Proceedings of the American Philosophical Society* CIV (1960), 668a.

17

REPUBLICS

REPUBLICANISM

Although much thought on government was transmitted from the early Middle Ages, real political literature was first seen in the thirteenth century. Ecclesiastical or lay, Italians were the most significant theorists. This was partly because they had the strongest literate lay professions and partly because they lived in both republics and monarchies, and hence were inspired to compare constitutions more than others. Some, however, were northerners, especially scholastics who commented on Aristotle's *Politics*, available in 1260 in William of Moerbeke's translation. Rather like an Italian, one such, John of Hocsem, a canon who had studied at Paris, was moved by the victory of the 'people' at Liège in the early fourteenth century to argue for democracy against oligarchy.

To turn first to the scholastics, two of the most significant ones who dealt with political thought, Marsiglio of Padua and William of Ockham (d. *circa* 1349), are only touched on here because their careers lie beyond the time assigned this volume. Still, earlier writers had prepared their way. The most significant of these were two: the monarchist Giles of Rome, and the republican Ptolemy of Lucca. Ptolemy's *On Princely Rule* of about 1302 benefited from the fact that he continued a tract begun by Thomas Aquinas around 1265, under whose name his thought spread throughout Europe. Enjoying even wider circulation (translated into English, French, German, Hebrew, Italian, Portuguese, Spanish and Swedish), Giles's tract with the same title written 1277–9 was almost the only systematic treatise favouring hereditary monarchy. It was also divided into the three parts of 'practical philosophy', ethics or self-government, economics and politics.

Thomas Aquinas shared the characteristic reserve of clerical intellectuals: he did not believe wholly in any one form of government, that is, in monarchy, aristocracy or democracy. Depending on his audience, he shifted: addressing a prince in his *Rule of Princes*, he does not praise electoral government; writing for scholars, however, he does, as when he lauded the ancient constitution of the Jews. These, he thought, had been governed by a prince aided by a group of elders, chosen by and from the people.

> This is the best of all polities, being a mixture of monarchy, in so far as one leads, of aristocracy, in so far as many rule according to virtue, and of democracy, that is, of the power of the people, because the rulers are chosen from the popular elements and the election of these rulers pertains to the people.[1]

Although a mere sketch, his celebrated 'mixed constitution' is similar to what moderns call constitutional monarchy. Elsewhere in the same book, he shows that he respected what the fathers of the Church had said about popular government. Everything depends on the people's virtue.

> Augustine tells us in the first book of his *On Free Will* that 'if a people is moderate and sober, a diligent guardian of the common good, then the law rightly says that such a people may elect the magistrates by whom the republic is administered. If, however, the same people gradually becomes depraved, sells its vote and commits its government to profligate and vicious persons, the power of giving office is rightly taken away from it and given instead to the judgment of a few good men.'[2]

Some disliked republicanism and, since this polity was widespread among Italians, detested them as well. Dreaming of a unified Europe in 1306, the French judge Peter Dubois complained that the Empire had been wrecked by the German princes and especially by Italian urban republics. 'Since these cities and many princes who recognize no superior on earth . . . will stir up disputes, before whom will they litigate or proceed in law?'[3] He proposed a general council to stop wars and order the parties to settle disputes by arbitration, final appeals going to the pope. As had his earlier compatriot Beaumanoir, this monarchist believed that the Lombard republics had been spawned by traitorous, forked-tongued rich urban patricians. Alexander of Roes in 1288 believed democracy to be a manifestation of Italian 'materialism'.

The republic of the Christian Faith resides principally in three nations, Italy, Germany and France . . . . Italians love to acquire, Germans to rule, and French to learn . . . . Because humanity is prone to evil . . . , Italians suffer from avarice and envy, Germans from rapacity and discord, and French from pride and lust . . . . This is why soldiers rule in Germany, the clergy in France and the people in Italy.[4]

'Rascism' apart, Italy's Ghibellines shared these suppositions. Although Dante Alighieri worshipped the Romans, it was because they exemplified the discipline needed for world empire and not because of their republican form of government. Freedom, for him, was no mere gratification of appetite's impulse, but instead due subordination to the common good, and he asserted that human free will is best exemplified in those 'who live under a monarchy'. Republicans like Boncompagno of Signa were forever prating about how Italy was no mere imperial province but instead the 'mistress of the other provinces', but the poet converted this into the 'mistress of a whorehouse'.[5]

Ptolemy of Lucca's vision reflected northern and central Italy where the republics were everything. Even if there was a tradition of monarchy, 'counts and other princes, unless they tyrannize by violence, must rule in the republican style. Certain titles to office derived from the Empire are found among them, also, giving them jurisdiction over their subjects, although today this authority is . . . almost wholly eliminated because of the power of the cities.'[6]

Republics were communities of citizens, and although heavy with religious overtones, citizenship could be casual. At Pisa in 1286 naturalization required twenty years' residence, but because industry needed labour this was reduced to three years by 1319. Rural inhabitants with a tax valuation above fifty pounds, moreover, were obliged to become citizens. In theory, all citizens were equal before the law and all could hold office. Discussing Aristotle, Ptolemy of Lucca rejected Crete's oligarchy in favour of Sparta's way, in which the king

was elected by the wise, chosen from all grades of the citizenry; and it appears reasonable that a king should be raised up to rule the people by the counsel of the whole population, as the cities of Italy commonly do today. This is what the word 'city' means, being, according to Augustine's *City of God*, 'a multitude of men bound together by a certain bond of society'.[7]

To persons of this commitment, this polity was better than monarchy. 'Because,' the Dominican John of Paris explained, 'of the great power conceded to kings, kingdoms easily degenerate into tyrannies.'[8] Monarchy is also inefficient because excellent subjects, when elevated, are sometimes incapable of ruling and hence must be quickly replaced. Bonaventure sourly noted that experience, not birth, makes ship's captains, and, like Ptolemy of Lucca, that Rome had risen under elected leaders and fell under hereditary emperors. A monarchist argument against this was expressed by Giles of Rome. As noted above, if an heir is defective, monarchy is more than a person because a prince would be aided by his council. Indeed, Humbert of Romans found councillors more useful than their kings. Giles also argued that the participation of the many in elections and legislation led to sedition. Ptolemy had earlier answered this objection by stating that, according to the ancients and practical experience, the appetite for honours is innate and makes men seditious if never sated, and that men best obey a law they have themselves proposed. In addition, no one, however wise or instructed, is superior to the whole population. The Franciscan Peter John Olivi defended a mixture of electoral monarchy plus councils:

> The regime in which the subjects participate in elections and councils is more acceptable to them, and, because of this, is better advised, more honourable and more authoritative because it would be unlikely, indeed incredible, for one acting together with many to err as much as one acting alone.[9]

Even monarchists like Giles of Rome knew that, in theory, republicanism was the better form of government. 'Speaking absolutely, it is better to choose a prince by election than by hereditary succession. Nevertheless, because men have corrupt appetites . . . it is better for a realm or city that its lord be chosen by heredity rather than by election.'[10] Fathers naturally want their sons to succeed to their place, and hence dynastic succession is more natural than is elective. As others also said, 'experience' showed that most states were hereditary monarchies. His and others' use of history's argument could, however, be subverted. Although he too thought monarchy better in the corrupted state after the Fall (before which mankind had been republican), Ptolemy cited special exceptions. God had ordered the ancient Jews to elect their leaders, setting a model for all peoples, and the virtuous Romans had created the paradigmatic republic praised in the *First Book of Maccabees*. God and history therefore confirmed the licity of this polity.

Ptolemy of Lucca noted that subordinate officers of princes usually held their charges hereditarily, whereas even lifetime office was viewed with suspicion in republics.

> In the regions of Liguria, Aemilia and Flaminia, which are today called Lombardy, no lifetime government is found except by way of tyranny, with the exception of that of the Doge of Venice who nevertheless has a temperate government. Whence government by short-term office is the one most suitable for these regions.[11]

Writing in the early 1260s, Brunetto Latini said that

> in France and other countries under the government of kings and other lifetime princes, they sell the governorships to those who buy them at the highest price, who then look after their own profit and not that of the citizens. In Italy, on the other hand, the citizens, bourgeois and commons of the town elect their *podestàs* . . . as they wish, and these are more profitable to the common good of the town.[12]

The Franciscan Salimbene even recommended that prelates of regular orders should be chosen like Italy's magistrates.

> Do we not observe in Italy's cities today that the Captains and *podestàs* are changed twice yearly, and that they give good justice and rule well? When they enter office, they swear to observe the statutes promulgated by the wise of the city to which they have come, and have with them judges and learned men who are governed by ancient [Roman] law . . . . For if 'the number of fools is infinite', so also 'is the multitude of the wise the health of the earth'. Therefore, if laymen rule their cities well by means of officers elected for short terms, how much more should the religious . . . be able to improve their government.[13]

Electoral government requires decisions as to who should participate. Writing a manual of town government before 1246, John of Viterbo counselled against choosing a *podestà* simply because he was noble or rich. He recommended, however, that if two candidates were otherwise equal, the richer could be chosen, because 'one presumes that [the poorer] might be more easily corrupted. I do not deny, however, that, if diligent . . . and tested, the latter may be elected.'[14] Following Aristotle, Ptolemy of Lucca found that those best suited for elected office and council were 'the middling folk of the city, that is, not those who are too powerful for they easily tyrannize over others, nor yet those of too low a condition for they straightway democratize or level everything'.[15] Experience at Liège seems to have taught John of Hocsem the same lesson: democracy's weakness was the notion that all were equal, since some were obviously worth more than others. According to Ptolemy, however, all should have a chance to rule: 'Praiseworthy therefore is that polity in which office and honours are distributed to each in turn according to merit, as did the ancient Romans.'[16]

Although leading citizens were often nobles, a vision of natural equality marked Italian republics. John Barixellus, liberator of Parma from the Ghibellines, was a tailor of peasant origins. The 'people' rewarded him: 'First, they made him, who had been poor, rich. Second, they gave him a wife of noble lineage . . . . Third he was always, without election, a member of the council because he had common sense and the gift of public speaking.'[17] Bonvesino of Riva told of Hubert delta Croce, a great soldier and athlete circa 1215. This Milanese was a huge eater, once devouring thirty-two eggs at one sitting with much pasta, and his mistress bore him a daughter of wondrous strength. Still, Hubert was democratic: always polite, he never vaunted his strength or injured anyone without reason.

Laws were issued differently in republics and monarchies. Although intellectuals said that kings were bound by law, hence distinguishing between good and despotical royal government, both Giles of Rome and Ptolemy of Lucca noted that princes enjoyed arbitrary power or free will when issuing law, something found in the inmost recesses of their hearts. Ptolemy found this capacity almost godlike:

> A king, society's artificer or architect, ought not fail to answer the needs of the realm, those that pertain to the conservation of human social life, and should repair society's every defect. We must therefore conclude that, if needed, princes can impose legitimate exactions or tributes, just so long as they do not transcend the bounds of need.[18]

Unlike princes, elected officers were bound by the laws of the communities in which they served, and changes in them were to be made only by the 'people' and their assemblies. Furthermore, since a retiring magistrate's record was examined in a public hearing (*sindicatio*) at his term's end, his service was judged by the 'people'.

Alberic of Rosate stated that, in republics, law was made by a public assembly of the people or by elected magistrates, the latter acting 'in two ways, either by executive act or by judicial sentence . . . because what these magistrates do . . . is done by the authority of the people which elected them, and so the people makes the law'.[19] Legislation was issued in three ways. Relatively rare, all males met in a public parliament and voted on a proposal of the rector or magistrates of the city. More frequently, the elected officers 'should be convoked [together with the councillors] . . . and among them should take place the proposal, discussion and enactment of statutes'.[20] A third way was to have the citizens or their councillors choose experts to formulate the statutes, a system naturally favoured by this jurist. Borrowing much from Albert Galeotti (*fl.* 1250s–72), Albert of Gandino described the process:

> There may be proposed in a council whatever its members think ought to be enacted, the *podestà* being present, because resolutions can only be introduced in his presence . . . . Second, any councillor may speak to what is proposed. Third, resolutions shall be discussed by the councillors to determine whether or not they wish them made into law.[21]

Public assemblies varied in size. The anonymous *Pastoral Eye* notes that princes favour small councils but that republics 'choose many for their councils, adhering perhaps to the rule that "what touches all should be agreed to by all" . . . . And Authority says that omnipotent God "sometimes reveals to the humble what he hides from the powerful" . . . . But truth is revealed more clearly by many [than by few].'[22] As to the size and social composition of such assemblies, Alberic of Rosate cites a question of the Bolognese doctor Martin Syllimani (d. 1306). To abrogate or change a law, could a *podestà* summon both his own council of the 600 and the 'people's council' of the Captain of the People? No! And for this reason: 'if the People's Assembly is mixed together with the Council of the 600, the people's councilmen, for fear or reverence, will not dare to speak their minds as freely as they would were they by themselves, and hence often follow the councilmen of the Council of the 600'.[23]

Monarchy and republicanism also differed in emotional tone. Ptolemy of Lucca confessed that kings were majestic because, since the State was theirs, it and they shared the same interest. Elected for a year or six months, political hirelings ran the government merely for personal profit or salary. Still, as noted above, they sat on thrones and carried sceptres as signs of the respect they were supposed to be accorded. Like the newly rich, however, hired politicians maligned their rivals, feared losing office and used the public treasury to buy friends. Dante's lawyer friend Cino speaks of 'a certain People's Captain in Pistoia who sold himself in the middle of the communal palace like a whore in her lupanar'.[24] Both temporary and mercenary, such officers were sometimes viewed disrespectfully. A Paduan chronicle in 1302 described one *podestà* as 'malicious' and next year called another an 'imbecile'.

As seen in the previous chapter, however, an advantage of salaried political officers was that they were both professional and experienced. More, their governments were more gentle than those of princes. Ptolemy remarked that 'the way of governing in a republic is usually mercenary because the lords are hired for a salary; and where salary is the object, the officer does not concentrate on ruling his subjects, and therefore the rigour of the law is tempered.'[25] This temperance allows us to understand why Brunetto Latini, roundly contradicting Aristotle's *Ethics*, claimed that 'seigniories are of three kinds: one is of kings, the second is of the aristocracy and the third of the commons, which is the best of all three'.[26]

Not all were equally suited for republican government. Moved by natural history, Ptolemy of Lucca opined that, because of the influence of the stars, climate and geography, there were naturally servile peoples, and to this north Italian, Corsicans, Sicilians and Greeks were among them. Reading Vegetius, John of Hocsem discovered that all southerners were servile, but not the good northern folk of Liège. Still, Ptolemy confessed that, certain unhappy peoples excepted, 'Republican government flourishes best in cities . . . . Large regions appear to pertain more to royal government, as is seen in many cases.' But he went on: 'The exceptions are Rome, which governed the world by its consuls, tribunes and senators . . . and certain Italian cities [of today] which, although they rule whole provinces, are nevertheless governed as republics.'[27]

Having thrown his sociology out of the window, Ptolemy reverted to patriotism:

> Some regions are servile by nature, and such should be governed by despotical government, and I include in 'despotical' royal as well. Those, however, who are virile in mind, bold in spirit and confident of their intelligence, cannot be ruled except by a republic, which term I extend to include aristocracy. This kind of government flourishes best in Italy.[28]

Boncompagno of Signa had put it more succinctly. Italians, he said, 'neither can nor ought live under tribute, because liberty has placed its principal seat in Italy'.[29]

THE 'PEOPLE'

Twelfth-century new towns were democratic because settlers were as yet undifferentiated in class. Needing solidarity to oppose princes, older cities veiled social differentiations. In 1164 the consuls of the 'company' of Pisa ordered that knightly clans not build towers higher than their neighbours. Revolutions against princes, moreover, stirred all social classes, and hence a measure of equality characterized towns when they sought freedom.

As they grew, however, so did social differences. Where knights resided, the developing conception of nobility gradually separated them from other social groups. Often oligarchies or plutocracies monopolized office. At Bruges in 1240 only members of the Hanse of London, the rich merchants' association, could hold public office. In Rouen in the late twelfth century the mayor and the twenty-four councillors were chosen from the Hundred Peers. At Freiburg in the Breisgau after 1218 the twenty-four consuls held almost lifetime office and were all patricians or knights. Co-optation was common. At Ghent three bodies of thirteen members each served in rotation as boards of governors, advisers and electors, their members being termed 'hereditary men'. In Cologne in 1297 the officers of the patricians' association chose the magistrates. In Genoa all town business was brought before the general assembly until 1157, but thereafter an aristocratic small council monopolized it, even electing the first *podestà* in 1190. Oligarchy, however, served a useful function for a time. By limiting political participation it reinforced the solidarity of those fighting for town liberty.

In regard to towns, it was noted above that princes were opportunist. They sometimes supported the rich, as the Capetians did in Flanders when weakening their feudatory, the count. At other times they aided the poor, as during Stephen Boileau's provostship of Paris from 1261 to 1269. Since town freedom had grown under patrician leadership, princes sided largely with middling or lower elements against the rich until self-government had been weakened. One of the few democratic electoral systems in Languedoc was that of Nîmes, installed by the count of Toulouse when he restored the power of his vicar in 1207: 'The whole people of the city or its larger part shall be summoned . . . to create consuls with our vicar, and, when assembled, shall elect five good men from each quarter, which twenty electors shall choose four consuls.'[30] Tailored to fit

Italy, Hohenstaufen policy was similar: divide in order to rule. Trying to split the rulers of Florence, the emperors supported knightly privileges. Where the rich ruled, as in the March of Treviso when Ezzelino of Romano was imperial vicar from 1239 to 1259, they supported the humble.

In Italy the attack on oligarchy was sparked by the militia service required by the Hohenstaufen wars. In 1260 the Florentines were defeated at Montaperto by the Sienese. Statutes issued by the town officers 'to the glory, triumph, honour, good state and praise of all the militia and people of Florence and to the detriment, confusion and death of all its enemies' fell into the hands of the victors.[31] Professional and militia formations were backed by pioneers, a siege train, notaries and medical doctors. An order of the day named a doctor 'to visit and cure the sick . . . with fever or other ailments . . . elected in Florence with certain others . . . to treat the wounded'.[32] Apart from the town's lion keeper, millers and a few others, all adult males were called up.

Taxes were almost equally draining. As already seen, sales taxes and import duties were favoured by the rich but unpopular with the people. At Genoa in 1164 and Venice by 1171, citizens were ordered to lend money to the city, being, in return, allotted shares in income from revenues, which shares became negotiable and alienable. Although the poor also put in their mites, the well-to-do (and monasteries) were especially drawn to these loan societies or *montes*. Reorganized in 1274, Genoa's Salt Company, so called because of a tax on that commodity, was managed by officers appointed by two representatives of town government and by the larger shareholders. Often themselves town councillors, shareholders set the rate of return on these 'forced loans', investments bringing anywhere from five to fifteen per cent annually. A similar system involving the sale of 'rents' on town revenue began in northern Europe about 1300. Popular with rich subscribers, the popular party in Liège abolished the system when they rose in 1302.

Middling and lesser folk favoured taxes based on property values. Well nigh universal was the Frenchman Beaumanoir's attitude, namely that taxes should vary according to the wealth of the taxed. As early as 1162 in Pisa, two stages were required before the actual collection of taxes: a public assembly determined revenue needs and public deposition under oath made an estimate of each household's wealth. At Volterra in 1239 town officers were to swear 'to impose the tax in good faith and without fraud on those in their quarters, the rich according to wealth, and the poor according to poverty, by examining equity carefully, and each inhabitant's convenience and inconvenience'.[33] Apart from cheating, there were problems. As in Pistoia in the mid 1280s, knights were often less taxed because of their military value. After much resistance, the popular party in Milan imposed in 1240 this kind of taxation in rural areas where town patricians and knights had property.

However oligarchic it may really have been, equality was a town's public cult, and hence the 'people' were never entirely forgotten. To hear the statutes read, general assemblies of the whole male population were held three or four times yearly. There was also a tradition, which oligarchies tried to obviate, that 'new law' needed the consent of all. At Arles around 1200 only 'the better and saner council of the consuls and the archbishop' may call a general 'public assembly . . . in which changes in the consulate are to be made, improvements, augmentations and diminutions in law introduced or taxes for the common utility raised for a war or reprisals'.[34]

Other than war's need, what gave muscle to the humble was the rise of the guilds because, if individuals were too weak, their collectivities were not. The popular movement was seen first in Italy where, beginning in Milan in 1198, the 'people' were given a larger voice. New offices appeared, the People's Captains for example, whose function was to defend popular legislation and, in the manner of Rome's tribunes, protect the 'people'. Like *podestàs*, captains were elected and had one or more councils, but unlike the former, they were often citizens. Popular victories began with the Peace of St Ambrose in Milan in 1258 and spread until the Most Sacred Ordinance of Bologna in 1282 and the similarly named law of Florence in 1293. By that date, moreover, the State had become corporate, the electorate being the guilds together with regional representation of town quarters or militia companies. Others were elected to protect the people, Florentine Standard-Bearers of Justice for example, and those of the guilds and militia companies. A group of six to twelve 'ancients' or priors chosen by lot or elected by the leading guilds often headed the State. Serving briefly (two months in Florence in the 1290s), this group rose above all other magistrates of the republic like the ancient Athenian prytany. Corporate structure had made the Italian republic hydra-headed.

As seen above, the rise of the people provoked the appearance of formal groups of nobles or magnates. These were sometimes expressly designed to limit the power of the whole community over these groups. In Pisa during the 1280s knights of both old lineage and new creation created a nobles' commune with marshals and officers to balance the popular one. In the late thirteenth century Pavia had three *podestàs*, each with his council, one for knights, one for the people and the other for notaries and jurists, all subordinate to the *podestà* of the commune and his council. Such separatism soon failed in the face of popular attack.

In Bologna in 1252, the semi-familial associations of the magnates were outlawed, carrying sidearms prohibited and not a few family towers demolished. Guilds also tried to limit magnate participation in political life. By 1282 in Bologna and Florence, a citizen 'who has not worked in a craft with his own hands' could not sit in the general council.[35] This law sometimes also led to excluding jurists – especially those who glossed popular statutes, one guesses! – and patrician families. A Bolognese law of 1288 granted the head of the Guelph popular party 'free will to exile magnates . . . and great commoner families, whenever and however often necessary for reason of crimes, rumours or rixation which they may or can commit . . . or which they may be suspected of being able to raise up'.[36] Exclusion of the wealthy and educated was to build a society in which the 'people' could live in peace. Bologna's Most Sacred Ordinance stated that, 'wishing and intending that rapacious wolves and gentle lambs walk with equal step', the gentle lambs obliged ninety-two well-to-do persons to put up monetary guaranties of good behaviour.[37] In a similar period of Florentine history, from 1293 to 1295, members of seventy-three magnate and great popular families were exiled, just under half of all in this category.

The 'people', moreover, were themselves divided. Corporations housed both entrepreneurs and crafts- and tradesmen, and some labourers were unable to acquire the right to form guilds. When these workers sought to participate politically, a familiar problem of democracy was posed: should the majority bow to what was a minority in social power and numbers? The exclusion of magnates was necessarily also incomplete because the popular party needed competent, experienced leadership: a knight, Giano della Bella, led the Florentine popular party in 1293. Laws excluding the educated upper classes were therefore subverted. Even after Giano's popular movement failed in 1295, the priors were to be chosen only 'from the more prudent, better and legal artificers . . . continuously exercising their profession or those who are recorded in the matricule of any profession of the city, as long as they are not knights'.[38] But the knightly Florentine Dante enrolled in the doctors' guild and even served as a prior.

Limitations aside, the popular party triumphed. As seen above, noble magnates petitioned to become commoners, and, writing about 1277–9, Giles of Rome was probably very near the truth:

> In Italy's cities the many, as the whole people, commonly rule. The consent of the whole people is required in establishing statutes, in electing *podestàs* and in correcting them. Although there is always a *podestà* or lord who rules the city, nevertheless the whole people rules more than he does, because it pertains to the whole people to elect him, to correct him if he acts badly and to establish statutes beyond which he is not permitted to go.[39]

In Florence in the 1290s, putting aside the elected Standard-bearer of Justice and the six priors, there were three councils, a financial one with 100 members, a second with 300 to serve with the *podestà* and a third with 150 to sit with the Captain of the People, all elected by or from the twelve major guilds and the twenty-one minor ones. Since councillors' terms were for a half year without re-election to the same council, and since the councils were elected at different times of the year, well over 1,000 citizens out of a population of under 50,000 helped legislate each year. Nor was Florence extraordinary. Lucca, a city with a population around 15,000, had a main council of 1,550 members.

A similar 'democratization' took place in the north, and sometimes paralleled the Italian experience strikingly. In Swabian, Burgundian and Alsatian towns the office of the Captain of the People or guild 'Overmaster' first appeared in Basel in 1280. In Freiburg in the Breisgau a popular rising against the patricians made the consulate into an annually elected board, basic financial power being given to another annually elected council chosen in 1293 from eighteen trade and artisan guilds presided over by the 'Overmaster'. At Liège, sixty governors of the crafts moved into the government beside the two burgomasters and their council of sworn men. The general assembly policed the new constitution, an act of 1311 stating that new law could not be issued nor new taxes raised without the consent of all citizens, big, middling and humble. Already weakened in 1297, Ghent's thirty-nine 'tyrants' or 'hereditary men' were replaced by a council recruited from three 'members'. First came the 'portmen', soon containing no less than twenty-six old patrician lines, second the crafts and third the cloth weavers.

The rise of popular parties prompts one to ask whether these parties were like those in modern republics or constitutional monarchies. During the Hohenstaufen wars, Italian parties had ideologies. Ghibellines favoured monarchy and Italian unity under the Empire and Guelphs decentralization and the republican form of government, and the rise of the popular parties grafted on them a quasi-democratic ideology. On winning, however, the victorious parties generally tried to exclude their opponents altogether. Defeated political leaders were often exiled, and only one party remained active, the other being abolished. Sometimes both parties continued to exist but were then robbed of meaning. At Todi, offices were equally divided between the parties annually, a practice having little to do with a party system. Victorious parties also often lost their initial ideological bent. In the late thirteenth century the Florentine Guelphs, once the people's party and still continuing as of old, for example, to force magnates to become commoners, fell into the hands of the wealthy. Dante, although a Ghibelline, served as a Florentine prior in 1300 in the White Guelph party, and was later exiled by the Blacks.

What stifled the party system is hard to fathom. A guess is that, after the Hohenstaufen defeat, the rising guilds spread a corporate social organization that eventually covered all society. To participate politically, citizens had to be guildsmen, members of professional colleges or of a formal social order like the magnates. Politics was reduced to determining what groups were allowed in government and how much representation each was to have. Within republics, therefore, the corporations had largely taken over the parties' role. Not that these had disappeared: they were still useful for describing diplomatic alignments. Florence's rivals in Tuscany were Siena and Pisa; Florence being Guelph, Siena and Pisa were Ghibelline. Moving from Florence to Siena, a Guelph liking politics became Ghibelline. Experience also taught Bartolo of Sassoferrato that, in fact, either party, Guelph or Ghibelline, could promote tyranny, and he therefore proposed that a good man's duty was, if the tyrant was Guelph, to be Ghibelline, and vice-versa.[40]

PRINCES AND OLIGARCHS

Although not readily discernible until about 1400, most of the changes marking the dawn of modern times were previsioned in the late thirteenth century. The political unit was becoming larger, and, most clearly in England but also visibly in France, the national state was being born. In the German Empire territorial states were beginning to consolidate, and in Italy larger centres like Milan, Venice and Florence were busy absorbing their neighbours. The independence that marked the medieval town was beginning to wane.

Italy's towns had also attained their closest approach to democracy and those of northern Europe began to move towards theirs. At the very same moment, however, princely government and stable oligarchy also began to appear. The first was more general. In France and most of northern Europe the building of monarchy, what Ptolemy of Lucca called 'despotical government', took place covertly, by reimposing the power of traditional princes on erstwhile free towns. This occurred in Italy as well, where the vestigial Empire was momentarily enlivened again, but on the whole this peninsula's peculiar destiny was to invent anew the monarchical or princely institution.

With the exception of Venice and its lifetime but powerless Doge, Italian magistrates held office for short terms, six months or a year. This began to fail in the combat between democratic and oligarchical elements in the latter thirteenth century. When a party won office, it tried to make sure it held it long enough to effect its aims. Azzo VII of Este was elected *podestà* of Ferrara in 1242, again in 1244, for three years in 1247 and again in 1258. At his death in 1264, his heir Obizzo was elected governor and 'perpetual' or lifetime lord. In Parma Gilbert of Gente became Captain of the People and of the guilds for a five-year term and took over the office of *podestà* as well. In 1254 he was elected for a ten-year term, with a proviso that if he died in office his son would fill out the remainder of his term. In 1303 a relative, Gilbert of Correggio, was elected perpetual Defender of the Peace and Protector and Defender of the Merchants, Arts and Guilds.

The powers granted the new magistrates were also vastly enlarged. Albert delta Scala at Verona in 1277 was given general and free authority to govern the city, change the statutes, alienate the town's properties, decide all cases, and generally handle all other matters

> by his free will and wish as it appears to him to be useful and better . . . and whatever is done, acted or decreed by him or by his command . . . will persist unchanged as if it had been done, acted or decreed by the *podestà* . . . the ancients . . . and the general and special council and by the whole people of the city of Verona.[41]

A similar grant to Guido Bonacolsi, captain of Mantua, in 1299 added that the captain should make war and peace, choose and remove *podestàs*, judges and other officers, summon councils and general assemblies, refuse permission to summon the same, and generally do anything 'with council or without, at his full, pure and general choice and will, no solemnity of law, custom, reform, decree or statute being observed'.[42] Although true dynastic succession awaited the fourteenth century, the Scaliger of Verona associated heirs in their offices in the 1290s. *In fine*, 'free will', traditionally a monarch's right, was given to elected officers, terms of office were lengthened and the beginning of dynastic succession was visible.

Of the larger Lombard towns, only Ferrara seems to have evolved the new magistracy, the basis of the later principate, from the old office of the *podestà*. Elected *podestàs* had appeared when the then aristocratic republics had recently broken free from imperial power. As noted earlier, fearing renewed monarchy these heads of state were chosen from outside the communities that hired them, and were allowed no social relationships with their citizens. Unlike the new extraordinary magistrates, also, *podestàs* were rarely elected in general assemblies, and at Bologna that body could not even praise this magistrate or his retinue. Their powers were carefully circumscribed. Although always judges of criminal cases, the *podestà* of Bologna in 1250, for example, could only enlarge fines, not reduce them. Nor could they summon general assemblies except, as at Siena, when this action was applauded by a two-thirds vote of the council. Although new towns were sometimes named after popular *podestàs* (Pietrasanta in 1255 after Guiscard of Pietrasanta, *podestà* of Lucca), anything that smacked of the hero on horseback, such as an equestrian statue, excited great alarm.

At Milan, Verona, Mantua and Padua the later princes derived from the Captains of the People, an office described above that was generalized by the rise of the popular party. Like John Barixellus of Parma seen above, Captains usually had a special corps of militiamen to serve as the 'people's guards'. Having been given extraordinary powers to enforce the popular will, in short, the captaincy was not limited by the anti-monarchical safeguards once placed around the *podestà*.

Stimulated by the Hohenstaufen wars, Salimbene remarked that Italy's little states were like children piling their hands atop each other's. The one who last slipped his hand out from below and slapped it on top felt happy. There is no doubt that, as in ancient Athens, the 'people' favoured war to weaken rival towns, exploit the countryside and spread the good word. Under the leadership of the Torre family from the 1240s to the end of the 1270s, Milan's popular party conquered Como, Lodi, Bergamo, Novara and Vercelli. There is also no doubt that parties, popular and aristocratic alike, were led by knights or squires, and that the ascendancy of particular families was built on military success. The hero of Milan's resistance after the defeat by the Hohenstaufen at Cortenuova in 1237 was Pagano of Torre, whose fame made his family the leaders of the popular party for the rest of the century. On the other hand, war and the ability to wage it does not explain the rise of the princes. War captains, even Roman-style dictators at Milan like Humbert Pallavicini in 1259 and William of Montferrat in the 1290s, had moments of puissance but did not found principates.

Because war with one's neighbour often expresses internal conflict, social war within the Italian town was more significant. Fear of it was a common literary theme about 1300. Although Ptolemy of Lucca asserted that despotical or royal government had no place among Lombardy's naturally free men, he added a quiet 'except by way of tyranny'. Bonvesino of Riva warned that division within the city could permit foreign tyrants to establish their sway over the free Milanese. The notion that tyranny derived from oligarchy was an Aristotelian commonplace found in Aquinas's *On the Rule of Princes*. What was harder to explain was how tyranny arose from democracy, but Plato helped out. The matter could be put bluntly. Aquinas argued that 'the government of the many has almost always ended in tyranny, as was shown in the Roman republic', and went on to state that 'if one studies past and present history one discovers that tyranny has been more frequent in lands ruled by the many than in those governed by one'.[43] Rector of Paris in 1275, Peter of Auvergne was convinced that where the many dominate, there is tyranny: 'Where the multitude rules, it does violence to the rich by confiscating their goods in the manner of a tyrant, and it is therefore obvious that the multitude is a tyrant.'[44]

It seems unlikely that tyranny or the principates derived from only one part of the population – from, for example, the rich or the poor – and some contemporaries knew it. When warning the Paduans of the rising tyranny of Can Grande della Scala in 1313 by likening him to Ezzelino of Romano, Albertino Mussato (d. 1330) employed these ideas. As he put it, Padua had begun as a mixed government of knights and commoners. It then became an oligarchy of the rich, 'the fat people', who oppressed the plebs, after which it became a plebeian democracy from which tyranny arose. Leaning on the astrological determinism of Peter of Abano (d. *circa* 1315), Mussato conjectured that, like the human body, the body politic maintained sobriety into its forties. Thereafter, fat, lustful, envious, insolent, the body sickened for twenty years, until finally freedom died, wasted by tyranny. A specific example will illustrate further dimensions. Milan's principate was established by the Visconti, whose first assumption of the town's lordship was by Archbishop Otto in 1277. This was followed by repeated five-year terms as Captain of the People granted to Matthew V Visconti from 1310 onwards. Although the Visconti originally represented a plutocracy or oligarchy, the restraints on the old magistracies had already been weakened by the Torre who played the role of the Gracchi in the Roman republic. The popular party of St Ambrose had created for Martin della Torre the extraordinary office of the *Podestà* of the People in 1256, had appointed him lifetime lord in 1259, and granted his brother Philip a lifetime term as head of the party and lord of Milan in 1264.

Having led the battle to free Italy's towns from the Empire, Milan epitomized the aspirations of the popular parties of many Lombard and Tuscan cities. The same city subsequently pioneered the development of the principate. The most likely reason for the choice of this form of government was that class conflict had become endemic. Talking about Florence, Remigio de'Girolami said the republic was being wrecked 'because the artisans speak evil of the rich, namely that they devour them, commit treason, protect the property of their enemies . . . and the rich say that the artisans wish to dominate and do not understand they are ruining the country'.[45] Moderates everywhere echoed Ptolemy of Lucca's advice to exclude both the very rich and powerful and the humble poor from the management of the republic, but the moderate centre itself lacked moderation. In Florence, for example, the regulations of entrepreneurial industrial guilds like the *Calimala* not only exploited humbler artisans economically but also exercised criminal jurisdiction over them. On the other end of the social scale, the attack on magnates and their commoner allies was pushed with great severity. So exacerbated had relationships become that anything harmful to the opposing party was permissible. Although the majority ruled, whenever defeat in war or economic difficulties supervened, its solidarity was shaken, creating breaches through which the excluded groups entered the scene again, fuelled with the rage of past rejection.

The history of these Lombard cities also illustrates that, no matter what its social origins or initial party affiliation, a principate, a complex composed of a leader, his family and agents, belonged to no one part of the republic. Until weakened in modern times, the advantage of this form of government was that it permitted no parties and favoured no member or social group at the expense of its neighbours, save only the prince himself. Writing in 1324 Marsiglio of Padua spoke of the sovereign people as the 'legislator' or 'defender of the peace'. In the sense that the people were choosing the principate he was right; but in the system that triumphed the 'legislator' or 'defender of the peace' was not the people but instead the prince.

To these reasons may be added another. It was remarked above that political units were becoming larger, hence involving the relationship of cities to the small towns and villages of the countryside. In northern Europe, monarchs used rural resistance to urban domination to control, or take power in, their towns. Something similar was seen in Italy where countryfolk aided the growth of the principate. Sometimes, in times of economic hardship or rapid industrial growth, countryfolk flooded into town, there to swell the disfranchized disrupting the political balance of the community, ready for violent action. Princes also derived from families with power, not only in the city but also in the villages and small towns of the countryside, an example being the Este in Verona, Mantua and Ferrara. In Ferrara the Este had beaten out the rival family of the Torelli, with whom they had long shared office, to become hereditary *podestà*s in the late thirteenth century. Similarly, south Piedmont and Lombardy saw the rise of the Montferrat family in Alessandria and Acqui whose leaders held offices in towns as far apart as Ivrea, Como and even Milan in the 1260s and 1280s. Still, although villages and small towns helped build principates, the durable ones were created inside large cities such as Milan.

Not all Italian republics evolved into principates; some were converted into relatively stable oligarchies. In Venice this process could be clearly discerned around 1300: the cloture in 1297 of the group participating in government, the abolition of the general assembly and the creation of a secret council. The defeat of a popular revolt in 1300 and a patrician rising in 1310 cemented oligarchical power. It may be noted here that the problem is to explain why Venice and, to a lesser degree, Florence and Genoa were able to build stable oligarchies when elsewhere this effort failed as the principate rose. What seems peculiar about these cities was the strength of their international connections. Both Genoa and Venice had maritime empires, and it was the governing cadre of these empires and of the fleets binding them together that constituted the oligarchy. In Florence the merchant bankers, richer than those of other cities and closely linked to papal finances, formed the base of her oligarchy. Her financial power, however, did not prove as reinforcing as the others' maritime empires.

However stable, these were surely oligarchies. As noted above, Bartolo of Sassoferrato borrowed from Aquinas, Ptolemy of Lucca and Giles of Rome to argue that large regions were best governed by kings, and the largest, the Empire, by an elected monarch. Cities of modest size, he thought, were best ruled by the multitude, excluding, of course, the magnates and the very poor. Large cities should be ruled neither by a king nor by the multitude.

> These should instead be ruled by a few, that is, by the rich and wise . . . . Both Venice and Florence are ruled in this way . . . and in these seditions [against oligarchy] play no role. For although they are said to be ruled by the few, I say that they are few with respect to the multitude contained in these cities, but many with respect to other cities. Since they are many the multitude does not object to being ruled by them, and also they cannot easily be divided against themselves because of the many middling folk who participate and uphold the law of the city.[46]

Deceit surely, but needed for oligarchical republicanism.

NOTES AND REFERENCES

1   *Summa theologiae* I–II, 105, 1 c.

2   *Ibid.* I–II, 97, 1c.

3   *De recuperatione terre sancte* 12 (ed. C.V. Langlois, Paris, 1891), 10.

4   *Noticia seculi* 12–14 in *Alexander von Roes Schriften* in *MGH Staatschriften*, 159–60.

5   *De monarchia* 1, 12 and *Purgatorio* 6, 78, cited with context in R.B. Benson, '*Libertas* in Italy (1152–1226)' in *La notion de liberté au moyen-âge: Islam, Byzance, Occident* (eds George Makdisi, Dominique Sourdel and Janine Sourdel-Thomine, Paris, 1985), 191–2.

6   *De regimine principum* 3, 22 in Spiazzi (ed.),*Opuscula philosophica*, 324a–b. The word 'republic' is often used here to translate his 'polity'.

7   *Ibid., 4, 18 in Spiazzi (ed.), Opuscula philosophica*, 347a, and Augustine's *De civitate dei* 15, 8, 2.

8   *De potestate regia et papali* 19 (ed. Bleienstein), 175.

9   *De renunciatione papae* in *Archivum franciscanum historicum* XI–XII (1915-19), 354–5.

10   *De regimine principum* 3, 2, 5 (Rome, 1607), 461.

11   *De regimine principum* 4, 5 in Spiazzi (ed.), *Opuscula philosophica*, 336a.

12   *Li livres dou tresor* 3, 73 (ed. Carmody), 392.

13   *De prelato* in his *Chronicon* in *MGH SS* XXXII, 156; Ecclesiastes 1:1, and Wisdom of Solomon 6:24.

14   *Liber de regimine civitatum* 5 in BIMA III, 221b.

15   *De regimine principum* 4, 8 in Spiazzi (ed.), *Opuscula philosophica*, 336a.

16   *Ibid.* 4, 7 in Spiazzi (ed.), 335a.

17   *Cronica* in *MGH SS* XXXII, 374–5.

18   *De regimine principum* 3, 11 in Spiazzi (ed.), *Opuscula philosophica*, 311b–12a.

19   *De statutis* 1, 3, 6 in *TUJ* II, 2va.

20   *Ibid.* 1, 4, 3–6 in *TUJ* II, 2va–b.

21   *Quaestiones statutorum* 2 in *BIMA* III, 157–8.

22   A composite quotation from the *Oculus pastoralis* 6, 5 and 2, 3 in Muratori (ed.), *Antiquitates Italicae medii aevi* IX, 856 and 806. See *Code* 5, 59, 5, 2.

23   *De statutis* I, 120 in *TUJ* 17va.

24   From his *In Codicem* in Sbriccoli, *L'interpretazione dello statuto*, 409.

25   *De regimine principum* 2, 8 in Spiazzi (ed.), *Opuscula philosophica*, 285a–b.

26   *Li livres dou tresor* 44 (ed. Carmody), 211.

27   *De regimine principum* 4, 2 in Spiazzi (ed.), *Opuscula philosophica*, 327a.

28   *Ibid.* 4, 8 in Spiazzi (ed.), 336a.

29   From his *Liber de amicitia* in Carl Sutter, *Aus Leben und Schriften des Magisters Boncompagno* (Freiburg im Breisgau, 1894), 5, a polemical use of Italy's tax exemption under Rome.

30   P.M. Viollet, 'Les communes au moyen-âge' in *Mémoires de l'Académie des inscriptions et belles-lettres* XXXVI, ii (1901), 436.

31   *Libro de Montaperti* (ed. Cesare Paoli, Florence, 1889), 369.

32   *Ibid.*, 75.

33   Enrico Fiumi, *'L'imposta diretta nei comuni medioevali della Toscana'* in *Studi in onore di Armando Sapori* (Milan, 1957) I, 332.

34   Kiener, *Verfassungsgeschichte der Provence*, 195.

35   Dahm, *Untersuchungen zur Verfassungs- und Straftrechtsgeschichte der italienischen Stadt*, 33.

36   *Ibid.*, 39n.

37   Salvemini, *Magnati e popolani in Firenze*, 327.

38   Dahm, . . . *Verfassungs- und Straftrechtsgeschichte der italienischen Stadt*, 33.

39   *De regimine principum* 3, 2, 2 (Rome, 1607), 455.

40   *De Guelphis et Gebellinis* 2 in *ibid.*, 135–6.

41   Salzer *Über die Anfänge der Signorie in Oberitalien*, 173.

42   Leicht, *Storia del diritto Italiano*, 338, No. 30.

43   *De regimine principum* 1, 6 in Spiazzi (ed.), *Opuscula philosophica*, 263a.

44   *VIII libri politicorum seu de rebus civilibus* 3, 8 in *Thomae Aquinatis opera omnia* (ed. S.E. Frette) XXVI, 234a cited by Gewirth, *Marsilius of Padua* I, 200n.

45   Davis, 'An early Florentine Political Theorist', 667a.

46   *De regimine civitatis* 2 in Quaglioni, *Politica e diritto nel trecento italiano* 164–5.

18

GOVERNMENT AND LAW

SCRIBES AND CHANCERIES

Other than the clergy, the largest literate profession in Italy and adjacent regions was that of the scribes. In 1293 Pisa, a substantial but not huge town, had at least 232 public notaries. At first close to judges, notaries evolved to become somewhat like modern solicitors. They not only wrote acts for their clients, but also informed them about the law. As towns gained freedom, also, princely controls over notaries diminished, and before 1200 their most significant affiliation was their town guild or college which examined and licensed them. In much-divided Italy, however, notaries were also instituted by imperial or papal authority, thus enabling a town notary to extend the area in which his acts had currency. Although imperial notaries were rare outside the Empire and Italy, papal notaries were found in much of Europe until the Reformation.

Licensed by public authority, a notary's signature or 'manual seal' sufficed to authenticate documents. Soon even the abbreviated entry he made in his notebook or register when he first recorded his client's wishes also became a valid proof of an action taken. An early notarial register is that of the Genoese scribe John of 1155, one written on paper, a substance beginning to replace expensive if durable parchment.

Although Italy's system was quickly imitated in nearby southern France and Catalonia, its implantation was slower in the north. Addressing John Peckham, archbishop of Canterbury, John of Bologna wrote: 'Tracts on instruments are widely diffused in Italy because Italians . . . wish to have a public record of everything, but . . .

almost the opposite is true in England, where, unless absolutely necessary, instruments are rarely requested.[1] Things were changing, however. By about 1300 there were town scribes in places as far apart as Lübeck and Metz. The system differed from Italy's because these scribes were tied more directly to town government. In England's Ipswich, for example, the town's customary rolls expanded to contain private transfers of property in 1255, testaments in 1281 and other personal actions in 1285.

In northern Europe, princely, episcopal and even seigniorial courts were also enlarged to accommodate society's growing need for records. Exercising 'gracious jurisdiction', these courts sold their seals, so to speak, to authenticate and register private documents. Northern charters were therefore usually sealed whereas southern ones, unless emanating directly from a prince, prelate or republic, were signed by notaries. A council held in London in 1237 edicted that, 'since the use of notaries is not customary in England and one has recourse instead to authentic seals . . . we ordain that not only archbishops and bishops, but also episcopal judges, abbots . . . [and] rural deans shall have . . . such seals'.[2] Both authentications were accepted by the popes. Alexander III told the bishop of Worcester that 'if witnesses have died, documents have no authority unless drawn by the public hand [of a notary] . . . or unless they have an authentic seal'.[3]

Scribal service expanded enormously. Under Philip the Fair, the Châtelet of Paris provided sixty notaries for public and private services. Northern episcopal Officials everywhere registered testaments and other documents. The French crown so profited from 'gracious jurisdiction' that it even tried to extend the system to southern France in 1291, but the flourishing public notariate there fought the project to a standstill within a year. In 1304, royal France was divided into two zones, that of the seal and that of the notarial signature.

Before the Gregorian age, titles to property were found mostly in ecclesiastical archives. Written by clerks of the institutions receiving the gifts, the documents were often compiled into cartularies or long rolls. By 1300 cartularies had become rare and documentation laicized, in that laymen collected their own records and instruments were written by lay scribes. Although this change was under way in the north, it was slower there, episcopal jurisdictions in northern France still providing much scribal service to layfolk. By 1300 most economic and social documentation was in notaries' registers or, in northern towns, those of bishops or lords possessing seals.

Ecclesiastical and secular chanceries provided much of the service described above, and also housed the bulk of public documents. The Church provided the model for all these chanceries, and a canon lawyer named Stephen of Tournai (d. 1203) truthfully wrote that at Rome, 'when a letter about a matter of importance is sent to anyone, a copy is retained, and such copies are compiled into books called registers'.[4] The archive was insecure, however, because the popes often moved from town to town within the patrimony and even went outside of Italy, and hence, save for some fragments, all was lost in the wars of the early thirteenth century and the extant series begins only with Innocent III (accession 1198). The popes' chancery was Europe's busiest. In the eighteen years of John XXII's pontificate about 65,000 papal letters were registered, and many were not so recorded. The chancery was sometimes awash in 'paper'. In 1183 Lucius III apologized to the serfs of Rosny sur Bois and restored a decision he had mistakenly reversed in favour of the chapter of Ste Geneviève of Paris. He told Rosny that

> because of the great quantity of business referred to the apostolic see, it is impossible to recall the contents of all our letters . . . . Trickery can therefore circumvent us, and we can unknowingly be induced to write things contradicting what we have written before.[5]

The papal court was imitated by prelates generally. In northern Europe, bishops' registers and those of their Officials were common, but not in Italy because episcopal business was inserted into the books of secular notaries. Churchmen registered almost everything. The visitations of his archdiocese by Odo Rigaud, archbishop of Rouen, stretching from 1248 to 1269, were registered. Perhaps less pleasantly, beginning in the 1230s the registers of the inquisitors of 'heretical pravity' recorded the interrogations of whole communities in southern France.

Secular princely chanceries were little organized until the later twelfth century. The first extant registers or rolls of letters sent from princes were those of John of England (accession 1199) and James I (accession 1213) in Catalonia–Aragon. Before that time, governments and princely courts left the preservation of the privileges and grants they issued to those who received them and concentrated on recording their own rights and revenues. The tally of what was owed the king, called *Domesday Book* (1086), was used by the English treasury and was supplemented by a record of actual income called the *Pipe Rolls*, a series continuous from the start of the reign of Henry II in 1154. Catalonia possessed a celebrated *Book of Fiefs* dating from the reign of Alfonso II (accession 1162).

Chancery registration provided not only a record but also a public source sometimes open to others than the prince. Introducing the *Book of Fiefs*, Raymond of Caldès, dean of Barcelona, stated that his prince had 'often publicly stated that you want all contracts drawn up between your predecessors, yourself and your men . . . recorded for the use of your subjects so that . . . each shall learn his rights, and hence . . . discord arising between you and your men shall be prevented'.[6] Specific governmental offices also early began to produce manuals treating the history, practices and legal implications of their functions. An early example was the *Exchequer Dialogue* of the English treasury, whose author was probably Richard Fitzneale (d. 1198).

As state authority grew during the thirteenth century, moreover, the Roman practice of inserting private documents into public archives was revived, thus supplementing with public repositories the private ones of the notaries. In 1289 'it was enacted at Bologna that legal instruments are to be inserted in the public registry, if valued at more than twenty-five pounds'.[7] Government required public registration of the statutes of business companies and partners' names. In 1303 a suit in Paris charging a firm for the debts of a presumed associate failed when it was found that the debtor was not listed as a partner in the register of the Florentine chamber of commerce. As urban taxation increased, also, registers containing careful statistics amassed under oath about household or family size and wealth were compiled and kept up to date.

Governments compiled books containing privileges, administrative orders, judicial decisions and legislation. The popes legislated by publishing the canons or laws decided on in council. The Constitutions of Melfi of 1231 issued by Emperor Frederick II reflected his right to issue law or legislation ('constitutions') in a general assembly of his realm. Statutes were published by town governments, especially in Italy. Often called 'reformations', statutes embodied the idea that princes or magistrates were restoring the right order of things, applying ancient principles to new circumstances. Collections designed to protect princely prerogatives and possessions or the liberties of towns contained a mass of diverse materials, privileges, judicial decisions and legislative enactments.

NOTARIAL TECHNIQUES

Public scribes produced grammars and letter-writing manuals for which the usual term in Latin is *ars dictaminis*. To these were added formulary books, some for general use and others specific to a given chancery or notariate. One written for the papal chancery of around 1270 contained nearly three thousand model letters. Linked to ecclesiastical and princely courts, northern manual writers and some of those in Italy, such as the imperial chancellor Peter of Vinea (d. 1249), favoured ornate Latin. Public notaries were simpler in their tastes, and invented the notarial manual. An example is Boncompagno of Signa who taught briefly at Bologna and was a famous wit. This Florentine wrote several grammars, two rhetorics – one containing humorous letters on simoniacal elections of abbots and bishops, another addressed to lawyers and public speakers – a humorous tract on how to write statutes and a blasphemous manual of love letters.

The difference between notaries and chancery clerks is seen in two careers. In 1167 Peter of Blois (d. 1205) was tutoring a Norman–Sicilian prince, and in 1173 entered the secretarial service of Henry II of England and his wife. He closed his career as archdeacon of London and chancellor of the archbishop of Canterbury. Peter wrote an elegant letter-writing manual, worldly and amatory Latin poetry, tracts on the Crusades and ecclesiastical discipline and the sacraments, and produced sermons and a spate of letters full of classical allusions.

Quite different was the Bolognese Rolandino Passaggeri. A notary in 1234, Rolandino entered the town chancery in 1238, becoming notary of the bankers' guild in 1245. Back in the town chancery in 1249 he penned a celebrated response to the threats against Bolognese liberty contained in a letter of Peter of Vinea, Frederick II's chancellor. In 1255 or 1256 he issued his *Summa of the Notarial Art*, the main textbook for this discipline for several centuries. In the 1280s he was busy teaching at the university and redacting the legislation of the Guelph party, including the famous

Most Sacred Ordinances of 1282, the crowning monument of popular legislation, and he may still have been alive in 1297.

Although testaments and court cases are sometimes exciting, private charters, administrative manuals and court records rarely entertain. So much dull work, however, made wit a mark of the legal and scribal professions. King John of England, to name one prince, was witty even in official correspondence. Bologna's Bulgarus (d. *circa* 1166), a widower marrying a widow, cracked up his students when he resumed his course on Roman law after his bridal night: 'I have entered a thing neither new nor unaccustomed.'[8] Boncompagno of Signa taught how *not* to use scripture in this manner:

> A fellow who carnally knew a nun said; 'I have not violated the divine bed, but, because the Lord delighted me by his creature, I have striven to exalt his horn.' Again, a nun might say to her lover; 'Thy rod and thy staff, they comfort me.' Or wives to their lovers; 'Give us of your oil, for our lamps have gone out.'[9]

LAW

Scribes and notaries were the lower ranks of the legal system, whose seniors generally went to universities in Italy or practical schools in other countries, such as England's Inns of Court. These technicians dealt with complex bodies of law. As in the sciences and letters, what was lacking were dictionaries of precedents or models and instead jurists had codes of law, sometimes huge. These were of two kinds: compilations of local customary law, and those of general, or common, law.

One common law was canon law. At Bologna the Camaldolese monk Gratian composed around 1140 the basic collection of conciliar canons, papal letters and patristic sources called the *Concordance of Discordant Canons* or *Decretum*. This collection soon drove out earlier compilations and gave rise to commentary, those who glossed it being called 'decretists'. Recent papal letters and conciliar canons were thereafter amassed into collections of 'extravagants' (laws and canons not yet encoded). One of these was assembled by the Dominican Raymond of Peñafort and published by Gregory IX in 1234, a collection regarded as authoritative. Since there were five books in this text, the next similar publication, that of Boniface VIII in 1298, was called the *Sixth Book*. Those who commented on these collections were called 'decretalists'. This mass of new law involved the usual conflict between old and new law. Boncompagno of Signa sourly described the difference between the two kinds:

> A decree is a holy canon promulgated by the authority of the highest pontiff with the assent of a council . . . . A decretal is the first born of the decrees, whence 'tis said: 'A decretal is named from decree and is its diminutive, but now 'tis trying to be its equal.'[10]

All these basic texts were glossed. The ordinary gloss on Gratian was by John Teutonicus around 1215–17, that on Gregory IX's collection was by Bernard of Parma from 1241 through 1266, and John Andreae did the *Sixth Book* from 1294 to 1303. The jurists also wrote epitomized surveys of the whole field. Among the most celebrated were those of Huguccio of Pisa (d. 1210), Innocent IV and Hostiensis. Certain problems received special treatment, as, for example, a tract on usury by Alexander Lombard written shortly before 1307. A manual of judicial procedure was published by the canonist professor Tancred of Bologna in 1216 whose work soon became standard.

Other than canon law, Europe's most universal law was Rome's Justinianic compilation, of which a good text save some novels had been reintroduced in the late eleventh century. It was studied in Italy, especially Bologna, where work initially was in the form of exegetical glosses. Azzo, a Bolognese professor, wrote glosses on the *Code* and *Digest*, *Summae* on the *Code* and *Institutes*, commentaries and questions on the principles of law and much else. Accursius, another Bolognese, wrote the great or ordinary gloss on Roman law, and his and Azzo's contemporaries extracted their treatments of specific problems, such as usury or arbitration, and published them separately. Specialization grew apace, a treatise on criminal law and another on statutes by Albert of Gandino being typical examples. Compilations of the debates of the doctors appeared and judges and professors rendered opinions, thereby creating a large literature, variously called 'counsels' or 'answers' (*consilia* or *responsa*). Like individuals, faculties at Bologna, Toulouse and elsewhere produced collections of opinions.

In the decentralized world of Latin Europe, jurisprudence was often based on regional customs. In France, codes of provincial law appeared, the first being Normandy in 1194. Local customary law ranged from village and town customals to monuments of jurisprudence such as the *Saxon Mirror* written by Eike of Repkow from 1215 to 1235 and the *Customs of Clermont in the Beauvaisis* published around 1283 by Philip of Rémi, lord of Beaumanoir, both encyclopaedias of legal and social lore. Although local customs were also seen, what was celebrated in relatively unified England was the 'common law'. Treatises on England's laws and customs begin about 1187 with a collection attributed to the then chief justiciar Ralph of Glanville. The second was compiled by English judges from 1220 to 1234 and was named after its reviser, Henry of Bracton (d. 1268). The attempt to unify Castilian customs resulted in a law code called the *Book of the Laws* (*Siete Partidas*). Written from 1256 to 1263 for the king of Castile, Alfonso X, this compilation won general currency only in the next century.

Political decentralization and the relationship between Church and State led to conflicts between canon and civil law. Although some Roman law titles were 'canonized', as churchmen said, and many prelates were themselves jurists, they shared the feeling that law was earthbound and theology heaven-directed. This conviction led Honorius III to grant theological study such great advantages at Paris in 1219 that law was driven to other centres such as Orléans and Toulouse.[11] William Durand the Elder in his *Judicial Mirror* noted the superiority of canon law over civil and listed the cases reserved to it – marriage, for example, and usury. Secular princes and republics nevertheless insisted on judging cases concerning these topics. Besides, although much canon law was received, some was expressly rejected. English law, confirmed at Merton in 1236, refused to receive legitimation according to canon law, stating that once a bastard, always so. In canon law, also, two witnesses sufficed to prove a marriage or a testament, but town statutes and civilian doctors insisted on more. Besides, canon law necessarily borrowed much from Roman jurisprudence. As Boncompagno put it: 'canon law leans on another's staff because it . . . is forced to beg the aid [of Roman law] in incepting and conducting trials and promulgating sentences'.[12]

Roman law's attraction for the schools was that it provided models. Enforceable nowhere, it ruled, as the tag had it, 'not for reason of Empire but because of the empire of reason'. Having been promulgated under a monarchy, it rarely mentioned limitations on princely power. In fact, if principles useful for other forms of government were conveyed there, they were veiled. The *Code* contains a law dated AD 446 wherein the emperors vowed to issue new laws only with the express consent of the high officers in their consistory and that of the senate, for example, but late Rome's great structure of provincial and urban assemblies has to be excavated from references dealing with other subjects. An example of this law's indifference to political matters is that the principle 'what concerns all shall be decided by all' is buried in a section on inheritance and tutorial rights and is not featured, as it was in canon law, among the 'rules of law'.[13]

The study of Roman law especially flourished in Italy partly because of Italy's anti-German 'nationality'. Proud of a Roman law they thought Italian, Bologna's jurists often even maligned their Lombard law that had been systematized at Pavia on the Roman model in the late twelfth century. Boncompagno and others called this law of Charlemagne's (!) a 'German stain' or 'blot', not to be called law but instead dung.[14]

Respect for Roman law, however, does not mean that it was above local custom or law. The superiority of the latter over Roman law was a commonplace among Italy's princes, republicans and jurists. Using the word 'custom' to refer to local law, lawgivers at Salerno in 1251 and Amalfi in 1274 insisted that 'although [Roman] laws were, are and will be holy, good customs are even more holy, and, where custom speaks, there the law ought be wholly silent'.[15] Boncompagno commented dryly: 'Civil law is of little worth because it does not govern a hundredth part of the earth, and is vituperable because villagers' statutes and popular plebiscites straightway obviate its authority.'[16] Notwithstanding the superiority of statute law, the schools' Roman law was a normative jurisprudence with which to harmonize the laws of the peninsula's many independent states. Rome's laws were Italy's 'common law', something they later became in the Empire.

Oddly, another local Italian customary law nearly became yet another European universal law. Typical is a Beneventan law of 1202 ordering judges to decide cases first by the statutes of the republic, then in regard to fiefs, Lombard law and lastly Roman law. In that region, Lombard law had been hard to replace because it regulated the fiefs and service of nobles. Although weakened by the hostility of the popular parties, it persisted in Italy, and its derivatives were to rule the duelling field in modern Europe.

The north was slower to accept Roman law. Not being as unified, France had no 'common law' like England's but instead provincial laws. As a result, Roman and canon law filled up the cracks, providing national uniformities. The custom of the Orléanais called *The Book of Justice and of Pleas* lifted 195 of its 342 titles from the *Digest* and thirty-one from Gregory IX's decretals, but disguised this fact by citing them in or as French enactments or judgments. As stated in a royal edict of 1312, Roman law took over the schools:

> Our kingdom is especially ruled by custom . . . not by written law; and although in certain parts . . . written law is used . . . it does not bind as such, but as custom introduced . . . following the model of written law. Just as the study of the liberal arts introduces a student to the science of theology, however, so does the study of . . . written law perfect reason's understanding . . . thus preparing [the mind] for local customs.[17]

By that date, indeed, French Roman lawyers even had something to teach the Italians. The work of James of Revigny (d. 1296) and of Peter of Belleperche, both teachers at Toulouse and then at Orléans, was influenced by the dialectics of the Parisian scholastics, a method transmitted to Cino of Pistoia, the teacher of the great Bartolo of Sassoferrato.

Oddly, the first northern centre of Roman legal studies was that of Vacarius in Oxford. Since Roman law was widely viewed as supporting monarchy, however, the feudal king Stephen of Blois expelled this Italian after 1149. In spite of repeated prohibitions, such as that for London's practical law schools in 1234, Roman law made its way in surreptitiously. Doctrines reinforcing the English monarch, such as the inalienability of royal property, were speedily picked up. The justiciar's manual ascribed to Glanville used Justinian's *Institutes* to define the majesty of England's king, and the author of the lawbook called *Fleta* (1290–1300) copied this earlier source together with the Roman style panegyrics accorded Frederick II Hohenstaufen. But there was more than monarchy involved. Bracton's case book made extensive use of Bologna's celebrated jurisconsult Azzo, especially when insisting on precedents derived from prior judicial decision. The code of laws bearing the same jurist's name was itself modelled on the *Institutes* in its division into books.

Other examples of this process are not hard to find. Alfonso X's Castilian *Book of Laws* was freighted with Roman law, and his compilers even incorporated whole sections of Vegetius's late–Roman manual on warfare. To turn north, Magdeburg law of 1300 (soon translated into Latin, Czech and Polish) explained servitude's origin and nature in these words: 'All men are either free or servile. Liberty . . . is the natural faculty of a man to do what he wants unless prohibited by force or law. Servitude derives from the positive law in which a man is subject to the rule of another against nature.' The source of this is the *Digest*.[18]

LAWYERS AND JUDGES

In past ages, most suits were brought against defendants by specific persons who, if they failed to prove their charges, were punished. Unlike servile folk, also, free defendants were tried by their peers and often by their own law. A result was that, although a prince or seignior presided and was often aided by a legal specialist, court decisions were made by persons of the same status or law as the defendants, and were often chosen by the parties. When resolution failed among the lower classes, ordeals such as grasping hot iron were imposed on defendants thought guilty. Among the quality, oaths were taken by family or social groups favouring defendants, and the military could claim trial by battle or duel. Both conjuration and duel often threatened to deteriorate into vendettas or small local wars.

The growth of government in both Church and State militated against the magic of earlier modes of proof. Churchmen like Peter Cantor and his contemporaries among Italian jurists detested oath, battle and ordeal. Oath taking or compurgation was durable. In 1262 an archidiaconal court of Rouen established the guilt of a clerk for having relations with his brother's wife. The archdeacon, 'fearing that the said Thomas, appearing in his court with compurgators, would lie, enjoined him to leave the country for two years and busy himself at the university of Paris or elsewhere'.[19] Although trial by battle was gradually exiled from the courts, gentlemen claimed the right to defend themselves by the sword, thus beginning the transformation of public judicial battle into private duel.

The ordeal was less resistant. A way of condemning one against whom there was much suspicion but insufficient proof, the ordeal – often avoided by exile – was brutal and led to abuses, especially against foreigners. Clerical participation in ordeals was formally prohibited by the fourth Lateran Council of 1215, which caused it to fade away. Barbarisms were discountenanced, slaughtering 'criminous' animals, for example, especially farmyard pigs. To Beaumanoir such actions were irrational and absurd; to his near contemporary Thomas Aquinas they were blasphemous.

Law's punishments were, however, neither rational nor gentle. In Burgundy if a horse or ox killed a person, the beast was sold for the lord's profit. 'But if other beasts or Jews do it, they are to be hanged by their hind feet.'[20] Awful punishments, furthermore, were characteristic of the age's tight little communities. 'Criminals' were normally run naked through the streets of towns before expulsion. Maiming and death were visited on condemned persons in extraordinary ways. Some time before 1246 in Fanjeaux near Carcassonne a young man sneaked a look into a house and witnessed the entry into Catharism of a condemned murderer. The murderer had wanted this ceremony in order to be purified. And why? Because he was about to be buried alive.

Horrors aside, the new law was more gentle than the old. John Bassiani repeated an old saw: the Romans 'thought it more equitable to release a criminal without punishment than to condemn an innocent person'.[21] As in canon law, imprisonment was sometimes substituted for the death penalty, and exile, already known in German Europe, was remodelled on analogous Roman institutions. Alberic of Rosate remarked that 'to be banned is to be ejected from the public good and is a secular excommunication'.[22] Civil courts and prisons were separated from criminal ones, and custodial or pre-trial imprisonment of those suspected of grave crime was distinguished from imprisonment as punishment. A system similar to bail appeared. Albert of Gandino proposed that, if one accused of grave crime denied guilt before trial, he should be imprisoned and the case hurried to its conclusion to limit the custody. If, however, 'the crime is not grave, the accused is to be given to his guarantors'.[23]

Legal personnel became increasingly professional and written procedure replaced verbal. From the mid twelfth century the old diocesan boards of laymen and clergy were replaced by an episcopal judge, the professional Official. Italy's lay consuls gave way to schooled jurists. Roffredo scorned seigniorial judges and jurors, and, mocking their lack of Latin and schooling, called them 'laymen and idiots'.[24] Judges at Verona in 1228 were required to have studied law at school. With increasing complexity, past judicial decisions or opinions became increasingly useful, hence the literature of opinions or counsels referred to earlier in this chapter. Culled from Roman law, the system was that, as jurists like Azzo said, judges should decide cases by precedent, that is, 'proceed from like to like'.[25]

Opposition was unremitting. The English reaction, seen above, was paralleled by churchmen who lamented the replacement of synodal justice by what they called Justinian's laws. Nor were they merely obscurantist. The literature of law had become vast. Boncompagno made fun of the first glossator Irnerius (d. by 1118), quoting Azzo saying: 'when a gloss requires a gloss, the [law's] sense is contemned and drowned in a labyrinth of double meaning'.[26] Jurists and lawyers were also usually upper class in interest if not in origin, as is seen in 1239 at Pistoia where the opposition to the popular party was called the 'knights and judges'. Popular parties therefore tried to protect their legislation against being glossed away, and Boncompagno suggests a model: 'this statute is composed for the common good, and we wish that . . . the whole of it be understood literally without any gloss or interpretation'.[27] A similar desire led Francis of Assisi to require that the rule he gave his order be obeyed 'to the letter' without gloss. Casuists, however, always had the last word. Alberic of Rosate quoted the paradigmatic popular legislation: 'Jacob Butrigarius [d. 1348] said that at Bologna, where the Most Sacred Ordinance was to be obeyed literally, anyone shedding blood in the town hall was to be beheaded. A certain barber phlebotomized a judge of the *podestà* there. Was he to be beheaded according to the statute'?[28] Besides, few citizens could question the maxim that 'in doubtful cases, the kinder interpretation is always to be preferred'.[29]

Professional judges were controlled in several ways. Entry into their ranks required education and corporate bodies tested aspiring members. By Roman tradition, judges usually had to choose trained assessors to sit with them, as William Durand the Elder described civil cases: 'If there is no assessor at the trial with whom the judge can deliberate, then, according to general Italian custom, learned men should be elected jointly by the litigants and the judge should pronounce according to their opinion'.[30] A statute at Vicenza in 1264 required judges to swear not to decide cases involving more than 100 shillings without assessors, and ecclesiastical inquisitors invariably chose lawyers or other notables to help them. As significant were political controls. In Italy judges were often elected and their decisions were examined by a council or even a general assembly at the end of their terms. Political controls were sometimes imposed. Albert of Gandino reports that at Cremona the *podestà* could not sentence anyone for high crime without the consent of the elected 'ancients' or four councillors.

As the new system grew, lawyers evolved from those chosen by the litigants as arbitral judges, and came to stand before the bar to speak for their parties. These specialists clearly advantaged the rich. Following Roman antecedents, *Peter's Excerpts* therefore recommended in the twelfth century that counsel be equalized to aid the poor, and John of Viterbo later urged *podestàs* to provide them with advocates. Around 1300 William Durand the Younger recommended that magistrates appoint not only advocates without cost but notaries as well.

The minute lawyers appeared, their enemies arose. Some asserted that, being court officers, lawyers were only to instruct clients in the law and help them answer questions truthfully. Judges especially sought to protect court serenity by trying to stifle lawyers' objections when questioning litigants. In theory, lawyers were to defend justice, helping only those litigants they thought right, but Boncompagno knew better: 'an advocate's function is to . . . palliate lies, veil falsity under the image of truth, instruct his party in his positions and answers and induce witnesses to corroborate whatever he wants proved or confuted'.[31] Jurists argued that even an excommunicate or one banished for treason should be represented by a lawyer in order to protect the law and public interest. In both canon and Italian urban practice, however, such aid was usually refused in cases of grave crime: treason, habitual violence and heresy.

Legal change also linked social utopianism to juristic professionalism to encourage an active eradication of crime. Accusation by an injured party was supplemented by other procedures, especially the inquisition, a judicial inquiry initiated by substantial evidence against a putative wrongdoer. This mechanism was favoured by institutions and communities with a vigorous sense of individual responsibility and membership. These prevented the protection of putative wrongdoers by family and local interests, and thus had the advantage of making all citizens equal, save for differences allowed for special functions. The modern nation state was to favour this procedure, and signs of its future development were already visible in Hohenstaufen southern Italy, Plantagenet England and Capetian France in the late thirteenth century. Typical of the period treated here, however, lead in developing the inquisition was taken by the ecumenical Church and Italy's urban republics.

The *Digest* had it that 'proof is incumbent on him who charges, not on him who denies the charge', but a well-conducted inquisition obviated this rule because there was no accuser.[32] An investigation was begun when persistent report reached the ears of a judge, a report obtained from many worthy and honest men, or, as Hubert of Bobbio (d. by 1245) put it, one 'not doubted by the people or a majority of the people'.[33] A result was that trials of usurers, traitors, violent criminals and heretics were usually initiated by public opinion. Once sufficient indications of guilt had been assembled to begin a trial, the report was converted into proof mainly by means of sworn witnesses or voluntary confession. Strong preliminary indications of guilt made it difficult for lawyers to protect defendants, and a papal law heavily influenced by contemporary Italian criminal law, *Ad extirpanda* of 1252, forbade legal counsel for those charged with heresy. Even when permitted, counsel was limited to giving the defendant general advice.

Two other qualities marked inquisitorial trials. When witnesses needed protection against a defendant reputedly violent, as Albert of Gandino states, the latter was not given the names of those testifying against him. Adapted from Roman law, also, the 'question', as torture was discreetly called, was introduced into Italian urban law at Verona as early as 1228. The crime had to be of unusual gravity, and as John of Viterbo wrote in the mid thirteenth century, torture was to be used only when a suspect was very probably guilty. It was also to be moderate, leaving no lesions or broken bones.

The 'question' was easily abused. *The Pastoral Eye* complains that 'when proof is lacking in a criminal case, you [a *podestà*] turn straightway to torture . . . nor do you consider how much trust should be put in this procedure'. Some stand it better than others 'and hence confessions extorted from defendants should not be considered as evidence of crime unless afterwards, having been free [from torture] for a time, they should persevere in confession'.[34] Although providing only a partial proof requiring supplementation, torture seemed so effective in lay criminal cases that *Ad extirpanda* recommended it for the inquisition against 'heretical pravity' in 1252.

A *podestà* . . . is required to force all heretics . . . short of breaking limbs and danger of death . . . expressly to confess their error and accuse all other heretics whom they know . . . and their receivers and defenders, just as thieves and robbers of temporal things are forced to accuse their accomplices and confess the crimes they have committed.[35]

Italian secular courts reflected the rise of the popular parties in the urban republics. Social utopianism joined democratic hope in accentuating community welfare, making crime utterly heinous. The establishment of guilt no longer sufficed, and a confession by a 'criminal' was required to confirm the laws or beliefs of the community from which he or she had diverged. From being passive and protective, justice had become active and penitential. So attractive was this law, indeed, that almost all Europe adopted it, even Italian-style torture. Employed by northern tribunals by about 1300, in France torture offered a partial proof confirming the results of an inquest, whereas in England it was used to make a defendant submit to an inquest. The English adaptation was known in France, but only in baronial courts.

Percipient though the new law was, it echoed harsh social relationships. The previous chapter noted that political thinkers thought it wise to exclude the very poor and very rich from the political community. A partial legal equivalent was the reintroduction into criminal law of the Roman distinction between the 'honest' well-to-do and the 'humble' or 'vile' poor. Albert of Gandino, a professional judge and *podestà*, asks the question whether

> both rich and poor ought be given like punishments. I answer that it depends on whether the penalties are pecuniary or corporal. If pecuniary, the law says that the penalty should be diminished for cause of poverty, as we see *podestàs* doing daily . . . . If corporal [save for false testimony, forgery, treason and desertion in war], the poor are to be more severely punished.[36]

Not that one may weep only for the humble. At Bologna in 1282 and Pisa in 1286 statutes of the popular party proposed proceeding against magnates on the basis of simple rumour, permitting condemnation as if a case 'had been fully proved'. Torture was to be used against them because history, if not action, indicated that their offences were treasonable. In Parma in 1316, for example, the 'question' could be used on commoners only in the presence of the elected 'ancients', the heads of the popular party and those of the guilds,

> saving and reserving that the *podestà* and the Captain [of the People] and their judges may torture magnates, nobles and powerful men . . . without the presence of the 'ancients'. . . . Against all others of whatsoever condition one must proceed rationally and with such moderation that none fall into danger of death from the severity or damage of torture.[37]

In social war, anything goes.

NOTES AND REFERENCES

1   *Summa notarie* prologue in *BuF* II, 603.

2   Matthew Paris, *Chronica majora* (Rolls Series) LVII, iii, 438.

3   *Liber extra* 2, 22, 2 in *CICan* II, 344.

4   Bresslau, *Handbuch der Urkundenlehre* I, 121.

5   Marc Bloch, 'De la cour royale à la cour de Rome' in *Studi in onore di Enrico Besta* (Milan, 1937) II, 153.

6   *Liber feudorum maior. Cartulario real que se conserva en el Archivo de la Corona de Aragòn* (ed. F.M. Rosell, 2 vols, Barcelona, 1945) I, 1.

7   Albert of Gandino's *Quaestiones statutorum* 69 in *BIMA* III, 189.

8   *Code* 3, 1, 14: '*Rem non novam neque insolitam aggredimur*', an incipit also used by Boniface VIII in *Extravagantes communes* 2, 3, 1 in *CICan* II, 1256.

9   *Rhetorica novissima* 8, 1 in *BIMA* II, 284a; 1 Samuel 2:10, Psalm 23:4 and Matthew 25:8.

10   *Rhetorica novissima* 2, 3 in *BIMA* II, 255.

11   *Super specula* in *Liber extra* 5, 5, 5 in *CICan* II, 770–1.

12   *Rhetorica novissima* in *BIMA* II, 290–1.

13   *Quod omnes tangit* in *Code* 1, 15, 8 for AD 446 and *ibid*. 5, 59, 5, 2 and *Liber Sextus* 5, 12, 5, No. 29.

14   The Latin pun is *lex* vs *faex*.

15   Cortese, *La norma giuridica* II, 139.

16   *Rhetorica novissima* 7, 3 in *BIMA* II, 259b.

17   Chénon, *Histoire générale du droit français publique et privé* I, 510n.

18   *Das sächsische Weichbildrecht. Jus municipale saxonicum* in A. von Daniels and Fr. von Gruben (eds.), *Rechtsdenkmäler des deutschen Mittelalters* I (Berlin, 1858), 66 from *Digest* 1, 5, 4. 'Positive law' translates *ius gentium*.

19   *Regestrum visitationum archiepiscopi Rothomagensis–Journal des visites paroissales 1245–69* (ed. Th. Bonnin, Rouen, 1852), 432.

20   *Coustumes et stilles de Bourgoigne* (1270–1360) in Esther Cohen, 'Law, Folklore and Animal Lore' in *Past and Present* 110 (1986), 12 and 20.

21   In his *De ordine judiciorum* in Rossi, *Consilium sapientis judiciale*, 143–4, citing *Digest* 48, 2, 4 and 48, 19, 5.

22   *De statutis* 4, 1, 8 in *TUJ* II, 66ra.

23   *Tractatus de maleficiis* 4 in Kantorowicz, *Albertus Gandinus und das Strafrecht der Scholastik* II, 155.

24   His commentary on the *Code* in Rossi, *Consilium sapientis judiciale*, 34.

25   *Digest* 1, 3, 12 and 13.

26   *Rhetorica novissima* 10, 1 in *BIMA* II, 292.

27   *Cedrus* 6 in *BuF* I, 123.

28   *De statutis* 1, 9 in *TUJ* II, 5rb.

29   *Digest* 50, 17, No. 56.

30   His *Speculum juris* 2, 2, 1 in Rossi, *Consilium sapientis judiciale*, 37.

31   *Rhetorica novissima* 3, 2 in *BIMA* II, 259.

32   *Digest* 22, 3, 2.

33   As in Albert of Gandino, *Tractatus de maleficiis* 17 (ed. Kantorowicz), II, 100.

34   *Oculus pastoralis* 6, 5, *Invectiva justitiae* in Muratori (ed.), *Antiquitates Italicae medii aevi* IX, 853–4.

35   Fiorelli, *La tortura giuridica nel diritto commune* I, 80.

36   *De maleficiis* 39, 22, 8 (ed. Kantorowicz), 253.

37   Dahm, *Untersuchungen zur Verfassungs- und Strafrechtsgeschichte der italienischen Stadt*, 35.

PART FIVE
Thought

19

INTELLECTUALS

UNIVERSITIES

Around 1300 William Durand the Younger summarized papal legislation dating from 1179 to 1215, proposing that

> bishops are to provide masters in cathedral churches and major parish churches to teach poor students without cost . . . and a tenth part of all ecclesiastical benefices, both secular and regular, are to be assigned poor scholars in the faculties of the university by whom God's Church will be illuminated.[1]

This system was amplified with the foundation of residential colleges ostensibly for poor pupils, the earliest being created at Paris in 1180. In spite of this very real effort, most good intellectuals came from families whose means bought supplementary or better education than most. Chaplains taught noble and patrician children, and young burghers and substantial villagers were instructed by hired teachers or became monastic oblates for education.

Church legislation attempted to improve lower-school education. Although none had been known before, testamentary bequests mention five parish schools in Toulouse between 1234 and 1257, and a similar number of village parish schools were seen in the Lauragais south of the town at mid-century. John Villani patriotically claimed that up to 10,000 Florentine boys and girls were learning to read and write. Up to 1,200 students attended six abacus schools for arithmetic, he added, and four great grammar schools housed up to 600 pupils of Latin and logic. Bonvesino of Riva, a teacher himself, states that Milan had about seventy teachers of

327

elementary letters and eight professors of grammar in 1288. Church and secular government divided this work. In 1253 the town of Ypres settled with St Martin's. The chapter was to provide the rector and masters of the 'great' schools whose costs were regulated. Under town licence 'small' schools, teaching reading and writing, could be secular. Some communities even ran public facilities. In 1253 Lübeck founded a long-lived municipal Latin school. In this period, universities and lower schools overlapped: Thomas Aquinas had completed six years in the faculty of letters at Naples at the age of sixteen.

The earliest university or 'high school' was the school of law at Bologna, privileged by the emperor in 1158 and confirmed by papal authority. The town of Bologna provided the teachers and the students, usually not citizens, organized to control and regulate the service sold them, eventually winning a decisive hand in choosing instructors. In Paris, where masters were not citizens, the king recognized their association in 1200. Although the pupils also organized, the masters' association, divided into faculties or nations within the large faculty of arts, was the real university. Curiously, it was more disturbed and torn by problems about academic liberty than the law school at Bologna. Differences aside, the two institutions had much in common. Both came under church law: the Lateran Council of 1179 regulated the licence for teaching, and degree requirements in both were formalized in the 1220s.

The university system expanded rapidly. Masters' associations like that of Paris formed schools at Oxford in 1214 and Cambridge in the 1230s. Montpellier built a faculty of medicine in 1220, and added one of law in the 1230s. In the north, Orléans evolved in the same decade, becoming northern France's centre for legal study after the eradication of Paris's law faculty in 1219. In 1229 a school was founded at Toulouse to attack heresy, but faltered before southern hostility. After the repression of Catharism by mid-century it resumed to become France's premier law centre.

Between 1204 and 1248 no less than nine high schools appeared in urbanized Italy, six in the north and three from Rome south. Founded and licensed in 1224 by Frederick II, Naples was Europe's first state university, serving the whole of this prince's southern kingdom, and the same was true of the ancient school of medicine at Salerno given royal privileges in 1231. Elsewhere, universities appeared slowly. Although initiatives date from as early as 1208–9 and Salamanca flourished from 1254 until its collapse in the 1280s,

Spain's schools did not get under way until around 1300. Germany lacked universities until the next century, but Dominican schools there were famous.

Excepting Paris and Bologna, these institutions were small. In 1262 a convocation of the liberal arts at Padua included two teachers in physics, one in logic and six in grammar and rhetoric. Alfonso X's ideal foundation at Salamanca in 1254 was to have two civilian jurists, three canonists, two logicians, two grammarians and two physicists. Academic ceremonies had appeared: in 1215 Boncompagno of Signa read a work before the doctors and students of Bologna, and was then crowned with laurel.

During the thirteenth century a curriculum of philosophy and theology became traditional. The schedule at Paris for a theology degree began with six years in the arts faculty, the last two as a bachelor attaining the master's degree. To become a theological doctor or 'divine', a student spent eight years in the theological faculty, devoting four years to biblical exegesis and Peter Lombard's *Sentences*, and four more as a bachelor disputant and teacher, the institution's basic teaching staff. For a time, commentaries on parts of the *Sentences* became the theological dissertation. Academic disputations (*quaestiones quodlibetales* or *disputatae*) embodied syllogistic methods used in such monumental works as Thomas Aquinas's *Theological Summa*. In addition, teachers wrote essays on various topics, as Aquinas's tracts on *Being and Essence* and *On the Rule of Princes*. Subjects requiring practical experience needed different methods. At Salerno medical students read logic for three years and then devoted five years to Hippocrates, Galen and surgery. They were licensed after a final year of practical experience under a working physician.

Secular clerks usually returned to parish work after a few years of study. In the deanery of Stow near Lincoln, only nine per cent of the rural priests had been touched by higher education in the 1230s, but by the 1270s twenty-one per cent had. Great careers required more. Thomas Aquinas studied arts at Naples and, between visits to pick up degrees at Paris, spent over ten years with Albert the Great (d. 1280) in the Dominican school at Cologne. Thereafter he taught regularly at Paris, with periods at the papal court, Bologna and Naples. He also counselled popes, princes, bishops and church courts, and died on his way from Naples to attend the second Council of Lyons in 1274.

Although hobbled by officers such as the chancellor at Paris and the archdeacon at Bologna, the masters' power was their monopoly of the right to examine students and thereby to control access to teaching. In 1231 the king at Melfi defined Salerno's doctorate:

> We order that no one seeking the title of doctor shall dare to practise or otherwise heal unless first approved at Salerno by the judgment of the masters in a public examination. He should then enter our presence . . . with letters . . . from the masters and other doctors, and receive from us . . . the licence to heal.[2]

The power of masters to conduct examinations was admitted even at Bologna where students often chose the teaching staff.

Masters published as well as taught. A biographer of Thomas Aquinas claimed that he had written nearly a hundred books. The Franciscan Ubertino of Casale (d. *circa* 1330) defended Peter John Olivi before the pope, saying: 'And your Apostolic Wisdom should know that the number of books by brother Peter . . . is twenty-seven times greater in quantity than Peter Lombard's *Sentences*.'[3] Writing a history of the Dominicans, Bernard Gui described the accomplishments of his order's scholarly luminaries. Not that divines were slavishly respected. The distinguished Parisian theologian William of Auxerre (d. 1230) was on a papal commission examining Aristotle's works, but Salimbene casually remarked that, although perhaps a great professor, he was an incoherent preacher.

Like many artists and architects, academic writers habitually signed their works. Few went as far as a jurist, the first letters of each chapter of one of whose works spelled out 'Roffredo of Benevento, professor of Roman law, author of this work'.[4] This curious example brings up plagiarism. Because learned pieces were directed to an audience already in the know, and because the sources were authorities whose opinions had to be attacked or relied on, both juristic and scholastic treatises cited authors, ancient and modern, by name. It was different when an audience was broader. Careful in his technical works, Thomas Aquinas did not bother to note his debt to Vegetius in his *On the Rule of Princes*, a work addressed to a lay audience. Other motives were also seen. Fearing to set his readers' teeth on edge before his argument had been swallowed, the secular master Henry Goethals of Ghent quoted but did not identify Aquinas when attacking his doctrine of original sin. The Dominicans spotted it anyway, and sprang to the defence of their doctor. Earlier authors were often shaved close. About a third of John Quidort of Paris's *On Royal and Papal Power* came from contemporaries like Aquinas. Unlike today's authors who are impeded by copyright, medieval ones not only lifted ideas but copied text as well.

Intellectuals are famed backbiters, and were so at this time. Roger Bacon claimed that divines like Alexander of Hales and Albert the Great, who were trained before Aristotle's natural history was studied and had little mathematics, were incapable philosophers. The Franciscan Peter Auriole (d. 1322) was notorious for acidulous views about contemporaries and teachers. William of Ockham later turned the tables on him, observing (probably falsely) that he had wasted barely a day reading Peter's works.

There was more here than envy: institutional pressure made for conflict. When, as shall be seen, the mendicant orders invaded the parishes, they were resisted at Paris by the secular masters. Supported by the popes, however, they forced their way in from 1229, when the first Dominican, Roland of Cremona, began teaching. The battle occasionally erupted, as in the 1250s when the career of the secular doctor William of St Amour (d. 1272) was ruined and he himself rusticated from Paris in 1260. During these combats, moreover, the mendicants split apart. The Franciscans attacked Aquinas, asserting the superior authority of their Bonaventure. In 1287 a general chapter ordered the Austin Friars to defend the opinions of their spokesman, Giles of Rome. Retarded by the Parisian condemnation of certain propositions expounded by Aquinas in 1277, his canonization in 1323 and the revocation of the articles attacking him in 1325 left no doubt as to the efficacy of Dominican pressure.

In spite of divisions, the masters of the faculties constituted an order, one able to withstand bishops and other ecclesiastical authorities. The issue was largely who had superior competence in theological and philosophical matters. Aided by divines, Bishop Stephen Tempier of Paris had condemned a series of Averroist and Aristotelian propositions, some Thomist, in 1277. Chancellor of the university in 1280, the theologian Geoffrey of Fontaines called this act scandalous because, as he said (without regard to the facts), the commissioners were ignorant.

The academics even took on Rome. Recalling William of St Amour's debates with the mendicants in the 1250s, the poet John of Meung called the university Christianity's guardian, far superior to the popes. When the mendicants' privilege of preaching was again attacked in 1290, the secular masters took up the cudgels under Henry of Ghent. Henry asked why, since masters could discuss scripture, they could not question the privileges. The papal legate Benedict Gaetani (later Boniface VIII) responded to the masters:

> You sit in your chairs and think that Christ is ruled by your reasons . . . . Not so, brothers, not so. Because the world has been committed to us [at Rome], we ought not think about what will humour you clerks, but about what is advantageous to the world . . . . You believe you have great glory and commendation at Rome, but we judge you to be fatuity and blather [*fumus* = smoke] . . . . I have seen your arguments, and they can be answered, and this is the answer . . .

Let there be no question of the mendicants' privileges. Warming up, he added:

> And I tell you that before the Roman court will withdraw this privilege, it would sooner confound the University of Paris. We have not been called to be learned or appear glorious, but instead to save souls. Because the said brothers' life and teaching saves many souls, their privileges will always be preserved.

After this peroration, a master sourly observed:

> Lo! So valid and firm were the masters' arguments built up over ten years that they have all been shattered by the statement of one cardinal. What d'you think they'll say at Rome when all the masters seated in their chairs were unable to answer one cardinal?[5]

The curial party won this battle because the mendicants and many French bishops stood behind it. It lost a later one because the French had defeated the papacy, the mendicants were divided and the conciliar idea of ecclesiastical government – often led by the bishops and divines of the Gallican Church – was threatening papal monarchy. In an attempt to buttress Franciscan conservatives, John XXII supported the opinion of a commission of theologians on the Beatific Vision in 1333 to the effect that those dying in a state of grace would not see God face to face but would repair to Abraham's bosom, there to await the Last Trump. Others had quite different opinions, Aquinas for example having even proposed that both Moses and St Paul had seen God briefly even while alive. In 1334, amid much excitement, twenty-nine Parisian masters informed the king that the pope's opinion was purely personal, having no other significance than that he held it. The king then supported 'his' university. During the fray, the usually peppery John XXII was very defensive indeed when he wrote to the king: 'Because someone will perhaps tell you that we are not a master of theology, hear what a wise man says: "Give ear not to who speaks, but rather to what he says."[6] And this embarrassed sage held an office whose doctrinal infallibility had been asserted at the second Council of Lyons in 1274! Before he died, John withdrew his opinion.

LEARNING AND FREEDOM

Education was to prepare humanity for heaven. Because most assumed that human reason was capable of comprehending some part of nature and even of glimpsing the deity, learning was almost idolized. This belief encouraged the Latins to explore the wealth of ancient and Islamic thought, and served a Church that was busy leading the world. Human reason, however, was inadequate. It did not obviate death, predict the morrow, explain the cosmos or define eternity, nor tell if behaviour was free or bound by fate. Some therefore favoured a different, non-rational way of looking at the world, one that had marked the Church from its earliest reaction against the thought of Greece and Rome.

Most intellectuals would have denied that they were balancing on a tightrope strung between the naturalism of reason's philosophy and the religion of man's need as expressed by theology. They were instead convinced that philosophy and theology combined together to argue for Christ. Thomas Aquinas put it thus:

> The gifts of grace are added to nature in such a way that they do not do away with it, but instead perfect it. Hence the light of faith freely infused into us does not destroy the light of natural knowledge implanted in us naturally. Although the . . . human mind cannot show us things made manifest by faith, it is none the less impossible that that which faith gives us is contrary to that implanted in us by nature. Were that the case, one or the other would be false, and, since God gave us both, He would be the author of untruth, which is impossible . . . . Just as sacred doctrine is founded on the light of the faith, so is philosophy founded on the light of natural reason, and hence it is impossible that philosophical things are contrary to things of the faith.[7]

Given his bent for natural science, the Franciscan Roger Bacon believed that 'the objective of philosophy is to know the creator by what He has created'.[8] Philosophy, he thought, could help make man understand the Eucharist which, he said, many deny, many doubt and many receive with repugnance. Writing earlier, before 1230, Roland of Cremona had explained: 'Because many believe that the human soul is corruptible and dies together with the death of man's organs . . . it seemed useful to me . . . to adduce philosophical reasoning.'[9] Even those questioning philosophy really favoured it. Bonaventure reminded his readers that Christians had always used non-Christian sources: 'Read [Augustine's] *On Christian Doctrine* where he shows that Holy Scripture cannot be understood without the skills of the other sciences, and that Israel's sons carried off Egypt's vases, just as [today's] divines appropriate philosophical teaching.'[10]

The question, however, was whether reason and philosophy were equal to authority and theology. To those repeating Gregory the Great's (d. 604) assertion that 'faith to which human reason lends proof has no merit', Abelard had long before a ready answer: if someone claims that an idol is the true God, who, without reason, can disprove it? Aquinas was more tactful: reason teaches faith. Certainly, if only doubt is to be removed, authority is to be used, but if auditors are to be persuaded 'then one must lean on reason to investigate the truth and to show how what is said is true'.[11]

New knowledge was often non-Christian. Preaching during the prohibition of the study of natural history at Paris, James of Vitry counselled scholars to avoid Plato and Aristotle. Theologians, he said, need no natural science and anyway Plato erred when saying that the planets were gods and Aristotle that the world was eternal. The Dominican general Humbert of Romans complained of ostentatious professors who always cited Plato, Aristotle, Algazel, Averroës, Alfarabi and other 'unworthy' philosophers. Some anti-Aristotelians rejected this extreme position. Bonaventure said that one should even study Christ's enemies: 'if studious persons study heretical writings to better comprehend the truth by refuting them, they would be neither idly curious nor heretical, but instead Catholic'.[12]

Intellectuals generally did not share this hostility, and showed it in two ways. First, translations of scientific and philosophical works from Greek and Arabic appeared, including the recent works of Averroës (d. 1198) and Maimonides (d. 1204). The translators from Arabic were Gerard of Cremona (d. 1187) and Michael Scot (d. before 1235), and those from Greek were James of Venice (*fl.* 1140s) and especially the Dominican William of Moerbeke, who died in 1286 as archbishop of Corinth. Substantial segments of

Greek theology by John Chrysostom (d. 403) and John of Damascus (d. 749) were also translated. Second, they tried to smooth the rough edges of non-Christian thought. Abelard likened Plato's 'world soul' to the third person of the Trinity because the Greek had comprehended the godhead. John of Salisbury thought Aristotle had awakened the Latin mind. In 1190 Daniel of Morley, worshipper at the Arabic shrine of Toledo, condemned Oxford and Paris for their hostility to natural science. Roger Bacon explained away the polytheism and sacrifices of his Roman favourites by asserting that 'these philosophers busied themselves with this because of the law and the multitude, not because of truth, as Seneca says in the book he composed about superstition'.[13] Excerpting whole sections from Seneca to build his moral philosophy, he distinguished between earth and heaven:

> Although . . . [pagan] philosophers did not know the virtues that lead to grace, that is, faith, hope and charity, we Christians nevertheless . . . do not equal them in elegance of statement about the virtues commonly required for . . . human society . . . . Christian philosophers therefore need to study attentively the [pagans'] great glory.[14]

The divines of the time were therefore syncretist. Alan of Lille proposed first to prove the unity of the Trinity's 'essence by reasoning, second, by the varied authority of gentile philosophers, and, third, by the authority of the holy fathers'.[15] He then cited anything that came to hand – ancient philosophers, hermetic writings, Arabs such as the astrologer Albumazar as well as Christian authors, old and new.

Even if contrary to the faith, therefore, non-Christian sources enjoyed authority. This did not lie only in the texts themselves but also in those who explicated them – the masters, a group enjoying a measure of autonomy with regard to the rest of the Church. Autonomy required self-police, however. Albert the Great, for example, did not agree with Peter Lombard on original sin, but said he would uphold Peter's view out of respect. There were, of course, dissenters. The contentious Roger Bacon wanted the Lombard's book replaced by the study of scripture, history, natural philosophy and mathematics. But in important matters solidarity existed. The revival of Aristotle was pushed just as avidly by Albert and Aquinas as by Parisian extremists, those known to moderns as the Latin Averroists after the great Arabic commentator Averroës. That the masters thought of themselves as authorities, even church fathers, is shown in a book 'that is all gold, because herein are contained the golden sentences and questions of the holy fathers Augustine, Jerome . . . and of the modern masters William of Champeaux, Yves of Chartres and Anselm of Laon'.[16]

Nor can the measure of intellectual freedom attained be described only as a conflict between authority and reason. Reason's defenders were not disinterested intellectuals but rather those whose claim to attention rested on their use of ancient and other non-Christian authorities. Theirs was, in short, the authority of the learned. Nor was authority simple. James of Vitry and others of Peter Cantor's circle were certainly opposed to Plato, Aristotle and natural philosophy, but they were no less revolutionary because of that. By trying to realize here on earth the utopia of the Acts of the Apostles, James and his colleagues turned the world on its ear. The same may be said of the later radical Franciscan Peter John Olivi, who stoutly maintained that Aristotle had nothing to do with Christ. In brief, those who loved authority were often more revolutionary than those who loved reason.

Besides, authority required constant redefinition. Although no one was permitted to doubt, few basic doctrines were not susceptible to interpretation. At the time of the controversy over the Eucharist in the late eleventh century, contemporaries noted that Augustine differed from Ambrose, and to reconcile them, reason was employed, however tortuously. Later, Aquinas perceived that the doctors who preceded the Arian heresy did not speak as clearly about the unity of the divinity as those who followed it. He also noted that Augustine had changed his mind: 'in his books written after the birth of the Pelagian heresy he spoke more cautiously of the power of free will than in those he wrote before the said heresy'.[17] Earlier, Alan of Lille admitted that authority has a nose of wax that can be bent in any direction, an opinion applicable also to scripture, the source of all authority. Around 1324 a manual for preaching friars and parish priests stated that 'Sacred Scripture is a soft wax that takes the impression of every seal,' now of the lion, now of the eagle, now of Christ, and now of the devil.[18] Authority, in fine, was like reason, being texts and traditions interpreted by persons using their wits to advance their favoured causes.

Mainstream thought oscillated between avowing the usefulness of natural philosophy and reason and the opposing position, an oscillation most marked during institutional crises in church life. Being static, somewhat anti-historical and inclined to justify whatever was, the naturalist position was not helpful when new institutions were needed. In moments of revolutionary effervescence, utopians summoned the irrational urges of Christian hope. Once old institutional impediments had been demolished, however, reason's philosophers harmonized conflicting viewpoints. An illustration is seen during the Gregorian revolution, when the Church underwent institutional recasting and rose to lead Latin Europe. The rationalist defenders of the symbolic interpretation of the Eucharist were then defeated by the spokesmen of the miraculous interpretation, and their champion Berengar of Tours silenced in 1059. The irrationalists won the day by claiming that priests miraculously renew the Incarnation, binding God to humanity and its institutions. By 1150, however, the Church's need for systematic organization led to the victory of the rationalists in all other matters. The great battles around scripture and dialectics typified by the names of those mentioned in Mr Brooke's volume – Peter Abelard, Gilbert of La Porrée and Bernard of Clairvaux – were stilled, but the victory went to the two 'rationalists'.

A similar crisis occurred around 1200. The repression of the great popular heresies and the opening of the Church to new forms of monasticism led to a general attack on all intellectual frontiers. Aristotelianism was assaulted at Paris in 1210 and 1215, and Amalric of Bène's (d. *circa* 1205–6) Platonic or pantheistic naturalism was repudiated there in 1210. Joachim of Fiore's utopian historicism was rebuked at the Lateran Council in 1215, and the Platonism of the Carolingian philosopher John the Scot Erigena's was outlawed in 1225. These traditions, however, were repressed only momentarily, and the mendicant professors of the Dominican order that rose during this crisis were among the greatest exponents of the new learning.

The last crisis considered here took place around 1300, when the pullulation of the mendicant orders and their utopian wings was attacked. Divided internally, church leadership was seriously questioned by lay society and the secular State. As exemplified in Olivi's work, Joachitic historical utopianism was condemned. Some Thomistic propositions, Aristotelian naturalism, and especially the Averroist interpretation of that philosophy, were questioned at Paris in 1270 and again in 1277 by the celebrated commission of Stephen Tempier, bishop of Paris. In Italy the positions of determinist astrologers like Peter of Abano, teacher of medicine at Padua, and Cecco of Ascoli, professor of astronomy at Bologna, were assaulted with great vigour. A pacific age followed, however, and the articles against Thomas Aquinas were retracted in 1325.

Intellectuals were sometimes punished for their opinions. William of St Amour was silenced and rusticated. Siger of Brabant (d. 1281–4) was on his way to Rome to clear himself when he died. Olivi had substantial parts of his work condemned from 1284 onwards but, in spite of formal submission, appears to have gone on writing as he saw fit until his death in 1298. Amalric of Bène suffered the obloquy of being anathematized after death, and the sect his teaching inspired, like that of the later Olivites, was hunted down. In spite of the death penalty so freely imposed on heretics, and book burning, however, no teacher in the schools was killed: no master before the astrologer Cecco of Ascoli in 1327, and no theological divine before John Hus in 1415.

Not dissimilar struggles rent the Jewish community. One crisis was precipitated by Maimonides's *Guide to the Perplexed*, an attempt to find accord between revealed religion and the somewhat Platonized Aristotle of Arabic philosophical circles. Europe's rabbinate reacted vehemently, especially in northern France and Germany. Although less successful than its parallel among Christians, the defence of the new thought was similar. A medical doctor from Barcelona and Rome, Seraiah son of Isaac, grandson of Salathiel, said about a celebrated rabbi of Barcelona: 'Nahmanides was a Talmudist who understood nothing of philosophy and therefore attacked Maimonides . . . . He would have done better to be silent because a judge must first understand what he is judging.'[19] Nahmanides had himself actually defended Maimonides, using terms that would have been familiar to Parisians favouring Aristotle and Averros. He asked the Talmudists: 'Did Maimonides seek to disturb your greatness in Talmudic studies when he wrote a book designed to be a refuge against the Greek philosophers Aristotle and Galen? Have you ever read these books, or have you been seduced by your own arguments?'[20] Led by Rabbi Solomon son of Abraham, Montpellier's Jews denounced the *Guide* to Dominican inquisitors, who obligingly burned it in 1233.

NOTES AND REFERENCES

1   *De modo generali concilii celebrandi* 2, 4, 16 in *TUJ* XIII, 165rb.

2   P.O. Kristeller, 'The School of Salerno' in *Studies in Renaissance Thought and Letters* (Rome, 1956), 528.

3   Douie, *The Nature and the Effect of the Heresy of the Fraticelli*, 95.

4   *Quaestiones sabbathinae* in F.C. von Savigny, *Geschichte des römischen Rechts im Mittelalter* (Heidelberg, 1829) V, 186.

5   Finke, *Aus den Tagen Bonifaz VIII*, Anhänge, V–VII.

6   Heinrich Denifle and E. Chatelain, *Chartularium universitatis parisiensis* (Paris, 1889) I, 436–7, No. 978.

7   *In Boetium de trinitate* 2, 3 cited in Chenu, *La théologie comme science au treizième siècle*, 88.

8   *Opus maius* 2, 7 (ed. Bridges), III, 51.

9   From his *Expositio in Job* by Chenu, *La théologie au douxième siècle*, 28.

10   *Epistola de tribus quaestionibus* 12 in *Opuscula varia* (Quaracchi, 1898) VIII, 336ab.

11   His *Homiliae in Evangelia* cited in Grabmann, *Die Geschichte der scholastischen Methode* I, 144.

12   *Epistola de tribus quaestionibus* 12 in *Opuscula varia*, 336a.

13   *Baconis operis maioris pars septima seu moralis philosophia* 1, 8 (ed. Eugenio Massa, Turin, 1953), 132.

14   *Ibid*. 3, 5, *proemium* (ed. Massa), 132.

15   *Quoniam homines* I, 1 prologue in Pierre Glorieux (ed.), *Archives d'histoire doctrinale et littéraire du moyen âge* XXVIII (1953), 122.

16   The *Liber Pancrisis* cited in Chenu, *La théologie au douzième siècle*, 358, dated to the second third of the century.

17   The *proemium* of his *Contra errores Graecorum* in *Opera omnia* (Rome, 1967) XL, A, 71a.

18   Prologue of the *Speculum humanae salvationis* (eds Lutz and Perdrizet), 3.

19   Güdemann, *Geschichte des Erziehungswesen . . . der Juden* II, 157–8.

20   *Ibid*. I, 72.

20

REASON AND RELIGION

HISTORY AND PROGRESS

History helped educate mankind towards the good. Gerald of Wales outlined its advantages:

> A careful reading of the histories of the ancients helps princes because it warns of the chancy outcome of war, of difficult and fortunate circumstances and of hidden traps and [needed] precautions. History teaching, princes may examine as though in a mirror past actions to see what is to be done, what avoided, what fled and what pursued.[1]

Godfrey of Viterbo addressed his versified history to the Emperor Henry VI with this monition: 'An emperor cannot attain true glory unless he knows the course and origin of the world . . . . An emperor learned in philosophy is thought to stand before other men, but, if ignorant, he appears to err or stray rather than reign.'[2] Apparent practicality aside, myth was intertwined with history as in Martin of Troppau who repeats the fictions that Charlemagne had visited Jerusalem and that Pope Sylvester II (Gerbert of Aurillac, d. 1003) had, like Faust, sold his soul to the devil to get Arabic mathematical and scientific knowledge. And Martin, papal penitentiary, prelate and counsellor of princes, provided historical information for intellectuals of the stature of Marsiglio of Padua and William of Ockham!

History was moralistic and programmatic. Godfrey of Viterbo, for example, repeated the myth that the Trojans had moved to Europe, where they founded Rome and the Frankish kingdom. From Carolingian times, Troy was thought to have given the

Franks, a people related to but unconquered by Rome, the natural right to govern others. John Quidort of Paris used this history to argue against putting the Church above the State. Among the Franks (that is, the French) royal power had clearly preceded ecclesiastical authority.

> Hence royal power is not from the pope either intrinsically or in terms of exercise, but instead from God and the people electing the king either in person or dynasty . . . . To say then that royal power derives first from God and afterwards from the pope is utterly ridiculous.[3]

But there was more to history than myth. In the days of the sainted Emperor Henry III (d. 1056), Quidort said, no pope was elected without imperial assent, and ecclesiastical unction, although mentioned in the Old Testament, is nowhere found in the New. Besides, unction was not used everywhere in his own day, at least not in Iberia.

From Abelard on, those of the rational or dialectical tradition viewed human history as something static in which great changes were unlikely to take place until the end of time. Times change, but not the faith; small things are mutable, but great ones unchanging. Historian of the early twelfth century, Otto of Freising divided history into three ages: that of the Old Testament and the law, the present age of the New Testament and the sacraments, and a third age, the end of the world. Today's age chronicled the histories of successive empires and was a time of senescence, awaiting the Antichrist and the Last Days. Thomas Aquinas also likened modernity to senescence:

> The last age is the present, after which there is no further age of salvation's [history], just as there is no further age after old age. Although men's other ages have a determined number of years, that is not so in old age, because it begins at the sixtieth year and some live for 120 years. Hence it is not determined how long this age of the world will last.[4]

Some, however, found modernity superior to earlier ages. Priscian's ancient tag 'the more recent, the more perspicacious' was often quoted, and John of Salisbury and Peter of Blois stated that, although mere dwarfs on the shoulders of giants, moderns see further than the ancients. In the early thirteenth century Boncompagno of Signa said that the old saw 'there's nothing new under the sun' was true only in a limited sense. God, after all, daily creates

341

new souls, putting them into new bodies, and, working with pri-
mordial matter, a common artisan shapes it into new forms at will.
Indeed, the Incarnation's renovation of grace proves that man,
God's creation, sees things with new eyes, whence the apostle Paul
'ordered him who came first to be silent when something has been
revealed to him who comes after'.[5]

Around 1255 Rolandino Passaggeri noted that old manuals on
contracts were useless because designed for the ancients, who were
perhaps more virtuous than moderns. The result was that their
authors

> were ignorant of the subtleties of modern man . . . . And 'because the more a
> thing is modern, the more it is perspicacious', our age brings with it in contract
> law as in other matters new and more subtle ways of doing things. It is therefore
> fitting that we should put old laws aside . . . because they are somehow foreign
> to, or lack congruence with, any or few modern subtleties. As in other things,
> we should make a new law reflecting today's ways and methods . . . in order to
> improve our way of life.[6]

Borrowing from Aristotle, Aquinas asked whether or not human
law can be changed. It could,

> because human reason naturally moves step by step from the imperfect to the
> perfect. Whence we see in the speculative sciences that those who first philosop-
> hized handed down imperfect results which afterwards made more perfect
> by their successors. Similarly in practical matters, those who first tried to find
> something useful for the human community, being unable to understand every-
> thing, introduced things in many ways deficient; but their successors replaced
> these with ones far less faulty.[7]

This moderate idea of man's advancement did not attract enthusiasts, who required stronger stuff. This vision was expressed by
Joachim of Fiore:

> When scripture says, 'the eye is not satisfied with seeing nor the ear filled with
> hearing', it means that full and unending pleasure is to drink not what has been
> tasted but instead what is yet to be tasted, nor to hear what has been heard and
> interpreted by the fathers, but rather to hear something new from God's inex-
> haustible treasure, something we lack of divine wisdom.[8]

To this was added history. The Parisian canon and teacher Hugh of
St Victor distinguished the spiritual character of each age in the
faith's history, each of them having within it the prophets of the
succeeding one, the men before their time.

The Premonstratensian Anselm of Havelberg, who died as archbishop of Ravenna in 1158, defended the multiplication of new orders by saying that spiritual progress was essential to the Church. Although humanity was living in the last of three ages, that initiated by Christ's coming, he found progress there. Seven seals, or periods, were delineated, of which humankind was in the fourth, and in spite of persecutions each age was one of fulfilment through which the Church wound its upward course. Praising new orders – Vallumbrosans, Cistercians and others – Anselm said: 'From generation to generation, God's wonderful dispensation causes the youth of the Church to be ever renewed by a new order, just as the youth of the eagle which seeks to fly higher in contemplation.'[9] Nor is it surprising that an unchanging God allows the Church to be changeable

> because it is necessary that, according to time's progression, the signs of spiritual grace should increase and increasingly declare the truth. Thus, together with the desire for, the knowledge of the truth will grow in the course of time, and so first good things were published, then better, and lastly the very best.[10]

Indeed, scripture revealed itself progressively. Richard of St Victor (d. 1173) glossed the text: 'And when he opened the third seal' – that is, when, according to the progress of time, the effect of the divine promise and the progress of human salvation more and more began to be discerned and known in scripture – 'I heard the third beast saying, "Come and see"!'[11]

By the latter part of the century these ideas had been elaborated. A Benedictine who likened Benedict of Nursia (d. *circa* 747) to John the Baptist, Odo, abbot of Battle (d. 1200), had a scheme of four ages. The 'first testament God gave men's hearts was called natural law, and, had they obeyed it, they would not have needed a second. But since men are habitual lovers of novelty, he gave them a second testament, that of circumcision.' A third time, the deity brought them out of indifference with the testament of

> baptism which was predestined to remain for all eternity. But because long and inveterate custom began to lead man again bit by bit into neglect, He gave a fourth testament, the monastic cowl, to which . . . novelty's lovers have now gravitated. There will be no fifth testament because, in a new and wonderful way, the blessings of all peoples are contained in [the fourth].[12]

Tied to an unfolding revelation in history of an ever purer morality of brotherhood in the procession of the three persons of the

Trinity, varieties of this monastic vision gave enthusiasts something analogous to the fervours of the modern idea of progress. The best example was the teaching of Joachim of Fiore and those who claimed to follow him. This abbot envisaged the successive ages of the Father, Son and Holy Ghost. Advancing from the slavery of the Mosaic law to the lighter burden of Christ's law, humanity was to be fulfilled in the spiritual freedom of the Holy Spirit, when all were to receive and live on earth some part of the monastic calling. As did the nearly contemporary 'Children's Crusade' and Francis of Assisi's exemplification of childhood's 'innocence', Joachim replaced old age with youth as the mark of the age to come. In Old Testament times the maturity of the aged taught mankind to shun the transitory and cleave to the lasting. In that of the New Testament the patience of the young became the teacher. In the third age leadership was surrendered to childhood's sincerity, uncorrupted by property and the flesh. Joachim believed not only that the Church, including Peter's see, was soon to be replaced and purified by spiritualized monks, but also that it would itself foster the change. 'For just as old Simeon lifted the boy [Christ] in his arms, so the successors of Peter . . . seeing this order following Christ's footsteps in spiritual virtue, will sustain it by [their] authority.' Indeed, the old order will rejoice in its replacement: 'Nor should it lament its own dissolution since it knows that it will remain in a better succession . . . and . . . what order can grieve that it lacks perfection in itself, when a universal perfection succeeds it?'[13]

Although progress was ineluctable, Joachim did not promise an easy victory. Before the angel pope ushered in paradise on earth, an apocalypse complete with Antichrist and Armageddon was to afflict mankind. Even before that, there were to be battles. Joachim attacked the static image of trinitarian unity found in Peter Lombard, insisting on the historical procession of the three persons. Showing that the old order was not prepared to step down as quietly as the abbot envisaged, this view was roundly condemned by the pope and the bishops meeting at the Lateran Council in 1215. Perhaps Joachim suspected this recalcitrance because he had not infrequently referred to the present Church as the 'great whore', a view warmly espoused by his sectaries. Indeed, although the abbot was vague about details, Joachites in Italy and elsewhere, like the earlier Amalricians at Paris, proclaimed the abolition of the old Church. William the Breton reported that the Parisians had argued that the power of the Father lasted as long as the Mosaic law; and, because it is written 'the old shall be cast out when new things come in', after Christ came, they abolished all the sacraments of the Old Testament, and the new law flourished up to this time. They said that today the sacraments of the New Testament are come to an end and the time of the Holy Spirit has begun, in which confession, baptism, the Eucharist and other sacraments without which salvation cannot be had have no longer any further place, but each man inwardly can be saved without any exterior act merely through the grace of the Holy Spirit.[14]

The Parisian Amalricians believed the age of the Holy Spirit had begun or would within five years, but Joachim of Fiore, according to the Franciscan Hugh of Digne (d. by 1257), never actually named a time, although it was imminent. Both his enemies and the later Franciscan Spirituals, however, were sure he had. When Joachitic views were condemned at Anagni in 1255, a judge stated:

> So much for the words of Joachim, by which he strives in a bizarre way to exalt I know not what order that will come, as he says, at the end of the second age, of which there now remain only five years . . . by which, I say, he seeks not only to exalt [this order] over all other orders, but also above the whole Church and the whole world, as is clearly stated in many passages of the above work.[15]

Explaining why the abbot's doctrines had failed to elicit broad support, Hugh of Digne put his finger on the truth. What prevented 'Abbot Joachim from being believed was that he predicted future tribulations. This was why the Jews had slain their prophets . . . . Carnal men do not willingly hear about future tribulations, only about consolations.'[16] Lastly, if Joachim had not named a date, his followers certainly had.

The idea of lost primal bliss also encouraged men like Robert of Curzon to envisage recovering the apostles' primitive community. Francis of Assisi and also the extremist wing of his order tried to imitate the Saviour or the apostles. Nor did restoration conflict with progress because human capacity to reproduce lost perfection shows that God had made the species perfectible. It obviously could not be stated that Francis equalled the Saviour or the Franciscans the apostles, but this impediment could be sidestepped. Borrowing from Peter John Olivi, Ubertino of Casale, a leader of the spiritual Franciscans, formulated a solution in 1305. Francis and his brethren were certainly not equal to Christ and the apostles, but there had been something unfulfilled about the apostolic age. Because of the synagogue's perfidy and because the gentiles were then incapable of understanding so spiritual an idea,

> the Holy Spirit showed the apostles that the perfection of the evangelical life was not at that time open to the multitude. Whence the apostles did not require perfection to be observed in the churches they ruled, that perfection they themselves accepted when imposed by Christ and which they fully followed.[17]

Referring to Joachim of Fiore, Ubertino observed that the apostolic mission was not to be spread to the multitude until a later time, the sixth seal of the seventh age, by his calculation. As John the Divine had prophesied in Revelation 7:2, that age was to see the coming of the angel ascending from the east, bearing the sign of the living God. To Ubertino and his followers this angel was Francis of Assisi, and he noted in passing that Bonaventure had also asserted this identity when preaching at Paris. In short, Francis was not Christ nor the Franciscans the apostles, but Christ's apostolate was to be made real only by the Franciscans in their own age.

Linked to a utopian view of man's relation to his neighbour, this idea of progress was expressed in the attack on usury, the growth of economic corporatism and the exaltation of poverty and communal living. The historical vision was also combined with the natural history and moral sociology of the Aristotelians. In Roger Bacon, inventions like flying machines and optical devices were to be joined to an accurate forecasting of astral and geographical influences, a correct ordering of law and society, the abolition of sexual and moral irregularity and educational reform. All were needed to defeat the Tatars, the Saracens and the soon-to-appear Antichrist.

> I do not wish 'to set my mouth against the heavens', but know that if the Church studied Holy Scripture, sacred prophecy, the predictions of the Sibyl, Merlin, Aquila, Joachim and others, and also the histories and books of the philosophers, and ordered astronomy to be studied, a sufficient or even certain estimate of the time of the Antichrist would be discovered . . . . All the wise believe that we are not far from that time. Because individuals, cities and whole regions can be changed for the better according to the aforesaid, life can be prolonged as long as necessary, all things managed functionally, and even greater things can be done . . . not only in the natural sciences, but also in the moral sciences and arts, as is evident from Moses and Aristotle.[18]

Intellectuals felt hopeful as they dealt with natural history, because, as seen above, they accepted the notion that, since nature begins with less perfect forms, the later the time, the more perfect the creature or thing. Reinforcing this vision was human success:

everywhere forests and swamps were being cleared, architecture and metalwork surpassed in quantity and quality the achievements of antiquity and contemporary cultures, and transport was taking decisive steps forward. Not that this age saw technological innovation on a scale comparable to modern times, but humankind could nevertheless imagine that nature beneficently welcomed human use. Exploitation is catching: just as the Latins plundered Greek and Islamic society economically, they did also intellectually. The spate of new translations of Arabic, Jewish, Byzantine and classical sources mentioned briefly above attests the Latins' ability to use others' ideas. Albert the Great may not have been inventive, but his encyclopaedic interest in the sciences – indeed, in all kinds of subjects and authors – exemplifies the aggressive confidence of the Latin mind.

SCIENCE AND DETERMINISM

A wide gap lay between the theoretical sciences of the schoolmen and the practical techniques of artisans, architects and others, but its size can be exaggerated. As the occasional act ennobling or granting privileges to architects or masters of works in Italy shows, the higher practical arts were not rigidly separated from the liberal ones. Practice and theory were necessarily distinguished but their relationship was also recognized in apprenticeship contracts recorded by Rolandino Passaggeri. Neophytes were instructed in both the practice and theory of their art or craft. Anent the medical profession, the translator Dominic Gundisalvo, archdeacon of Segovia (d. after 1190), paraphrased Alfarabi:

> The royal virtue is composed of two virtues, one consisting of the knowledge of universal rules and the other of observation and assiduity in working and testing. A medical doctor does not become a perfect physician unless he knows universal rules or theory and unless he also shows ability in healing the sick with medicines, which is called practice.[19]

Some humanists played with science. Essentially literary, Alexander Neckham, who had taught at Paris and died as abbot of Cirencester in 1213, compiled not only a moralized account of natural history but also a dictionary of tools and domestic implements. The age's great mathematician, Leonard Fibonacci of Pisa (d. after 1240), whose own work, although theoretical, was not philosophical or speculative, kept in touch with those who were. He dedicated his manual of geometry to an astronomer and his *Book of the Abacus* to the translator and astrologer Michael Scot.

Still the gap was wide. And the lack of an efficacious technology is its principal explanation. The inability to do much with what knowledge there was led minds interested in natural science towards metaphysical speculation or to play with magic. Their difficulty was not that they postulated a necessary interlinking of all of nature's parts from the stars to the earth and a common quality, or essence, within all the elements. It was rather that neither natural philosophers nor magicians could use their possibly valid ideas to transmute metals, predict the course of nature or, save for the most obvious phenomena, show the effects of the heavenly movements on human life. Both common sense and anti-intellectualism therefore lay behind the widespread mockery of such persons, popular though they often were. To Boncompagno alchemy was futile: its adepts never accomplished anything, because, as he put it, their subject contained nothing, and nothing is true about nothing. More, 'intelligent sailors know more about the changes of the weather than learned astrologers'. Mathematicians also excited his scorn: 'you really have little or nothing to boast about because you merely count other people's money, and in this you're like common moneychangers. So don't boast about the science of numbers because there's scarcely anyone so stupid that he can't count his own money.'[20]

The vulgarities of common sense were combated, however, by strong intellectual traditions, Platonic and Aristotelian. Although Aristotle wrote the basic textbook, he was too secular, too narrow to encompass man's moods or inspire utopian hope and feelings of certitude, but Plato added an emotional melodiousness to his monotone intellectualism. The marriage of the two led to useful work, as is exemplified by the study of optics by Robert Grosseteste and his followers, including the great popularizer Roger Bacon. Trying to harmonize the illuminative mysticism of Platonic Augustinianism with Aristotelian naturalism, these latter-day Boethians linked dialectics, the experiential side of the natural sciences and mathematics to create something like a scientific method. Bacon summed it up:

There are two ways of knowing, argument and experience. Argument demonstrates and makes us concede conclusions, but it does not certify or remove doubt . . . until truth is discovered by experience . . . . Since arguments do not verify [propositions], abundant experiences are to be carefully examined by means of instruments . . . for all depends on experience.[21]

And mathematics was the science that lent experience certainty:

In mathematics we attain full truth without error and certitude without doubt in all things because mathematics provides a demonstration by means of its own necessary cause . . . . In sciences without mathematics, there are so many doubts, so many opinions, so many errors that they cannot be explained . . . since a demonstration by their own necessary causes is absent in them . . . . In natural entities there is no necessity because of the generation and corruption of their own causes and therefore of their effects . . . . In mathematics alone is there certitude without doubt.[22]

Natural science, like history, posed the problem of determination. In his *Introduction to Astronomy*, translated by John of Seville around 1133, Albumazar argued that the planets 'show that a man can choose only what they prognosticate because his choice of a thing or of its contrary is made by the spirit of reason which is implanted in the individual's living mind by means of planetary influences'.[23] John of Salisbury apprehended that this emphasis on nature or the stars' role in determining human and natural history subsumed God into nature, thus depriving both God and humanity of free will. John's opposition was nevertheless moderate. Like Aquinas later on, he saw value in astrology:

Although no trust should be put in auguries, I do not deny the value of those signs which divine disposition has given to educate God's creatures. 'For in many places and many ways, God instructs his creatures', . . . making clear what will happen now by the voices of the elements, now by the evidences of sensible and insensible things.[24]

Accommodation aside, fears inspired by astrological and natural determination helped provoke the assault on Aristotelian naturalism in Paris in the early thirteenth century.

In spite of opposition, astral, geographical and climatological theories of determination invented by the ancients and elaborated by the Arabs were accepted among intellectuals. So familiar were these by 1300 that they were used to explain the natural liberty of one's own people, as Peter Dubois did for the northern French, and the slavishness of others, as Ptolemy of Lucca did for the Greeks. Much could be accepted if, as did Aquinas, natural determination was restricted to man's lower nature. It was even permissible to find human morals determined by climate or the stars, if these were limited by man's free will, God's grace, the devil and even, as Bacon quaintly added, good or bad advice, especially in childhood. Both Albert the Great and Bacon thought the practical weakness of astronomical determination could be avoided and its value affirmed by broadening its focus. Bacon said: 'It was not Ptolemy's intention for an astrologer to render sure judgment in specific cases . . . he can, however, render a limited judgment in a general matter, one midway between the necessary and the impossible.'[25]

Such advice rarely restrained those whose inclinations were totalitarian or who responded to the human need for predictability. Bacon's own utopianism led him not only to believe in indemonstrable relationships between astronomical conjunctions and historical events, such as the 'Children's Crusade', but also to predict that astrology would be a useful tool in the forthcoming war against the Antichrist.

NATURE AND FREEDOM

In Paris, Henry Goethals of Ghent observed about the relationship of divine and natural law to positive law that 'our design is to live according to nature'.[26] An Augustinian critic of Thomistic Aristotelianism, Henry did not mean what a modern or an ancient would by this phrase, but clearly conceived of a world in which it was meaningful to link God, nature and man. Even stronger were Aquinas's opinions. Philosophy

> first proves things one needs to know in order to understand the faith . . . things proved by natural reason concerning God, namely, that He exists, that He is one, or similar things concerning Him or his creatures. Second, to make known things of the faith by means of analogy, just as Augustine in his book *On the Trinity* used many analogies taken from philosophy in order to explain the Trinity.[27]

The masters faced real quandaries. Perhaps because of Platonic influence, those who elevated nature claimed that the deity endowed mankind with intellect and matter with individuality and particular form. This was the root of the varied pantheisms attributed to Amalric of Bène and David of Dinant early in the thirteenth century, and also of the doctrine described as the unity of the intellect, assigned to Averroës and the Latin Averroists, especially Siger of Brabant. Such doctrines not only weakened a Christian's conviction of corporeal and personal immortality, but also, by making both individuation and the individual's capacity to think dependent on the emanations of a necessarily uniform divine spirit, threatened individual responsibility. Writing in 1323, Thomas Aquinas's biographer, William of Tocco, congratulated his hero:

> Quite apart from the said great volumes . . . in which he confuted the ancient heresies, he . . . destroyed the heresies of his own time, of which the first was that of Averroës, who said that there was one intellect common to all men. This error encouraged the crimes of the wicked and detracted from the virtues of the saintly, since, if there is but one mind in all men, there is no difference between men or distinction of merits. This [teaching] even penetrated the minds of the ignorant and spread so dangerously that when a certain knight was asked in Paris if he wished to purge himself of his crimes, he answered: 'If the soul of the blessed Peter is saved, mine will be also, because, since we know everything by one intellect, we share the same fate.'[28]

To defeat Platonizing Aristotelians, Aquinas turned to Aristotle and followed him in locating the source of individuation and cognition in the matter initially created and then enlivened by the divine spirit. Since no two things in nature are exactly alike, this seemed to resolve the problem of individuation and intellection. It required, however, that Thomas play again a game that had been earlier played in antiquity and Islam. The perception given to an individual by his material corporeality had somehow to be linked to the uniform divine intellect that sparked the matter into being. This was done by postulating a series of intermediary intellects – active, possible, and so on. Not only was this cumbersome, but it also indicated to some that the Thomistic solution did not differ much from that of the Averroists. From Bonaventure through the condemnations at Paris in the 1270s, the so-called Augustinians tarred the Thomists with the brush used on the Averroists.

The Augustinians also searched for a way out of the quandary. Although retaining much of the apparatus of the active and possible intellects, they simplified matters and based man's intellectual endowment on God's intervention through special illumination. Pushed far enough, the cure was as bad as the malady. On the one hand, the direct application of God's illumination to seemingly random and particular cases had the advantage of freeing a theologian from having to explain the unexplainable by means of reason, but it left him with two worlds, that of divine intellection and that of human or natural perception, linked only by unpredictable divine initiatives. This helped not at all to justify human institutions: it is lovely when God loves sinners, but ugly when he does not love those who, in human terms, are good. Confounding the regularities of divine illumination with the arbitrariness of grace, this teaching served to comfort only those who believed they had found in particular institutions – as did Joachite Franciscans – or even in their own lives – as did Francis of Assisi and some heretics – the tracks of divine intervention that had not illuminated other institutions or persons.

The other side of the illuminist argument, however, brought the theologian back to where he had come from. To assert that God had so endowed humanity that all possessed a capacity to understand and live according to moral truths was equally unsatisfactory. Theoretically, this position's weakness was that, since everyone had the capacity to be good and yet only some exercised it, an individual's free will was what enabled him or her to be good. As was later charged against Ockham, this opinion smacked of the Pelagian heresy because it weakened the primal motivating force of divine election or predestination. God endowed mankind with a capacity to be free, but, like Aristotle's deity, he had left it up to the individual to make the choice. And what did that choice have to do with grace?

Because God was the source of all lovable things like freedom, truth and beauty, it was necessary to define His freedom. Divine freedom had always posed insoluble problems, ones so weighty and frightening that they invited playfulness. The Latin father Jerome, Peter Damian, Alan of Lille and Thomas Aquinas all debated whether God could wholly restore a violated woman's virginity. Could, in short, God undo what He had done? Augustinians of Damian's stripe replied that, although God generally acted predictably, He could do what He wanted because to bow to necessity is offensive to divine omnipotence. Alan of Lille argued the other side:

> Opposing this, I say that God cannot change what has taken place, because, if He did, He would obviate His own will and orderly arrangement of things. For since He willed that there be a world, if He now wishes that there never had been one, He would go against His own will, which God forbid![29]

God's will, in sum, was so strong that He could not change His mind!

To bind divine freedom to what had been created satisfied some. Writing around 1310–13, Dante Alighieri, who elsewhere praised both Thomas Aquinas and the Averroist Siger of Brabant, overturned Augustine's celebrated denial of a moral foundation for the Roman State. Justifying secular authority, he applauded the virtue of the Romans, the spread of whose Empire was, in his opinion, divinely ordained. Derived from ancient sources, the notion that God justified the Romans was stated at length by Jordan of Osnabrück around 1281, and Ptolemy of Lucca expounded Roman natural virtue shortly thereafter. Dante copied this idea but added nature to the equation. For him, God's will was expressed in the world by the principle of right. Rome's capacity to conquer and to govern proved that its Empire was in accord with nature's right order.

> It is clear that nature ordains things with respect to their capacities, which respect is the basic right placed in things by nature. From this it follows that the natural order cannot be conserved in things without right, since the fundamental principle or right is annexed to [nature's] order . . . . The Roman people was ordained by nature to rule.[30]

What was, then, was right!

This was awkward. Since the past is the precondition of the present, the creator is bound to his creation. As Averroists were said to have put it, God cannot but produce and create, and that creation is necessarily good. Although this description of God and nature could be greeted with complacency when circumstances were happy, it relies on a limited segment of experience. Not only dualist sectarians like the Cathars believed that not everything in creation was good. Some of the orthodox were also not convinced by the familiar arguments that evil was merely the absence of good and human misery merely a punishment for sin. In a manual of love letters, Boncompagno of Signa repeated a common theme. Writing to a nun who said he was proposing to commit adultery at the expense of the Lord of Hosts, the annoyed lover replied that he would 'rather violate the bed of Him who has slain my parents and relatives, and who visits us with storms, hail and tempests, than that of any human who can harm few or none'.[31]

To describe the divine principle, moreover, as bound to its creation and prior ordinances fails to account for the unpredictable and, for each mortal, the unknowable in life. Augustinians like John Duns Scotus (d. 1308) argued that, since God is the first cause, were He bound by a necessity derived from His own nature or subject to a pressure exerted by His creation, all freedom and judgment would be destroyed among men and women. God must be free for humanity to have a hope of freedom.

Averroist or Thomist, the adherents of Aristotelian thought were aware of the insufficiencies of the teaching they espoused. Thomists escaped its limitations by emphasizing God's freedom to perform miracles – in short, by insisting on God's magic and man's free will. Their Augustinian critics dismissed such exceptions, keeping their eyes glued on the general system. What made it worse for Aquinas and other innovators of what a modern has called 'natural theology' was that Aristotelian teachings often conflict with the faith. Opposed to the Christian's historical view, with its creation, its Incarnation and other clear demarcations of human and divine history, was the static Aristotelian human and natural history, a teaching insisting on the eternity of the world or cosmos. Having extended an analogy derived from present experience back into eternity, their position was ostensibly the stronger of the two, but it clearly contradicted the faith. Never one to insist on theory to the exclusion of obedience, Aquinas recognized the problem in several debates, where he opined that the creation of the world at a given moment in time must be believed but cannot be proved by human reason.[32] Christians, he went on, who insist on trying to prove otherwise merely make themselves the laughing stock of unbelievers.

That fun could be poked at revelation's historical scheme is shown by John of Jandun (d. 1328). Commenting on the Jewish and Christian creation, he wrote:

> The gentile philosophers did not know this method of creation, and this is not astonishing because it cannot be known from sensible evidence . . . especially because it . . . only occurred once, and it is now a very long time since that happened. Those therefore who understand this kind of creation know it by another way, that is, by the authority of the saints, by revelation and by things of the sort.[33]

Elsewhere John went on to assert about a similar matter that this kind of belief is best learned in childhood by dint of repetition. Critics of Averroist Aristotelianism and Thomistic theology hunted for ways to release God from bondage to his own creation. From Augustinians of Bonaventure's persuasion through Duns Scotus to the later Ockhamists, they criticized past attempts to demonstrate the deity's existence and qualities by arguing from analogies seen in the natural world. To cease to argue back from effect to cause was costly, however. What appeared good to man could no longer be said to be necessarily God's good. Only the moral injunctions and ecclesiastical institutions explicitly found in scripture were beyond question. Since the Bible offered only the Deuteronomic code, Christ's laws of love and Paul's recommendations, it directly bolstered few ecclesiastical institutions. How this threatened the institutional structure of the Church and its claimed superiority over the secular State was already clear in John of Paris's tract *On Royal and Papal Power* of 1302.

DEITY AND CERTITUDE

The excision of the accretions of the somewhat naturalist theology required care. It was impermissible to assert, as did a proposition condemned at Paris in 1277, 'that nothing can be known about God save that He exists or has being', since scripture revealed many of His actions.[34] The proponents of the deity's freedom could get pretty close to this proposition, however, by falling back on orthodox thought. In the Lateran Council of 1215 where Joachim of Fiore and Amalric of Bène were castigated, it was asserted that 'there is no similarity to be discerned between the creator and his creatures that is not overtopped by a discernible dissimilarity'.[35] Even Alan of Lille, a leader among those expanding the role of reason in theology, said that the terms with which God is described differ from those with which mankind is, hence there is no true similitude of God and man. Humans may be rational, but God is reason itself. Although such distinctions also appealed to Aquinas, the Augustinians and Duns Scotus used them to weaken naturalist theology irreparably. If much can be learned from faith and divine illumination, Scotus said, unaided human reason can know no more than the fact that both God and man have being. The analogies derived from humanity's brief life cannot define that wilful, all-perceiving and eternal principle of freedom.

Intellectuals turned back to views like those with which Bernard of Clairvaux assailed Abelard:

Since he was prepared to use reason to explain everything, even things which were above reason, he presumed against both reason and faith. What is more hostile to reason than to try to transcend reason by means of reason? And what is more hostile to faith than to refuse to believe what cannot be attained by reason?[36]

To Bernard, as to the later Augustinians, believing derived from direct divine illumination and therefore produced certitude. Against the rationalists' belief that theology had to lean on the crutch of philosophy for its proofs, Bernard asked the question:

How do we understand [the truth]? Disputation does not understand it; holiness does, if, in some way, the incomprehensible can be understood. But unless it can be comprehended, the apostle would not have said, 'that we be able to comprehend with all the saints'. The saints therefore understand. Do you want to know how? If you are holy, you understand and know. If not, be holy, and you will know by experience.[37]

Bernard's opinion that Abelard misused reason attracted others than irrationalists. Describing the debates in the theological faculty of Paris about the character and origin of human intellect and other matters, the 'Averroist' John of Jandun wrote in 1323: 'Of what use these are, and how they advance the Catholic faith, God alone knows. Anyone can see this for himself, anyone, that is, who [honestly] seeks . . . from [these divines] the rationale of their arguing in this way.'[38] Bacon remarked that theologians overstepped their bounds when they discussed such problems as matter, species, being and ways of knowing; they should merely accept philosophers' solutions. John of Jandun said in effect that each discipline, theology and philosophy, was autonomous in presuppositions, methods and results, and would have agreed with the earlier Boethius of Dacia, whose opinions had been questioned in 1277 by Stephen Tempier's commission at Paris. In his *On the Eternity of the World* Boethius had separated the spheres comprehensible by philosophy or reason from those comprehensible by faith or theology. Debating the familiar difference between the Christian creation in history and the philosopher's eternity of the world, he concluded that 'two things are clear: one is that natural [reason]'s eternity of the world cannot contradict the Christian faith, and the other is that natural reason cannot prove that the world . . . was ever new'.[39] There were, he said in effect, two truths, one in theology, the other in philosophy.

Although double truth was called an Averroist heresy, the separation of the disciplines was going on apace, and even the censure in

1277 of the Parisian Averroists had the inadvertent effect of strengthening it. Some severed the disciplines by finding languages appropriate to each, and by giving to one, theology, the possession of a higher truth. The Parisian Peter of Poitiers (d. 1205) observed that an opinion of the ancient Boethius, a philosopher and not a theologian, reflected probability more than certainty. Earlier, Bernard of Clairvaux had chided Abelard for applying philosophy's probabilities to theology, in which only certitude ruled. The Cistercian's opinion was like that of the later Bonaventure and was used to attack Thomistic theology. Around 1300 the majority of the schoolmen limited natural philosophy to the production of probable propositions.

Natural philosophers, however, refused to be deprived of certitude. Astrologer and medical doctor, Peter of Abano was reported to say that he and others dealt with things describable 'by human certitude' and not, as did theologians, with those held by simple credulity. This view was not devoid of tradition. Alan of Lille earlier wrote that 'properly speaking, there is no science of God. For when it is said that the science of God is known, reference is being made rather to the knowledge of the faith and of credulity than to the knowledge of certitude.'[40] Besides, the results of Robert Grosseteste's repeated experiences in optics gave him a feeling similar to Bernard's illumination by divine light.

Nor could theology do without probability. The rising tide that sought to cut away all authorities, ancient or modern, other than scripture actually encouraged theological probabilism, that is, the weighing of one authority or historical precedent against another. Arguing from scripture against Bernard of Clairvaux's stand that the secular sword was to be used at the behest of the Church, John of Paris blandly remarked that the Cistercian's opinion was of little weight. When the same Dominican's treatise on the Eucharist was being examined by the bishop and doctors of Paris in 1305–6, they reported that John

asserted in the presence of the college of the masters of theology that he holds that either way of assuming the body of Christ to be on the altar is a probable opinion, and that he finds both approved by Holy Scripture and the opinions of the saints. Furthermore, he says that nothing [concerning the Eucharist] has been determined by the Church, and that nothing therefore falls under the faith, and that, if he had said otherwise, he would not have spoken correctly. And he who would pertinaciously assert either one of these options of itself to fall under the faith should incur anathema.[41]

The attempt to separate philosophy from theology, 'learning' (*scientia*) from 'wisdom' (*sapientia*), by giving the latter certitude's superiority and the former probability's inferiority was bound to fail. Of course, nobody doubted that the two spheres were distinct. The glosses on Plato's *Timaeus* by William of Conches (d. 1153–4) had long ago distinguished between the Creator's and nature's work: the former created 'from nothing' and performed miracles; the latter only according to the rules placed in it at its creation. Albert the Great observed in his commentary on Aristotle's *On the Heavens and the World* that the business of a philosopher was not to discuss God's omnipotence or his miracles but rather what happens in nature by reason of its inherent causes.

This simple distinction became significant when it touched on moral life here on earth. In his *On Monarchy*, Dante defined humanity's aims:

> Unerring providence has ordained two objectives man must seek: the bliss of this life which consists in the use of his own powers and is configured by the terrestrial paradise, and the bliss of eternal life which consists in the enjoyment of the vision of God to which man's own powers cannot ascend unless aided by divine illumination, and which is made understandable by the celestial paradise.[42]

Like Aquinas, Dante believed that the former objective was attained by the exercise of moral and intellectual virtues and the latter by the theological virtues and spiritual teaching transcending human reason. Unlike the heavenly objective, the earthly objective could never be perfectly achieved. Writing shortly before 1310, Engelbert of Volkersdorf, abbot of Admont, said: 'The objective of present felicity in the temporal kingdom is to labour continuously with zeal and joy to build its peace . . . even if it can never really be obtained fully.'[43] The objectives, then, were clear, but the problem was to determine whether moral and political virtues were valid of themselves or only in terms of their relation to celestial ends.

A limited autonomy was traditionally allowed to humankind's natural moral virtues. Ever moderate, Thomas Aquinas felt that political virtues were not morally indifferent but intrinsically good, and were meritorious if informed by God's grace. An anonymous commentary produced in the arts faculty at Paris just after 1277 advances the case that God helps those who help themselves, the author contending that

> felicity derives from both a divine cause and a human one. It derives . . .

originally from God as a primal and remote cause; in an immediate sense, however, this same felicity is from a human cause. Whence happiness is not immediately from God, but instead from God when man works with Him. Whence
felicity consists in human actions, because it is necessary for man to labour if he
would be happy.[44]

John of Paris reinforced this by affirming that, pagan or Christian,
humans are God's 'assistants', and 'it can be said that the moral
virtues [they] acquire [on earth] can be perfect without the theological virtues, nor, except for a certain accidental perfection, are
they made more perfect by the [latter] virtues'.[45] A secular morality
free of Christianity had begun to appear, and with it the ambition
of discovering a firm link between God and humanity, between
heaven and earth, began to fade.

Utopians, however, did not give up easily, and the years around
1300 witnessed the assault of their forlorn hope. Raymond Llull's
scheme of universal knowledge lent certitude to natural philosophy
and theology by means of mathematics. So did Roger Bacon's:
'Since it is proved that philosophy cannot be known unless mathematics is known, and everybody knows that theology cannot be
known unless philosophy is known, it is necessary for theologians
to know mathematics.'[46] This unified knowledge will be useful because, by means of it,

faithful Christians will attain the reward of future blessedness . . . . The republic
of the faithful shall so dispose its temporal goods that all things useful both to
individuals and the multitude for conserving bodily health and a wonderful pro-
longation of life shall be effected in material and moral goods and in discretion,
peace and justice . . . . All nations of the infidels predestined to eternal life shall
be converted to the great glory of the Christian faith . . . . Those foreknown to
be damned who cannot be converted shall be restrained by the ways and works
of wisdom rather than by civil wars.[47]

But humanity's natural endowment was not up to the task, and
direct divine illumination was required. Bacon confessed 'that,
through his own industry, man cannot know how to please God . .
. nor how to deal with his neighbour or even with himself, but is
wanting in those things until the truth is revealed'. What was
needed was

that a revelation should be made to one man only that he is to be the mediator
between God and man and the vicar of God here on earth, a man to whom the
whole human race should be subject and who ought to be believed without
contradiction . . . . He is [to be] the legislator and the highest priest, who has

the plenitude of power in spiritual and temporal things, a 'human God' as Avicenna says commenting on . . . the *Metaphysics* 'whom it is licit to adore after God'.[48]

This curious fantasy shows how utopians rejected rational theology and philosophy, and instead tried to force God and nature to be one. Others, like John of Jandun and the Ockhamists, found reason limited, and resigned themselves to thinking that God and nature were worlds apart. From whichever side they approached the problem, however, they had one thing in common. They no longer believed that unaided human reason could construct a Christian synthesis of God, humankind and nature, and hence the confidence that had animated intellectuals from Peter Abelard to Thomas Aquinas was beginning to weaken.

NOTES AND REFERENCES

1   *De principis instructione* 1, 11 in *Rolls Series* XXVIII, viii, 42–3.
2   *Memoria seculorum*, prologue in *MGH SS* XXII, 103.
3   *De potestate regia et papali* 10 (ed. Bleienstein), 113.
4   *In epistolam ad Hebraeos* 9, 5 cited in Chenu, *La théologie au douzième siècle*, 76.
5   *Rhetorica novissima*, prologue in *BIMA* II, 252.
6   *Summa artis notariae* I *praefatio* (Venice, 1583) I, 2v, and *Code* 3, 38, 3.
7   *Summa theologiae* I–II, 97, 1c.
8   *Tractatus super quatuor evangelia* (ed. Ernesto Buonaiuti, Rome, 1930), 195, and Ecclesiastes 1:8.
9   *Dialogus* I, 10 in *PL* CLXXXVIII, 1157.
10 *Ibid.*, 1160.
11 Kamlah, *Apokalypse und Geschichtstheologie* 118, and Revelation 6:5.
12 Letter to a novice in Jean Mabillon, *Vetera analecta* (Paris, 1723, rprt), 477b.
13 *Tractatus super quatuor evangelia* (ed. Buonaiuti), 80, and Luke 2:25 ff.
14 *De gestis Philippi II* by Grundmann, *Religiöse Bewegung im Mittelalter*, 365–6, and Leviticus 26:10.
15 Second article in Heinrich Denifle, 'Das Evangelium aeternum und die Commission zu Anagni' in *Archiv für Litteratur- und Kirchengeschichte des Mittelalters* II (1900), 112.
16 Recounted in Salimbene's *Cronica* 15 in *MGH SS* XXXII, 238.
17 *Arbor vitae crucifixae Jesu Christi* 5, 1 (Venice, 1485, rptd), 422a.
18 A composite quotation from the *Opus maius* 4, 16 on Mathematics and Astrology (ed. Bridges), I, 269 and 402, and Psalm 72 (73):9.

19   *De divisione philosophie, de partibus practice philosophie* in Ludwig Baur (ed.), *Beiträge zur Geschichte der Philosophie des Mittelalters* (Münster, 1903) IV, ii–iii, 135.

20   *Rhetorica novissima* 8, 3 in *BIMA* II, 289b.

21   *Opus maius* 6, 1 and 12 (ed. Bridges), II, 166 and 201, a composite quotation.

22   *Ibid.* 4, 1, 13 (ed. Bridges), I, 105–6.

23   *Abu Ma'Shar and Latin Aristotelianism in the Twelfth Century*, 128n.

24   *Policraticus* 2, 2 (ed. Webb), I, 417a. See Hebrews 1:1.

25   *Opus maius* 4, *judicia astronomiae* (ed. Bridges) I, 245.

26   *Quodlibet* 2, question 17, cited in Lagarde, *La naissance de l'esprit laïque* III, 253.

27   *In Boetium de trinitate* cited in Chenu, *La théologie comme science au treizième siècle*, 89.

28   *Vita S. Thomae Aquinatis* 4 in *AA SS*, 1 March 664 BC.

29   *Quoniam homines* 1, 2, 4 in Glorieux (ed.), *Archives d'histoire doctrinale et littéraire du moyen âge* XXVIII (1953), 233.

30   *De monarchia* 2, 6 (ed. Gustavo Vinay, Florence, 1950), 148.

31   *Rota veneris* (ed. Baethgen), 21–22.

32   *Quodlibetum* 12, 6, 1 and *Quodlibetum* 3, 15, 2, 2 in Spiazzi (ed.), *Opuscula philosophica*, 277b and 68b–9a.

33   *Quaestiones super libros physicorum* cited in MacClintock, *Perversity and Error: Studies on the 'Averroist' John of Jandun*, 91–2 and 173–4n.

34   Denifle, *Cartularium universitatis Parisiensis* I, 553: Error No. 215 of Item No. 473.

35   *Liber extra* 1, 1, 2 in *CICan* II, 6–7.

36   *Contra quaedam capitula errorum Abaelardi* 1, 1 in *PL* CLXXXII, 1055.

37   *De consideratione* 5, 14 in *Sancti Bernardi opera* III, 492. See Ephesians 3:18.

38   Chapter II of his *Tractatus de laudibus Parisius* (eds Taranne and Leroux de Lincy, Paris, 1856).

39   MacClintock, *Perversity and Error*, 100.

40   *Quoniam homines* 1, 1 in Glorieux (ed.), *Archives d'histoire doctrinale et littéraire du moyen âge* XVIII (1953), 136.

41   Denifle, *Cartularium universitatis Parisiensis* I, 120, No. 656.

42   *De monarchia* 3, 16 (ed. Vinay), 280–2.

43   From his *De ortu et progressu et fine regnorum et precipue regni et imperii Romani* 18, in Vinay's edition of Dante's *De monarchia*, 284–5n.

44   A Paris manuscript quoted in MacClintock, *Perversity and Error*, 165n.

45   *De potestate regia et papali* 18 (ed. Bleienstein), 163.

46   *Opus maius* 4, 4 (ed. Bridges), I, 175.

47   *Compendium studii philosophiae* I in Brewer (ed.), *Opera Fr. Baconi hactenus inedita*, 395.

48   *Baconis operis maioris pars septima seu moralis pholosophia* 1, 1 (ed. Massa), 8.

21

ENTHUSIASM AND HERESY

DOUBT AND HERESY

Quoted by the cardinals at Anagni in 1255 examining the works of Joachim of Fiore, Gratian defined heresy as when 'each man chooses for himself the teaching he thinks best. Whoever understands Holy Scripture in a manner other than is required by the judgment of the Holy Spirit by whom it was written, is to be called an heretic even if he does not leave the Church.'[1] The Holy Spirit had inspired the Church Militant, that is, the popes, hierarchy and 'divines' here on earth. Heresy was to diverge from them.

But people did diverge, and scepticism, doubt and simple disbelief were pervasive. Since the days of Gregory VII, for example, clerical celibacy had been prized and enforced, but the lively dissent seen around 1100 in such tracts as that of the Norman Anonymous was never stilled. It echoed through the Platonic school of Chartres into the thirteenth century, becoming popular among the laity or those who wrote what laymen read. The type of argument employed may be seen in Andrew the Chaplain's *On Love* of 1184–6. Condemned by Stephen Tempier's commission of theologians in 1277, and thereafter enthusiastically translated from Latin into vernacular tongues, Andrew's tract affirmed that, even for clerks, from love comes virtue.

> I believe that God cannot be gravely offended by love, for what is done because nature obliges us to can easily be purged by expiation. Besides, it is unsuitable to call criminal the [act] in which the greatest good in this life has its origin and without which no one on earth can be considered worthy of praise.[2]

Besides, the idea that celibacy was unnatural was widespread, especially among layfolk. A poet of the quality and popularity of the Parisian John of Meung pronounced in his *Romance of the Rose* that almost all the virtues of the religious were unlovely: poverty was ugly, abstinence and chastity unnatural and humility and obedience refused humanity's high place in nature's order.

People were also ambivalent about miracles. Because chronicles and histories propagated a Christian view of the world, they were crowded with references to these events. All the same, a common lament was that they no longer happened because of the 'corruption' of the Church. Anti-Hohenstaufen, Caesarius of Heisterbach loved telling stories against Philip of Swabia, king of the Romans. According to this Cistercian, Philip, hearing that the Templars were miraculously hidden from the Saracens who surrounded them by singing a verse from Psalm 26, sourly observed that, had he been there, he'd have dropped that psalm and run for it. Salimbene records how Boncompagno of Signa made fun of the Dominican miracle worker and preacher John Schio of Vicenza. At the time of the Alleluia of 1233, a widespread political and religious movement against the Hohenstaufen, Boncompagno announced at Bologna that he would fly. When the crowd assembled, he, having worn wings but not flown, drily congratulated its members on their credulity. When Florentine wiseacres heard that John was about to visit their town, they said: 'For God's sake, don't let him come here. He raises the dead, and we're already so many that our city can't hold us.'[3]

To scepticism as a source of hostility to miracles may be added dislike of clerical manipulativeness. Joinville tells that Louis IX praised Simon of Montfort, commander of the Albigensian crusaders, because he refused to rush out to witness a nearby miracle whereby the Lord's body had become flesh and blood in the hands of a priest, thus confuting Catharism. His faith being firm, said the king, Simon had no need of proof. Besides, what soldier enjoys the cries of those who both urge him to risk his life and draw attention to themselves?

The Franciscan Salimbene exemplifies the age's mixture of credulity and disbelief. Franciscan saints were sound in his opinion, but he happily recounted stories against Dominican ones and against those of the Friars of the Sack. Cults fostered by the secular clergy were invariably frauds, and he was especially hostile to plebeian holy men. Speaking of Albert, the Lion Banner Bearer for the wine-porters' guild of Cremona, he ascribed the spread of his cult to Parma and Reggio around 1279 'partly to the hope of the sick to become well, partly to the desire of the curious to see novelties, partly to the secular clergy's envy of the modern orders and partly to the profit gained by bishops and canons from such a cult'.[4] This Guelph then added politics: exiled Ghibelline nobles hoped to return home during the wave of plebeian good feeling precipitated by the elevation of a worker to sanctity. He was here referring to the kind of social alliance between the top and bottom of society that threatened the mixed aristocratic and middle-class Guelph popular parties ruling so many Italian town republics after 1250.

The faith itself evoked doubt. Joachim of Fiore likened doubt about predestination to the devil's temptation of Christ during the forty days. This was especially hard on monks, who had surrendered so much.

> If you are not elected, you vainly exhaust yourself by sustaining such labours, for no one can be saved who is not chosen; if, however, you are chosen, even if you spare yourselves so that you are idle when the Lord comes, you will be saved, because no man of the elect can perish.[5]

Joachim's solution was dour. If you seek profit from your faith, you breach the law of Matthew 4:7: 'You shall not tempt the Lord your God.' The abbot then sounded what he thought was a more hopeful note: 'Although we cannot be certain in this life whether we are reprobate or chosen, nevertheless just as the sign of election is to act strongly and be strengthened, so is the sign of reprobation to fall from rigour with one's power of justice enervated.'[6] This teaching of the external signs of salvation required believers to show by a dogged happiness that they did not despair. The deity, so to speak, was keeping mum. As a manual for parish clergy put it: 'Nobody should presume to investigate why God wished to create men who he knew would fall or why he wished to create angels whose fall he certainly foreknew . . . . These works of God and others are beyond human understanding.'[7]

The *Book against Heresy* produced between 1184 and 1207 by Durand of Huesca's Waldensians reported that the Cathars argued that Catholic teaching on predestination meant that, since God created everything and foreknew what it was, He had created evil. In a work composed between 1241 and 1250, the Lombard Cathars said that Lucifer and the fallen angels could not have been good before they fell from heaven, because, if they had been,

> from the very beginning, God [had] knowingly created his angels of such imperfection that they were unable to resist evil. Hence God, who is good, holy, just, wise and fair . . . is the cause and beginning of evil, an opinion which must be wholly rejected. Hence one must believe that there are two first principles, one good and the other evil, the latter being the cause of angelic imperfection and likewise of all evil.[8]

Orthodox Christians and moderate dualists countered this argument by asserting that it deprived humanity of free will, thus inducing despair and destroying individual responsibility. Yet dualist doctrines were hardly more destructive of human optimism than orthodoxy. Discussing those predestined to salvation, Thomas Aquinas wrote:

> It may be said that a good proportionate to the ordinary state of nature is found in many and is lacking in few, but that a good that exceeds that ordinary state is discovered only in very few. It is evident that there are many who have knowledge sufficient for governing their own lives, and few, who are called fools or idiots, who lack this knowledge, but there are also very few who are able to attain a profound knowledge of intelligible things [that is, of philosophy]. Since, therefore, eternal blessedness, which consists in the vision of God, exceeds the ordinary state of nature (especially because grace has been weakened by the corruption of original sin) there are very few indeed who are saved.[9]

Faced with this vision, some dualists such as the Rhenish Luciferians lauded the fallen angels, proclaiming that Lucifer was God's brother who had been unjustly cast out of heaven, and that the fraternal victor was too cruel to be worshipped.

If philosophical learning was like salvation, damnation was like death. The Luciferians cursed God for damning Lucifer as did the orthodox Boncompagno of Signa for condemning mankind to death. Caesarius of Heisterbach tells about Landgrave Lewis II of Thuringia (d. 1168). Literate and hard on the clergy, as Caesarius puts it, he loved Psalm 115:16: 'The heavens, even the heavens are the Lord's: but the earth has he given to the children of men' − thence arguing that there is no link between heaven and earth. He was wont to say that, if predestined to salvation, no evil deed would cost him heaven; and, if foreknown to damnation, no good one would gain it for him. Urged to repent lest he die in sin, he replied: 'When the day of my death comes, I will die. I cannot delay it by living well nor advance it by living evilly.'[10]

365

Anti-Christian polemic reinforced natural scepticism. Muslims ridiculed monogyny, clerical celibacy and trinitarian 'polytheism'. Much of the evidence about this kind of thought, at least that which concerns princes and prelates, comes from the mouths of their enemies. Gregory IX's letter of 1239 condemning Frederick II Hohenstaufen was widely distributed. The pope closed this lengthy missive by asserting that Frederick enjoyed repeating that three impostors, Moses, Jesus and Mohammed, had deceived the world. Nor did he believe in the Virgin Birth because none is born save of the carnal commerce of man and woman, 'and a man ought not believe anything he cannot prove by natural means and reason'.[11] According to hostile witnesses deposing before Clement V in 1310–11, Boniface VIII when a cardinal observed that, although the mob may think otherwise, no educated person could believe in the Trinity, Virgin Birth or the real presence in the Eucharist. These questions had surfaced when discussing the relative validity of Christian and Muslim law, wherein the cardinal had observed that

> no law is divine; all has been invented by men. Eternal penalties are there included for only one reason, namely that men shall be restrained from evil deeds by fear of punishment. Therefore this law has no truth other than that, because of fear of punishment, men will live peacefully.[12]

These tales were not pure fabrications. Anent Frederick II's incredulity, the Muslim historian Sibt ibn al-Jauzi of Damascus (d. 1257) remarked that the emperor was known to be an atheist who poked fun at Christianity. Such scepticism had a popular base. In 1288 the harangue of a Bolognese statute stated that

> Because it often happens that barmen and dice players in the streets and public squares of the commune of Bologna . . . utter truly detestable and horrible words against God and His Mother, and their tumult puts many difficulties in the way of the preachers who announce the word of God in these squares,[13]

such vile persons were threatened with punishment.

In 1299 a student at Bologna told the inquisitors that a farmer from a nearby village said that the proposition that Merlin was God's son was as easily demonstrable as it was about Jesus. The sceptical naturalism of the statements attributed to Frederick II and Boniface VIII is paralleled by Boncompagno of Signa's remark about Tuscans who denied the afterlife. They imitated the ancient Athenians by 'mendaciously asserting that, because it can be shown demonstratively, everything proceeds from the elements and all individual things individually revert into their elements'.[14] Caesarius of Heisterbach speaks of a female recluse who, urged by an abbot to recover her faith in God, asked: 'Who knows if God exists or if he has angels, souls or the kingdom of heaven? Who has seen them? Who has returned thence and told us what he has seen?'[15] No less an intellectual than Siger of Brabant averred that all the world's philosophers could not convince anyone of personal immortality, and Aquinas confessed that unaided human reason could not know what the beatitude of the future life really was. The Parisian condemnations in 1277 also record that university artists asserted that bliss was found only in this life and that bodily death was so awful that it was silly to worry about hell.

The Church was powerless against this kind of doubt. Attempts to confront it often leaned on vulgar reasoning. Alexander Neckham praised the efficacy of dialectics, telling about a Parisian scholar who lay dying. The youth asserted that, unless convinced by reason, he could not believe in personal resurrection. A fellow student argued in this wise:

> If you believe in the future resurrection, this resurrection will either be or will not be. If you believe it will be and it is not, this belief will not harm you. If you believe it will be and it is, this belief will be of advantage to you. Now, if you do not believe and there should be a future resurrection, eternal woe will fall on you. It is therefore better to believe than not to believe.[16]

According to Alexander, the youth closed his eyes in happy belief.

If so, his awakening must have been rude. John of Joinville tells of an old woman of Acre carrying a brazier of coals and a bucket of water. She wished, she said, to burn heaven up and douse hell's fires so humanity would act not for reward but rather for love of God. The Franciscan Jacopone of Todi (d. *circa* 1306) said he cared not if he were saved or damned, just so long as God would tell what he could do for Him. Jacopone was saying that those who love either love or freedom should love them for themselves and not for any good they may do them or their world. To both the elegant seneschal of Champagne and the one-time lawyer of Todi, Alexander's Parisian had broken the law: 'You shall not tempt the Lord your God.' With Him, there is no *quid pro quo*.

What held doubt in check was not the ability of churchmen to prove personal resurrection, free will, man's freedom to make moral choices or similar propositions. Such can be believed but, as was often then stated, they assuredly cannot be proved. The reason for belief seems to have been twofold. First, church teaching was no less capable of gaining the trust of its adherents than other systems also based on indemonstrable propositions that had preceded it or were to follow. Second, the period from 1150 to 1300 was one when the relatively beneficent material conditions of life combined with the newness of the Church's institutional and mental mechanisms to reinforce Latin cultural confidence. Wishing not to disbelieve, many were bemused for a time.

Although their genesis had something to do with the above, most divergent ideas and sects replaced orthodoxy with variants of a similar metaphysical character. If Cathars usually mocked miracles, they also used them. Around 1320 a Cathar preacher tried to prove the truth of metempsychosis, or transmigration of souls, by telling of a Perfect who, 'while standing next to a fountain, declared he recalled that, when he was a horse, he lost one of his shoes in the bed of the said fountain while drinking. He had the said horseshoe looked for and there it was!'[17] Heretics, in short, were not those who believed too little, but rather those who believed too much, and scepticism helped orthodoxy almost as much as it did heresy. Initially Joachite, Salimbene provides a good example. His ardent friends persuaded that the new age would begin in 1260, the date on which the death of 'their' Antichrist, Frederick II, was prophesied. When the Hohenstaufen suddenly died ten years before the projected date, Salimbene, already out of his depth among these sectaries, dropped the teaching, resolving never again to believe anything he had not actually seen – unless, of course, it was safely orthodox.

DIVERGENCE

Several sects showed Judaic influence, and one such, the Passagians of around 1200, were clearly judaizers, defending circumcision, the Jewish sabbath and the primacy of the Mosaic law. The partial parallel between Cathar teachings and those of the Kabbalah, strong among Mediterranean Jews at this time, with its metempsychosis and dualism, has often been noted. Since the Kabbalah often reinforced attacks on Maimonidean rationalism, it paralleled the hostility to Aristotelian natural reason so strongly expressed by many

Christian utopian enthusiasts, both orthodox and heretic. Of contacts between Jews and Cathars little is known except that the orthodox claimed that there were such. The main outside influence on Latin Cathars was probably Byzantine. Before 1167, for example, they held to the Bogomil or Bulgar doctrine that Lucifer, cast out of heaven by God, founded evil. In that year, however, Niketas, a Cathar bishop of Constantinople, visited the Lombard churches and is said to have assembled a council at St Felix de Caraman near Toulouse. Ordaining bishops in both areas, he persuaded the Cathar clergy to adopt his church's rigorous dualism whereby Lucifer was regarded as the creator of the material world and co-eternal with God. In spite of the reality of foreign influences, gnostic dualism was undoubtedly an innate part of Latin Christianity and required little external stimulus in order to flower.

Most critical enthusiasts were antisacerdotal. Hugh Speroni of Piacenza averred around 1177 that merit and not office gave priests their power, and merit was hard to come by. Writing between 1179 and 1202, Alan of Lille remarked that the Waldensians quoted Pope Gregory I to argue 'that the power to bind and loose was given only to those who preserve and live both the teaching and the life of the apostles'.[18] So far, thought some, had the clergy fallen from the apostolic life that their sacraments were all vitiated. This view turned enthusiasts into heretics: the true believer must cleanse the corrupt Church or secede to found a purer one. According to the ex-heretic Buonacorso of Milan, writing between 1176 and 1190, this was the opinion of the Arnoldists, a pre-Waldensian sect deriving its name from Arnold of Brescia, the companion of Abelard, radical reformer and leader of Rome's revolt against the temporal dominion of the popes, executed in 1155.

Such assaults could be nipped in the bud, the orthodox believed, by insisting that the merit of the officiant was not the basis of sacramental validity. An argument appealing to ordinary penitents came from Alan of Lille:

> All priests have the power of binding and loosing, but those only who adhere to the life and teaching of the apostles use this power justly. . . . Absolutely speaking, however, the remission or retention of sins is also performed by those who are not holy, for God gives his blessing to the worthy seeker even by means of an unworthy minister.[19]

This was codified at the time of Innocent III in the doctrine *ex opere operato*, wherein grace was conferred by a sacrament irrespective of the merit of the person administering it.

If the moral quality of the officiant bore no relation to sacramental validity, however, this teaching destroyed individual responsibility and hence society. Reinforcement was needed, and that turned out to be the idea of intention. In the moralizing excitements of the Gregorian revolution, this ancient idea was revived, being expressed, for example, in Peter Abelard's *Ethics*, where he pronounced that an individual's merit or demerit does not lie so much in what he or she does as in what they intend to do. Hugh of St Victor applied this teaching to the sacraments: for efficacity, a priest must intend to perform them. By the time of the great scholastics the matter was complex. Some, like Bonaventure, opined that God would supply man's deficiencies; others, like Aquinas, that habitual or virtual intention – that is, the lack of a positively perverse intention – was enough. But few indeed cared to maintain that, even with God supplying, one who did not believe in the faith or was a heretic could perform or receive a valid sacrament. In short, however hard the doctors tried to lock the door, it always came unlatched again; the problem was, as of old, to define what was a heretic.

Enthusiasts, both orthodox and heretical, found simony to be a heresy. This attitude derived from the Gregorian age when the 'reformers' had disinterred this ancient weapon to beat the clergy loyal to the old state churches. Simony could also be broadly construed, occurring not only when a sacrament was purchased or an office bought, but also when they were obtained by means of, or exercised under the shadow of, family influence, favour, vice or even hypocrisy. Since simony was heretical, enthusiasts could say that believers should not attend heretical conventicles and sacraments. Had not, as Peter Damian reported, the Vallumbrosan radicals in Florence in the mid eleventh century asserted that, because of simony, there was no pope, no king, no archbishop and no priest, and had not thousands of men, deceived by the 'trumpery and incantations' of false sacraments, died without a valid sacrament? In 1218 two branches of the Waldensian movement, the Lombard Poor of Christ and the French Poor of Lyons, met to heal differences at Bergamo. The French accepted the orthodox position on sacerdotal authority; the Lombards refused, alleging that Christians must obey God, not man. Although admitting that God would supply deficiencies, the Lombards cited Gratian who attributed to Gregory I a statement that simoniacs

> cannot be priests, whence it is written: damnation of the giver, damnation of the receiver. This is the heresy of simony. In what way, therefore, can they who are not holy and are damned sanctify others? How can they transmit or receive the body of Christ? He who is cursed, how can he bless?[20]

It was but a short step from this to propose that only good men, those predestined to salvation, were true priests, that, in short, there was a priesthood of all true believers, lay and clerical alike. This view was attributed to the Arnoldists and to later groups among the Waldensians. According to Stephen of Bourbon, an inquisitor in the Rhone valley between 1232 and 1249, some Waldensians held that women could be priests. At the conference of Bergamo in 1218 the Lombard Poor charged that the extreme views of their French associates on this point would lead them to admit not only women but also whores to the priesthood.

Lay antisacerdotalism was restrained by the fact that enthusiasts lived within a Church in which, until after 1300, lay religious passions were normally channelled into monastic or quasi-monastic groups. Even for the orthodox religious, sacraments were of limited importance, the way of life almost everything. Thus, for example, the French Waldensians at Bergamo accepted the sacerdotal authority of priests ordained by Rome. Vital things, preaching and exemplaristic living in common like the apostles, however, they entrusted to lay rectors and ministers elected by the community. The compromise reached at Bergamo provided that the community 'gathered together in one body . . . may jointly choose provosts for life or rectors for a set term whichever seems more useful to the community or the maintenance of peace'.[21]

Lay direction usually faltered as time went on. In orthodox movements, this was exemplified by the Franciscan order. Among the divergent, the larger sects seem to have evolved towards hierarchy and sacerdotalism, and would surely have gone further had they been allowed to grow freely. The Cathars were early divided into simple believers and Perfects, and higher officers appeared – bishops, for example – as early as 1164. These were initially elected but, in the thirteenth century, were chosen by the hierarchy. Perfects were celibate, and women, although permitted into this grade and even into the diaconate, were never admitted to higher office.

Among sects of Waldensian type this evolution did not always take place, but when Bernard Gui summed up available information in his manual of 1323–4, he noted that the sect had a self-perpetuating celibate cadre of bishops, priests and deacons from which women were excluded. Practical need may also have encouraged this tendency. The Latin father Jerome, the Norman Anonymous of the late eleventh century and Marsiglio of Padua all said that the threat of schism had prompted the growth of the hierarchy in antiquity. All divergent movements, including the Cathars, suffered from scission, and hierarchy based on priestly magic and socio-sexual differentiations was a way to combat this tendency.

Hierarchy and sacerdotalism were, however, braked by the enthusiasts' belief that they had a way of living or knowing that made them superior to others. This élitism derived from the monks who thought of themselves as already citizens of the supernal Jerusalem. Significant here was the teaching of Joachim of Fiore and the later Joachites about historical progress. The 'spiritual men' of the third age were to live the contemplative life, enjoying an understanding of scripture granted by the Holy Spirit, one far above that of the clergy of the second age who, bound by the compromises of the active life, enjoyed only a rational understanding. This gnosis made the theology of such sects somewhat inconsistent. The learned Amalricians crushed at Paris in 1210 were inspired by a Platonic pantheism presumably taught by the Parisian master Amalric of Bène and remotely derived from John the Scot Erigena. Although believing that God was everything, they nevertheless did not conclude that all men were equal but rather that he who knows with the Apostle Paul that 'God worketh all in all' cannot sin. Many sectaries thought of themselves as God's special vessels into which the Holy Spirit or the Saviour had been or was about to be poured.

Divergent gnosticism spiritualized religious conceptions in wonderful ways. The Amalricians held that 'hell is nothing other than ignorance, and paradise nothing but the knowledge of the truth . . . and this full knowledge is the resurrection, nor is any other resurrection to be expected'.[22] The one-time heretic and later inquisitor Rainier Sacconi reported in 1250 that John of Lugio of Bergamo (one of the few Cathar intellectuals known by name) said that

'the primal principle of evil has many names in Holy Scripture: evil, iniquity, cupidity, impiety, sin, pride, death, hell, calumny, vanity, injustice, perdition, confusion, corruption and fornication'. [John] even says that all the aforesaid vices are gods or goddesses deriving from the evil he claims to be the primal cause.[23]

Although orthodox utopians were usually hostile to Muslims and Jews, heretical ones, members of persecuted minorities, were often not so. The Amalricians thought that, had Jews their knowledge of the truth, they would need no baptism, and Prous Boneta, a later Olivite, added the Saracens as beneficiaries of her dispensation. Some Joachites shared these views. In 1254 the Parisian divines examined the *Eternal Evangel*, a compilation of Joachim of Fiore's tracts introduced and glossed by Gerard of Borgo San Donnino. This Franciscan was said to have believed his book would serve as the New Testament of the age of the Holy Spirit now nearly ushered in. Among the propositions purportedly found, and certainly condemned, was the following: 'However greatly the Lord will afflict the world's Jews, he will nevertheless reserve some to whom he will impart benefits at the end, even those who remain Jews, whom he will liberate.'[24]

Some gnostic sectaries emphasized nature's inherent goodness and others its malevolence. The Amalricians accented the natural moral purity of those who know or learn the way, linking this to progress: within five years, the world would become a sinless natural paradise. Cathars, especially the rigid dualists among them, contrasted the unalterable sinfulness of the material world with the bliss of the spiritual world, the two being linked only by the slow ascension of purified souls to heaven. Both visions suffered from contradictions. The Amalricians said, in effect, that whatever is is good, or shortly to be so. Writing thirteen years after the eradication of their sect, Caesarius of Heisterbach remarked that their predicted five-year term was long past and things had not come off as foretold. The Cathars went to the other extreme. The material world was all bad: created by concupiscence, meat could not be eaten (fish could!), and sin was so pervasive that some consoled (a ceremony of forgiveness and entry into the ranks of the Perfects) when sick are said to have fasted to death for fear of relapsing. Dour though they may have been, however, the Cathars were not without heart. Burned in 1321, the Perfect William Belibasta taught that 'it was a good work to give charity to anyone, so much so that, if a man gives charity to the devil because of God, God would remunerate that act', and that, if a man fell away, he should remember that

'God will indulge all men's sins, except desperation, that is, when a man despairs of God's having pity'.[25]

THE IDEAL WORLD

Rome's police maintained that élitist divergences led to moral antinomianism. Garnier of Rochefort wrote in 1208–10 that the Amalricians were wont to say: '"He who knows that God does everything cannot sin even when fornicating because he should not attribute what he does to himself, but rather to God." O shameless opinion! Why do they hold it? In order to persuade girls to fornicate more easily.'[26] Inquisitors at Bologna in 1299 reported that Gerald Segarelli of Parma, head of the Apostles or Poor of Christ, taught that, regardless of marriage, nude necking and even copulation were without sin. The notion that a soul annihilated in God's love may do anything without remorse was among the opinions for which the Beguine Margaret, called Porrette, was condemned in Paris in 1310, and a charge of moral antinomianism was also used at the Council of Vienne in 1311 to impugn all Beguines and Beghards.

Variations of sexual expression were also condemned. A Bolognese statute of 1259 directed the *podestà* to assist the Confraternity of the Blessed Virgin's war on sodomy and heresy. These two 'crimes' were frequently linked in polemic, but proof is lacking that homosexuals were more than usually heretical. What the literature indubitably shows is that men saw all crimes or deviations as analogous. The charges against Boniface VIII peddled by the French party after his death in 1303 include heresy, simony, usury and the more common sexual divergences, including a defence of masturbation.

Although the voices are ones inimical to them, some dissidents may well have been libertine, but others were surely not. The Amalricians were perhaps the former, but the Ortliebians, an Italian sect sharing many of their views, were moral rigorists. The Cathars were perhaps those who most rejected nature and the flesh, even calling marriage no better than disguised fornication. This teaching cost the sect adepts. In 1246 a noblewoman from Avignonet, south of Toulouse, told the inquisitors that she quit Catharism because she thought she heard them say that 'a man could not be saved if he slept with his wife'.[27] Cathar arguments nevertheless appealed to others than moral rigorists. According to Alan of Lille, 'they even say that marriage contradicts nature's law, because natural law dictates that all should be in common, and marriage appropriates to one what ought to be shared'.[28] Besides, theory and life overlap only partially. A hidden advantage of the sharp separation of Cathar believers from the Perfects was that the former were not expected to eschew marriage, usury or the other 'faults' of ordinary living save that, when dying, they were to forgive their enemies. In short, although hard on their clergy, theirs may have been an easy religion for believers because they lacked orthodoxy's penitential police.

Like the orthodox monks of Fontevrault, Cathars and Waldensians placed women higher than did most Catholics. The former, for example, emphasized the spiritual equality of women and men, a Perfect named William Belibasta saying that 'the souls of men and women are the same and without difference, and the whole difference between men and women is in their bodies which Satan made'.[29] In divergent belief, also, women could lead and are known to have attracted followings. Such a one was Willelma of Milan, whose cult was supported by the monks and aged pensioners of the Cistercian monastery of Chiaravalle near Milan, but whose followers – this annuity set included a Visconti! – were charged with heresy after her death in 1281. Another was Prous Boneta of Montpellier, a woman condemned for her version of the Olivite heresy in 1325. She was, she said, the spiritual Mary through whom God would send the Holy Spirit to humanity. A study in woman's guilt overcome, she reported that 'just as Eve, the first woman, was the beginning and cause of the damnation of all human nature and of all the human race through the sin of Adam, so,' the Lord had told her,'"you will be the beginning and cause of the saving of human nature and the human race by means of the words I make you say, if they are believed".'[30']

Enthusiasts believed the world was upside down, certain that contemporary Christian life was far from noble. William Pelisson, a Dominican inquisitor, reported that a Toulousan weaver in the late 1220s, who later hereticated and was burned, cried out when first arrested: 'Sirs, hear me! I am not an heretic because I have a wife, lie with her, have children, eat meat, lie and swear, and am a faithful Christian.'[31] The sectaries blamed the corruption of the Church, and within the Church the attack on heresy evoked campaigns in which churchmen, starting at the top, condemned other ecclesiastics for deserting Christ's path and falling into avarice and lubricity. The problem is to discover what all this shouting was about.

Self-criticism among churchmen was a way the Church mobilized itself to combat heresy. By blaming individuals for falling short, churchmen allayed anxiety about the inherent impossibility of attaining the ideal. A result was that much polemic was misdirected or untruthful. Polemists said the clergy of Languedoc, beset by Catharism, were luxurious and rich. Some were, but their church was a poor one. In the diocese of Toulouse the bishop was so indigent that, in 1206, he was hounded by lay creditors and even by his own cathedral's canons. Papal letters and even public opinion claimed that heresy was victorious there because Languedoc lacked Christian devotion. But the rise of divergent belief everywhere paralleled the growth of orthodox enthusiasm. A rector of the Dalbade alleged that the parish revenues had fallen off 'both because of the heretics whose perverse sects abound in the area of Toulouse and because of the newly built churches in the parish to which everybody goes on festivals'.[32] Nor could the Church expect to meet its critics' objections, since their demands were contradictory. On one hand, for example, the clergy were often condemned for failing to live up to clerical celibacy. On the other, many sectarians, especially Waldensians, were sure the requirement was a perversion of scripture.

These polemics reflected inherent contradictions, because it was hard to agree on what the Christian republic should be. Some were convinced that humanity was neither perfect nor perfectible. They accepted the endowment of the Church with wealth and power to enable it to rule men for their good. Worrying about this, Gerhoh, provost of the Augustinian chapter of Reichersberg, in 1155 or 1156 saw Jesus standing before Pontius Pilate clad in both the white robe of the priesthood and imperial purple. He then sadly observed: 'It would indeed please me if Caesar's things could be rendered to Caesar and God's things to God, but with this caution, that the Church be not ravaged or stripped of its white robe if the purple is taken off too rashly.'[33]

Some spoke out against such voices, trying to free the Church from the world's contamination. Peter Cantor praised Bernard of Clairvaux for his dislike of expensive churches and lauded Peter Abelard for insisting that the gifts given by the count of Champagne to his monastery called The Paraclete not come from money tainted by usury or violence. Others, such as Peter Waldes, who converted in 1173 and died in 1216, and Francis of Assisi comprised the utopian wing of the Christian republic. Naked to follow the naked Christ and, like the apostles, having all in common, they wanted to live the communism described in the *Acts of the Apostles*. Having no property and not saving for the morrow, they were to earn their bread by preaching, begging and working. Clergy and laymen were inspired by grand visions of this kind. One sect, the Amalricians, was led by secular clergy from in and around Paris. Of its thirteen leaders, at least three were masters at the university, and all but two had studied arts or theology there. Among them were four parish priests, and all the others were clerks in minor orders. The monastic or mendicant orders also frequently provided leadership for both enthusiastic and deviant movements. Many, however, such as Waldes and Francis mentioned above, were layfolk, inspired by texts and ideas from the clergy, but layfolk none the less.

Clerk, monk or layman and laywoman, those who diverged from orthodoxy were to change the character of the Church. The next chapter will discuss how these enthusiasts or disbelievers were either won back to orthodoxy, suppressed or driven underground.

NOTES AND REFERENCES

1 *Decretum* 24, 3, 27 in *CICan* I, 997–8, from Jerome and Isidore of Seville.
2 *De amore* 1, 6, H (ed. Trojel), 94.
3 *Cronica* in *MGH SS* XXII, 83.
4 *Cronica* in *MGH SS* XXXII, 503–4.
5 *Tractatus super quatuor evangelia* (ed. Buonaiuti), 159. The 'at the moment when the Lord comes' translates 'ad horam' because Joachim was thinking of Matthew 24:42–50 and Apocalypse 3:3.
6 *Ibid.* (ed. Buonaiuti), 160.
7 *Speculum humanae salvationis* I, prologue (eds Lutz and Perdrizet), 5.
8 *Liber de duobus principiis* (ed. A. Dondaine, Rome, 1939), 84.
9 *Summa theologiae* 1, 23, 7 *ad* 3.
10 *Dialogus miraculorum* 1, 37 (ed. Strange), I, 33.
11 *Historia diplomatica Friderici Secundi* (ed. Huillard- Bréholles) V, i, 350.

12 Dupuy, *Histoire du différend d'entre le pape Boniface VIII et Philippe le Bel*, 531 (testimony No. 7 quoted above) and 534 (testimony No. 12).
13 Charles du F. DuCange, *Glossarium mediae et infimae latinitatis* s. v. *incisor*.
14 *Rhetorica novissima* 8, 1 in *BIMA* 11, 278b.

15   *Dialogus miraculorum* 4, 39 (ed. Strange), I, 207.

16   *De naturis rerum* 2, 73 in *Rolls Series* XXXIV, 297.

17   *Le registre d'inquisition de Jacques Fournier, 1318–1325* (ed. Jean Duvernoy, Toulouse, 1965) III, 221.

18   *Quadripartita editio contra hereticos, Waldenses, Judaeos et Paganos* or *Contra haereticos* 2, 6 in *PL* CCX, 383. To Alan, Cathars were heretics and Muhammedans pagans.

19   *Contra hereticos* 2, 7 in *PL* CCX, 353–4.

20   *Decretum* 2, 1, 1, 12 in *CICan* I, 361. Cardinal Deusdedit had attributed this passage to Pope Pascal I. The Waldensian source is the *Rescriptum heresiarcharum Lombardie ad pauperes de Lugduno qui sunt in Alamania* in Giovanni Gonnet, *Enchiridion fontium Valdensium* (Torre Pellice, 1958) I, 181–2.

21   *Ibid.* (ed. Gonnet) I, 171–3.

22   *Ibid.* 3 and 7 (ed. Baeumker), 13 and 21.

23   *De Catharis et Pauperibus de Lugduno* in *Liber de duobus principiis* (ed. Dondaine), 72.

24   Denifle, *Chartularium universitatis Parisiensis* I, 273, No. 243.

25   *Le registre d'inquisition de Jacques Fournier* (ed. Duvernoy) II, 481 and 515, in reverse order.

26   *Contra Amauricianos* 2 in Clemens Baeumker, *Beiträge zur Geschichte der Philosophie des Mittelalters* XXIV (1926), v–vi, 12, putatively attributed to Garnier.

27   My *Men and Women at Toulouse in the Age of the Cathars*, 42.

28   *Contra hereticos* 1, 63 in *PL* CCX, 366.

29   *Le registre d'inquisition de Jacques Fournier* (ed. Duvernoy) III, 223.

30   W.H. May, 'The confession of Prous Boneta' in *Essays in Medieval life and Thought Presented in Honor of A.P. Evans* (eds J.H. Mundy, R.W. Emery and B.N. Nelson, New York, 1955, rprt) 29.

31   *Chronicon* (ed. Charles Molinier, Aniché, 1880), 17.

32   See my 'Charity and Social Work in Toulouse' in *Traditio* 11 (1966), 237n.

33   *De novitatibus huius temporis* 12 in *MGH Ldl* III, 296–7.

22

REPRESSION AND PERSUASION

DIVERGENT THOUGHT AND SOCIETY

Most Christian radical ideas had been heard before 1100, especially during the Gregorian revolution. At that time, however, the radicals themselves remained relatively orthodox because of the expansion of the monastic orders and types of life to which the new religious and their associated layfolk devoted themselves. Afterwards frictions increased. Remembering the earlier Gregorian disorders, the secular clergy wanted to claustrate the monks again and limit lay participation in preaching. Once established, the new religious orders prized 'stability', and tried to prevent their members going off to found or join more exciting ones. Formulated in the third Lateran Council of 1179 and again in the fourth of 1215, restrictive legislation voiced this worry. The aristocracies of the Church, so to speak, had combined to repress the people, and, because of this muzzling, secession from the Church swelled in the late twelfth century.

But the prince of the Church came to the aid of 'his' people and derived great profit therefrom. Although insisting on episcopal control, Alexander III embraced Waldes in 1179, and in 1181 the latter swore loyalty. Innocent III opened the gates wider. Negotiations starting in 1198 led to a papal rule for the Lombard Humiliati in 1201. Some Waldensians, Durand of Huesca's Poor Catholics and Bernard Prim's Poor Lombards, were legitimated in 1208 and 1210, and thereafter fought the Cathars. In 1216 James of Vitry persuaded Honorius III to license Mary of Oignies's Beguines, a group begun at Liège around 1207. The Franciscans received verbal approval in

1209 and a rule in 1223, followed by the Dominicans in 1216. Rome privileged these orders to perform sacramental, penitential and preaching services. They opened the way for lay enthusiasm and, by this, diverted the flood from the threatening popular heresies.

The expansion continued until the counter-attack of the secular clergy and the older orders clamped on the lid again from 1245 to 1311. Before that, however, the spread of preaching and the formation of lay devotional groups associated with the new orders had created a lay religious literacy equalled again only during the Reformation of the sixteenth century. Anent the Lombard Humiliati whom he visited in 1216, James of Vitry praised their preaching, remarking that almost all their male members were literate, meaning they had some Latin. Those with vernacular also knew much religion. Prous Boneta of Montpellier, for example, commented on the earthly paradise soon to come, then briefly held up by 'her' Antichrist, Pope John XXII. She noted that Franciscans and Dominicans had prepared the way for a new church, a spiritualized Eve, whose fabric was, however, temporarily rent asunder. From Eve, God, a spiritualized Adam, had had two sons, Cain and Abel, the latter being the Franciscan Peter John Olivi and the former the recently canonized Dominican Thomas Aquinas. 'Just as Cain slew his brother Abel in the flesh, so did this brother Thomas slay his brother, namely the said brother Peter John, spiritually, that is, in his writings.'[1]

Most sectarians used the vernacular. Waldes employed a priest to translate scripture and commentaries, and translations of Jerome, Augustine, Gregory I and Bernard of Clairvaux were seen. By the end of the 1230s, papal letters, local conciliar legislation and the Inquisitors had begun to prohibit translations because sectarian biblical interpretations combated orthodox ones. Some rejected not only the scholastics but even the Latin fathers and based their arguments on scripture alone. Not a few were hostile to Latin, partly because ordinary layfolk could not understand it and partly because it was the language of the clergy. Not to flourish until the Reformation, the notion that Latin slavery was opposed to vernacular freedom was already known.

In 1178 a cardinal examining heretics at Toulouse was horrified at having to discuss the faith in the vernacular and not in Latin, the language of the clergy, its liturgy and thought since the long-ago German invasions. The cardinal's fears were well founded because some clearly wished the vernacular to replace Latin. As noted above, vernacular poetry and literature invaded the world of ideas, and, after an initial period when lay scribes and notaries revived and popularized a vulgarized Latin, vernacular legal documents penetrated into the arcana of law and contract. Although far in the future, this change portended the defeat of the ecumenical Church by Europe's regional states and the subordination of the clergy to secular magistrates and princes. Heresy failed, but the extremists had won the battle. To defeat them, churchmen had been obliged to use the vernacular, thus popularizing religious culture immensely by 1300.

As long as monasticism expanded to admit new devotions and functions, however, lay utopians could express their hopes by entering religion without too greatly disturbing civil society with its many necessary but unhappy institutions. Churchmen often said that they alone could live according to natural and divine law – that is, sharing property communally in apostolic communism's true freedom and equality. In the world, laymen were obliged to live by the civil law, the law that instituted slavery and private property. Perhaps because they could exist alongside and not within secular society, also, the Humiliati, Beguines and mendicants were able to build relatively durable institutions, durable, that is, when compared with short-lived ancient or modern utopian settlements or revolutionary societies.

There were limits to the discreteness of the social orders, which were, in fact, already breaking down. As seen above, the spread of the monastic calling to layfolk began to empower men and women to live in the cloisters of their hearts while inhabiting the world and going about its business. Although the full weight was not felt until nearly two centuries had passed, secularism or the lay spirit was therefore already alive. Ecclesiastical visions were similar to secular ones. Although some churchmen insisted on distinguishing between ecclesiastical and secular things, some went pretty far in the other direction. When discussing the sin or heresy of simony, Peter Cantor said that princes derive their authority from consecration. 'When someone is too young, as a boy to whom as heir a kingdom falls, or someone is insufficient in life and merit, does the prelate sin who grants him consecration? It seems so. For does he not consent? He can and ought resist.'[2] Since justice is sacred, it is simony to sell it or buy its exercise, just as it is simony to buy a kingdom or a duchy because princes have the care of souls.

One wonders whether the royal dignity should be conferred by election. It appears iniquitous that, as though forced by necessity, men should be obliged to receive unjust princes by reason of succession. Jerome says: 'Joshua the son of Nun is chosen from another tribe that it may be known that the government of the people is to be conferred not because of blood but because of life.'[3]

Is then hereditary monarchy heretical?

That enthusiasts' beliefs reached into political and social realms is not surprising. War and coercion were to be abolished. The Passagians, for example, urged Christians to beat their swords into ploughshares and nations not to learn war any more. 'That for which kings were created, namely to wage war, to wield the material sword and administer punishment, has no further place among Christians.'[4] Exploitation was condemned and economic brotherhood prized: all must labour honestly and not live by others' sweat. The primitive communism of the apostles was the model for Christian organization.

Robert of Curzon's utopian message and the propaganda against usury of his contemporary Stephen Langton provided arguments for economic brotherhood useful to guildsmen in their attacks on exploitative entrepreneurs and rich masters. It will be recalled that craft and trade guilds were beginning to be organized only after 1150, and that the full flood of this movement was not attained until the late thirteenth century. Although few guilds were directly affiliated with the Church, the spectacular growth in the number of hospitals and confraternities offering burial and hospital care shows how close the explosion of religious passion was to the emergence of a guild economy. These services were especially needed by working-class people, and charitable institutions evoked less resistance from the rich than economic ones. Although often founded by nobles or patricians, early Beguine settlements in the Low Countries and Rhine valley attracted female workers in the cloth industry, women who continued to work after conversion. Widespread in northern and central Italy, the Humiliati were initially industrial workers, and craftsfolk exploited by entrepreneurs had an unusual affinity for religious enthusiasm. Among these were weavers, whose very name became a popular synonym for 'heretic'.

Christ's or the apostles' poverty had a natural appeal to such groups because it asserted the moral superiority of the poor. William Cornelis, a secular canon of Antwerp, resigned his prebend, preached poverty and died in the odour of sanctity in the early 1250s. On his demise, his followers were charged with heresy because they were said to maintain that the poor were automatically saved and the rich damned. Being in a state of grace, indeed, the poor could fornicate and commit prostitution without sin. Working-class commitment to enthusiasm emphasized labour's purifying force, an idea exemplified by the Waldensians, Humiliati and Beguines. Although begging, or mendicancy, taught the virtue of humility, Francis of Assisi's rule of 1221 urged his friars to work at the trades they knew, and, using all the New Testament passages on manual labour, James of Vitry reported in 1216 that the early Franciscans worked with their hands.[5] Utopian ideas die hard. Later on, Bishop Robert Grosseteste of Lincoln preached to the Franciscans at Oxford and, after praising mendicancy, went on to observe that there was a higher calling, 'namely, to live from one's own labour. Whence he observed that the Beguines are the most perfect and holy of religious because they live of their own labour and do not burden the world.'[6]

For several reasons, however, labour was minimized and, in the case of the Franciscans, replaced with mendicancy. Not all churchmen were happy about replacing work by begging. Aiming his shafts against Beguines and Beghards, William of St Amour, a secular master at Paris, complained that the world was crowded with unproductive people.

> What I have said above concerning mendicity I have said especially because . . . of youths called Good Workers and young women called Beguines, who are spread throughout the whole kingdom. They are all perfectly capable of work but instead wish to do little or no labour and live from alms in bodily sloth under the pretext of praying.[7]

But this was a lost cause. Early on, some argued against the Waldensian requirement of manual labour by noting that the Lord had exempted his apostles from it because he wanted them instead to preach, pray and save souls. The decline of religious economic utopianism also coincided with the political and economic triumph of artisan guilds. Fearing competition once they had won their place in the world, they no longer needed utopian aid, and turned against celibate workers.

Utopian enthusiasm was also linked to society's assault on usury. Just as the religious mind joined sodomy to heresy, so it did usury, the offence against economic brotherhood. The attack on these two 'crimes' by the White Confraternity established in Toulouse in 1209 under Bishop Fulk of Marseilles, mentioned earlier, is a paradigm of ecclesiastical propaganda and action. Caesarius of Heisterbach reports that around 1200 heretics from Montpellier came to preach in Metz, and were there protected by patricians who hated the bishop because he had refused burial to one of their usurious relatives. But usurers were not necessarily inclined towards heresy. At Toulouse Pons of Capdenier, whose testament of 1229 included restitution for usury, was described by the historian Bernard Gui as the 'patron' of the newly founded Dominican order. As with sodomy, so with usury; it was risky enough without adding heresy. Heretics, moreover, answered orthodox charges by charging churchmen with profiting from usury. In Bologna in 1299 they claimed that the Dominicans buried usurers for a share of their filthy lucre, all to keep their concubines in style!

Usury had class connotations. Usurers was not merely those who lent money at interest, but those who became infamous. As noted above, the poor were sometimes preserved for virtue by incapacity to be evil and the old rich by lack of need or antipathy to the counting house; usurers denominated infamous were usually new men making their fortunes. Especially in the twelfth century, when episcopal lords of cities were charging the proponents of urban liberty with heresy, it is sure that some of them were inclined to divergent thought. In the Inquisitorial registers of Languedoc, however, middle-class burghers were not heavily represented.

URBAN OR RURAL?

Nobles and patricians – the great bourgeois of Metz, for example, or the merchant bankers of Tuscany – were more involved in divergence. An example is Hugh Speroni, a consul of Piacenza and schoolmate of the jurist Vacarius at Bologna, who wrote against the Church around 1177 and whose sect was still alive in the 1220s. Another was Peter Maurand of Toulouse who confessed and underwent penance in 1178, involving a trip to the Holy Land, restitution of usury and surrender of tithes to the Church. A patrician whose family was unusually Cathar, Peter owned a towered town house and large rural properties including a castle or fortified village. An Inquisitorial register of 1245–7 shows that the mixed rural and urban aristocracy of the area around Toulouse was deeply implicated in this belief. These wealthy folk were surely attracted to divergent thought for many reasons. One may have been that, being used to having their own way, to have a variant spiritualism to set against the authority of orthodoxy was naturally appealing. They may also have had fears, notably worry over the rise of new wealth and popular parties threatening their leadership. The latter possibility tinctures with truth the common Guelph charge that Italian Ghibelline magnates were heretical. Still, all that can be said is that the imperialist party in Milan, Brescia and Bologna had heretical overtones, and that Ghibelline chiefs in Lombardy, like Humbert Pallavicini and the proto-tyrant Ezzelino of Romano in his lordships of Treviso, Padua and Vicenza, actively protected heretics against the Inquisitors.

Divergent belief or heresy, it is rightly reported, was strongest and most inventive where urban life was vigorous. Northern and central Italy were its most vibrant centres, and Milan, the very symbol of industry and self-government, was often described as heresy's capital. Other lively areas were western Languedoc, the Rhone valley, the Rhine with its western confluents and the relatively heavily urbanized region extending from Liège through Brabant to Flanders. These were also, however, the same regions where Gregorian enthusiasm had been liveliest, where most monastic innovations were first introduced, where the mendicant movements had their initial success and where orthodox learning flourished most brightly. In other words, regions marked by relatively heavy urbanization were in the forefront of everything, orthodox or heterodox.

Not that rural populations were untouched by divergent thought. Rural Flanders and the villages of Champagne, whose fairs were visited by Italians and other foreigners, were influenced by Catharism. Languedoc and adjacent regions offer the best examples of rural heresy, where it followed a pattern later repeated in the Protestant movement in that region. Catharism flourished among nobles in the early thirteenth century, and even penetrated the local princely houses of Foix, Béziers and possibly St Gilles-Toulouse. The Crusade of 1209–29 and the repression by the Inquisitors through the decades prior to 1250 drove it out of the aristocracy, both rural and urban, and confined it to the humbler classes. Nobles and patricians were too visible and exposed and more attracted by careers in civil and ecclesiastical office than ordinary folk. Oliver of Termes, member of a heretical family and militant opponent of the Crusade and the Inquisitors in Narbonne during the 1230s, gave up, went on crusade with Louis IX in 1248 and entered royal service.

When attacked, divergent belief lost its hold first in rich areas. In Languedoc, for example, Catharism was strongly implanted in both town and countryside in the early thirteenth century. By about 1230 it was irreparably damaged in Toulouse, western Languedoc's capital. Even before 1250 it weakened rapidly in the more populous and cultivated plains, being driven into the foothills of the Pyrenees. Impoverishment affected its intellectualism. The historian Matthew Paris reported that Lombard and Tuscan Cathars had sent members to study at the university of Paris, and three such students were condemned in 1241 and 1247. By 1300 Catharism had long since ceased to grow intellectually and was reduced to a somewhat primitive dualism. In Italy, dissent was also pushed out of the towns and plains into isolated geographic pockets: the Piedmont, the Alps above Lake Como and the Apennines. An example is Gerald Segarelli's sect called the Apostles, who distilled a mixture of Franciscan poverty, Joachitic optimism and dualism. Starting in Parma and the Romagna about 1260, the sect spread throughout Lombardy. By 1308, when its leaders were executed, it was strong only in a few villages in the mountain piedmont above Vercelli.

The fact that a local seignior hostile to the town of Vercelli initially aided the Apostles shows that there was more to this than mere flight. As among the offshoots of mendicant extremism and Waldensians, inhabitants of marginal lands, especially uplands, seem to have favoured secession. Waldensian spread from the Rhone valley to the hills of Dauphiny, Savoy and Piedmont. In 1210 the bishop of Turin launched against them the first of a series of small punitive expeditions that lasted throughout the century. In the meantime these sects spread through the Alps to Austria, Moravia and Bohemia (where Waldes died in 1216). In the early fourteenth century they began moving down the Apennines to southern Italy. The endemic social conflict between hill and plain seen in much of Italy in the later Middle Ages was already developing, a reflection of the combat between town and countryside and between agriculture and herding. Hillfolk resisted ecclesiastical and secular government, tax collectors and the repression of smuggling designed to protect a corporatized economy. A primitive version was earlier seen in the forested plains and marshes around the Weser river in northern Germany. The rural Stedingers were charged with heresy and defeated in 1234 by a holy war launched by nearby towns, seigniors, bishops and papal pronouncements. Vestigially pagan, perhaps, and surely reluctant to pay tithes, the Stedingers were really resisting commercial penetration and centralizing government.

Divergent belief also demarcated cultural frontiers. An example was Bogomil Catharism proselytized from Byzantium through Bulgaria into the south-east marches of Latin Christendom. This cult became the religion of a Bosnian local prince in 1199, a status it held well after 1300 in spite of campaigns launched by Hungarians, Venetians and popes.

To conclude this brief section on the regional history of divergent belief, although rural populations rarely invented or developed it to its highest intellectual pitch, they were as much given to it as urban ones. It is clear, moreover, that urban growth does not wholly explain its incidence because it was stronger in lightly urbanized Languedoc than in heavily urbanized Flanders. Something other than urbanization must also have counted.

The Low Countries, the Rhine and the Rhone valleys, Languedoc and northern and central Italy generated most new enthusiasm for orthodoxy as well as for heterodoxy. These were also the regions where the devolution of political power into small principalities and urban republics was most marked. Areas in which the older monarchies held on better or were renewing their power, such as England, royal and Plantagenet France, Aragon, Castile and Norman and Hohenstaufen southern Italy, were famed for neither heresy nor (save for academic) inventive orthodoxy. Although ecclesiastical liberty had everywhere increased since Gregorian days, the greater princes of these regions had retained much power over their local churches, and therefore were interested in defending institutions in which they still enjoyed presidency. Where the link between secular power and the Church was weaker, religion was both more inventive of new forms of orthodoxy and more liable to heretical secession.

FORCE AND CONVERSION

Churchmen fought to preserve their faith's unity. Although some hated the practice – Peter Cantor, for example, cited Abelard, Bernard of Clairvaux and Gilbert of La Porrée as though all opposed it! – schoolmen often charged that their rivals' opinions smacked of heresy. In spite of this, from 1150 to 1300 no ecclesiastical intellectual was more than censured, rusticated or briefly imprisoned for divergent opinions. This contrasts sharply with the burning or perpetual immurement frequently meted out to the lay members of heretical sects. Although, then, the charge of heresy was thrown about loosely, ideological divergence on the part of single individuals or intellectual groups rarely invited serious repression. John of Joinville tells us that a bishop of Paris consoled a university teacher who doubted the sacraments by likening him to a soldier at the front and himself to a man back home where it was safe.

Dissent by select intellectuals differs from mass secession, and how extensive such was is seen in western Languedoc. In 1207 at Montréal near Carcassonne a papal legate was obliged to debate publicly with a group of Cathars, his performance being 'judged' by four laymen, knights and burghers. In the same year Pons Ademar of Roudeille, a 'wise knight', told Fulk of Marseilles, bishop of Toulouse, that he could not act against the Cathars 'because we have been raised with them, have kindred among them and see them live virtuously'.[8] Although surely minorities amidst presumably passive orthodox majorities, this large scale secession was threatening.

The Church defeated popular divergent belief mainly by opening its arms to the initiators of new devotions, enthusiasms and utopianisms. However dangerous these were, their success in undermining heresy is evident. When Bishop Fulk of Toulouse visited the Low Countries in 1212 to raise money and men for the Albigensian Crusade, he was impressed by the success against heresy of the Beguines, a group introduced to him by Robert of Curzon and James of Vitry. Four years later James, on his way to Rome, where he had the Beguines approved, and the Holy Land, stopped off in Milan,

which is the womb of heresy, where I remained for some days and preached . . . . One can scarcely find anyone in the whole city who resists the heretics save for certain holy men and religious women called Patarines by the malicious and worldly, but Humiliati by the pope who gave them the right to preach to fight the heretics, and who confirmed their order. These people leave all for Christ, assemble in communities, live by manual labour and preach God's word . . . . So greatly has this order multiplied in the diocese of Milan that they have founded 150 conventual congregations, men in some and women in others, without counting those who remain in their own homes.[9]

The Church, it may be said, defeated the popular heresies partly by means of persuasion, that is, by preaching or providing seemingly attractive alternatives.

Many believed that coerced belief was not true belief, and therefore hoped that persuasion would succeed. Bernard of Clairvaux preached in Languedoc in 1145, and although his effort was much lauded, he was hooted down at Verfeil near Toulouse and his tour had no lasting result. Later Cistercian missions saw preaching reinforced by coercion. The third Lateran Council of 1179 asked laymen to help, promising crusaders' protections, and two years later Henry of Marcy, abbot of Clairvaux, cardinal and papal legate, raised a small force while preaching in Languedoc and captured the town of Lavaur. In 1209 the Albigensian Crusade was launched, at first under the command of the legate Arnold Amalric, abbot of Cîteaux. A similar change took place in the Dominicans. The founder, Dominic of Caleruega, had preached in Languedoc with modest success from 1206 to 1208. In 1221 the pope instructed the friars to combat heresy, and ten years later they were referred to as Inquisitors in a law applicable in Rome that passed into imperial legislation the next year. Thereafter the Dominicans (and occasionally the Franciscans) produced not only famed preachers but also inquisitor-judges. From the 1230s onwards Dominican lay associates or tertiaries were brigaded into confraternities of Jesus Christ or the Blessed Virgin to hunt heretics, and the Dominicans denounced as unprofitable the public debates with heretics and Jews that had been common around 1200. Teachers were not reluctant to use coercion. Roland of Cremona has been mentioned as the first Dominican to teach in France and, for a time, at the new university in Toulouse. In 1231 he led a mob on Christmas day that burst into a house where a Waldensian had died, tore it down, converted it into a latrine, disinterred the body and dragged it off to be thrown on the town dump. Preaching was similar to what is seen in today's one-party states. In 1247, the count of Toulouse repeated ecclesiastical injunctions by ordering his subjects to assemble and hear the preaching of mendicant friars not only on feast days and Sundays, but whenever they came to town. Churchmen had clearly come to believe that persuasion without coercion was inefficacious.

The penalties visited on those of divergent belief – mainly exile and confiscation of property – were found in Roman law. Gratian also borrowed from Roman law the notion that heresy was a crime against the State, and since war defended that entity, lawyers recommended the death penalty for pertinacious heretics.

Not all were happy about this revival of old law, but it won out. An example of changing attitudes is seen in comments on the execution of Arnold of Brescia at Rome in 1155. At the time, this act was attributed to the civil prefect of Rome and not to the pope, but contemporaries knew that this was mere legalism. Gerhoh of Reichersberg wept:

> How I wish he had been punished for his admittedly evil doctrine by exile or imprisonment or by any other penalty than death, or, at least, that he had been killed in such a way that the Roman Church or its court should not bear the responsibility for his death.[10]

By the time the canonist Huguccio of Pisa (d. 1210) wrote, Arnold's fate was no longer bewailed but instead used as an example. To be tried, degraded, hanged and then burned on order of the pope, as Huguccio describes it, was a justifiable punishment and shows that 'when incorrigible, [heretics] are to suffer the extreme penalty, as was done in the case of Arnold of Brescia'.[11]

Secular law on this 'crime' was old, but publication and enforcement were required, and here local princes took the lead. Other than profiting from the confiscation of property, their motives were various. Some fought to protect their profitable local churches; others desired to appear more Catholic than the pope. England was off to an early start. In 1165–6 a group of Flemish or German Cathars was condemned by a local synod at Oxford, 'relaxed' to the secular court and there branded and exiled. One of Henry II's attempts to impose a settlement on Thomas Becket, the Constitutions of Clarendon of 1166, ordered punishment for those aiding heretics. The kings of Aragon moved ahead, imitating Roman law by assimilating heresy to treason, and ordering exile, confiscation and, in 1197, death by fire. In edicts issued from 1224 to 1239, Frederick II Hohenstaufen extended the death penalty from Lombardy to all his dominions. His laws were 'canonized' by Innocent IV in 1254, thus making ecumenical what had been local.

Some churchmen resisted this severity. Before heresy became widespread, they could afford to be tolerant, largely because the people and princes almost thoughtlessly slew those who diverged from the Church. About such a lynching, Bernard of Clairvaux said that 'we approve the [people's] zeal, but do not persuade them to do it because faith is a matter of persuasion not to be imposed by force'.[12] Long before Innocent IV, this curious position was untenable, and moderates like Peter Cantor were reduced to insisting on due process and easier punishment. Peter blamed a prelate for condemning as Cathars women who had refused the advances of a priest. He may have had in mind an event in the late 1170s when Gervase of Tilbury precipitated the extirpation of a sect in Rheims because a maiden refused his overtures by rashly asserting that the loss of her virginity would be tantamount to immediate damnation. Still, the Chanter did not want heretics to circulate freely and corrupt others. Imprisonment was best, but if death was to be imposed, a heretic should be given time to think it over. The Romans, he thought, were gentler than the judges of his own day.

> Even the infidels used to allow Christians a thirty-day delay . . . to think over whether or not they wished to sacrifice to the idols . . . . Why then does the Church presume to examine men's hearts with this strange and uncouth judgment? Why are Cathars immediately burned and not given legitimate delays to think the matter over?[13]

In the past, deviance had been pursued and punished by episcopal and secular authorities. Reliance on the latter was unsatisfactory because it gave laymen power over the clergy, and because laymen were either indifferent or excessively severe, action against heretics, for example, being like lynching. Episcopal action was impeded because prelates were recruited from local society and reflected local moods, something obviously harmful to the Church in Languedoc, where the well-to-do were often heretical. Even the forced retirement and replacement of bishops by the popes was inefficacious because a local man was eventually bound to be elected as successor. With Inquisitors appointed by the popes in the 1230s, however, systematic pressure could be applied.

Inquisitors were usually the new mendicants, especially Dominicans. Armed with papal letters instructing them to 'reform the Church' as well as purge heretics, their missions initially evoked popular support and, one imagines, got caught up in local issues and hysterias having little to do with heresy. Aided by mendicants, Conrad of Marburg, a canon of Mainz, spread fire and death in much of western Germany from 1227 until he and three companions were assassinated in 1233. The Dominican Robert the Bugger (so called because he was a converted Cathar or Bulgar) was active from Flanders to Champagne. The apex of his career was reached in 1239 when he is said to have burned just under 200 inhabitants of the village of Montwimer in one day. He was shortly thereafter sentenced to life imprisonment as mad. Occasional excesses, however, were not the principal reason for opposition. The heretical minority resisted being rooted out and the relatively orthodox majority wearied of the disruption caused by probing investigations. The history of Peter of Verona may stand as an example of the curious ambivalence with which this problem was fraught. The first Inquisitor at Milan (from 1233), this Dominican was assassinated in 1252. Within ten months of his death, he, who had saved souls by slaying bodies, was canonized as St Peter Martyr.

Although accepting the help against heretics, the secular clergy were rarely enthusiastic. Meeting in councils, French and German bishops arrested the missions of Conrad of Marburg and Robert the Bugger. The papacy, however, had its way, and the mendicant Inquisition was introduced along with mendicant preaching and teaching. Princes and self-governing communities also often resisted the papal Inquisition. Frederick II Hohenstaufen promulgated the harshest laws against heresy, but his Ghibelline supporters actively impeded Inquisitors. Where heresy was weak and the State's power over the local church strong, the papal Inquisition never really penetrated. This was the case in Castile, England and much of central, northern and eastern Germany. Inquisitors were to be found in France, but were especially busy in autonomous or frontier provinces like Flanders, Champagne and Languedoc.

The repression of heresy was tied to politics. Around 1250 the Inquisitor Rainier Sacconi estimated that there were about 2,500 Cathar Perfects in northern and central Italy as against some 200 in southern France, but the Crusade was launched against Languedoc, not Lombardy. The popes were tempted to attack Milan, but dropped the idea when Emperor Frederick II actually proposed it, because this Lombard capital headed the towns who were the popes' best allies in the struggle against the Empire. All the same, although townsfolk everywhere fought the first introduction of the Inquisitors in the 1230s (and as late as 1256 in Genoa and 1289 in Venice), the frequency with which their advent was hailed by the Guelph, or popular, parties shows that the majority of the inhabitants in Italy's urban republics favoured the Inquisitors.

To the vast literature against heresy the Inquisitors added their own. Partial manuals appeared in the 1240s, but the first large one was written around 1256, an anonymous work later expanded by the Franciscan David of Augsburg (d. 1272). In 1178 it was still possible for a council headed by a papal legate to have a Cathar at Toulouse recant by repeating the oath exacted from Berengar of Tours in 1059 in favour of the real presence in the sacramental host. This worked, because Cathars also did not believe in the real presence, but was rough and ready. With manuals came sophistication: the basic beliefs of each sect were described and lines of interrogation suitable for each suggested. The surgical tenor of this literature is illustrated by Bernard Gui's discussion of what to do about a heretic who wants to retract when being led out to execution. Unless a recidivist, he or she is to be received into penance, and for two reasons: mercy is to be preferred to rigour, and, adds the policeman, the fainthearted would be scandalized were a penitent refused. The sincerity of the penance, however, is to be expressed by a prompt confession of the names of all associates.

Resistance angered these policemen. Inquisitors were sometimes one-time heretics, and some, like the Bugger, were driven mad by their work. Even Bernard Gui, perhaps provoked by the Franciscan Bernard Délicieux's (d. 1320) attacks on Dominican Inquisitors, abandoned judicial calm to record with joy the gruesome slaughter of Dolcino of Novara and Margaret, the last leaders of the Italian Apostles in 1307. Margaret was cut to pieces before Dolcino's eyes, and he was himself chopped up immediately afterwards.

These punishments should not leave the impression that Inquisitors were uniquely brutal. As seen above, awful corporal punishments were normal in Latin jurisprudence, and the savagery was reinforced by the educational publicity given public executions. By partially replacing the death penalty with imprisonment, however, the Inquisitors were even progressive. The Catharism of western Languedoc was broken in three stages. A vehement attack often close to lynching rooted it out of the capital city of Toulouse by the mid 1230s. Two better organized Inquisitorial campaigns, those of 1245–6 and 1256–7, then broke the back of the heresy in rural districts around town. The first was directed against a heresy still widespread and was more gentle than the second, which pursued stubborn remnants. In the year 1246, 945 heretics were sentenced. None was killed; eleven per cent were imprisoned and eighty-nine per cent were given various penances, including pilgrimage and crusade service. In 1256–7 about fifteen per cent of 306 sentences were levied against those previously dead in heresy or in flight, seven per cent were death penalties and seventy-eight per cent life sentences.

Although an awful weight on the society it afflicted, Inquisitorial professionalism had 'reformed' apprehension, investigation and punishment of divergent belief. Brutality remained, but lynching had largely disappeared. The judicial inquiry against putative wrongdoers known as the Inquisition was the procedure relied on. Discussed above, this method began with popular deposition under oath, insisted on the secrecy of witnesses and refused to allow counsel to the defendant. Its design was to elicit proof, principally by witnesses or voluntary confession. Initially in Italy, torture was introduced by *Ad extirpanda* in 1252.

The Inquisitors always elicited opposition. In and after 1245 episcopal power rose in the general councils, and as the conciliar fathers usually attacked the mendicants' preaching and teaching, so also did they attack the Inquisitors. Upset by the condemnation of 156 inhabitants of Limoux south of Carcassonne in 1248, Innocent IV intervened and precipitated the Inquisitors' resignation. A late result of this pressure was that Boniface VIII allowed legal representation and publication of the names of witnesses. In spite of an attempt to regulate the various missions by the appointment in 1262 of an Inquisitor resident at the papal court, Inquisitors gradually fell under the secular State. In 1255 Alphonse of Poitiers, first Capetian count of Toulouse, replaced south French Dominicans by others from Paris. Similar to his largely northern civil officers, this recruitment was a late stage in the French absorption of Languedoc. In spite of the failure to organize a real papal Inquisition, the popular heresies of 1200 had been broken by Inquisitors, some, like the Cathars, nearly extirpated, and others, like the Waldensians and illuminist sects, gravely weakened.

Divergent or secessionist belief, however, was changing. Impossible to camouflage, the dualism of the Cathars – who, it is worth recalling, thought of themselves as the true Christians – never again played much of a role, and of these early groups, only the Waldensians persisted into modern times. The Inquisitor Bernard Gui said that they were 'foxy', but they were hard to nail down simply because they had so much in common with orthodoxy. Later divergent thought, moreover, was both more parishional and academic and therefore less monastic and popular than before. This had advantages. The theological probabilism of the schools disguised the dangerous thrust of new ideas. The academic or sacerdotal grades of the spokesmen of what seemed a 'reforming' orthodoxy made it possible to build a party before silence was imposed. In the post-monastic age of the later Middle Ages, Waldes's eventual successors were John Wycliffe, John Hus and Martin Luther. The final chapter of this book will attempt to describe the start of the great transition, one in which the lay and clerical constituencies of the later Reformation were first beginning to identify themselves.

This said, it is wise to recall what was said before, namely that twelfth-century popular heresy was beaten not only by force but also by opening the Church to new devotions and orders and by preaching and teaching. One without the other, force or persuasion, would surely not have worked. Also, great though it seemed at the time, the victory did not arrest the spread of divergent thought for very long.

NOTES AND REFERENCES

1   W.H. May, 'The confession of Prous Boneta, Heretic and Heresiarch' in *Essays in Medieval Life and Thought* (eds. Mundy, Emery and Nelson), 24.

2   *Liber casuum conscientiae* 185 in *Summa de sacramentis et animae consiliis* III, 2a (ed. Dugauquier), 102.

3   *Liber casuum conscientiae* 185 (ed. Dugauquier), 101. Jerome in *Decretum* 2, 8, 1, 6 in *CICan* I, 591.

4   *Summa contra haereticos* ascribed to *Praepositinus of Cremona* 21 (eds J.N. Garvin and J.A. Corbett, Nôtre-Dame, 1957) 225–6. See Micah 4:3.

5   See *Lettres de Jacques de Vitry* (ed. Huygens), 76, and, in Letter No. 1, Ephesians 4:28, 1 Thessalonians 4:10–21 and 2 Thessalonians 3:7–12.

6   Thomas of Eccleston, *Tractatus de adventu fratrum minorum in Angliam*, 15 (ed. Little), 99.

7   Alphandéry *Les idées morales chez les hétérodoxes latins au début du XIIIe siècle* (Paris, 1903), 12–13n. 'Good workers' translates *boni valeti* meaning journeymen.

8   *Guillaume de Puylaurens Chronique* 8 (ed. Jean Duvernoy, Paris, 1976), 48–50.

9   *Lettres de Jacques de Vitry* (ed. Huygens), 72–3, No. 1. 'Patarin' meant heretic in Lombardy.

10 *De investigatione Antichristi* in *MGH Ldl* III, 347–8.

11 Maisonneuve, *Etudes sur l'origine de l'Inquisition*, 88.

12 *Ibid.*, 105n.

13 *Verbum abbreviatum* 72 in *PL* CCV, 320.

PART SIX
Church and State

23

POPES, CLERGY AND LAYFOLK

LAY POWER AND THE PAPACY

The secular State strove to appoint, tax, control and judge the local clergy. The Church, especially the papacy, attempted to regulate the action of secular governments. After the Hohenstaufen defeat, the first combat was between King Philip IV of France and Pope Boniface VIII. It began in 1296 and continued intermittently until the election of the Frenchman Clément V in 1305 and the removal of the papacy from Italy to Avignon on the Rhone river in 1309. The second began in the teens of the fourteenth century, involved a civil war in Germany and resulted in the election of an imperialist antipope. It reached its peak in the 1320s but dragged on until 1347. The two principal protagonists were John XXII and the emperor (or, rather, king of the Romans) Lewis of Bavaria. This second combat is to be treated in the next volume of this series.

To turn back a bit, Alexander of Roes said that the Empire fell victim to Rome and France. When Conradin was executed in 1268, the Hohenstaufen cause seemed obliterated. It had, however, left a legacy: Frederick II's polemics. The curialists were aware of this and even invented the verb 'to frederize'. One lively centre of 'frederization' was the court of Philip IV the Fair.

The French were especially dangerous heirs of the Hohenstaufen because, from Philip Augustus's latter years, France was Rome's principal ally. The alignment of the Capetian cadet house of Anjou–Provence with the popes and the Guelph popular parties of Italy enabled the French to conquer south Italy and Sicily and spread their influence throughout the peninsula. Although second thoughts abounded as Angevin power was cemented, most Italians admired the French, their manners, arts and institutions. Medieval France was at its peak. The Plantagenets were defeated and Louis IX even arbitrated England's civil troubles at Amiens in 1264. Although suffering one severe defeat and gaining no territory, his expeditions bore the burden of the Crusades and helped stabilize the Islamic frontier from the 1240s until his death at Tunis in 1270. Louis exemplified monarchy's glory for all Europe. Noted above, the Florentine Remigio de'Girolami stated that, in comparison with France's king, all other western princes were mere kinglets. Even northern French heretics were loyal, Caesarius of Heisterbach remarking that the Amalricians believed Latin Europe would be ruled by France's king in the forthcoming age of the Holy Spirit.

So useful were the French that the pontiffs converted Capetian and Angevin wars into Crusades financed by clerical taxes. The popes also helped convince this nation that it was special. Although the title 'Most Christian King' was liberally bestowed, Innocent III declared in 1215 that this honorific was a special mark of France's kings. Alexander III told the archbishop of Rheims in 1171 that his kings had always helped St Peter in his hour of need and possessed unshatterable faith. In 1239 Gregory IX glorified the people, writing that, on earth as in heaven,

> the son of God . . . according to the divisions of tongues and of races . . . has constituted diverse kingdoms, among which, just as the tribe of Judah was granted the gift of a special benediction among the sons of the patriarch, so the kingdom of France is distinguished from all other peoples on earth by a privilege of honour and grace.[1]

As a pacific gesture between the already embroiled monarchy and papacy, Boniface VIII canonized Louis IX in 1297.

As France aided Rome, the number of cardinals representing French and Angevin south Italian interests gradually increased. Of the thirteen reigning popes from the accession of the French Urban IV in 1261 until that of Clément V in 1305, four were French, the first breach of the Italian monopoly of that office since 1159. For years – since the decretal *Per venerabilem* of 1213 referring to a king of France, as seen above – the popes argued that a king is emperor in his own kingdom, thereby contradicting Frederick I Barbarossa's observation that Europe's kings were mere 'kinglets' under the emperor. In 1303 Rome abruptly reversed its long-held position. Shortly before he was seized at Anagni by France's Roman allies,

Boniface VIII remarked anent his tentative alliance with the German king Albert I of Habsburg that all kings, and especially the vainglorious king of France, ought be subject to the emperor. This attempted diplomatic revolution had no morrow. The brief pontificate of Boniface VIII's Italian successor was followed by the Frenchman Clement V, who moved the papal court from Rome – actually from the patrimony because the court had spent most of its time in Viterbo, Orvieto and elsewhere – to Avignon. There new troubles began. The renewed marriage of French and papal policies helped precipitate the battle between John XXII and Lewis of Bavaria. French influence had long been penetrating southern and western Germany, and the Capetian court was dreaming of having its king elected emperor. Although with reservations, John XXII advocated that policy.

French power did not precipitate these conflicts; in fact, the reverse was true. The loss of Constantinople in 1261, the collapse of the union of the Byzantine and Roman churches in 1282, the fall of Acre in the Holy Land in 1291 and the shrinking of Europe's 'first colonial empire' in the face of Islamic and Byzantine attacks affected the French with peculiar intensity. They had led the Crusades and their language was implanted in the Near East and Aegean. They sought scapegoats, blaming not only the Templars, the first military order and a French foundation, but also their Roman ally. Much that exacerbated relationships between France and Rome was due to the arrest of French expansion, as well as the domestic crises foreshadowing France's internal breakdown in the later Hundred Years' War. In 1296 the issue between Boniface VIII and Philip (as well as the king of England) was the secular government's right to tax the clergy without papal approval. The crown needed money to suppress the revolt of the Flemish cities and battle their English ally. Its penury was worsened by the refusal of its own aristocracies, rural and urban, to finance the government adequately.

The rivalry of France and England threatened Boniface VIII because it drew church revenue away from causes dearer to his heart. Foremost was the hope of resuming Crusades against the infidel, a cause still believed in, at least formally, by the people. But priorities differed. The pope wanted to get on with Crusades, but first had to settle Italy; the French wanted the same, but first had to settle the Anglo-Flemish question. Another issue was Catalonia–Aragon. The revolt of the Sicilians against the Angevin French in the Vespers of 1282 had established a Catalan–Aragonese dynasty in that island. By the early fourteenth century, Catalan fleets and armies penetrated an Aegean Sea once ruled by the French and Italians and weakened Angevin Marseilles' commerce. The rise of this Iberian kingdom encouraged the still lively separatism of the recently absorbed provinces of the Midi reaching from once imperial and now Angevin Provence to Capetian Languedoc.

Catalonia–Aragon's emergence as a main player in Europe's affairs encouraged Boniface VIII to try to escape the French alliance. The repulse of repeated Angevin attempts to reconquer Sicily and the failure of the Capetians against Peter III of Aragon led the pope (who had earlier assisted these efforts because of the link between Peter and the Sicilian Hohenstaufens) to think of an alliance with Barcelona. At least one Catalan spokesman, Raymond Llull, had plans for renewing the Crusades that were more attractive to the pope than French ones. Lull's strategy did not appeal; indeed, it must have seemed bizarre. Whereas French and Italians usually proposed conquering Egypt or Syria as a start, Lull preferred to begin at Granada in Spain, and thence move through north Africa to Egypt and Syria. What did appeal was the institutional side of Lull's scheme. While the French talked about uniting the military orders of the Church under their king, Lull proposed unifying these shock troops under Rome. Even more enticing was his notion 'that the pope and cardinals should assign the tithe of the Church to the Crusade until the Holy Land is conquered, the tithe which they now give to Christian kings. This tithe has its origin in, and is contributed by, those who labour so that the Church be honoured and sustained, but kings wickedly divert it to secular causes.'[2] The pope's attempt to work out something with Catalonia–Aragon together with the unrest in Languedoc precipitated Philip IV's attack on the papacy. In 1301 he arrested Bernard Saisset, bishop of Pamiers and papal legate. He also asked Rome to degrade the bishop and hand him over to his court to be charged with high treason and collusion with Catalonia and dissident southern French. The pope refused and issued the famous bull *Unam sanctam*, on which more anon.

At the time of Lewis of Bavaria, also, the pope's adhesion to French policies hurt the papacy. Even before the 1290s, Franciscan radicals from southern France shared politics earlier seen in Italy, where, as the Hohenstaufens failed and the Angevins rose, utopians viewed the Franco-papal alliance as wicked. Hostile to the Crusade as an irruption of naked force into religion, they had prayed for the defeat of Louis IX's Crusades. When the Catalans revived the Hohenstaufen dream in 1282, Franciscan radicals joined them along with other sectaries. In southern France this ideology was linked to regional separatism. Franciscans like Bernard Délicieux intrigued with Catalonia-Aragon, and were consequently pursued by both pope and king in the 1320s. The result was that the Franciscan 'left' sided with Lewis of Bavaria.

France experienced more intensely what happened to all Europeans affected by the cessation of expansion and Islam's counter-attack. Because the German frontier continued expanding and the full extent of the Turkish threat was not yet apparent, it was hard to read the signs. Men still followed the same old roads, blaming others when they led nowhere, as Boniface blamed the French, who in turn blamed him.

CHURCH DIVISIONS

Although the clerical order had often split during past struggles with secular authority, it was unusually lacking in solidarity around 1300. Although fearfully, France's prelates adhered to their king in the north French assembly of 1302. The secular clergy and the older regular orders had fought for nearly a century against the invasion of their parishes and prerogatives by the mendicant orders fostered by the popes. They were also linked to local interests, and had long resisted Rome's appointment of university-trained clergy or Italian absentees. Cardinal Matthew of Aquasparta's statement in consistory that the French had no grounds for complaint because only two French prelates were Italian, and these were famous men (one was Giles of Rome) who had spent much of their lives in France, was not heard over the Alps. The abbots of older orders, bishops and provosts of cathedral chapters traditionally summoned to general councils also favoured a conciliar constitution, whereas the pope stood for monarchy. The secular clergy's shaky loyalty would not have been decisive, however, had not the mendicants failed to help. A reason for this was that the growth of these new orders was being slowed by the clergy assembled in the general councils to which the popes were being forced to bow. Although indirectly represented by members who had been elevated to prelacies, the mendicants had no direct conciliar representation. The squeeze was already felt at the first Council of Lyons in 1245, but the legislation of second Lyons in 1274 was more drastic. Several recent orders of friars were there abolished, one being the Friars of the Sack, an order founded in Provence in 1248 and granted a rule in 1251, which boasted about eighty houses at its abolition. The culminating legislation was the canon *Cum de quibusdam mulieribus* at the Council of Vienne in 1311 which cut off further expansion by the Beguines. By that time, what had been viewed as progressive was seen as disorderly and dangerous. This opinion, moreover, was not idiot: monasticism was laicizing with a vengeance. In 1310 Augustine Trionfo, an enemy of Peter John Olivi, inveighed against the world of the lay enthusiasts, having in mind perhaps the Franciscan tertiary, philosopher, missionary and utopian Raymond Lull and the medical doctor, divinator and lay theologian Arnold of Villanova: 'When we see these fellows mobile in their status, now married, now continent, now secular, now monks, now overseas, now at home, now spurning the world, now belonging to it, this is a sign that their visions are not divine revelations but rather diabolical illusions.'[3]

Nor could the conciliar fathers have had their way had not the mendicants themselves been divided. There were conflicts between the orders, especially between Dominicans and Franciscans, and also an increasingly intense battle within the latter order. By far the largest mendicant order, it was also the most unstable and tumultuous, partly because it was the major orthodox equivalent of the Waldensians described above. Francis and his early companions differed from other extremists because they obeyed bishops and popes, thereby playing a 'counter-revolutionary' role. The initial lay leadership of the order and the express desire to imitate Jesus's life and poverty enabled it to attract utopian spirits who would have otherwise leaned towards divergent thought. They hoped to rebuild in the Franciscan order a world modelled on the supernal Jerusalem.

In its early days, the principal conflict in the order concerned lay leadership. Francis was a layman and so was Elias of Cortona who, having served as the practical Martha to Francis's spiritual Mary until the latter's death in 1226, assumed the office of minister general at that date. Elias tried to maintain lay predominance, but as he slowly lost out to the clerical brethren he became increasingly arbitrary, especially during his second generalship beginning in 1232. The lay principle could protect him in Italy, but the opposition was led by friars from ultramontane houses where there was no mass lay recruiting. This foreign pressure obliged or enabled the pope to depose him in 1239. Although Francis and his companions provided an example of the eremitical life and personal fulfilment, only the brethren in orders could provide the sacramental services necessary for Franciscan success in the lay world.

As in early Christianity, moreover, spontaneity and equality were lost in emphasizing the mission. Francis, for example, suspected that education created invidious distinctions between equals. His rule of 1223 therefore stated that the brethren should not busy themselves learning Latin. How this anti-intellectualism failed is seen in a statement of the general Bonaventure. When discussing the origin of the order, this famous and learned doctor asked:

> Does it not move you that the brothers were simple and unlearned in the beginning? . . . . I confess that what has made me love the life of Francis is that it is like the beginning and perfection of the Church, which first began with simple fishermen and afterward advanced to famous and learned doctors . . . . [Our order] was not invented by man's prudence, but instead by Christ . . . because learned men did not disdain to descend into the company of simple ones, bearing in mind the apostle's message: 'If there is a wise man among you, let him become a fool, that he may be wise.'[4]

Francis's *Testament* of 1226 had also insisted that the rule God had given him should not be glossed away but instead obeyed 'to the letter, to the letter, to the letter'! Commenting on this, Bonaventure glossed it:

> The rule does not prohibit study for those with letters, only for the unlettered and lay. Following the apostles, [Francis] wants each one to remain in the vocation to which he has been called so that no one should ascend from the laity into clerical orders, but he did not want clerks to become laymen by refusing to study.[5]

Although lay rule vanished with Elias's fall, the tertiary lay brethren were often truculently radical in the late thirteenth century.

Few layfolk espoused the eremitical life of a Francis, but instead wanted the preaching, sacramental, burial and charitable services the order could offer. To provide these, the Franciscans invaded the secular clergy's parishes, battled with rival mendicants and acquired bishops' mitres and cardinals' hats. This had angered the founder, but it is fair to say that his friend Cardinal Hugolino of Ostia, the later Gregory IX, was of real value to him, and that he himself revealed a talent of manipulating others. He stilled the opposition to his *Second Rule* by having God speak to him directly, so that he appeared like another Moses on Sinai. Unlike the founders of other orders, including the Dominicans who settled for a version of the so-called Augustinian rule, Francis's insistence on promulgating his own rule served to foster an aggressive sense of his order's peculiar fitness. This led later brethren to use papal privileges to get their way with the parish clergy, thus disobeying Matthew 10:23: 'when they persecute you in this city, flee into another', a passage repeated in the founder's testament of 1226. Again, the more the Franciscans defeated the popular heresies, the more vehemently they pursued their mission.

Missions require sustenance. Ideally, the Franciscan was to acquire, by begging or working, only enough for the day with no accumulation for the morrow, and neither member nor order was to have property. Even before mid-century, the idea of Franciscan poverty split into rigorous and lax interpretations: the poverty of the *usus pauper* as against moderate use. The austerity demanded by John of Parma, general from 1247 to 1257, or by the later Spiritual Franciscan, Ubertino of Casale, was beyond most brethren and alienated them by favouring the ascetical minority. However moderate, use required property.

Property held in trust by other than the friars offered a way of both avoiding poverty and endowing the mission. The mission required the predictable use of economic means. It also needed cult centres, and the convents and churches erected in Francis's name, beginning with the basilica raised over his tomb in Assisi by Elias, were costly. Without predictable use, libraries, scheduled preaching, sacramental services and charity could not be maintained. Missions also required specialists whose training required time, time bought by property's fruits. Working men were sometimes wise and inspired but had little time to learn and teach. Behind Prous Boneta stood Olivi, whose work on the *Apocalypse* she had read (or had read to her) in a vernacular translation. Behind Salimbene's stammering day labourer of Parma, Master Benvenuto, stood those who had translated or read him sections from the Bible, Joachim of Fiore, Michael Scot and anonymous prophetic works of the time.

The Franciscan quandary, in brief, was how to reconcile an aggressive mission with an ideological unwillingness to endow it. Starting with Gregory IX's *Quo elongati* of 1230, the pontiffs provided ways around the rigour of Francis's rule and testament. While the predictable use of the fruits accrued to the Franciscans, the ownership of the property from which the fruits derived was vested in Rome entrusted to a cardinal protector, two proctors in each province and associated layfolk. Writing shortly after 1312, the conservative Bonagratia of Bergamo argued that, 'since by natural and divine law the use of all things pertaining to human life ought to be common to all men, and, since it came about by iniquity that this is said to be mine and that yours' the Franciscan's right to use nature's fruits fulfilled the natural communism of the apostolic community.[6] After Nicholas III issued the decretal *Exiit qui seminat* in 1279, moreover, which declared that Christ and his apostles owned nothing severally or in common, some believed that the Franciscans fulfilled Christian utopian hope.

Poverty became an obsession among Franciscans, perhaps because the defeat of their lay brethren had made them so similar to other mendicants. It became their special claim to attention, a substitute for the early order's social radicalism, and a way of beguiling its eremitical and laic wings. Although there were serious battles about poverty as early as the 1240s, the split between the minority radicals, soon to be called Spirituals (and when they really diverged, Fraticelli), and the majority or Community awaited the end of the generalship of Bonaventure in 1272. Following the *usus pauper* guideline, the radicals first charged that the majority was not as austere as the founder wished. They then moved to a more telling point: the distinction between use and ownership was deceitful, because one who enjoys a predictable use of the fruit of a good is surely the 'moral' owner of the good in question. Composing his letter *Sanctitas vestra* just after 1312, the Spiritual Ubertino of Casale observed:

> Surely the blessed Francis did not wish that the possession would be the pope's and the use ours. Quite the contrary, he wanted ownership to be vested in the hands of prelates, donors or communities, so that no tenure be given the brethren . . . . In his testament and legend he says that the brothers should not inhabit their poor homes as their own, but live as pilgrims and strangers in others' homes.[7]

Under Boniface VIII and John XXII, the popes' usual policy was to aid the Community against the Spirituals, sometimes with inquisitorial prosecution. The spirit of this effort is seen in a phrase from John XXII's bull *Quorundam exigit* of 1317: 'Great is poverty, but greater still is blamelessness and the greatest good of all is obedience.'[8] The radical Franciscans were therefore hostile to Boniface

VIII in his French troubles and actively sided with Lewis of Bavaria against John XXII, and both the secular clergy, the Dominicans and some other mendicants, none of whom enjoyed the privilege of poverty, united to oppose them. Besides, the Community's position on use and ownership obliged the papacy to uphold a dubious case at the cost of some bloodshed and much turbulence. In the decretal *Ad conditorem canonum* of 1322 John cut the Gordian knot and used the Spirituals' argument to weaken the Community's position. He there denied that there was any substantial difference between the predictable use of fruits and the ownership of the property whence they derived. With minor exceptions, therefore, Franciscans were to hold property as other orders did. Following Thomas Aquinas, John asserted that not poverty but charity or love was the basis of a perfect life. Spurred on by the Dominicans, the same pontiff declared in his *Cum inter nonnullos* of the next year that to aver that Christ and the apostles did not own and have free use of property was heretical. Having thus been stripped of their order's claim to attention, the Community's leaders went over to the side of the Bavarian, there to rest in uneasy proximity to their brothers of the radical wing. In brief, the largest and most popular order actively harmed both the papacy and Church liberty in the struggle with the secular State.

The loss to the Church was more than tactical. Bonaventure reports that when Francis asked Innocent III for the right to be poor, Cardinal John Colonna said that he could not 'refuse the request of this poor man as being too hard and unheard of . . . . If anyone should say that the observance of evangelical perfection or the vow of this man is strange, irrational or impossible, he blasphemes against Christ, the author of the Gospel.'[9]

Nor did this failure merely involve the way of life. As poverty's partisans became aware of the resistance facing them, they began seeking assurances that their cause was inevitably going to win, and that shortly. In the 1240s, the Joachitic idea of spiritual progress penetrated radical Franciscan circles, and consequently each crisis over poverty was accompanied by one over Joachitic historicism. The first of these occurred during the generalship of John of Parma when Gerard of Borgo San Donnino's *Introduction of the Eternal Evangel*, a glossed compilation of Joachim's works, was published. Gerard thought these texts would replace both the Old and New Testaments in the forthcoming age of the Holy Spirit. The storm provoked by this publication resulted in a hasty condemnation of

Joachim's teaching by a papal commission at Anagni in 1255, the resignation of John of Parma in 1257 and real but moderate repression under Bonaventure.

The lid on the Spirituals was lifted when Raymond Gaufridi became general in 1289, and hope bloomed again until Celestine V resigned in 1294 and was replaced by Boniface VIII. Thereafter things worsened. Languedoc's Olivites were wiped out in the 1320s and Olivi's work on the Apocalypse was condemned in 1326. This Franciscan's enemies claimed he said that Francis and his twelve companions had founded the Church of the Final Age. The constitution of this new evangelical church was the several rules dictated by Francis, his testament and the bull *Exiit qui seminat* on the poverty of Christ. So infallible were these precepts believed to be that no authority, of pope or general and ecumenical council, could ever change them. If the Inquisitor Bernard Gui's understanding of what they had to say is correct, they asserted that a self-designated élite could reject the opinions of the Church in the name of spiritual progress. Anent *Exiit*, they may also have helped to invent the notion of papal infallibility. To them, the bull was so infallible that no successor on Peter's throne could change its teaching.

Some churchmen reacted by denying that the radical Franciscans were the vehicle of spiritual progress, and by questioning the idea of progress itself. John of Anneux, a secular clerk silenced in 1279 at the time of *Exiit*, sprang up to defend the pope in 1328, tripping over his tongue in his rage:

> How could this witless fellow Francis discover a new way of living which so many doctors, Augustine, Gregory and other saints inspired by the Holy Spirit didn't know, and which the Church that lasted before him for a thousand years didn't have, which was then more perfect, just as the men of that time were a hundred times more perfect than they are now; nor can this Francis's way of life be lived except by hermits in the desert.[10]

Others said the same with moderation, and hence it seems that the Franciscan failure marked a recession of the hope of spiritual progress that had fired the Church from the Gregorian period until Avignon. That hope had not vanished, however, but instead became attached to the secular State – as in the time of Cola di Rienzo (d. 1354) – to flower again in modern times as an obsession of secular dreamers.

The Franciscan failure also served to advance secularization, to bring nearer the moment when all true Christians, whatever their worldly vocation, equalled the religious. In his *Ad conditorem canonum* John XXII argued that, without charity, a monk or friar derived no spiritual advantage from his vow of poverty unless he was free from the solicitude or care incumbent on those who seek to use property. Such was clearly not the Franciscan case or, indeed, that of any monk. Later on in 1334, Ockham angrily responded:

> This error opposes the religious who profess to live without their own property. According to it, if monks . . . are solicitous to acquire, conserve and dispense temporal goods after taking their vow of poverty . . . their [personal] surrender of goods . . . confers no advantage so far as [spiritual] perfection is concerned. From this error there follows a certain ancient error . . . namely, that it is not better to do good works with the vow than without it.[11]

Ockham was right: John XXII had taught that there was no spiritual or moral advantage to being in a religious order. The doctrine of charity or love, moreover, could be treated similarly. A later defender of John's position, John of Celle, a Tuscan gentleman who retired to a hermitage in 1351, told the Fraticelli that they had made poverty their idol and lost sight of mercy and love. In urging the elders of Ephesus to be charitable, Paul had reminded them of Christ's injunction: 'It is more blessed to give than to receive.' John drew from this the corollary: 'And if this is true, and it surely is, the rich who give deserve more than the poor who receive.'[12] A rich lay donor was therefore more blessed than a poor monk who received. A utopian hope that had seemed about to penetrate all society at the time of the Humiliati, Robert of Curzon and others had been channelled into the Franciscan order, and had there failed once again.

LAY PRESSURE

Clerks would not have vacillated had not layfolk pressed so hard, and they did so because Latin society was in difficulty. Overpopulation had led to the cultivation of marginally productive land. By 1300 social and economic corporatism had maximized rights and profits in agriculture, industry and commerce, and society was divided into interest groups flying at each other's throats in efforts to realize their ambitions. Men responded with anger and utopian fancies to this *rallentando* of their dreams' realization. The potentiality of social and economic corporatism for mobilizing larger units of production and government was known, but had yet to win support. To give that, people had to be convinced by the harsh experience of domestic and foreign war that private right and property should be diminished and the liberties and privileges of individuals, localities and social groups restricted. They were not yet ready to surrender these in order to erect the unitary monarchies or principates that were to harness and police their passions in early modern times.

Real princely government was already emerging around 1300. The idea of the 'arbitrary power' or 'free will' that empowered princes to act without the constraints of prior law or public assemblies was already well defined. Princely prerogatives were nevertheless still everywhere impeded by particularist elements, and, indeed, were not to be freed – and then never wholly so – until the efforts of ecclesiastical conciliarism and secular parliamentarianism had been defeated in the fifteenth century. Still, the restraints on the powers of princes and their unitary states were already visibly weakening. Before 1300 Latin Europe had been ruled by an alliance of the ecumenical Roman Church with local rural and urban aristocracies. At the time of Boniface VIII this combination faltered and the aristocracies, hard pressed by the rise of the plebs beneath them and by the growth of princely power above, sought to escape by sacrificing Rome.

Layfolk reacted for many reasons: they spoke of resistance to ecclesiastical domination, and how heavily the Church weighed on them. It did. The attack on usury, the exercise of tighter controls over marriage and the family, and the regulation of just war in the forum of conscience paralleled the Church's attempt to police Europe's states, to call for service against heretics and Crusades. The Church's call also inadvertently summoned lay magistrates and princes to examine, and intervene in, its workings. Layfolk were not merely meretricious in their desire to control the behaviour, services and appointments of the clergy. Having been called to serve, their consciences or fears were as deeply involved in the affairs of the Church as those of the clergy. To witness executions was normal in the thirteenth century, but to light the fire, as Inquisitors asked them to do, was different. Laymen were also more capable. The growth of lay literacy and professionalism began to give them the ability to intervene in the clerical sphere, and the spread of the monastic vocation to those living in the world convinced them that they were the spiritual equals of churchmen.

Human conscience is related to interest. Responding to petitions from Languedoc in 1301, Philip the Fair complained to the bishop of Toulouse about the Inquisitors' pursuit of the Spiritual Franciscans, charging the Dominicans with committing the most abhorrent crimes under the guise of protecting the faith. The king later changed his tune on learning that the Spirituals were in touch with Catalonia–Aragon. In 1308 the same prince mounted his campaign against the Templars and asked the theologians of Paris if lay magistrates could proceed against heretics without ecclesiastical permission. They said not, 'except when evident and notorious danger threatened, in which case secular power could [intervene], if it had a sure hope of ecclesiastical confirmation'.[13] The king's hope soon became sure because the Templars collapsed under torture and he leaned on the pope at Avignon. Nor were princes unique. All kinds of groups tried to limit ecclesiastical power and direct the Church. Typical was the clergy's lament at a synod held in 1258 at Ruffec (between Poitiers and Angoulme) about leagues of 'knights, communities and barons, farmers and townsmen' combating ecclesiastical jurisdiction.[14]

Quarrels between towns and churchmen reflected the issues that embroiled Rome and larger states. An extreme but revealing example is a complaint against the knights and citizens of Eichsätt brought before an archiepiscopal council held at Mainz. It was there reported that the townsmen, aided by some rural seigniors, had remained almost a year under excommunication, plundered the church's treasure, continued burial services and, 'with heretical and diabolical presumption and perversion, cruelly and violently expelled the bishop together with the clergy who supported him, and chose laymen to serve as bishop, provost and dean', thus continuing the Church's administrative services.[15] Describing the divisions rending Florence in the early fourteenth century, Remigio reported that the clergy called laymen 'traitors, usurers, perjurers, adulterers, robbers . . . . And laymen say that clerks are fornicators, gluttons and idle and the religious vainglorious thieves.'[16]

Apart from the clergy's right to trial in its own courts, what angered the laity was the enlargement of the papal right to appoint to posts in local churches, the increased control of church courts over testaments, the consequent appeals to Rome and Rome's taxation of local churches. The bone of contention was partly gold.

That Rome was avaricious had long been a commonplace. In 1245 Louis IX protested the taxes paid by the Gallican Church to Rome, claiming that his kingdom was being impoverished and foreigners enriched by its spoils. A despatch in 1301 from an Aragonese ambassador at Rome said that the French embargo was bringing the pope to his knees. France had ordered, he reported, that

> no one shall take from the kingdom gold, silver, cloth, wool, horses and money even in letters of exchange or deposit contracts. Thus have the French prelates summoned by the pope been wholly prevented from coming. Whence you should know, famous lord, that fear and tremors have gripped not a few, especially if the way of gulping down the gold of France should be closed to them.[17]

The pope combated the charge. Boniface VIII remarked in consistory that Capetian revenues had more than doubled since the days of Philip Augustus because of favours granted by the Holy See. An argument that might also have carried weight – but did not – was that the communities and seigniors who protested losing business to ecclesiastical courts were losing far more to royal tribunals. In regard to taxes, the French crown had been assigned substantial ecclesiastical subsidies by the popes in every year from 1284 to 1296, and Boniface's attempt to stop this haemorrhage precipitated the first crisis between him and Philip. As seen above, a reason for this was that the monarchy had not yet been able to impose regular taxation on France's nobles and communities; nor did it, in fact, until the latter part of the Hundred Years War. Even so, what can be said of that later time can probably be said of 1300: the fiscal demands of the secular State were growing more rapidly than those of Rome. Unused to the costs and constraints required and threatened by the quasi-democratic urgings of the plebs, the aristocracies of town and countryside did not wish to pay for the growing central State but were nevertheless obliged by circumstances to favour the growth itself. For a time, then, they willingly joined prince and people to make the Church pay.

Arising from natural solidarity, the idea of the nation provided an alternate focus of loyalty. In the letter of Gregory IX of 1239 cited above, the idea was twofold: a people was defined by language and race. When Edward I summoned the archbishop of Canterbury to the Model Parliament in 1295, this French-speaking prince cited the threat of the French, whose king, he said, intended to obliterate the 'English tongue'. Race ideas are seen in the Rhinelander Alexander of Roes. To him, as noted above, Italians were ruled by the love of gain, Germany by that of ruling and Frenchmen by the desire to know. These natural qualities determined their different governments: in Italy the people ruled, in Germany the soldiery and in France an arrogant and lustful clergy. The word 'Gaul' derives from cock, and Frenchmen share that bird's qualities, being 'handsome of body, but more handsome feathered than plucked, that is, when clothed not naked'. The French erroneously said that 'Gaul' comes from the Greek *galla* which means milk, and that they were called so because their colour is white. 'It is true that, when compared with Spaniards or Moors [variant: Greeks], they were white, but . . . their whiteness cannot compare with that of the Saxons and English.'[18]

France naturalized the same ideas. Peter Dubois insisted that, by geographical and astral determination, northern France was the cradle of those naturally capable of ruling others. Stealing his text from the Hohenstaufen propaganda of Godfrey of Viterbo (who had taken it indirectly from Carolingian Frankland), John of Paris found that the French, heirs of ancient Troy, had never been subject to Rome and hence were naturally free. Assembled in 1247 to protest Church policies, the French baronage, headed by the magnates of Burgundy, Brittany and St Pol, used arguments prefiguring those of the Monarchomachs of the late sixteenth century. Proclaiming Roman servility and Frankish liberty – the liberty, that is, of the French aristocracy – they implied that the Gallo-Roman 'plebs' indicated servility.

> Because the superstition of clerks does not consider that the kingdom of France was converted from the error of the gentiles to the Catholic faith by the wars and blood of not a few under Charlemagne and other princes . . . [and that clerks have by now] so absorbed the secular jurisdiction of the magnates that sons of slaves judge by their law the children of freemen; and because they ought rather be judged by us according to the laws of the original victors, our ancestors' customs ought not be superseded by [their] constitutions . . . therefore we, barons of the kingdom, perceiving with attentive mind that the kingdom was not acquired by the written law nor by the arrogance of clerks, but by the sweat of soldiers, declare . . . [19]

that, except for usury, marriage and heresy, no case may go to an ecclesiastical tribunal.

In France for a time the monarchy embodied the sentiments of the nation. The ideas of the king as emperor in his kingdom and as 'most Christian' and ever orthodox were repeated again and again in the manifestos issued by Philip's ministers William of Nogaret and William of Plaisans. So faithful was this prince that a sermon delivered at court during the Flemish war congratulated the enemy on the opportunity of being defeated, thus to be brought back to the ways of Jesus and right reason. Indeed, to this perfervid preacher the king's interests were identical to those of the faith: 'Whoever inveighs against the king combats the whole Church, Catholic doctrine, sanctity, justice and the Holy Land.'[20]

Addressing the French clergy in 1303, Nogaret contended that his prince's duty was to reform the Church. He had borrowed the idea from the Hohenstaufen when in 1239 Frederick II proposed to emend the Church 'to the better', a phrase taken from the canon of the mass. Repudiating his condemnation at the Council at Lyons in 1245, his *Illos felices* of 1246 declares that the emperor

> most especially intends that the prelates and clergy should be returned to that state of poverty in which they were at the time of the primitive church . . . . For clerks of that time contemplated the angels, and, coruscate with miracles, cured the sick, raised the dead and subjected kings and princes by sanctity and not by arms.[21]

By 1247 north French barons borrowed this rhetoric to justify reducing clerical power. They acted, they said, so that

> our jurisdiction thus revived should breathe again, and that [churchmen], up to now enriched by our impoverishment . . . should be reduced to the state of the primitive church, so that, living in contemplation while we, as is fitting, lead the active life, they will again perform miracles, those miracles that have so long departed from this earth.[22]

Many loved the Christian republic, but each wished to defend it after first purging the others. In 1301 Boniface VIII issued two bulls, *Ausculta, fili* and *Ante promotionem*, in which he summoned a council of French prelates and masters of law and theology. To reconquer the Holy Land, he proposed, royal policies, such as the debasement of coinage, were to be rescinded and much was to be done 'for the augmentation of the Catholic faith, the conservation of ecclesiastical liberty, the reformation of the king and kingdom, the correction of past excesses and the good government of the kingdom'.[23] French anger may be gauged from a passage in a tract by Peter Dubois probably of 1303: 'You, noble king, by inheritance above all other princes defender of the faith and destroyer of heretics, can, ought and are obliged to require . . . that the said Boniface be held and judged as an heretic.'[24] In June 1303 the court adopted and publicized a plan suggested long before in 1239 by Frederick II: convene a general council to judge the crimes attributed to the pope. Even with the split among the cardinals, the adhesion of the French clergy to the crown, and France's power, it is unlikely that this council would have carried much more weight than the one summoned later at Rome against John XXII by Lewis of Bavaria, but in the meantime Boniface had been seized at Anagni by France's Roman allies. He was shortly thereafter released by his friends, but died suddenly in October 1303. Before his end, however, the pontiff had issued in November 1302 the great *Unam sanctam*. It is to this bull and the polemics around it that attention will now be turned.

NOTES AND REFERENCES

1   Huillard-Bréholles, *Historia diplomatica Friderici secundi* V, i, 457–8.

2   *Disputatio Raymundi christiani et Hamar saraceni* 2 in *Beati Raymundi Lulli opera* IV, 477b.

3   *Tractatus contra divinatores et sompniatores* 1 in Richard Scholz, *Unbekannte kirchenpolitischen Streitschriften aus der Zeit Ludwigs des Bayern* (Rome 1914) II, 483–4.

4   *Opusculum XII: Epistola de tribus quaestionibus ad magistrum innominatum* 13 in *Opera omnia: Opuscula varia ad theologiam mysticam et res ordinis fratrum minorum spectantia* VIII (Quaracchi, 1898), 336a–b, and 1 Corinthians 3:18.

5   *Ibid.*, 10, *Opera omnia*, 334b, and 1 Corinthians 7:24.

6   Douie, *The Nature and Effects of the Heresy of the Fraticelli*, 158. Bonagratia used Gratian's paraphrase from Augustine and a letter attributed to Clement I in *Decretum* 1, 8, 1 and 2 and 2, 1, 2 in *CICan* I, 12–13 and 676.

7   Leff, *Heresy in the Later Middle Ages* I, 148, derived partly from Bonaventure's *Legenda Sancti Francisci* 7, 2 in *Opera omnia* VIII, 523b.

8   *Extravagantes Johanni XXII* 14, 1 in *CICan* II, 1223.

9   *Legenda S. Francisci* 3, 9 in *Opera omnia* VIII, 512a.

10   Douie, *The Nature and Effects of the Heresy of the Fraticelli*, 170.

11   *Tractatus contra Johannem* 23 in H.S. Offler, *Opera politica* (Manchester, 1956) III, 89.

12   Felice Tocco, 'L'eresia dei fraticelli e una lettera inedita del beato Giovanni delle Celle' in *Studi francescani* (Naples, 1909), 460, and Acts 20:35.

13   Denifle, *Chartularium universitatis Parisiensis* I, 126, No. 664.

14   Lagarde, *La naissance de l'esprit laïque* I, 169n.

15   *Annales erphordenses fratrum praedicatorum* in the *Monumenta Erphesfurtensia, MGH SS in usum scholarum* 44, 97.

16   Davis, 'Remigio de'Girolami' in *Proceedings of the American Philosophical Society* CIV (1960), 667a.

17   Finke, *Aus den Tagen Bonifaz VIII*, lv.

18   *Memoriale* 15 in *MGH Staatsschriften* I, i, 107.

19   Matthew Paris *Chronica majora* in *Rolls Series* LVII iv 595-98. See Lagarde *La naissance de l'esprit laïque* I 161 and Wieruszowski *Vom Imperium zum nationalen Königtum*, especially *Verzeichnis* 222ff.

20   In Kantorowicz, *The King's Two Bodies*, 254.

21   Huillard-Bréholles, *Historia diplomatica Friderici secundi* VI, 393, and Eduard Winkelmann, *Acta imperii inedita* II (Innsbruck, 1880), 50.

22   Matthew Paris, *Chronica majora* in *Rolls Series* LVII, iv, 593.

23   *Ante promotionem* in *Les registres de Boniface VIII* III, 336, No. 4426.

24   *La supplication du peuple de France* cited in Wilks, *The Problem of Sovereignty in the Later Middle Ages*, 236.

24

UNAM SANCTAM

POLEMICS

During this threatening time, the enthusiast Roger Bacon said that an angel pope would mobilize the Latins against the Antichrist, launch Crusades again and convert the infidel, Jew and pagan. Fearing that the vast realms of the Tatars would fall to Islam or Judaism, Raymond Llull wanted them converted, saying that '[God] has given the Latins power to acquire the whole world, if they wish to.'[1] The opinions of another Catalan, Arnold of Villanova, sometime medical doctor of Boniface VIII, were close to Llull's. His politics were vehemently anti-French and he was an especially forthright adherent of the radical Franciscans. He believed in an early version of the secular idea of progress in which a new church or spiritual order of a Franciscan type was joined to mystic medicine and natural science.

Some favoured secular leadership. The Norman lawyer Peter Dubois proposed reforming and financing the Church by entrusting its property to lay management. Latin Europe was to unify under France's king, who was to direct the 'reconquest' of the Holy Land and the Near East. As a first step, the pernicious freedom of the Italian city republics and the resistance of King Peter of Aragon and the Sicilians to the Angevin French were to be crushed. These utopian schemes were contradictory: some favoured clerical leadership, others secular; some favoured the French, others their enemies. Although Llull's work was approved at Paris in 1310 and influenced later great men such as Nicholas of Cusa (d. 1464), some thought him mildly mad. Suspected of being a Joachite, Roger

Bacon was shunted aside in his later years, perhaps imprisoned. An ardent defender of the losing cause of the Spiritual Franciscans, Arnold of Villanova was convinced that the clergy had it in for him because, although a married medical doctor, he wrote about theology. He was probably correct, but the reserve greeting him is understandable. Responding to attacks on his tract proclaiming the immediate coming of the Antichrist, Arnold warned churchmen that,

> just as they rejected John [the Baptist] and Christ . . . so do they now defame these two modern messengers. For they said of him who [God] first sent, namely, Master Raymond Llull, that he was an illiterate idiot ignorant of grammar. Then he sent them the second messenger [Arnold himself], not only a true and splendid expert in the Latin language, but admirably competent in many subjects, and they said he was a rash fantast, and a magician or necromancer.[2]

Besides these unrealizable fancies, there were two main and somewhat practical issues. The first was the conflict between monarchism and conciliarism. It was noted that both Boniface VIII and Philip IV tried to summon councils in which to condemn the other. This conflict of political ideologies has been rehearsed in the chapters of Part Four above and will be referred to here only in so far as it concerns the second. The second issue is the familiar one: the relationship of Church to State, the prospects of the independence of the latter from the former, and its insistence on the subordination of the laity to the clergy. Of those who addressed this problem, the two greatest, Marsiglio of Padua and William of Ockham, escape the scope of this volume. Those on whom attention is centred are worthy forerunners, John Quidort of Paris, whose *On Papal and Royal Power* appeared in 1302, and Giles of Rome, whose *On Ecclesiastical Power* was issued the year before.

To John, a Dominican divine at Paris, the Church was to keep the mean between the Waldensians and the Herodians. The former wished it to surrender all property and coercion. The latter – Herod had mistakenly thought that Christ was an earthly king – wanted the Church to rule the world. Following Bernard of Clairvaux, John argued that the pope is not a master of souls, but rather a steward. Just as Jesus ruled men's hearts and not their possessions, so the pope accepts 'the keys of the kingdom of heaven, not because of power over [material] possessions but because of power over [moral] crime'.[3] Whatever temporal authority the Church enjoys was given it by the people or their governments. The very fact that Constantine gave the Church the 'Italian empire' and that the Church accepted the gift proves that it did not have civil dominion of its own right. Like Marsiglio later, John denied Henry of Cremona's allegation of 1302 that 'those saying that the pope lacks power in temporal matters are heretics because they are saying that the Church cannot coerce heretics by the secular arm'.[4]

The Church has powers, John says: the power to consecrate, the medicinal power of the keys in the forum of conscience and the power to teach or to preach. Although great, the power to teach cannot rely on coercion, only on persuasion. The Church can also punish spiritually: it can exclude, for example, heretics from its community. Unless the secular State freely lends its coercive force, however, this capacity to punish is devoid of earthly sanctions.

> An ecclesiastical judge cannot impose a . . . penalty for a crime as can a secular judge, unless the criminal wishes to accept it. If he does not, an ecclesiastical judge can compel by excommunication or other spiritual penalty, which is the most he can do: he cannot do anything more.[5]

Unless there is firm scriptural precept, especially in the New Testament, moreover, the Church may not even render judgments about moral matters. Usury can be judged, for example, but the larger issue of private property cannot. Although both moral and natural law clearly favour the common possession of property, John says, practical experience teaches that it leads to civil strife among sinful men and women. The Church is therefore not to interfere here, following Augustine's recommendation: 'Remove,' the great African said, 'the law of the emperor and one cannot say that this thing is mine, because in natural law there is one liberty for all and the common possession of all things.'[6] After the Fall, both the coerciveness of the State and private property became necessary; heaven, the monastic communism of the apostles, is not for this earth. But, to John, there was an advantage here: the sanctity of private property protected layfolk against tyrannical efforts by the Church to impose its solutions on them.

John's separation of the spheres is not as daring as it seems. Many had justified secular authority, even that of pagans or infidels, and John never tried to equal the earlier Peter Damian. Enraged by a summons to arms to protect the Church, Peter had insisted on the difference between the spiritual and material:

> If therefore for the faith by which the universal Church lives it is impermissible

to take up arms of iron, how then do armoured hosts rage with their swords for the earthly and transitory riches of the Church? Indeed, when the saints prevail, they will surely not destroy heretics or worshippers of idols, but will instead *not flee* being slain by them for the Catholic faith.[7]

An Aristotelian, John allows an exception to the Church's abstention from the employment of coercion described above: the case of dire need, when good people can transcend their normal roles to act for equity or epiky. The pope may never dispose of lay properties 'except in the ultimate need of the Church, in which case he acts not as a dispensator [with ordinary jurisdiction], but rather as one who declares the law'.[8] And so can any good person.

The secular State, then, is independent of the Church. Although the Church is more worthy, the State preceded it in history. 'Whence the Empire is from God alone . . . . As the pope does not have the [spiritual] sword from the emperor, so the emperor does not have the [temporal] one from the pope: "For the army makes the emperor." '[9] Corresponding to their different ends, the organization of Church and State differed. Contradicting the tradition that led Dante to favour universal monarchy, John maintains that, although God's ordinance made the faith one and unified, the same is not true of civil society.

> Laymen do not have it from divine law that they must be subject in temporal matters to one supreme monarch. By the natural instinct implanted by God, it is instead recommended that they live in a civil community, and, as a result, choose diverse kinds of governors in order to live well according to the diversity of their communities.[10]

This difference derived partly from nature: religion is naturally more unified than civil dominion because the word of persuasion travels faster than coercion's sword. Borrowing an idea of Augustine's, also, John argued that Rome's experience and that of other empires did not show that a universal state was necessarily beneficial. He concluded that, although the rule of one man is probably the best for any one people (a point later contradicted by Marsiglio who argued that true unity was the oneness of a community and not the number of its magistrates), 'it is nevertheless better that many should rule in many realms than that one should rule the whole world'.[11] Again, although ecclesiastical unity best protects church property which is held in community, the existence of private property in secular society pleads rather for diversity than unity. The basic reason John took this position, however, was that, in the natural sphere where the State operates, varieties of tongues, peoples and climates make it obvious that 'what is virtuous in one people is not so in another'.[12]

Ideally, for John, each nation is possessed by its inhabitants, who entrust government to elected or permitted magistrates – an example of the latter being the hereditary monarchs of France. So also is the Church an assembly of the faithful who continue to possess its government while attributing its exercise to ecclesiastical magistrates. Although, for example, the papacy is of divine foundation, the person holding the office is not divine. God's rule of the world

> does not exclude our work, for we are his co-workers. Although the papacy is from God, it is nevertheless placed in this or that person through human co-operation, namely, by the consensus of the electors and the elected, and, as a result, it can cease to be vested in this or that particular person by human consensus.[13]

A pope or other magistrate can therefore be removed, and the question boils down to how and for what reasons. Everyone agreed that the reasons should not be minor. Writing in 1295, Peter John Olivi stated that one must defer somewhat to princes: 'Thus minor mistakes or frauds may be committed by a monarch as long as he is obliged to use the advice of the many and the good in important matters.'[14] Monarchists went far further than this. In about 1308, an anonymous defender of Boniface VIII commented on a report that the pope had asserted that he, theoretically both emperor and pope, could not commit simony because everything was his anyway. Taking this as a probable proposition, the author argued that, if Boniface had said it, 'he should be understood in the good sense and not the bad, especially because, when we do not know with what intention things are done, we ought always give the benefit of the doubt'.[15] Accepting a moderate version of this permissive thought, John stated that a pope could be removed if he were mad, heretical or wholly inept.

John spelled out how popes could be removed. Like Olivi, he thought that if, for good cause, a pontiff were willing to resign, the cardinals could stand for the people and accept the decision. Were he unwilling, his deposition required a larger 'consensus of the people', and therefore followed Gratian 'where it is said that a general council was convoked to depose Pope Marcellinus,' a pope suspected of capitulating to the pagans during Diocletian's persecution.[16] And if a pope violently resists, a secular prince may be called in, 'nor does he act against the pope as pope, but against . . . the enemy of the republic'.[17] John went on to praise Emperor Henry III for removing three rival popes and replacing them with another at Sutri in 1046 – an action that had infuriated Gregorians. John also opined that the cardinals could invite secular intervention if a pope were notoriously heretical or simoniacal. Then, 'as an aid to law . . . the emperor, requested by the cardinals, ought to proceed against the pope and depose him', an idea that was later to appeal to the conciliar fathers in 1415.[18]

Employed together with the idea of the king as emperor in his own kingdom, John's doctrine was obviously useful to France's king. The difficulty was that the Church was made dependent on the secular sword, and it turned out that those who wielded that weapon subordinated the Church in return for their service. Unlike the far more secular Marsiglio, however, John tempered his advocacy. He viewed the accidental power 'in aid of law' as a double-edged sword, one that could be employed by the Church as well as by the State. Just as a prince invited by the clergy could act against a pope, so could a pope requested by the barons act against a prince. In John's imagination, everything depended on the people:

> I also say, however, that the pope acts *per accidens* because, if a prince is heretical, incorrigible and a contemner of ecclesiastical censures, the pope can do something among the people so that the prince will be deprived of his office by the people and be deposed. The pope does this for ecclesiastic crimes, which cases pertain to him, by excommunicating those who obey the prince as a lord, and thus the people deposes the prince [directly] and the pope indirectly.[19]

Wise about princes, this Dominican did not perceive that the people's affections were shifting. From the Gregorian age until about 1300, the people and the popes had together judged and limited princes. From 1300 onward the people, their princes and magistrates were to judge the popes and clergy. In that context, Boniface VIII's remark in 1301 that 'we have both spiritual and material power!' elicited a truthful rejoinder from a Frenchman: 'Indeed so, sir, but your power is verbal; ours is real.'[20] Aided by his contemporary Dante, John also provided a justification for laymen. Observing that temporal ends and virtues were distinct from spiritual ones and good in themselves, he averred that 'moral virtues acquired [on earth] can be perfect without theological ones', and went on to draw the corollary that on earth, 'without Christ governing, there is true and perfect justice', that is, true and perfect government.[21]

Defenders of ecclesiastical autonomy and the popes thought otherwise. Cardinal John Lemoine defended the bull *Unam sanctam* because there were four ends in life: physical health, personal moral virtue, the good of the multitude or society and the good of the sempiternal soul. These ends are in ascending order, but without the last the others are of no consequence. Giles of Rome was more subtle. He followed Thomas Aquinas in admitting that human and natural goods – health, a sufficiency of means, education and peace – were intrinsically good. Following Augustine, however, he argued from experience that things beneficial in themselves are not necessarily good for humanity because by itself it is incapable of using them to advantage. Without God's grace they are of no value, and he therefore concluded: 'If therefore neither our end nor our bliss is to be found in temporal things but only in spiritual ones, it follows that temporal things are good only in so far as they are directed toward spiritual objectives.'[22] Also, although the secular State is needed to provide a peace in which Christians may be educated toward blessedness,

> we say with Augustine that true justice cannot be found except in that republic whose founder and governor is Christ. Now, the pagan Romans talked much about justice and pontificated about the republic, but that republic, as Augustine says . . . was not alive in behaviour but merely painted in colours . . . . Hence Augustine asserts that the Roman republic was not a true republic because true justice never ruled there.[23]

In 1302 James of Viterbo not unfairly epitomized his master Giles: 'No community can be called a true republic save the ecclesiastical one, because true justice, utility and community exist in it alone.'[24]

It is true, says Giles, that secular power derives from God, and that directly. But then, so do fire, water, human bodies and human learning – indeed, everything in the natural world. Since good things may be put to evil use, however, the thing itself is not the same as the use made of it. The search for salvation is the only justification of all natural things, and for that the sacraments of the Church are required. It is therefore true that

> since none are worthy of honour, dominion, power or, indeed, of any good

except by ecclesiastical sacraments through the Church and under the Church, what our chapter heading said was well said, namely that, even if there is no power except that derived from God, no one is worthy of having any power unless he becomes worthy under the Church or through it.[25]

Although John of Paris appears not to have known it, Giles contradicted one of the Parisian's practical objections to ecclesiastical power (one later much developed by Ockham) by stating that secular princes or laymen should not grumble about the yoke placed on their necks by the Church, because this yoke is not servitude, but instead liberty.

> Because faithful Christians are redeemed by the Church from the power of the devil, they ought confess themselves to be ascript slaves of the Church . . . . This servitude is meritorious because it is more of love than of fear, of devotion than of coercion. By this servitude nothing is lost, but much is gained because what is given by the faithful to the Church will be returned a hundred times over, and they will possess eternal life.[26]

As Ockham and Marsiglio were to point out, to Giles and his followers the Church Militant was not merely an institution of divine foundation but also a godlike one.

So immense is Church power in this view that one wonders what was left to laymen. According to Giles, the Church had obeyed the injunction to render to Caesar what is Caesar's by attributing to the laity a particular and lower form of lordship or ownership, while reserving to itself a superior and universal one. He also applauds the view that, since all power is really vested in the spiritual sword, it was percipient to invent the material sword because 'a certain dignity in government should be given to the laity lest laymen perceive themselves to be wholly contemptible. This would cause murmurs and quarrels between the laity and the clergy in the Church.'[27] Here, glossing over Bernard of Clairvaux's earlier caveats, Giles asserts that the Church exercises both the lord's 'jurisdictional' right and the tenant's 'use' right in all temporal things. Still, as is evident, the Church grants laymen the tenant's right – that is, the right to raise fruits from temporal things – and this for good reason: as payment for their souls' care, the laity will support the clergy. This is especially advantageous because scripture teaches us that, in order to occupy themselves with spiritual solicitude, the apostles were enjoined to avoid earthly care. 'It was therefore the glory of the apostles that they possessed nothing at all as far as responsibility or anxiety are concerned, but everything as far as lordship,' and the clergy are the apostles' heirs.[28]

Without a general, an army is nothing and doomed to defeat. By analogy, the good of the Church is embodied in the pope. 'The Church must be feared and its commands obeyed, and the highest pontiff, who holds the apex of the Church and who verily can be called the Church, must be feared and his commands obeyed, because his power is spiritual, celestial and divine, and is without weight, number and measure.' Lay or clerical, all other offices have weight, number and measure, but, like God, the papal plenitude of power cannot be weighed or measured.[29] This vision of the pope as a quasi-God or 'image of Christ' infuriated both Marsiglio and Ockham, and had already elicited much opposition. In 1295 Olivi, although a moderate defender of practical papal authority, remarked: 'They say that he is uncreated, immense, impeccable, infallible and prescient in all things, like Christ, an opinion which no one would state or even hint at, except a lunatic.'[30] Giles tried to circumvent this objection by separating office and person. A truly spiritual man can judge all others and never be judged, and there are two kinds of spiritual men. One is spiritual because of personal perfection; another, like the pope, because of office. 'He who is spiritual according to his status and perfect in the highest degree according to the jurisdiction and plenitude of his power will be the spiritual man who judges all things and cannot be judged by anyone.'[31]

To believe otherwise, as was said in *Unam sanctam* by John Lemoine and others, is to substitute a heretical Manichaean duality for a divinely ordained unity. It is therefore, as Giles says, 'indeed well said that the power of the supreme pontiff is that sublime power to which every soul should be subject', or, as the princely Boniface VIII put it in *Unam sanctam*: 'We declare, state, decide and pronounce that it is altogether necessary for the salvation of every human creature to be subject to the Roman pontiff.'[32]

CONCLUSIONS

It has long been known that there was little original in *Unam sanctam*, and often observed that both John of Paris and Giles of Rome drew heavily on Thomas Aquinas. Yet from that central teaching, two very different doctrines were derived to feed the fires of institutional conflict. One, that of John of Paris, was to lead to Ockham's endless doubting questions and the secularism of Marsiglio of Padua. It thus served to open the way for secular magistrates and lay philosophers to replace churchmen and theologians as the vessels holding the basic religion of western man. The other, that of Giles of Rome, so hardened a once somewhat flexible doctrine that, in spite of its occasionally perceptive cynicism about laymen, it no longer rang true to life. To use the monk's image, Giles's clerical Marys were to be supported by unnaturally subservient lay Marthas. As seen in the order of Grandmont, the attempt to deprive the Marthas of some exercise of leadership had never really worked even among the religious. When applied to monarchies and republics and to their subjects and citizens (all fired by the spread and laicizing of the monastic vocation), this deprivation was not likely to fare half as well.

Perhaps the problem should be put differently. Perhaps it is true that the people support only those intellectual or religious leaders who sing the tunes they wish to hear; and that, as the lay spirit became more powerful and capable, layfolk threw priests and monks on to the dump. Against this one may argue with Jean-Jacques Rousseau that there is a true religion of intellectual and spiritual freedom, and that its levites can raise humanity above its mundane concerns, even against its will, and that, because of their vices, the clergy failed to do that. There are difficulties here, however. When discussing voluntary poverty, Aquinas remarked that he who seeks to live virtuously with no means of his own and who depends on the generosity of others has a problem:

> Freedom of the mind is most especially required for the attainment of perfect virtue, for, if this is weakened, men very easily become 'partakers of other men's sins' either by expressly agreeing, being adulatory or hiding their true feelings. Hence this way of living is prejudicial to freedom because there is no man who does not fear to offend him from whose kindness he lives.

Aquinas's answer was that those who give themselves to voluntary poverty are of such perfection that they would not be suborned by 'the little' they need in order to live.[33] But 'little' is a relative term, and it seems from the history of the Church in this period that the objection the saint thus hastily disposed of was the more probable or safer opinion. Even among the best, even among

the Franciscans and their radical offshoots, few or none were perfect, and consequently, few or none were free.

The quandary was much discussed at the time. A solution had
twice been tried, once at the time of the attack on heresy and usury
around 1200 and once again among the Franciscan rigorists around
1300: the utopian solution. When discussing 2 Thessalonians 3:7–
12, Peter Cantor urged the clergy to follow Paul:

> When preaching in Achaia, the apostle accepted no charity from [the people],
> partly because they were covetous and hated him to whom they gave . . . and
> partly because he did not want the idle – who, seeing him labour with his own
> hands and eat the bread of his own labour, were no longer able, as had been
> their wont, to eat the bread of sloth [that is, the bread of other's labour] – to
> have bought impunity by thinking: 'We have filled Paul's hands, and now we
> can do what we want.'[34]

But the history of the Church and indeed of society had shown
that the ascetic's or utopian's solution, although momentarily
possible for individuals, was impossible for the many. The attempt
to realize this ideal had twice failed, once in the world at large and
once within the narrower confines of the Franciscan order, and
with this failure the solidarity of the Christian republic and its ecclesiastical leadership had begun to crumble.

It serves no purpose to declare – in the moralizing language
often employed by today's historians – that churchmen failed because they were corrupt. Such views overlook the fact that the
clergy, although seemingly ruling, was only one group or one 'nation' in the Christian republic whose citizens permitted or created
their leadership. They are also untruthful because they encourage
one to forget that, although Christian ideals were useful because
they helped men both develop their talents and reconcile themselves to their misery, they could not possibly be attained. To dilate
only on the beauty of the hope of living the 'apostolic life' or of
creating here on earth a perfect society on the model of the supernal Jerusalem obscures a function of espousing impossible social and
religious ideals. That function is to give ideologues a way of condemning their neighbours for failing to live up to what they could
not reasonably be expected to. An aspect of this social idealism is,
then, an instrument for both personal aggrandizement and social
warfare because it deprives one's neighbours of rectitude and therefore of rights. Utopian dreams, untinged by resignation, soon
become nightmares. A historian should therefore eschew judgment

and instead try to understand, viewing those neighbours of the past, not as those others, but rather as brothers. Concerning a special aspect of utopian hope, Peter Cantor once remarked: 'In nature's law, all things are in common: earth for treading, air for breathing, water for drinking and bathing. Why then do princes and clergy hold as private goods what should be in common?' But in spite of his utopian hopes, a thousand experiences echoed in Peter's mind and finally made him say: 'It is difficult to advise princes on this matter and hard indeed to condemn the whole Church.'[35]

That their world had begun to fall apart was not because they were corrupt, but rather because churchmen, like their lay fellow citizens of the Christian republic, were not perfect. In judging them, one had best follow Gaius's rule: Semper in dubiis benigniora praeferenda sunt.[36]

– – –

However truthful it may be, the above runs ahead of history's schedule. To go back to the battles between Church and State in the early fourteenth century, Philip the Fair undoubtedly defeated Rome: the French party in the Roman court triumphed and brought the papacy to Avignon. In spite of this, little institutional power was surrendered to the secular State, and even the effect of the papacy's move to the Rhone valley was soon dissipated by the French collapse in the Hundred Years' War. The later battle with the Empire was almost a papal victory. When Lewis of Bavaria died in 1347, the emperor's pope had long disappeared while the pope's imperial candidate remained on the throne. Such being the case, who, in 1300 or 1330, would have believed that, following Europe's diplomatic alignments, the Church was to split into two or more obediences during the Great Schism, and that, in the Conciliar Age, it would begin to surrender institutional power to the State? What contemporaries did see, however, was that a pope had stumbled badly in his attempt to control the Capetian king, and could compare this with Innocent IV's earlier resounding victory over the Hohenstaufen emperor.

NOTES AND REFERENCES

1   *Disputatio Raymundi Christiani et Hamar Saraceni* 3 in *Beati Raymundi Lulli opera* IV, 477a.

2   *Tractatus quidam in quo respondetur obiectionibus que fiebant contra tractatum Arnaldi de adventu Antichristi* in M. Batllori, *Analecta sacra Tarraconensia* XXVIII (1955), 68.

3   *De potestate regia et papali* 10 (ed. Bleienstein), 110, from Bernard's *De consideratione* 1, 6.

4   *Ibid.* 11 (ed. Bleienstein), 126.

5   *Ibid.* 13 (ed. Bleienstein), 138.

6   *Ibid.* 13 (ed. Bleienstein), 136, a rough quotation from *Decretum* 1, 7, 1 in *CICan* I, 13.

7   Book Four, Letter 4 in *PL* CXLIV, 316a.

8   *De potestate regia et papali* 7 (ed. Bleienstein), 96.

9   *Ibid.* 10 (ed. Bleienstein), 111 and *Decretum* 1, 93, 24 and 96, 11.

10   *Ibid.* 3 (ed. Bleienstein), 82.

11   *Ibid.* 21 (ed. Bleienstein), 190.

12   *Ibid.* 3 (ed. Bleienstein), 83.

13   *Ibid.* 25 (ed. Bleienstein), 202.

14   *De renunciatione papae* in *Archivum franciscanum historicum* XI–XII (1918–19) 354–5.

15   Cited in Finke, *Aus den Tagen Bonifaz VIII*, lxxiv.

16   *De potestate regia et papali* 201 (ed. Bleienstein), 201. See *Nunc autem* in *Decretum* 1, 21, 7 in *CICan* 1, 71.

17   *Ibid.* 22 (ed Bleienstein), 196.

18   *Ibid.* 13 (ed. Bleienstein), 140.

19   *Ibid.* 13 (ed. Bleienstein), 138.

20   Dupuy *Histoire du différend*, 130.

21   *Ibid.* 18 (ed. Bleienstein), 163.

22   *De ecclesiastica potestate* 2, 4 (ed. Richard Scholz, Leipzig, 1929, rprt) 49.

23   *Ibid.* 2, 7 (ed. Scholz), 73; Augustine, *De civitate dei* 2, 21 and 19, 21.

24   *De regimine christiano* 1, 4 cited in Wilks, *The Problem of Sovereignty*, 18.

25   *De ecclesiastica potestate* 2, 9 (ed. Scholz), 85.

26   *Ibid.* 2, 10 (ed. Scholz), 95.

27   *Ibid.* 2, 15 (ed. Scholz), 136.

28   *Ibid.* 2, 1 (ed. Scholz) 37–8; 1 Corinthians 7:32.

29   *Ibid.* 3, 12 (ed. Scholz), 209, Wisdom of Solomon 11:21.

30   *Epistola ad Conradum de Offida* in *Archivum franciscanum historicum* XI–XII (1918–19) 368.

31   *De ecclesiastica potestate* 1, 2 (ed. Scholz) 6.

32   *Ibid.* 1, 4 (ed. Scholz), 11, and *Extravagantes communes* 1, 8, 1 in *CICan* II, 1246.

33   *Contra gentiles* 3, 132, 4, 4 and 3, 135, 4, 4 (Rome, 1934), 386b and 391b. 1 Timothy 5:22.

34   *Liber casuum conscientiae* 3, 50 in *Summa de sacramentis et animae consiliis* 3, 2a (ed. Dugauquier) 342.

35   *Ibid.: Liber casuum conscientiae* 3, 2 (ed. Dugauquier), 162, para. 208.

36   *Digest* 50, 17, 56.

BIBLIOGRAPHY

In addition to this bibliography, readers may also consult an alphabetical list of books appended at its end called the Bibliographical Supplement. This second list is for readers who need full bibliographical references for the works cited in the footnotes of this textbook.

A useful survey, though in need of updating, is R.H.C. Davis, *Medieval European History. A Select Bibliography* (3rd edn, 1977). More comprehensive is G.C. Boyce (ed.), *Literature of Medieval History. 1930–75*, 5 vols (New York, 1981). For England, see C. Gross, *A Bibliography of English History to 1485*, ed. E.B. Groves (Oxford, 1975).

For recent publication, there are helpful summaries in the *Annual Bulletin of Historical Literature* (published by the Historical Association), and more specialized listings in the biannual *International Medieval Bibliography*. A number of historical journals have bibliographical supplements, in particular *Cahiers de civilisations médiévales, Revue d'histoire ecclésiastique, Historische Zeitschrift* and *French Historical Studies* (the last two commendable for the speed with which new works are noted). Most of the books listed below contain their own bibliographies, and it is also worth consulting those in the volumes in the present series by C.N.L. Brooke and D. Hay.

INTRODUCTION: SOURCES

Many of the writings of key figures such as Thomas Aquinas, Bonaventure and Roger Bacon have at some time been translated into

English. Poems, romances and not a few histories are also available in translation, often in such well-known series as Columbia University's *Records of Civilization, Oxford Medieval Texts* or *Penguin Classics.*

For translations published before 1967, see:

C.P. Farrar and A.P. Evans, *Bibliography of English Translations from Medieval Sources* (New York, 1946);

M.A.H. Ferguson, *Bibliography of English Translations from Medieval Sources, 1943–1967* (New York, 1974).

See also:

R.C. van Caenegem, *Guide to the Sources of Medieval History* (Amsterdam, New York and Oxford, 1978).

PART ONE: EUROPE

1. Social orders

R.Folz, *The Concept of Empire in Western Europe from the Fifth to the Fourteenth Century* (1969).

R. Fossier (ed.), *The Cambridge Illustrated History of the Middle Ages*, vol. 3: *1250–1520* (Cambridge, 1986).

E.H. Kantorowicz, *The King's Two Bodies. A Study in Medieval Political Theology* (Princeton, 1957).

J. Le Goff, *The Birth of Purgatory* (Chicago, 1984).

C. Morris, *The Discovery of the Individual, 1050–1200* (1972).

A. Murray, *Reason and Society in the Middle Ages* (Oxford, 1978).

E. Rosenstock-Huessy, *The Driving Power of Western Civilization: The Christian Revolution of the Middle Ages* (Boston, 1950).

R.W. Southern, *The Making of the Middle Ages* (1953).

G. Tellenbach, *Church, State and Christian Society at the Time of the Investiture Contest.* (Oxford, 1940).

2. The Jews

R.W. Emery, *The Jews of Perpignan in the Thirteenth Century. An Economic Study* (New York, 1959).

W.C. Jordan, *The French Monarchy and the Jews* (Philadelphia, 1989).

G. Kisch, *The Jews in Medieval Germany. A Study of their Legal and Social Status* (2nd edn, New York, 1970).

H.G. Richardson, *English Jewry under the Angevin Kings* (1960).

3. The Crusades and Europe's frontiers

P. Alphandéry and A. Dupront, *La chrétienté et l'idée de croisade* (2 vols, Paris, 1954–59).

E. Christiansen, *The Northern Crusades. The Baltic and the Catholic Frontier, 1100–1525. (1980)*.

P.W. Edbury (ed.) *Crusade and Settlement* (Cardiff, 1985).

C. Erdmann, *The Origin of the Idea of the Crusade* (Princeton, 1977).

P.M. Holt, *The Age of the Crusades. The Near East from the Eleventh Century to 1517* (1986).

N. Housley, *The Italian Crusades the Papal–Angevin Alliance and the Crusades against Christian Lay Powers, 1254–1343* (Oxford, 1982).

B.Z. Kedar, *Crusade and Mission. European Approaches toward the Muslims* (Princeton, 1984).

H.E. Mayer, *The Crusades* (2nd edn, Oxford, 1988).

J.R.S. Phillips, *The Medieval Expansion of Europe* (Oxford, 1988).

J. Prawer, *Crusader Institutions* (Oxford, 1980).

J. and L. Riley-Smith, *The Crusades. Idea and Reality* (1981).

G.V. Scammell, *The World Encompassed. The First European Maritime Empires, c. 800–1650* (1981).

PART TWO: ECONOMY

1. Population and technology

P. Bairoch, J. Batou and P. Chèvre, *La population des villes européennes de 800 à 1850* (Geneva, 1988).

R.H. Bautier, *The Economic Development of Medieval Europe* (1971).

M. Beresford, *New Towns of the Middle Ages* (2nd edn, 1988).

The Cambridge Economic History of Europe, vol. 2: *Trade and Industry in the Middle Ages*, ed. M. Postan and E. Miller (2nd Edn, 1987), and vol. 3: *Economic Organization and Policies in the Middle Ages*, ed. M. Postan, E.E. Rich and E. Miller (1963).

N.J.G. Pounds, *An Economic History of Medieval Europe* (1974).

L. White, *Medieval Technology and Social Change* (Oxford, 1962).

2. Agriculture, industry, trade and urbanism

D.S.H. Abulafia, *The Two Italies. Economic Relations between the Norman Kingdom of Sicily and the Northern Communes. (Cambridge, 1977)*.

M. Balard (ed.) *Etat et colonisation au mayen âge (Lyon, 1989)*.

A.R. Bridbury, *Medieval English Clothmaking. An Economic Survey* (1982).

E.H. Byrne, *Genoese Shipping in the Twelfth and Thirteenth Centuries* (Cambridge, Mass., 1930).

The Cambridge Economy, History of Europe, vol. 1: *The Agrarian Life of the Middle Ages*, ed. M. Postan (2nd edn, Cambridge, 1966).

P. Döllinger, *The German Hanse. (1970)*.

G. Duby, *Rural Economy and Country Life in the Medieval West* (1968).

E. Ennen, *The Medieval Town* (Amsterdam and Oxford, 1979).

R. Fossier, *Peasant Life in the Medieval West* (Oxford, 1988).

R.S. Lopez, *The Commercial Revolution of the Middle Ages, 950–1300* (Englewood Cliffs, 1971).

C. Platt, *The English Medieval Town* (1976).

A. Sapori, *The Italian Merchant in the Middle Ages* (New York, 1970).

B.H. Slicher van Bath, *The Agrarian History of Western Europe, 500–1850* (1963).

3. Economic corporatism and usury

J.W. Baldwin, *Masters, Princes and Merchants. The Social Views of Peter the Chanter and his Circle.* (2 vols, Princeton, 1970).

E. Coornaert, *Les Corporations en France avant 1789* (Paris, 1941).

G. Mickwitz, *Die Kartelfunktionen der Zünfte und ihre Bedeutung bei der Entstehung des Zunftwesens* (Helsinki, 1936).

B.N. Nelson, *The Idea of Usury. From Tribal Brotherhood to Universal Otherhood. (2nd edn, Chicago, 1969).*

J.T. Noonan, *The Scholastic Analysis of Usury* (Cambridge, Mass., 1957).

P. Spufford, *Money and Use in Medieval Europe* (Cambridge, 1988).

PART THREE: SOCIETY

1. Women and men

P. Ariès and G. Duby (eds), *A History of Private Life,* vol. II, *Revelations of the Medieval World* (Cambridge, Mass., 1988).

J. Boswell, *Christianity, Social Tolerance nnd Homosexuality. Gay People in Western Europe from the Beginning of the Christian Era to the Fourteenth Century* (Chicago, 1980).

C.N.L. Brooke, *The Medieval Idea of Marriage* (Oxford, 1989).

J.A. Brundage, *Law, Sex and Christian Society in Medieval Europe* (Chicago and London, 1987).

E. Ennen, *The Medieval Woman. (Oxford, 1989).*

E. Le Roy Ladurie, *Montaillou. Cathars amd Catholics in a French Village, 1294–1324* (1978).

F.X. Newman (ed.), *The Meaning of Courtly Love* (Albany, 1969).

J. Roussiaud, *Medieval Prostitution* (Oxford, 1988).

S. Shahar, *Childhood in the Middle Ages* (New York and London, 1990).

2. Farmers and townsmen

B.A. Hanawalt, *The Ties that Bound. Peasant Families in Medieval England. (Oxford, 1986).*

M. Mollat, *The Poor in the Middle Ages* (New Haven, 1986).

J.A. Raftis, *Tenure and Mobility. Studies in the Social History of the Medieval English Village* (Toronto, 1964).

F. Rörig, *The Medieval Town* (1967).

3. Nobles and patricians

B. Arnold, *German Knighthood, 1050–1300* (Oxford, 1985).

R. Barber and J. Barker, *Tournaments, Jousts, Chivalry and Pageants in the Middle Ages* (Woodbridge, 1989).

M. Bloch, *Feudal Society* (2 vols, Chicago, 1961)

J.A. Brundage, *Medieval Canon Law and the Crusader* (Madison, 1969).

P. Contamine, *War in the Middle Ages* (Oxford, 1984).

D. Crouch, *William Marshal* (1990).

G. Duby, *The Knight, the Lady and the Priest* (1984).

M. Keen, *Chivalry* (1984).

T.A. Reuter (ed.), *The Medieval Nobility* (Amsterdam and Oxford, 1978).

4. Ecclesiastics

R.B. Brooke, *The Coming of the Friars* (1975).

G.G. Coulton, *Five Centuries of Religion* (4 vols, Cambridge 1929).

B. Hamilton, *Religion in the Medieval West* (1986).

L.K. Little, *Religious Poverty and the Profit Economy of Medieval Europe* (1979).

J.H. Lynch, *Simoniacal Entry into Religious Life from 1000 to 1260. A Social, Economic and Legal Study* (Columbus, 1976).

E.W. McDonnell, *The Beguines and Beghards in Medieval Culture* (New Brunswick, 1954).

G. Schnürer, *Church and Culture in the Middle Ages* (Patterson, 1956).

PART FOUR: GOVERNMENT

1. The Church

G. Barraclough, *Papal Provisions, Aspects of Church History: Constitutional, Legal and Administrative* (Oxford, 1935).

B. Bolton, *The Medieval Reformation* (1983).

J. M. Ferrante, *The Political Vision of the Divine Comedy* (Princeton, 1984).

K. Pennington, *Pope and Bishops. The Papal Monarchy in the Twelfth and Thirteenth Centuries* (Philadelphia, 1984).

B. Tierney, *Foundations of the Conciliar Theory. The Contribution of the Medieval Canonists* (Cambridge, 1955).

W. Ullman, *A Short History of the Papacy in the Middle Ages* (1972).

2. Monarchies and parliaments

D. Abulafia, *Frederick II. A Medieval Emperor* (1988).

J.W. Baldwin, *The Government of Philip Augustus* (Berkeley and Los Angeles, 1986).

F. Barlow, *The Feudal Kingdom of England, 1042–1216* (2nd edn, 1961).

G. Barraclough, *The Origins of Modern Germany* (3rd edn, Oxford, 1988).

T.N. Bisson, *The Medieval Crown of Aragon* (Oxford, 1986).

M.T. Clanchy, *England and its Rulers, 1066–1272* (1983).

J. Dunbabin, *France in the Making, 843–1180* (Oxford, 1985).

H. Fuhrmann, *Germany in the High Middle Ages, c. 1050–1250* (Cambridge, 1986).

B. Guenée, *States and Rulers in Later Medieval Europe* (Oxford, 1985).

E.M. Hallam, *Capetian Frane, 987–1328* (1980).

A. Haverkamp, *Medieval Germany 1056–1273* (Oxford, 1988).

F. Kern, *Kingship and Law in the Middle Ages* (Oxford, 1945).

A. MacKay, *Spain in the Middle Ages. From Frontier to Empire, 1000–1500* (1977).

A. Marongiu, *Medieval Parliaments. A Comparative Study* (1968).

H. Mitteis, *The State in the Middle Ages. A Comparative Constitutional History of Feudal Europe* (Amsterdam, 1975).

J.F. O'Callaghan, *The Cortes of Castile-León, 1188–1350* (Philadelphia, 1988).

F.M. Powicke, *The Thirteenth Century* (Oxford, 1962).

M. Prestwich, *War, Politics and Finance under Edward I* (1972).

M. Vale, *The Angevin Legacy and the Hundred Years War, 1250–1340* (Oxford, 1990).

3. Villages, towns, republics and political thought

J.H. Burns (ed.), *The Cambridge History of Medieval Political Thought, c. 350–c. 1450* (Cambridge, 1988).

M.V. Clarke, *The Medieval City State. An Essay on Tyranny and Federation in the Late Middle Ages* (Cambridge, 1926).

O.Gierke, *Political Theories of the Middle Ages* (Cambridge 1913).

J.K. Hyde, *Society and Politics in Medieval Italy. Evolution of Civilian Life, 1000–1350* (1973).

C.H. McIlwain, *The Growth of Political Theory in the West* (New York, 1933).

H. Pirenne, *Early Democracies in the Low Countries. Urban Society and Political Conflict in the Middle Ages and Renaissance* (1915).

S. Reynolds, *Kingdoms and Communities in Western Europe, 900–1300* (Oxford, 1984).

D. Waley, *The Italian City Republic* (3rd edn 1988).

M. Wilks, *The Problem of Sovereignty in the Later Middle Ages* (Cambridge, 1963).

4. Scribes, lawyers and society

R. Bartlett, *Trial by Fire and Water. The Medieval Judicial Ordeal* (Oxford, 1986).

M.T. Clanchy, *From Memory to Written Record. England 1066–1307* (1979).

H. Kantorowicz, *Studies in the Glossators of the Roman Law* (Cambridge, 1938).

F. Kern, *Kingship and Law in the Middle Ages* (Oxford, 1945).

S.F.C. Milsom, *The Legal Framework of English Feudalism* (Cambridge, 1976).

PART FIVE: THOUGHT

1. Intellectuals

R.L. Benson and G. Constable (eds), *Renaissance and Renewal in the Twelfth Century* (Oxford, 1982).

A.B. Cobban, *The Medieval Universities. Their Development and Organization* (1975).

A.C. Crombie, *Augustine to Galileo* (2 vols, 1959).

S.C. Easton, *Roger Bacon and his Search for a Universal Science* (New York, 1952).

G. Leff, *Medieval Thought. St Augustine to Ockham* (1958).

H. Rashdall, *The Universities of Europe in the Middle Ages* (3 vols, new edn, Oxford, 1936).

M. Reeves, *The Influence of Prophecy in the Later Middle Ages. A Study in Joachimism* (Oxford, 1969).

B. Smalley, *The Study of the Bible in the Middle Ages* (Oxford, 1952).

2. Enthusiasm and repression

R. and C.N.L. Brooke, *Popular Religion in the Middle Ages* (1984).

A. Gurevich, *Medieval Popular Culture. Problems of Belief and Perception* (Cambridge, 1988).

B. Hamilton, *The Albigensian Crusade* (1974).

– *The Medieval Inquisition* (1981).

M. Lambert, *Medieval Heresy. Popular Movements from the Bogomils to Hus* (1976).

R.E. Lerner, *The Heresy of the Free Spirit in the Later Middle Ages* (Berkeley and London, 1972).

R.I. Moore, *The Formation of a Persecuting Society. Power and Deviance in Western Europe, 950–1250* (Oxford, 1987).

M. Reeves, *Joachim of Fiore and the Prophetic Future* (1976).

PART SIX: 1300

M. Barber, *The Trial of the Templars* (Cambridge 1978).

G. Leff, *Heresy in the Later Middle Ages. The Relations of Heterodoxy to Dissent* (New York, 1967).

M.D. Lambert, *Franciscan Poverty. The Doctrine of the Absolute Poverty of Christ and the Apostles in the Franciscan Order, 1210–1323* (1961).

D.L. Douie, *The Nature and the Effects of the Heresy of the Fraticelli* (Manchester, 1932).

J. Rivière, *Le Problème de l'église et de l'état au temps de Philippe le Bel* (Louvain, 1926).

J.R. Strayer, *The Reign of Philip the Fair* (Princeton, 1980).

BIBLIOGRAPHICAL SUPPLEMENT

Books from which primary text passages have been excerpted.

P. Alphandéry, *Les idées morales chez les hétérodoxes latins au début du XIIIe siècle* (Paris, 1903).

S.W. Baron, *A Social and Religious History of the Jews* (vols III to XII, 2nd edn, New York, 1957–67).

W. Berges, *Die Fürstenspiegel des hohen und späten Mittelalters* (Stuttgart, 1958).

R. Bezzola, *Les origines et la formation de la littérature courtoise en occident* (3 vols, Paris, 1944–63).

M. Bloch, *Rois et serfs: un châpitre d'histoire capétienne* (Paris, 1920).

K. Bosl, *Die Reichministerialität der Salier und Staufer* (2 vols, Stuttgart, 1950–51).

W. Braunfels, *Die staatsbaukunst in der Toskana* (Berlin, 1959).

H. Bresslau, *Handbuch der Urkundenlehre* (3 vols, Berlin and Leipzig, 1912–60).

E. Chénon, *Histoire générale du droit français publique et privé* (2 vols, Paris, 1926–29).

M.D. Chenu, *La théologie au douzième siècle* (Paris, 1957).
—, *La théologie comme science au treizième siècle* (Paris, 1957).

E. Cortese, *La norma giuridica: spunti teorici nel diritto comune classico* (2 vols, Milan, 1962–64).

E. Cristiani, *Nobilità e popolo nel comune di Pisa dalle origini del podestariato alla signoria dei Donoratico* (Naples, 1962).

G. Dahm, *Untersuchungen zur Verfassungs-und Straftsrechtsgeschichte des italienischen Stadt in Mittelalter* (Hamburg, 1941).

D.L. Douie, *The Nature and the Effects of the Heresy of the Fraticelli* (Manchester, 1932).

G. Duby, *La société aux XIe et XIIe siècles dans la région Mâconnaise* (Paris, 1959).

R.W. Emery, *The Jews of Perpignan in the Thirteenth Century: An Economic Study* (New York, 1959).

E. Ennen, *Frühgeschichte der europäischen Stadt* (Bonn, 1953).

H. Finke, *Aus dem Tagen Bonifaz VIII* (Münster, 1902).

P. Fiorelli, *La tortura giuridica nel diritto comune* (2 vols, Milan, 1953).

H. Fitting, *Das castrense peculium in seiner geschichtlichen Entwicklung und heutige gemeinrechtlichen Geltung* (Halle, 1871).

L. Gauthier, *La chevalerie* (Paris, 1884).

O. Gierke, *Das deutsche Genossenschaftsrecht* (3 vols, Berlin, 1861–81).

C. Giraud, *Essai sur l'histoire du droit français* (2 vols, Leipzig, 1846).

M. Grabmann, *Die Geschichte der scholastischen Methode* (2 vols, Freiburg, 1900–10).

R. Grousset, *L'empire du Levant: histoire de la question d'orient* (Paris, 1946).

H. Grundmann, *Religiöse Bewegungen im Mittelalter: Untersuchungen über die geschichtlichen Zusammenhange zwischen der Ketzerei, Bettelorden und der religiösen Frauenbewegung im 12 und 13 Jahrhunderts* (2nd edn, Hildesheim, 1961).

M. Güdemann, *Geschichte des Erziehungswesens und der Kultur der abendländischen Juden während des Mittelalters und der Neueren Zeit* (2 vols, Vienna, 1880–84).

P. Guilhermoz, *Essai sur l'origine de la noblesse en France au moyen âge* (Paris, 1902, reprtd).

J. Haller, *Vier Kapitel zur Geschichte des ausgehenden Mittelalters: Papsttum und Kirchenreform* (2 vols, Berlin, 1903).

J. Hashagen, *Staat und Kirche vor der Reformation: Eine Untersuchung der vorreformatorischen Bedeutung der Laieneinflüsses in der Kirche* (Essen, 1931).

A. Hauck, *Kirchengeschichte Deutschlands* (8th printing, Berlin, 1954).

E.H. Kantorowicz, *The King's Two Bodies: A Study in Medieval Political Theology* (Princeton, 1957).

W. Kamlah, *Apokalypse und Geschichtstheologie: Die mittelalterliche Auslegung der Apokalypse vor Joachim von Fiore* (Berlin, 1935).

F. Kiener, *Verfassungsgeschichte der Provence* (Leipzig, 1900).

G. de Lagarde, *La naissance de l'esprit laïque au déclin du moyen âge* (5 vols, 2nd edn, Louvain, 1962).

C.V. Langlois, *La Vie en France au moyen-âge* (4 vols, Paris, 1926, rprtd).

G. Leff, *Heresy in the Later Middle Ages; the Relation of Heterodoxy to Dissent* (New York, 1967).

R. Lemay, *Abu Ma'Shar and Latin Aristotelianism in the Twelfth Century* (Beirut, 1962).

E. Lousse, *Société d'ancien régime* (Louvain, 1943).

S. MacClintock, *Perversity and Error: Studies on the 'Averroist' John of Jandun* (Bloomington, 1956).

H. Maisonneuve, *Etudes sur l'origine de l'Inquisition* (Paris, 1960).

R. Michel, *L'administration royale dans la sénéchaussée de Beaucaire* (Paris, 1910).

J.H. Mundy, *Liberty and Political Power in Toulouse, 1050–1230* (New York, 1954).

——, *Men and Women at Toulouse in the Age of the Cathars* (Toronto, 1990).

H. Planitz, *Die deutsche Stadt im Mittelalter von der Römerzeit bis zu den Zunftkämpfen* (Graz-Cologne, 1954).

J. Plesner, *L'Emigration de la campagne à la ville libre de Florence au XIIIe siècle* (Copenhagen, 1934).

G. Post, *Studies in Medieval Legal Thought: Public Law and the State, 1100–1322* (Princeton, 1964).

J.P. Ritter, *Ministérialité et chevalerie: Dignité humaine et liberté dans le droit médiéval* (Lausanne, 1955).

G. Rossi, *Consilium sapientis, judiciale* (Milan, 1958).

G. Salvemini, *La dignità cavelleresca nel comune di Firenze* (Florence, 1896, reprtd).

——, *Magnati e popolani in Firenze dal 1280 al 1295* (Florence, 1899, rprtd).

E. Salzer, *Über die Anfänge der Signorie in Oberitalien* (Berlin, 1900).

M. Sbriccoli, *L'interpretazione dello statuto: Contributo allo studio della funzione dei giuristi nell'età comunale* (Milan, 1969).

G. Scholem, *Jewish Mysticism* (New York, 1967).

G. Schreiber, *Gemeinschaften des Mittelalters – Recht und Verfassung: Kult und Frömmigkeit* (Münster, 1948).

B. Tierney, *Foundation of the Conciliar Theory: The Contribution of the Medieval Canonists* (Cambridge, 1955).

L. Verriest, *Institutions médiévales* (vol. 1, Mons, 1946).

P. Villari, *I primi due secoli della storia do Firenze* (Florence, 1905).

H. Wachendorf, *Die wirtschaftliche Stellung der Frau in den deutschen Städten des späteren Mittelalters. (Quakenbrüch, 1934)*.

H. Wieruszowski, *Vom Imperium zum nationalen Königtum* (Munich, 1933).

M. Wilks, *The Problem of Sovereignty in the Later Middle Ages* (Cambridge, 1963).

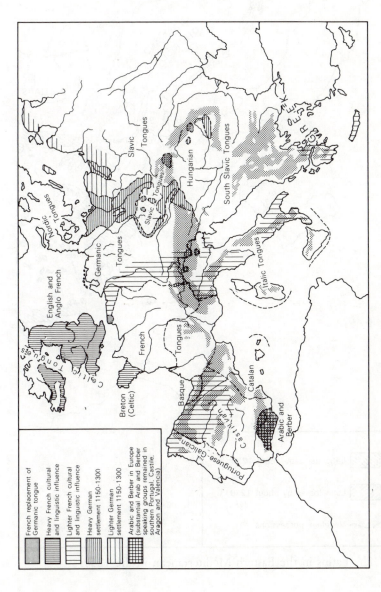

1. Europe's languages and patterns of settlement *circa* 1300

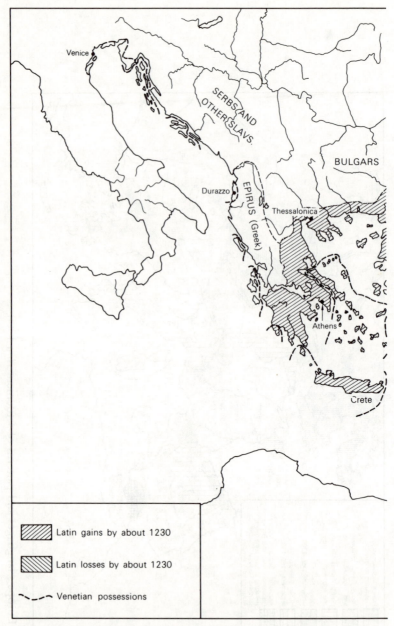

2. The Latins in the Eastern Mediterranean in the 1230s

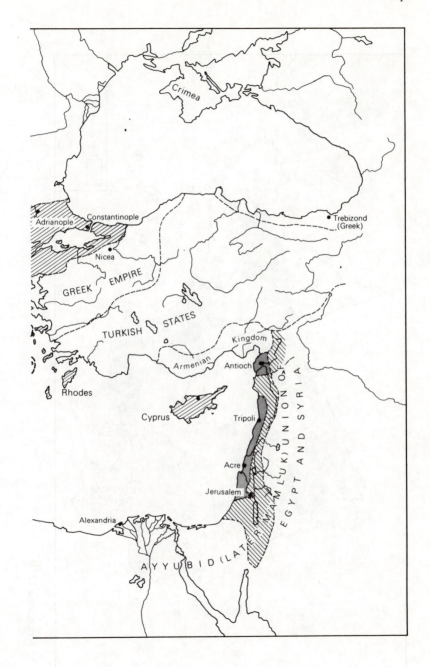

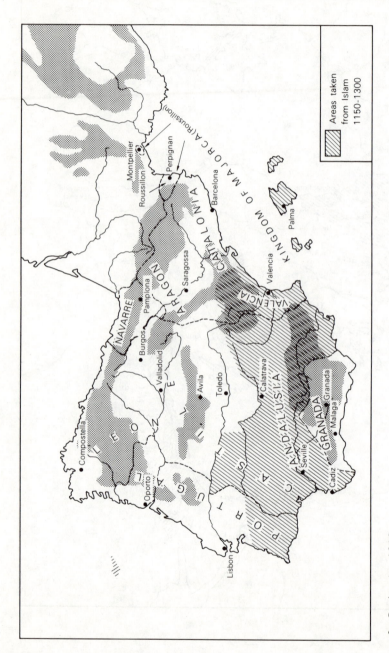

3. Spain *circa* 1310

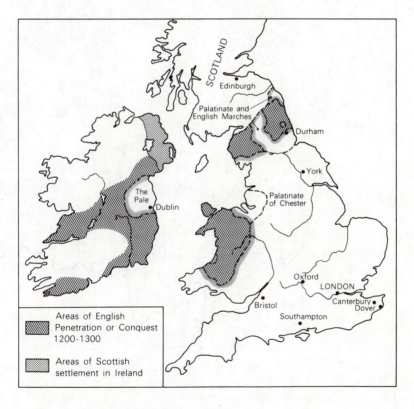

4. The British Isles *circa* 1300

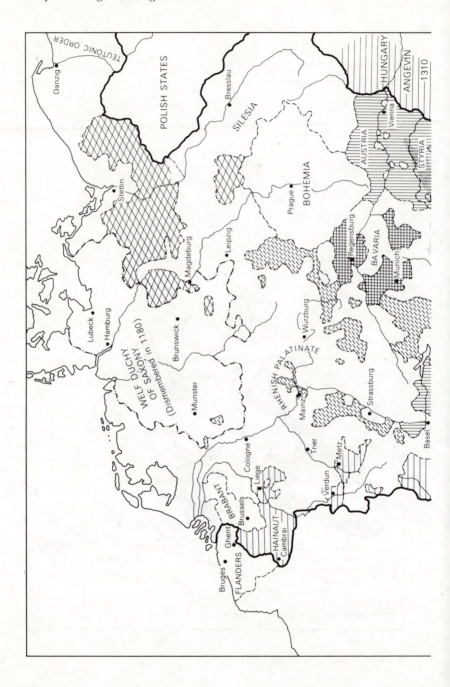

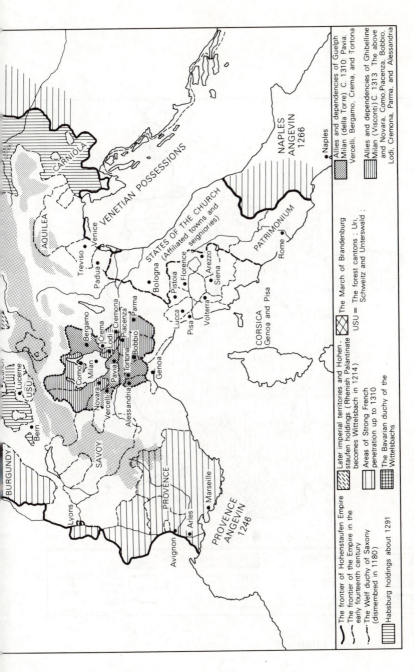

5. The Empire and Italy *circa* 1300

Allies and dependencies of Guelph Milan (della Torre) C. 1310: Pavia. Vercelli, Bergamo, Crema, and Tortona

Allies and dependencies of Ghibelline Milan (Visconti) C. 1313 The above and Novara, Como, Piacenza, Bobbio, Lodi, Cremona, Parma, and Alessandria

• Naples

The March of Brandenburg

USU = The forest cantons : Uri, Schweitz and Unterswald :

The frontier of Hohenstaufen Empire

The frontier of the Empire in the early fourteenth century

The Welf duchy of Saxony (dismembered in 1180)

Habsburg holdings about 1291

Later imperial territories and Hohen-staufen holdings (Rhenish Palatinate becomes Wittelsbach in 1214)

Areas of Strong French penetration up to 1310

The Bavarian duchy of the Wittelsbachs

NAPLES ANGEVIN 1266

PROVENCE ANGEVIN 1246

STATES OF THE CHURCH (Affiliated towns and seigniories)

VENETIAN POSSESSIONS

CARNIOLA

AQUILEA

BURGUNDY?

SAVOY

PROVENCE

PATRIMONIUM

CORSICA Genoa and Pisa

Treviso

Venice

Padua

Bologna

Bergamo

Crema

Lodi

Cremona

Parma

Piacenza

Bobbio

Como

Milan

Pavia

Tortona

Novara

Vercelli

Alessandria

Genoa

Lucca

Pisa

Volterra

Florence

Pistoia

Arezzo

Siena

Rome

Lucerne

Bern

USU

Lyons

Marseille

Arles

Avignon

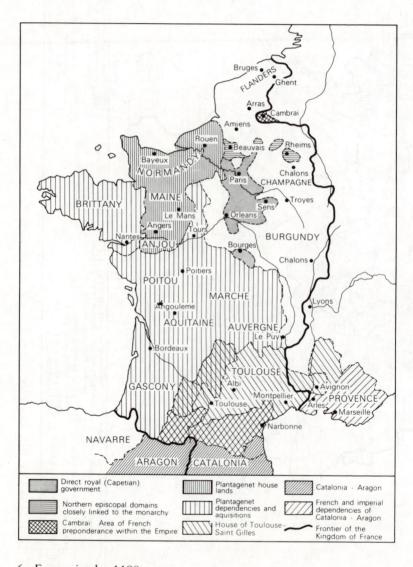

6. France in the 1180s

7. France *circa* 1310

INDEX